MW00975802

Documents in United States History

Volume II:
Since Reconstruction

PEARSON

Prentice Hall

UPPER SADDLE RIVER, NEW JERSEY 07458

© 2004 by PEARSON EDUCATION, INC.
Upper Saddle River, New Jersey 07458

All rights reserved
10 9 8 7 6 5 4 3 2 1

ISBN 0-13-150256-5
Printed in the United States of America

CONTENTS

Contents

Part Twenty-One

THE PROGRESSIVE ERA

Part Twenty-Two

WORLD WAR ONE

Part Twenty-Three

THE 1920S AND MODERN AMERICA

Contents

PART SIXTEEN
RECONSTRUCTION

16-1 "Address from the Colored Citizens of Norfolk, Virginia, to the People of the United States" (1865)

The end of the Civil War left African Americans in a state of uncertainty. The Emancipation Proclamation and the impending Thirteenth Amendment to the Constitution promised legal abolition of slavery, but this Address shows that freedom remained more a dream than a reality for the ex-slaves who asked for protection against discriminatory action by state and local governments.

We believe our present position is by no means so well understood among the loyal masses of the country, otherwise there would be no delay in granting us the express relief which the nature of the case demands. It must not be forgotten that it is the general assumption, in the South, that the effects of the immortal Emancipation Proclamation of President Lincoln go no further than the emancipation of the Negroes then in slavery, and that it is only constructively even, that that Proclamation can be said, in any legal sense, to have abolished slavery, and even the late constitutional amendment, if duly ratified, can go no further; neither touch, nor can touch, the slave codes of the various southern States, and the laws respecting free people of color consequent therefrom, which, having been passed before the act of secession, are presumed to have lost none of their vitality, but exist, as a convenient engine for our oppression, until repealed by special acts of the State legislature. By these laws, in many of the southern States, it is still a crime for colored men to learn or be taught to read, and their children are doomed to ignorance; there is no provision for insuring the legality of our marriages; we have no right to hold real estate; the public streets and the exercise of our ordinary occupations are forbidden us unless we can produce passes from our employers, or licenses from certain officials; in some States the whole free Negro population is legally liable to exile from the place of its birth, for no crime but that of color; we have no means of legally making or enforcing contracts of any description; we have no right to testify before the courts in any case in which a white man is one of the parties to the suit, we are taxed without representation, and, in short, so far as legal safeguards of our rights are concerned, we are defenceless before our enemies. While this is our position as regards our legal status, before the State laws, we are still more unfortunately situated as regards our late masters. The people of the North, owing to the greater interest excited by war, have heard little or nothing, for the past four years, of the blasphemous and horrible theories formerly propounded for the defence and glorification of human slavery, in the press, the pulpit and legislatures of the southern States; but, though they may have forgotten them, let them be assured that these doctrines have by no means faded from the minds of the people of the South; they cling to these delusions still, and only hug them closer for their recent defeat. Worse than all, they have returned to their homes, with all their old pride and contempt for the Negro transformed into bitter hate for the new-made freeman, who aspires for the suppression of their rebellion. That this charge is not unfounded, the manner in which it has been recently attempted to enforce the laws above referred to proves. In Richmond, during the three days sway of the rebel Mayor Mayo, over 800 colored people were arrested, simply for walking the streets without a pass; in the neighboring city of Portsmouth, a Mayor has just been elected, on the avowed platform that this is a white man's government, and our enemies have been heard to boast openly, that soon not a colored man shall be left in the city; in the greater number of counties in this State, county meetings have been held, at which resolutions have been adopted *deploring*, while accepting, the abolition of slavery, but going on to pledge the planters composing the meeting, to employ no Negroes save such as were formerly owned by themselves, without a written recommendation from their late employers, and threatening violence towards those who should do so, thereby keeping us in a state of serfdom, and preventing our free selection of our employers; they have also pledged themselves, in no event, to pay their late adult slaves more than $60 per year for their labor. In the future, out of which, with characteristic generosity, they have decided that we are to find clothes for ourselves and families, and pay our taxes and doctors' bills; in many of the more remote districts individual planters are to be found who still refuse to recognize their Negroes as free, forcibly retaining the wives and children of their late escaped slaves; cases have occurred, not far from Richmond itself, in which an attempt to leave the plantation has been punished by shooting to death; and finally, there are numbers of cases, known to ourselves, in the immediate vicinity of this city, in which a faithful performance, by colored men, of the duties or labor contracted for, has been met by a contemptuous and violent refusal of the stipulated compensation. These are facts, and yet the men doing these things are, in many cases, loud in their professions of attachment to the restored Union, while committing these outrages on the most faithful friends that Union can ever have. Even well known Union men have often been found among our oppressors; witness the action of the Tennessee legislature in imposing unheard of disabilities upon us, taking away from us, and giving to the County Courts, the right of disposing of our children, by apprenticing them to such occupations as the court, not their parents, may see fit to adopt for them, and in this very city, and under the protection of military law, some of our white friends who have nobly distinguished themselves by their efforts in our behalf, have been threatened with arrest by a Union Mayor of this city, for their advocacy of the cause of freedom.

Fellow citizens, the performance of a simple act of justice on your part will reverse all this; we ask for no expensive aid from military forces, stationed throughout the South, overbearing State action, and rendering our government republican only in name; give us the suffrage, and you may rely upon us to secure justice for ourselves, and all Union men, and to keep the State forever in the Union.

While we urge you to this act of simple justice to ourselves, there are many reasons why you should concede us this right in your own interest. It cannot be that you contemplate with satisfaction a prolonged military occupation of the southern States, and yet, without the existence of a larger loyal constituency than, at present, exists in these States, a military occupation will be absolutely necessary, to protect the white Union men of the South, as well as ourselves, and if not absolutely to keep the States in the Union, it will be necessary to prevent treasonable legislation. . . .

You have not unreasonably complained of the operation of that clause of the Constitution which has hitherto permitted the slaveocracy of the South to wield the political influence which would be represented by a white population equal to three-fifths of the whole Negro population; but slavery is now abolished, and henceforth the representation will be in proportion to the enumeration of the whole population of the South, *including people of color*, and it is worth your consideration if it is desirable or politic that the fomentors of this rebellion against the Union, which has been crushed at the expense of so much blood and treasure, should find themselves, after defeat, more powerful than ever, their political influence enhanced by the additional voting power of the other two-fifths of the colored population, by which means four Southern votes will balance in the Congressional and Presidential elections at least seven Northern ones. The honor of your country should be dear to you, as it is, but is that honor advanced, in the eyes of the Christian world, when America alone, of all Christian nations, sustains an unjust distinction against four millions and a half of her most loyal people, on the senseless ground of a difference in color? You are anxious that the attention of every man, of every State legislature, and of Congress, should be exclusively directed to redressing the injuries sustained by the country in the late contest; are these objects more likely to be effected amid the political distractions of an embarrassing Negro agitation? You are, above all, desirous that no future intestine wars should mar the prosperity and destroy the happiness of the country; will your perfect security from such evils be promoted by the existence of a colored population of four millions and a half, placed, by your enactments, outside the pale of the Constitution, discontented by oppression, with an army of 200,000 colored soldiers, whom you have drilled, disciplined, and armed, but whose attachment to the State you have failed to secure by refusing them citizenship? You are further anxious that your government should be an example to the world of true Republican institutions; but how can you avoid the charge of inconsistency if you leave one eighth of the population of the whole country without any political rights, while bestowing these rights on every immigrant who comes to these shores, perhaps from a despotism, under which he could never exercise the least political right, and had no means of forming any conception of their proper use? . . .

It is hardly necessary here to refute any of the slanders with which our enemies seek to prove our unfitness for the exercise of the right of suffrage. It is true, that many of our people are ignorant, but for *that* these very men are responsible, and decency should prevent *their* use of such an argument. But if our people are ignorant, no people were ever more orderly and obedient to the laws; and no people ever displayed greater earnestness in the acquisition of knowledge. Among no other people could such a revolution have taken place without scenes of license and bloodshed; but in this case, and we say it advisedly, full information of the facts will show that no single disturbance, however slight, has occurred which has not resulted from the unprovoked aggression of white people, and, if any one doubts how fast the ignorance, which has hitherto cursed our people, is disappearing, 'mid the light of freedom, let him visit the colored schools of this city and neighborhood, in which between two and three thousand pupils are being taught, while, in the evening, in colored schools may be seen, after the labors of the day, hundreds of our adult population from budding manhood to hoary age, toiling, with intensest eagerness, to acquire the invaluable arts of reading and writing, and the rudimentary branches of knowledge. One other objection only will we notice; it is that our people are lazy and idle; and, in support of this allegation, the objectors refer to the crowds of colored people subsisting on Government rations, and flocking into the towns. To the first statement we reply that we are poor, and that thousands of our young and able-bodied men, having been enlisted in the army to fight the battles of their country, it is but reasonable that that country should contribute something to the support of those whose natural protectors that country has taken away. With reference to the crowds collected round the military posts and in the cities, we say that though some may have come there under misapprehensions as to the nature of the freedom they have just received, yet this is not the case with the majority; the colored man knows that freedom means freedom to labor, and to enjoy its fruits, and in that respect evinces at least an equal appreciation of his new position with his late owners; if he is not to be found laboring for these late owners, it is because he cannot trust them, and feels safe, in his new-found freedom, nowhere out of the immediate presence of the national forces; if the planters want his labor (and they do) fair wages and fair treatment will not fail to secure it.

In conclusion, we wish to advise our colored brethren of the State and nation, that the settlement of this question is to a great extent dependent on them, and that supineness on their part will do as much to delay if not defeat the full recognition of their rights as the open opposition of avowed enemies. Then be up and active, and everywhere let associations be formed having for their object the agitation, discussion and enforcement of your claims to equality before the law, and equal rights of suffrage. Your opponents are active; be prepared, and organize to resist their efforts. We would further advise that all political associations of colored men, formed within the limits of the State of Virginia, should communicate the fact of their existence, with the names and post office addresses of their officers, to Joseph T. Wilson, Norfolk, Va., in order that communication and friendly cooperation may be kept up between the different organizations, and facili-ties afforded for common and united State action, should occasion require it.

1. *According to this document, what have been the effects of the Emancipation Proclamation upon the lives of African Americans in America?*
2. *What "simple act of justice" is requested? What would be the results of granting this plea?*

16-2   Carl Schurz, Report on the Condition of the South (1865)

At the end of the Civil War, the issue of the reconstruction of the South stimulated animated discussion among northerners. For some, including Carl Schurz, reconstruction had initiated a social revolution in a land experiencing severe economic distress. Especially regarding developing a free labor systems, the question arose over who would control the process of change for what ends.

We ought to keep in view, above all, the nature of the problem which is to be solved. As to what is commonly termed "reconstruction," it is not only the political machinery of the States and their constitutional relations to the general government, but the whole organism of southern society that must be reconstructed, or rather constructed anew, so as to bring it in harmony with the rest of American society. The difficulties of this task are not to be considered overcome when the people of the south take the oath of allegiance and elect governors and legislatures and members of Congress, and militia captains. That this would be done had become certain as soon as the surrenders of the southern armies had made further resistance impossible, and nothing in the world was left, even to the most uncompromising rebel, but to submit or to emigrate. It was also natural that they should avail themselves of every chance offered them to resume control of their home affairs and to regain their influence in the Union. But this can hardly be called the first step towards the solution of the true problem, and it is a fair question to ask, whether the hasty gratification of their desire to resume such control would not create new embarrassments.

The true nature of the difficulties of the situation is this: The general government of the republic has, by proclaiming the emancipation of the slaves, commenced a great social revolution in the south, but has, as yet, not completed it. Only the negative part of it is accomplished. The slaves are emancipated in point of form, but free labor has not yet been put in the place of slavery in point of fact. And now, in the midst of this critical period of transition, the power which originated the revolution is expected to turn over its whole future development to another power which from the beginning was hostile to it and has never yet entered into its spirit, leaving the class in whose favor it was made completely without power to protect itself and to take an influential part in that development. The history of the world will be searched in vain for a proceeding similar to this which did not lead either to a rapid and violent reaction, or to the most serious trouble and civil disorder. It cannot be said that the conduct of the southern people since the close of the war has exhibited such extraordinary wisdom and self-abnegation as to make them an exception to the rule.

In my despatches from the south I repeatedly expressed the opinion that the people were not yet in a frame of mind to legislate calmly and understandingly upon the subject of free negro labor. And this I reported to be the opinion of some of our most prominent military commanders and other observing men. It is, indeed, difficult to imagine circumstances more unfavorable for the development of a calm and unprejudiced public opinion than those under which the southern people are at present laboring. The war has not only defeated their political aspirations, but it has broken up their whole social organization. When the rebellion was put down they found themselves not only conquered in a political and military sense, but economically ruined. The planters, who represented the wealth of the southern country, are partly laboring under the severest embarrassments, partly reduced to absolute poverty. Many who are stripped of all available means, and have nothing but their land, cross their arms in gloomy despondency, incapable of rising to a manly resolution. Others, who still possess means, are at a loss how to use them, as their old way of doing things is, by the abolition of slavery, rendered impracticable, at least where the military arm of the government has enforced emancipation. Others are still trying to go on in the old way, and that old way is in fact the only one they understand, and in which they have any confidence. Only a minority is trying to adopt the new order of things. A large number of the plantations, probably a considerable majority of the more valuable estates, is under heavy mortgages, and the owners know that, unless they retrieve their fortunes in a comparatively short space of time, their property will pass out of their hands. Almost all are, to some extent, embarrassed. The nervous anxiety which such a state of things produces extends also to those classes of society which, although not composed of planters, were always in close business connexion with the planting interest, and there was hardly a branch of commerce or industry in the south which was not directly or indirectly so connected. Besides, the southern soldiers, when returning from the war, did not, like the northern soldiers, find a prosperous community which merely waited for their arrival to give them remunerative employment. They found, many of them, their homesteads destroyed, their farms devastated, their families in distress; and those that were less unfortunate found, at all events, an impoverished and exhausted community which had but little to offer them. Thus a great many have been thrown upon the world to shift as best they can. They must do something honest or dishonest, and must do it soon, to make a living, and their prospects are, at present, not very bright. Thus that nervous anxiety to hastily repair broken fortunes, and to prevent still greater ruin and distress, embraces nearly all classes, and imprints upon all the movements of the social body a morbid character.

In which direction will these people be most apt to turn their eyes? Leaving the prejudice of race out of the question, from early youth they have been acquainted with but one system of labor, and with that one system they have been in the habit of identifying all their interests. They know of no way to help themselves but the one they are accustomed to. Another system of labor is presented to them, which, however, owing to circumstances which they do not appreciate, appears at first in an unpromising light. To try it they consider an experiment which they cannot afford to make while their wants are urgent. They have not reasoned calmly enough to convince themselves that the trial must be made. It is, indeed, not wonderful that, under such circumstances, they should study, not how to introduce and develop free labor, but how to avoid its introduction, and how to return as much and as quickly as possible to something like the old order of things. Nor is it wonderful that such studies should find an expression in their attempts at legislation. But the circumstance that this tendency is natural does not render it less dangerous and objectionable. The practical question presents itself: Is the immediate restoration of the late rebel States to absolute self-control so necessary that it must be done even at the risk of endangering one of the great results of the war, and of bringing on in those States insurrection or anarchy, or would it not be better to postpone that restoration until such dangers are passed? If, as long as the change from slavery to free labor is known to the southern people only by its destructive results, these people must be expected to throw obstacles in its way, would it not seem necessary that the movement of social "reconstruction" be kept in the right channel by the hand of the power which originated the change, until that change can have disclosed some of its beneficial effects?

It is certain that every success of free negro labor will augment the number of its friends, and disarm some of the prejudices and assumptions of its opponents. I am convinced one good harvest made by unadulterated free labor in the south would have a far better effect than all the oaths that have been taken, and all the ordinances that have as yet been passed by southern conventions. But how can such a result be attained? The facts enumerated in this report, as well as the news we receive from the south from day to day, must make it evident to every unbiased observer that unadulterated free labor cannot be had at present, unless the national government holds its protective and controlling hand over it. It appears, also, that the more efficient this protection of free labor against all disturbing and reactionary influences, the sooner may such a satisfactory result be looked for. One reason why the southern people are so slow in accommodating themselves to the new order of things is, that they confidently expect soon to be permitted to regulate matters according to their own notions. Every concession made to them by the government has been taken as an encouragement to persevere in this hope, and, unfortunately for them, this hope is nourished by influences from other parts of the country. Hence their anxiety to have their State governments restored *at once*, to have the troops withdrawn, and the Freedmen's Bureau abolished, although a good many discerning men know well that, in view of the lawless spirit still prevailing, it would be far better for them to have the general order of society firmly maintained by the federal power until things have arrived at a final settlement. Had, from the beginning, the conviction been forced upon them that the adulteration of the new order of things by the admixture of elements belonging to the system of slavery would under no circumstances be permitted, a much larger number would have launched their energies into the new channel, and, seeing that they could do "no better," faithfully co-operated with the government. It is hope which fixes them in their perverse notions. That hope nourished or fully gratified, they will persevere in the same direction. That hope destroyed, a great many will, by the force of necessity, at once accommodate themselves to the logic of the change. If, therefore, the national government firmly and unequivocally announces its policy not to give up the control of the free-labor reform until it is finally accomplished, the progress of that reform will undoubtedly be far more rapid and far less difficult than it will be if the attitude of the government is such as to permit contrary hopes to be indulged in.

The machinery by which the government has so far exercised its protection of the negro and of free labor in the south-the Freedmen's Bureau-is very unpopular in that part of the country, as every institution placed there as a barrier to reactionary aspirations would be. That abuses were committed with the management of freedmen's affairs; that some of the officers of the bureau were men of more enthusiasm than discretion, and in many cases went beyond their authority: all this is certainly true. But, while the southern people are always ready to expatiate upon the shortcomings of the Freedmen's Bureau, they are not so ready to recognize the services it has rendered. I feel warranted in saying that not half of the labor that has been done in the south this year, or will be done there next year, would have been or would be done but for the exertions of the Freedmen's Bureau. The confusion and disorder of the transition period would have been infinitely greater had not an agency interfered which possessed the confidence of the emancipated slaves; which could disabuse them of any extravagant notions and expectations and be trusted; which could administer to them good advice and be voluntarily obeyed. No other agency, except one placed there by the national government, could have wielded that moral power whose interposition was so necessary to prevent southern society from falling at once into the chaos of a general collision between its different elements. That the success achieved by the Freedmen's Bureau is as yet very incomplete cannot be disputed. A more perfect organization and a more carefully selected personnel may be desirable; but it is doubtful whether a more suitable machinery can be devised to secure to free labor in the south that protection against disturbing influences which the nature of the situation still imperatively demands.

1. *Summarize Schurz's opinion of the state of the South. How is the South dealing with reconstruction?*
2. *What difficulties and dangers are present as the South attempts to make the transition from slavery to free labor?*

16-3 Clinton B. Fisk, Plain Counsels for Freedmen (1865)

After emancipation, questions arose about African American labor. In this document, Clinton B. Fisk counsels African Americans on the value of free labor and the judicious use of the income generated by work.

I come to speak to you this evening about work; yes, work, good, honest, hard work. Do not turn away, and say you will not hear me,-that you know all about it, and that it is not a good subject for a lecture.

Listen! The very first verse of the Holy Bible tells us that God is a worker,-that in six days he made all this great world on which we dwell, and the sun and moon and stars.

All the holy angels in heaven are very busy. They go forth to do the will of the Great Being, and find their greatest bliss in action.

Good and great men are all hard workers. And do you know what it is that makes a free state so rich and strong? It is, above all things save God's blessing, *patient, honest work.*

There is nothing degrading in *free* labor,-nay, it is most honorable. Why, when God placed Adam and Eve in the garden of Eden, before either of them had ever done any wrong thing, and while they were as pure as the angels, he made gardeners of them. He required them to dress the garden and keep it nice and in good condition.

The blessed Saviour himself worked at the bench, at the carpenter's trade, until he was about thirty years of age.

And yet, some very silly people are above work,-are ashamed to have hard hands,-and do their best to get through the world without honest toil.

But this was not the case with Abraham Lincoln, the man who wrote the Proclamation of Emancipation. He used the hoe, the ax, and the maul, cleared ground, and fenced it with the rails he had split, and was ready to turn his hands to any honest work.

I know that it is quite natural that you should associate work with slavery, and freedom with idleness, because you have seen slaves working all their lives, and free people doing little or nothing. And I should not blame you if you should ask, "What have we gained by freedom, if we are to work, work, work!"

Now, let me explain. A slave works all his life for others. A free man works for himself,-that is, he gets pay for his labor; and if he saves what he earns and manages well, he can get on so well that he may spend the afternoon of his life in his own pleasant home, and never want for any thing. . . .

If you earn twelve dollars in a month, and spend thirteen, you are on the road to misery, for you will get into debt, deeper and deeper, until after awhile it will be a load you can not carry.

You should make it a rule, therefore, to spend less each month and each year than you make. If you do this, you will become well to do in the world.

A free man should always consider before he buys an article, whether he can afford it. He would like a new hat,-price five dollars,-but if he needs the five for other and more pressing uses, to make a payment, for example, for something he has bought, then he should deny himself the pleasure of the new hat, and brush up the old one. A new coat might be very desirable, but if its purchase would create a debt, better keep the old one in good repair as possible, and stick to it another season. It is much pleasanter to wear the old clothes than to have the constable chasing you in the new ones.

Many a poor man has been driven almost out of his wits by constables, who were pursuing him for the payment of debts made to gratify the vanity of his wife. She wanted a handsome breastpin, and begged him to buy it. He could not resist, and bought it with the proceeds of a week's hard toil, and, as a consequence, was obliged to go in debt for meat and bread. Then she wanted a fine dress; then this, and then that; and so he sank into debt, step by step, until he was ruined.

A wife can soon destroy her husband's good name, by urging him to buy her things she could do without, and for which he is unable to pay.

It is a good plan for a man and woman who are just setting out as you are to make a living, to balance their accounts-that is count up what they earn and what they spend, and see how they compare-a great many times in the year. It will not take them long to do it, and the task will be both pleasant and useful.

Resolve that you will, by the blessing of God, live within your means. This is one of the most important secrets of success. It may cost you a struggle, but stick to it resolutely, and the day will come when you will be able to purchase not only the necessaries, but the luxuries of life.

I am not counseling you to be mean and stingy,-by no means; but no man has a right to be liberal with another man's money and at another man's expense.

For the sake of your good name, do not make a splurge in society with jewelry and fine clothes which have not been paid for, and for which you will never be able to pay. That is almost as mean as theft.

"The borrower," says the Bible, "is servant to the lender," and, let me assure you, a creditor is a very hard master. Do not put your necks in his iron yoke.

I am acquainted with many white persons who commenced married life twenty-five years ago with as little as you have now, and who worked with their hands for less than is given to you, who are now owners of handsome houses and farms, and are in very easy circumstances. They made it a rule to spend less than they earned.

1. What are the rewards of work in the opinion of the author?
2. What advice does the author have for those who may be earning wages and handling money for the first time in their lives?

16-4 Mississippi Black Code (1865)

In the aftermath of Emancipation, southern states passed a variety of laws known as "Black Codes". Although these codes varied from state to state, they were all aimed at tightly controlling the lives and labor of newly freed people. The codes angered Congress and the northern pubic, who viewed them as southern attempts to roll back Emancipation and subvert Reconstruction. The Civil Rights Act of 1866, the Fourteenth Amendment, and the Military Reconstitution Act of 1867 were all designed in part to counter the Black Codes.

The Civil Rights of Freedmen in Mississippi

Section 1. Be it enacted by the legislature of the State of Mississippi, That all freedmen, free Negroes, and mulattoes may sue and be sued, implead and be impleaded in all the courts of law and equity of this state, and may acquire personal property and choses in action, by descent or purchase, any may dispose of the same, in the same manner, and to the same extent that white persons may: Provided that the provisions of this section shall not be so construed as to allow any freedman, free Negro, or mulatto to rent or lease any lands or tenements, except in incorporated town or cities in which places the corporate authorities shall control the same.

Sec. 2. Be it further enacted, That all freedmen, free Negroes, and mulattoes may intermarry with each other, in the same manner and under the same regulations that are provided by law for white persons: Provided, that the clerk of probate shall keep separate records of the same.

Sec. 3. Be it further enacted, That all freedmen, free Negroes, and mulattoes, who do now and have heretofore lived and cohabited together as husband and wife shall be taken and held in law as legally married, and the issue shall be taken and held as legitimate for all purposes. That it shall not be lawful for any freedman, free Negro, or mulatto to intermarry with any white person; nor for any white person to intermarry with any freedman, free Negro, or mulatto; any person who shall so intermarry shall be deemed guilty of felony and, on conviction thereof, shall be confined in the state penitentiary for life; and those shall be deemed freedmen, free Negroes, and mulattoes who are of pure Negro blood, and those descended from a Negro to the third generation inclusive, though one ancestor of each generation may have been a white person.

Sec. 4. Be it further enacted, That in addition to cases in which freedmen, free Negroes, and mulattoes are now by law competent witnesses, freedmen, free Negroes, or mulattoes shall be competent in civil cases when a party or parties to the suit, either plaintiff or plaintiffs, defendant or defendants, also in cases where freedmen, free Negroes, and mulattoes is or are either plaintiff or plaintiffs, defendant or defendants, and a white person or white persons is or are the opposing party or parties, plaintiff or plaintiffs, defendant or defendants. They shall also be competent witnesses in all criminal prosecutions where the crime charged is alleged to have been committed by a white person upon or against the person or property of a freedman, free Negro, or mulatto: Provided that in all cases said witnesses shall be examined in open court on the stand, except, however, they may be examined before the grand jury, and shall in all cases be subject to the rules and tests of the common law as to competency and credibility.

Sec. 5. Be it further enacted, That every freedman, free Negro, and mulatto shall, on the second Monday of January, one thousand eight hundred and sixty-six, and annually thereafter, have a lawful home or employment. . . .

Sec. 6. Be it further enacted, That all contracts for labor made with freedmen, free Negroes, and mulattoes for a longer period than one month shall be in writing and in duplicate, attested and read to said freedman, free Negro, or mulatto, by a beat, city or county officers, or two disinterested white persons of the country in which the labor is to be performed, of which each party shall have one; and said contracts shall be taken and held as entire contracts, and if the laborer shall quit the service of the employer, before expiration of his term of service, without good cause, he shall forfeit his wages for that year, up to the time of quitting.

Sec. 7. Be it further enacted, That every civil officer shall, and every person may, arrest and carry back to his or her legal employer any freedman, free Negro, or mulatto who shall have quit the service of his or her employer before the expiration of his or her term of service without good cause, and said officer and person shall be entitled to receive for arresting and carrying back every deserting employee aforesaid, the sum of five dollars, and ten cents per mile from the place of arrest to the place of delivery, and the same shall be paid by the employer, and held as a set-off for so much against the wages of said deserting employee.

Sec. 8. Be it further enacted, That upon affidavit made by the employer of any freedman, free Negro, or mulatto, or other credible person, before any justice of the peace or member of the board of police, that any freedman, free Negro, or mulatto, legally employed by said employer, has illegally deserted said employment, such justice of the peace or member of the board of police shall issue his warrant or warrants, returnable before himself, or other such officer, directed to any sheriff, constable, or special deputy, commanding him to arrest said deserter and return him or her to said employer, and the like proceedings shall be had as provided in the preceding section. . . .

Sec. 9. Be it further enacted, That if any person shall persuade or attempt to persuade, entice, or cause any freedman, free Negro, or mulatto to desert from the legal employment of any person, before the expiration of his or her term of service, or shall knowingly employ any such deserting freedman, free Negro, or mulatto, or shall knowingly give or sell to any such deserting freedman, free Negro, or mulatto, any food, raiment, or other thing, he or she shall be guilty of a misdemeanor and, upon conviction, shall be fined not less than twenty-five dollars and not more then two hundred dollars and the costs, and, if said fine and costs shall not be immediately paid, the court shall sentence said convict to not exceeding two months' imprisonment in the county jail, and he or she shall moreover be liable to the party injured in damages: . . . .

Sec. 10. Be it further enacted, That it shall be lawful for any freedman, free Negro, or mulatto to charge any white person, freedman, free Negro, or mulatto, by affidavit, with any criminal offense against his or her person or property and upon such affidavit the proper process shall be issued and executed as if said affidavit was made by a white person, and it shall be lawful for any freedman, free Negro, or mulatto, in any action, suit, or controversy pending, or about to be instituted, in any court of law or equity of this state, to make all needful and lawful affidavits, as shall be necessary for the institution, prosecution, or defense of such suit or controversy.

Sec. 11. Be it further enacted, That the penal laws of this state, in all cases not otherwise specially provided for, shall apply and extend to all freedmen, free Negroes, and mulattoes. . . .

Approved November 25, 1865

1. Identify and explain the actual freedoms and rights that are granted under the Mississippi Black Code.
2. What restrictions and laws enacted by the Black Code effectively extend the racist doctrines of pre-Civil War slavery? What freedoms are notably denied under the Code?

16-5   James C. Beecher, Report on Land Reform in the South Carolina Islands (1865, 1866)

The controversial Reconstruction of the South after the Civil War was a difficult time for African Americans. Though given the right to voice political opinions for the first time, their voices often went unheeded. As southern whites regained control of political offices after Reconstruction, African Americans slowly lost much of their newfound political freedom.

November 29, 1865
Maj. Gen. R. Saxton

General:

I am to leave for Edisto Island in the morning. It seems that some of the planters whose lands have been restored were driven off by the freed people. Gen. Sickles immediately ordered that a company of white troops be sent there. Gen. Devens agreed with me that my troops were the ones to send if any and so I take a company with me.

I have apprehended trouble ever since the Govt determined to rescind the authority to occupy those lands. It is true that the War Dept. did not, in so many words, approve Gen. Sherman's order, but it certainly did *act* upon it, and there is an apparent bad faith in the matter which I am sure the freed people will feel. I cannot refrain from expressing grave fears of collisions on the island. The same difficulty is affecting the Combahee plantations. I hope to visit that section by Monday next.

James C. Beecher
National Archives

January 9, 1866

I . . . called the people together and carefully instructed them in their rights and duties. They said they had been assured by certain parties that Mr. Heyward [a local white planter] would be obliged to lease his land to them, and that they would not work for him at any price. They were perfectly good natured about it but firm. I then announced Mr. Heyward's offer:

That they were to retain their houses and gardens, with the privilege of raising hogs, poultry, etc. That he would pay for full hands, men $12, women $8 per month. They to find themselves-or he would pay $10 per month to men, $4 to women and ration them.

I am satisfied that no higher wages will be offered this year. Therefore I told the people that they could take it or leave it, and that if they declined to work the plantation the houses must be vacated. I proceeded to call the roll of all the able bodied men and women, each of whom responded "no." I then notified them that every house must be vacated on or before the 18th inst. I propose to remain and see everyone outside the plantation lines on that date.

Today I have pursued the same course on another large plantation, with the same results. Of course I anticipated this. It could not be otherwise considering the instructions which these people have received. I do not blame them in the slightest degree, and so long as they show no violence, shall treat them with all possible kindness. But it is better to stop the error they are laboring under, at once.

January 31, 1866

I am informed that on or about 12th inst a meeting was called on Wadmalaw Island to take measures to prevent white persons from visiting the island-that the Captain Commanding (very properly) forbade the proceeding, and notified the actors that in future no meetings could be held until notice of the same should be given him.

I am further informed that certain parties immediately proceeded to Charleston and returned with a document signed "By order Maj. Gen. Saxton" stating that the military authorities had nothing to do with them and they were at liberty to hold meetings when and where they pleased. This document was brought by three colored men calling themselves Commissioners from Edisto Island, attended by an escort of forty or fifty freedmen, and exhibited to the Officer. They then proceeded to Rockville, and held the meeting.

It is to be regretted that the Bureau should seem to bring the freed people in collision with the Military Police of the islands. Already in two instances the freed people have committed themselves seriously by acts of stupid violence and I have record of hurtful advice given by speakers at the meeting in question. I shall be exceedingly grieved to find myself in collision with the [Bureau] but being responsible for the military police of these islands cannot do otherwise than prevent disorder by any means in my power.

I respectfully request that instruction be sent to the same "Commissioners" to the effect that the order in question must be respected on Wadmalaw and Johns Island. Such instructions will prevent collision between the [freedmen] and the U.S. forces.

1. What difficulties are reported by Beecher regarding the settling of land disputes in the South Carolina Islands? Describe the two different views of the dispute.

16-6 The Memphis Riot (1866)

The Memphis riot began on May 1, 1866, when the horse-drawn carriages of a black man and a white man collided. Fighting broke out as a group of black soldiers from nearby Fort Pickering tried to intervene to stop the arrest of the black man by the mainly Irish-American police. Passions escalated into three days of racially motivated violence between the police and black residents of Memphis. When peace was restored, forty-six blacks and two whites had been killed, five black women raped, and hundreds of black homes, schools, and churches had been vandalized or destroyed. The following is the report of an investigation into the riot prepared for General Oliver Otis Howard, Commissioner of the Bureau of Refugees, Freedmen and Abandoned Lands.

Source: The Freedmen's Bureau Online, *Records of the Assistant Commissioner for the State of Tennessee, Bureau of Refugees, Freedmen, and Abandoned Lands, 1865–1869.* National Archives Microfilm Publication M999, roll 34 "Reports of Outrages, Riots and Murders, Jan. 15, 1866–Aug. 12, 1868".
http://www.freedmensbureau.com/tennessee/outrages/memphisriot.htm

Memphis, Tenn. May 22 '66

Maj. Genl. O.O. Howard
Commissioner B.R.F. & A. L.
Washington, D.C.

General,

In accordance with the instructions contained in S. O. No. 64, Ex. II, War Dept., B. R. F. & A. L. dated Washington, D. C. May 7, 1866 and your letter of "confidential instructions" of the same date, I have the honor herewith to submit a report of an investigation of the late riots in Memphis.

I reached Memphis May 11th and I found General Fisk, the Asst. Commissioner for Ky. and Tenn, here. He had already directed his Inspector General Col. C. T. Johnson to institute an investigation and I found the Colonel had commenced his work and was well advanced.

At the suggestion of General Fisk I immediately conferred with Colonel Johnson and we determined to make a joint investigation and report. We have taken some affidavits and as many more could have been procured if we could have taken the time.

I have the honor to be
Very Respectfully
Your Obdt. Servant
(sd) T. W. Gilbreth
Aid-de-Camp

Report of an investigation of the cause, origin, and results of the late riots in the city of Memphis made by Col. Charles F. Johnson, Inspector General States of Ky. and Tennessee and Major T. W. Gilbreth, A. D. C. to Maj. Genl. Howard, Commissioner Bureau R. F. & A. Lands.

The remote cause of the riot as it appears to us is a bitterness of feeling which has always existed between the low whites & blacks, both of whom have long advanced rival claims for superiority, both being as degraded as human beings can possibly be.

In addition to this general feeling of hostility there was an especial hatred among the city police for the Colored Soldiers, who were stationed here for a long time and had recently been discharged from the service of the U.S., which was most cordially reciprocated by the soldiers.

This has frequently resulted in minor affrays not considered worthy of notice by the authorities. These causes combined produced a state of feeling between whites and blacks, which would require only the slightest provocation to bring about an open rupture.

The Immediate Cause

On the evening of the 30th April 1866 several policemen (4) came down Causey Street, and meeting a number of Negroes forced them off the sidewalk. In doing so a Negro fell and a policeman stumbled over him. The police then drew their revolvers and attacked the Negroes, beating them with their pistols. Both parties then separated, deferring the settlement by mutual consent to some future time (see affidavit marked "A"). On the following day, May 1st, during the afternoon, between the hours of 3 and 5, a crowd of colored men, principally discharged soldiers, many of whom were more or less intoxicated, were assembled on South Street in South Memphis.

Three or four of these were very noisy and boisterous. Six policemen appeared on South Street, two of them arrested two of the Negroes and conducted them from the ground. The others remained behind to keep back the crowd, when the attempt was made by several Negroes to rescue their comrades. The police fell back when a promiscuous fight was indulged in by both parties.

During this affray one police officer was wounded in the finger, another (Stephens) was shot by the accidental discharge of his pistol in his own hand, and afterward died.

About this time the police fired upon unoffending Negroes remote from the riotous quarter. Colored soldiers with whom the police first had trouble had returned in the meantime to Fort Pickering. The police was soon reinforced and commenced firing on the colored people, men, women and children, in that locality, killing and wounding several.

Shortly after, the City Recorder (John C. Creighton) arrived upon the ground (corner of Causey and Vance Streets) and in a speech which received three hearty cheers from the crowd there assembled, councilled and urged the whites to arm and kill every Negro and drive the last one from the city. Then during this night the Negroes were hunted down by police, firemen and other white citizens, shot, assaulted, robbed, and in many instances their houses searched under the pretense of hunting for concealed arms, plundered, and then set on fire, during which no resistance so far as we can learn was offered by the Negroes.

A white man by the name of Dunn, a fireman, was shot and killed by another white man through mistake (reference is here made to accompanying affidavit mkd "B").

During the morning of the 2nd inst. (Wednesday) everything was perfectly quiet in the district of the disturbances of the previous day. A very few Negroes were in the streets, and none of them appeared with arms, or in any way excited except through fear. About 11 o'clock A.M. a posse of police and citizens again appeared in South Memphis and commenced an indiscriminate attack upon the Negroes, they were shot down without mercy, women suffered alike with the men, and in several instances little children were killed by these miscreants. During this day and night, with various intervals of quiet, the nuisance continued.

The city seemed to be under the control of a lawless mob during this and the two succeeding days (3rd & 4th). All crimes imaginable were committed from simple larceny to rape and murder. Several women and children were shot in bed. One woman (Rachel Johnson) was shot and then thrown into the flames of a burning house and consumed. Another was forced twice through the flames and finally escaped. In some instances houses were fired and armed men guarded them to prevent the escape of those inside. A number of men whose loyalty is undoubted, long residents of Memphis, who deprecated the riot during its progress, were denominated Yankees and Abolitionists, and were informed in language more emphatic than gentlemanly, that their presence here was unnecessary. To particularize further as to individual acts of inhumanity would extend the report to too great a length. But attention is respectfully called for further instances to affidavits accompanying marked C, E, F & G.

The riot lasted until and including the 4th of May but during all this time the disturbances were not continual as there were different times of greater or less length in each day, in which the city was perfectly quiet, attacks occurring generally after sunset each day.

The rioters ceased their violence either of their own accord or from want of material to work on, the Negroes having hid themselves, many fleeing into the country.

Conduct of the Civil Authorities

The Hon. John Park, Mayor of Memphis, seemed to have lost entire control of his subordinates and either through lack of inclination and sympathy with the mob, or on utter want of capacity, completely failed to suppress the riot and preserve the peace of the city. His friends offer in extenuation of his conduct, that he was in a state of intoxication during a part or most of the time and was therefore unable to perform the high and responsible functions of his office. Since the riot no official notice has been taken of the occurrence either by the Mayor or the Board of Aldermen, neither have the City Courts taken cognizance of the numerous crimes committed.

Although many of the perpetrators are known, no arrests have been made, nor is there now any indication on the part of the Civil Authorities that any are meditated by them.

It appears the Sheriff of this County (P. M. Minters) endeavored to oppose the mob on the evening of the 1st of May, but his good intentions were thwarted by a violent speech delivered by John C. Creighton, City Recorder, who urged and directed the arming of the whites and the wholesale slaughter of blacks.

This speech was delivered on the evening of the 1st of May to a large crowd of police and citizens on the corner of Vance and Causey streets, and to it can be attributed in a great measure the continuance of the disturbances. The following is the speech as extracted from the affidavits herewith forwarded marked "B" . . . "That everyone of the citizens should get arms, organize and go through the Negro districts," and that he "was in favor of killing every God damned nigger" . . . "We are not prepared now, but let us prepare and clean out every damned son of a bitch of a nigger out of town . . . "Boys, I want you to go ahead and kill every damned one of the nigger race and burn up the cradle."

The effect of such language delivered by a municipal office so high in authority, to a promiscuous and excited assemblage can be easily perceived. From that time they seemed to act as though vested with full authority to kill, burn and plunder at will. The conduct of a great number of the city police, who are generally composed of the lowest class of whites selected without reference to their qualifications for the position, was brutal in the extreme. Instead of protecting the rights of persons and property as is their duty, they were chiefly concerned as murderers, incendiaries and robbers. At times they even protected the rest of the mob in their acts of violence.

No public meeting has been held by the citizens, although three weeks have now elapsed since the riot, thus by their silence appearing to approve of the conduct of the mob. The only regrets that are expressed by the mass of the people are purely financial. There are, however, very many honorable exceptions, chiefly among men who have fought against the Government in the late rebellion, who deprecate in strong terms, both the Civil Authorities and the rioters.

Action of Bvt. Brig. Genl. Ben P. Runkle, Chief Supt., Bureau R.F. and A.L. Sub-District of Memphis

General Runkle was waited upon every hour in the day during the riot, by colored men who begged of him protection for themselves and families, and he, an officer of the Army detailed as Agent of the Freedmen's Bureau was suffered the humiliation of acknowledging his utter inability to protect them in any respect. His personal appearance at the scenes of the riot had no affect on the mob, and he had no troops at his disposal.

He was obliged to put his Headquarters in a defensive state, and we believe it was only owing to the preparations made, that they were not burned down. Threats had been openly made that the Bureau office would be burned, and the General driven from the town. He, with his officers and a small squad of soldiers and some loyal citizens who volunteered were obliged to remain there during Thursday and Friday nights.

The origin and results of the riot may be summed up briefly as follows:

The remote cause was the feeling of bitterness which as always existed between the two classes. The minor affrays which occurred daily, especially between the police and colored persons.

The general tone of certain city papers which in articles that have appeared almost daily, have councilled the low whites to open hostilities with the blacks.

The immediate cause was the collision heretofore spoken of between a few policemen and Negroes on the evening of the 30th of April in which both parties may be equally culpable, followed on the evening of the 1st May by another collision of a more serious nature and subsequently by an indiscriminate attack upon inoffensive colored men and women.

Three Negro churches were burned, also eight (8) school houses, five (5) of which belonged to the United States Government, and about fifty (50) private dwellings, owned, occupied or inhabited by freedmen as homes, and in which they had all their personal property, scanty though it be, yet valuable to them and in many instances containing the hard earnings of months of labor.

Large sums of money were taken by police and others, the amounts varying five (5) to five hundred (500) dollars, the latter being quite frequent owing to the fact that many of the colored men had just been paid off and discharged from the Army.

No dwellings occupied by white men exclusively were destroyed and we have no evidence of any white men having been robbed.

From the present disturbed condition of the freedmen in the districts where the riot occurred it is impossible to determine the exact number of Negroes killed and wounded. The number already ascertained as killed is about (30) thirty; and the number wounded about fifty (50). Two white men were killed, viz., Stephens, a policeman and Dunn of the Fire Department.

The Surgeon who attended Stephens gives it as his professional opinion that the wound which resulted in his death was caused by the accidental discharge of a pistol in his hands (see affidavit marked "B"). Dunn was killed May 1st by a white man through mistake (see affidavit marked "B"). Two others (both Policemen) were wounded, one slightly in the finger, the other (Slattersly) seriously.

The losses sustained by the Government and Negroes as per affidavits received up to date amount to the sum of ninety eight thousand, three hundred and nineteen dollars and fifty five cents ($98,319.55). Subsequent investigations will in all probability increase the amount to one hundred and twenty thousand dollars ($120,00.00).

(signed) Chas. F. Jackson
Col. And Insptr. Genl. Ky. & Tenn.
T. W. Gilbreth
Aide-de-Camp.

1. *According to the investigation, how widespread was white animosity toward the black community in Memphis in 1866? In addition to outright violence, how was this animosity manifested? Why do you think Irish-Americans in Memphis might have felt particularly threatened by freedmen?*
2. *According to the investigation, who should be held accountable for the death and destruction during the riot? Although not directly addressed in the report, how might future incidents such as this be prevented?*

16-7 The Fourteenth Amendment (1868)

Southern attempts to deprive African Americans of their rights stimulated constitutional remedies. Congressional radical reconstruction hoped that constitutional guarantees of citizenship and federal protection of rights would alleviate oppressive state laws.

Sec. 1. All persons born or naturalized in the United States, and subject to the jurisdiction thereof, are citizens of the United States and of the State wherein they reside. No State shall make or enforce any law which shall abridge the privileges or immunities of citizens of the United States; nor shall any State deprive any person of life, liberty, or property, without due process of law; nor deny to any person within its jurisdiction the equal protection of the laws.

Sec. 2. Representatives shall be apportioned among the several States according to their respective numbers, counting the whole number of persons in each State, excluding Indians not taxed. But when the right to vote at any election for the choice of electors for President and Vice President of the United States, Representatives in Congress, the Executive and Judicial officers of a State, or the members of the Legislature thereof, is denied to any of the male inhabitants of such State, being twenty-one years of age, and citizens of the United States, or in any way abridged, except for participation in rebellion, or other crime, the basis of representation therein shall be reduced in the proportion which the number of such male citizens shall bear to the whole number of male citizens twenty-one years of age in such State.

Sec. 3. No person shall be a Senator or Representative in Congress, or elector of President and Vice President, or hold any office, civil or military, under the United States, or under any State, who, having previously taken an oath, as a member of Congress, or as an officer of the United States, or as a member of any State legislature, or as an executive or judicial officer of any State, to support the Constitution of the United States, shall have engaged in insurrection or rebellion against the same, or given aid or comfort to the enemies thereof. But Congress may by a vote of two-thirds of each House, remove such disability.

Sec. 4. The validity of the public debt of the United States, authorized by law, including debts incurred for payment of pensions and bounties for services in suppressing insurrection or rebellion, shall not be questioned. But neither the United States nor any State shall assume or pay any debt or obligation incurred in aid of insurrection or rebellion against the united States, or any claim for the loss or emancipation of any slave; but all such debts, obligations and claims shall be held illegal and void.

Sec. 5. The Congress shall have power to enforce, by appropriate legislation, the provisions of this article.

1. Explain the focus, scope, and effect of the Fourteenth Amendment.

16-8 Albion W. Tourgee, Letter on Ku Klux Klan Activities (1870)

Founded by former Confederate general Nathan Bedford Forrest in Tennessee, the Ku Klux Klan spread across the South. As this excerpt shows, southern whites in the Ku Klux Klan used brutality and violence against those who supported Reconstruction governments and efforts to improve conditions for African Americans.

Some of the Outrages-Letter from Judge Tourgee to Senator Abbott

Greensboro, N.C. May 24, 1870.
Gen. Jos. C. Abbott

My Dear General:

It is my mournful duty to inform you that our friend John W. Stephens, State Senator from Caswell, is dead. He was foully murdered by the Ku-Klux in the Grand Jury room of the Court House on Saturday or Saturday night last. The circumstances attending his murder have not yet fully come to light there. So far as I can learn, I judge these to have been the circumstances: He was one of the Justices of the Peace in that township, and was accustomed to hold court in that room on Saturdays. It is evident that he was set upon by some one while holding this court, or immediately after its close, and disabled by a sudden attack, otherwise there would have been a very sharp resistance, as he was a man, and always went armed to the teeth. He was stabbed five or six times, and then hanged on a hook in the Grand Jury room, where he was found on Sunday morning. Another brave, honest Republican citizen has met his fate at the hands of these fiends. Warned of his danger, and fully cognizant of the terrible risk which surrounded him, he still manfully refused to quit the field. Against the advice of his friends, against the entreaties of his family, he constantly refused to leave those who had stood by him in the day of his disgrace and peril. He was accustomed to say that 3,000 poor, ignorant, colored Republican voters in that county had stood by him and elected him, at the risk of persecution and starvation, and that he had no idea of abandoning them to the Ku-Klux. He was determined to stay with them, and either put an end to these outrages, or die with the other victims of Rebel hate and national apathy: Nearly six months ago I declared my belief that before the election in August next the Ku-Klux would have killed more men in the State than there would be members to be elected to the Legislature. A good beginning has been made toward the fulfillment of this prophecy. The following counties have already filled, or nearly so, their respective "quotas:" Jones County, quota full, excess 1; Orange County quota full; excess, 1. Caswell County quota full; excess, 2; Alamance County quota full; excess, 1. Chatham County quota nearly full. Or, to state the matter differently, there have been twelve murders in five counties of the district during the past eighteen months, by bands of disguised villains. In addition to this, from the best information I can derive, I am of the opinion that in this district alone there have been 1,000 outrages of a less serious nature perpetrated by the same masked fiends. Of course this estimate is not made from any absolute record, nor is it possible to ascertain with accuracy the entire number of beatings and other outrages which have been perpetrated. The uselessness, the utter futility of complaint from the lack of ability in the laws to punish is fully known to all. The danger of making such complaint is also well understood. It is therefore not unfrequently by accident that the outrage is found out, and unquestionably it is frequently absolutely concealed. Thus, a respectable, hard working white carpenter was working for a neighbor, when accidentally his shirt was torn, and disclosed his back scarred and beaten. The poor fellow begged for the sake of his wife and children that nothing might be said about it, as the Ku-Klux had threatened to kill him if he disclosed how he had been outraged. Hundreds of cases have come to my notice and that of my solicitor. . . .

Men and women come scarred, mangled, and bruised, and say: "The Ku-Klux came to my house last night and beat me almost to death, and my old woman right smart, and shot into the house, 'bust' the door down, and told me they would kill me if I made complaint;" and the bloody mangled forms attest the truth of their declarations. On being asked if any one knew any of the party it will be ascertained that there was no recognition, or only the most uncertain and doubtful one. In such cases as these nothing can be done by the court. We have not been accustomed to enter them on record. A man of the best standing in Chatham told me that he could count up 200 and upward in that county. In Alamance County, a citizen in conversation one evening enumerated upward of 50 cases which had occurred within his own knowledge, and in one section of the county. He gave it as his opinion that there had been 200 cases in that county. I have no idea

357

that he exceeded the proper estimate. That was six months ago, and I am satisfied that another hundred would not cover the work done in that time.

These crimes have been of every character imaginable. Perhaps the most usual has been the dragging of men and women from their beds, and beating their naked bodies with hickory switches, or as witnesses in an examination the other day said, "sticks" between a "switch" and a "club." From 50 to 100 blows is the usual allowance, sometimes 200 and 300 blows are administered. Occasionally an instrument of torture is owned. Thus in one case two women, one 74 years old, were taken out, stripped naked, and beaten with a paddle, with several holes bored through it. The paddle was about 30 inches long, 3 or 4 inches wide, and 1/4 of an inch thick, of oak. Their bodies were so bruised and beaten that they were sickening to behold. They were white women and of good character until the younger was seduced, and swore her child to its father. Previous to that and so far as others were concerned her character was good.

Again, there is sometimes a fiendish malignity and cunning displayed in the form and character of the outrages. For instance, a colored man was placed astride of a log, and an iron staple driven through his person into the log. In another case, after a band of them had in turn violated a young negro girl, she was forced into bed with a colored man, their bodies were bound together face to face, and the fire from the hearth piled upon them. The K. K. K. rode off and left them, with shouts of laughter. Of course the bed was soon in flames, and somehow they managed to crawl out, though terribly burned and scarred. The house was burned.

I could give other incidents of cruelty, such as hanging up a boy of nine years old until he was nearly dead, to make him tell where his father was hidden, and beating an old negress of 103 years old with garden pallings because she would not own that she was afraid of the Ku-Klux. But it is unnecessary to go into further detail. In this district I estimate their offenses as follows, in the past ten months: Twelve murders, 9 rapes, 11 arsons, 7 mutilations, ascertained and most of them on record. In some no identification could be made.

Four thousand or 5,000 houses have been broken open, and property or persons taken out. In all cases all arms are taken and destroyed. Seven hundred or 800 persons have been beaten or otherwise maltreated. These of course are partly persons living in the houses which were broken into.

And yet the Government sleeps. The poor disarmed nurses of the Republican party-those men by whose ballots the Republican party holds power-who took their lives in their hands when they cast their ballots for U.S. Grant and other officials-all of us who happen to be beyond the pale of the Governmental regard-must be sacrificed, murdered, scourged, mangled, because some contemptible party scheme might be foiled by doing us justice. I could stand it very well to fight for Uncle Sam, and was never known to refuse an invitation on such an occasion; but this lying down, tied hand and foot with the shackles of the law, to be killed by the very dregs of the rebellion, the scum of the earth, and not allowed either the consolation of fighting or the satisfaction that our "fall" will be noted by the Government, and protection given to others thereby, is somewhat too hard. I am ashamed of the nation that will let its citizens be slain by scores, and scourged by thousands, and offer no remedy or protection. I am ashamed of a State which has not sufficient strength to protect its own officers in the discharge of their duties, nor guarantee the safety of any man's domicile throughout its length and breadth. I am ashamed of a party which, with the reins of power in its hands, has not nerve or decision enough to arm its own adherents, or to protect them from assassinations at the hands of their opponents. A General who in time of war would permit 2,000 or 3,000 of his men to be bushwhacked and destroyed by private treachery even in an enemy's country without any one being punished for it would be worthy of universal execration, and would get it, too. How much more worthy of detestation is a Government which in time of peace will permit such wholesale slaughter of its citizens? It is simple cowardice, inertness, and wholesale demoralization. The wholesale slaughter of the war has dulled our Nation's sense of horror at the shedding of blood, and the habit of regarding the South as simply a laboratory, where every dema-gogue may carry on his reconstructionary experiments at will, and not as an integral party of the Nation itself, has led our Government to shut its eyes to the atrocities of these times. Unless these evils are speedily remedied, I tell you, General, the Republican party has signed its death warrant. It is a party of cowards or idiots-I don't care which alternative is chosen. The remedy is in our hands, and we are afraid or too dull to bestir ourselves and use it.

But you will tell me that Congress is ready and willing to act if it only knew what to do. Like the old Irish woman it wrings its hands and cries, "O Lawk, O Lawk; if I only knew which way." And yet this same Congress has the control of the militia and can organize its own force in every county in the United States, and arm more or less of it. This same Congress has the undoubted right to guarantee and provide a republican government, and protect every citizen in "life, liberty, and the pursuit of happiness," as well as the power conferred by the XVth Amendment. And yet we suffer and die in peace and murderers walk abroad with the blood yet fresh upon their garments, unharmed, unquestioned and unchecked. Fifty thousand dollars given to good detectives would secure, if well used, a complete knowledge of all this gigantic orga-nization of murderers. In connection with an organized and armed militia, it would result in the apprehension of any number of these Thugs *en masque* and with blood on their hands. What then is the remedy? *First:* Let Congress give to the U. S. Courts, or to Courts of the States under its own laws, cognizance of this class of crimes, as crimes against the nation, and let it provide that this legislation be enforced. Why not, for instance, make going armed and masked or disguised, or masked or disguised in the night time, an act of insurrection or sedition? *Second:* Organize militia, National-State militia is a nuisance-and arm as many as may be necessary in each county to enforce its laws. *Third:* Put detectives at work to get hold of this whole organization. Its ultimate aim is unquestionably to revolutionize the Government. If we have not pluck enough for this, why then let us just offer our throats to the knife, emasculate ourselves, and be a nation of self-subjugated slaves at once.

And now, Abbott, I have but one thing to say to you. I have very little doubt that I shall he one of the next victims. My steps have been dogged for months, and only a good opportunity has been wanting to secure to me the fate which Stephens has just met, and I speak earnestly upon this matter. I feel that I have a right to do so, and a right to be heard as well, and with this conviction I say to you plainly that any member of Congress who, especially if from the South, does not support, advocate, and urge immediate, active, and thorough measures to put an end to these outrages, and make citizenship a privilege, is a coward, a traitor, or a fool. The time for action has come, and the man who has now only speeches to make over some Constitutional scarecrow, deserves to be damned.

1. Summarize some of the actions described in this letter that are attributed to the KKK? Why, do you think, Tourgee goes into such detail?
2. What is the tone of this letter? To whom does Tourgee turn in his plea?
3. Explain Tourgee's ultimate purpose in this letter. What remedy is suggested?

16-9 The Nation, "The State of the South" (1872)

The end of the Civil War left the South in dire economic straits. Despite efforts to revive the southern economy, by 1872, conditions had improved little. The Nation suggested the corrupt actions of carpet-baggers were exacerbating the situation.

The indolent excuse for our failure to understand the condition of the South is that nobody can very accurately comprehend it who has not been there to see for himself. With regard to troubles of a social character, this excuse is valid; but there are some plain statistical facts recently brought to light and published which it is our duty to recognize and confront. We must acknowledge that the condition of the South from almost every point of view is extremely wretched. The property of the eleven States in 1860, exclusive of slaves, was valued at $2,728,825,006. At the end of the war their increased liabilities and loss, exclusive of slaves, was $1,272,900,390, nearly one-half the assessed value of their property at the beginning of the war. This, however, was only the State loss. Secretary Belknap fixes the rebel debt, on the 1st of April, 1865, at $2,345,297,823. This estimate would make the total loss of the rebellious States by the war $5,262,303,554. This sum, it will be seen, is about twice the assessed value of all Southern property in 1860, exclusive of slaves. Five-eighths of Southern property is gone, and the taxes upon the remainder are four times that upon the original property before the war. How much of the money wrung from this impoverished country is expended upon public improvements, it is difficult to tell; but it is likely that most of it, and certain that much of it, goes to feed the vulgar and rapacious rogues who rob and rule a people helpless and utterly exhausted.

With the exception of Virginia and Tennessee, the debts of all the States have been increased since the end of the war. The near neighborhood of those communities to the Ohio may have had some influence in driving rogues further south. The real reason, however, is the comparative fewness of the negroes. The debt of Alabama in 1866 was $5,000,000; under the rule of the enlightened and disinterested economists who have undertaken to repair her finances, that debt has been increased to $24,000,000. In North Carolina the new government was established in 1868. In 1860, the State debt was $14,000,000; in 1865, $20,000,000; in 1868, $24,000,000; and in 1871, $34,000,000. Thus the increase of debt since the war has been more than twice the increase during the war-which looks as if war were a cheaper and more prosperous condition than peace. At any rate, reconstruction seems to be morally a more disastrous process than rebellion. Guile is the strength of the weak, and the carpet-baggers have taught the Southern people to meet rogues with trickery. The Ku-klux Committee, commenting upon their dreadful poverty at the close of the war, says that manifestly they must have at once succumbed under their loss of $5,000,000,000 had it not been for the benefactions of the North. It states that the Freedmen's Bureau has spent $13,000,000 upon Southern sufferers of both colors. This does not seem a considerable sum when we think that the increased debt since the war in North Carolina has been $14,000,000. Certainly, our charities have done less good than our carpet-baggers have done damage. The theory, of course, is that something remains from the enormous sums raised by taxation, that they have been expended upon needed public improvements. In North Carolina, it was alleged, the large subsidies given to railroads would encourage immigration. There has been no immigration, however; the bonds have been sold at a disadvantage; some of the money has been stolen, and a few of the rogues have been indicted. It is impossible to say how much of the sums raised remain to the States. The carpet-baggers have had it pretty much their own way. If they chose to rob, there was nothing to prevent them. Give men a chance to be tyrants or scamps, and there is no fear that some will not be found who will avail themselves of it. Here in New York, where we have all the rascals and all the plunderers within a radius of five miles, we know how long we have been in bringing the Ring to bay. The carpet-baggers have an immense extent of country to rifle; they do not buy the legislatures, they constitute them; they enact their own registration acts and vote their own supplies. The persons they rob are not of that apathetic and well-to-do class too indifferent to go to the polls, but people who could not go if they would.

All accounts agree as to the widespread misery and penury. In Mississippi, a large planter testified that it took all his cotton for the year 1871 to pay his taxes. It is South Carolina, however, that enjoys the unenviable eminence of being the worst-robbed State of the whole eleven. In the single county of Kershaw, possessing a population of only 11,000, there were 3,600 tax-executions issued. The taxation during 1870, $2,365,047, was more than the whole taxation on double the property for five years before the war. In order to change the fiscal year, they proposed to double this, and, in 1871, to levy a tax of $4,730,094; whether this law was executed we do not know, but the fact remains that it was enacted. Peculation and corruption are as universal as poverty and distress. In 1860, South Carolina paid for offices and salaries, $123,800; in 1871, the State expended on these $581,640. In two years, $1,208,577 67 have been paid out, for which no vouchers are to be found in the Treasury. According to the minority report of the Ku-klux Committee, the disbursements exceed the appropriations by $170,683. This report, though spoiled by some rather low allusions to "ebony legislators," "men and brothers," etc., brings to light some amusing facts. Money voted with which to fit up committee-rooms has been expended on the private apartments of the colored members of the legislatures. Their rooms were furnished with Brussels carpets, sofas, mirrors, etc. About seventy-five imported porcelain spittoons, bought for the South Carolina State-House, likewise adorned their private apartments. This fact seemed to affect the democratic minority of the committee even more profoundly than the vast robberies and excessive taxations. They remark, with rugged, Spartan simplicity, that they themselves, in "the splendid capital of the nation," had never had anything but "an article of common, plain brown earthenware, of domestic manufacture." This striking disparity between fortune and desert does not excite in us any feeling of indignation against the negroes. Emerging from a long night of slavery and cruel bondage, who can grudge them their fantastic lease of liberty and luxury? Did not graver considerations check us, our humor would be to vote them State barbers and the most delightful of oriental baths. We suspect the truth to be that in the distribution of spoils the poor African gets the gilt and plush, the porcelain spittoons, the barbaric upholstery, while the astuter Caucasian clings to the solider and more durable advantages. The negroes by themselves would be but little to be feared; yet, in the hands of the carpet-baggers, they have been the unwitting instruments of most of the harm that has been done. The swindlers could not have so got the control of things without the help of the negroes. They have made numerically the largest part of the conventions and legislatures in South Carolina. The Convention of 1868, which drew up a State constitution, was composed of 72 negroes and 49 white men. This convention made provision for a levy of $2,230,950 upon the State, which would necessitate taxation at the rate of 6 per cent; yet but 13 of the 72 negroes paid taxes. In the Legislature of 1869, there were twelve black and twenty white senators; eight of the twelve black senators paid no taxes. In the House, there were 86 black and 37 white members; 68 of the 86 black members paid no taxes. As things are at present, there seems to be no limit to the power of the carpet-baggers to plunder the South as they choose. The only ray of hope is in the passage of an act of universal amnesty. We have given the negro the ballot to protect him against his old master; we need now to give the white citizen the vote to protect him against the carpet-bagger.

Seven years have gone over us since the close of the war, and, instead of occupying this precious season with endeavors to re-establish prosperity and to sow the seeds of a peace which, in another generation, would ripen into goodwill and forgetfulness, we have averted our eyes from the whole problem, refused to listen to the complaints of men whose hands we have tied, and have fallen back upon the lazy belief that in some way this great country is bound to go through. The unconscious syllogism working in the indolent Northern mind seems to be: "Things are no doubt very bad-how bad, we haven't the time or the inclination to ascertain. Examination of such unpleasant matters, if a duty at all, is a disagreeable one. After all, the rebels have made their own bed, and they must lie in it." Perhaps their sufferings are only the just punishment of their crimes; but at any rate, there can be no reason for giving over the criminals into the hands of the carpet-baggers. What services have these persons rendered the country that we should grant them the monopoly of robbing rebels? It would be better to levy tribute-money, and get some national advantage from the merciless exactions inflicted upon the Southern people. Let us make up our minds one way or the other-do we or do we not propose further to punish the rebel States for their rebellion? If we do, let us at once proceed to devise some intelligent means for that purpose. If we do not, let us make haste to protect society from the ravages of ignorance and rapacity, or give society the means to protect itself. We thought it worth four years of war to retain the Southern States in the Union, now we hardly deem it worth an act of Congress to preserve them.

1. *Summarize the South's economic situation as it is represented in this document.*
2. *What, in the opinion of the author, has been the effect of Reconstruction policies upon the South? What attitude is voiced in this document toward carpetbaggers? What have carpetbaggers done? What is the solution to this problem?*

16-10   Susan B. Anthony and the "New Departure" for Women (1873)

During the early 1870s, Susan B. Anthony and Elizabeth Cady Stanton engaged in a strategy that they believed would secure the right to vote for women. This "New Departure" was based on the belief that the Fourteenth and Fifteenth Amendments guaranteed all citizens the right to vote regardless of gender. Anthony tested its constitutionality by casting a ballot in the 1872 presidential election. Anthony was arrested, indicted by a grand jury and placed on trial in June 1873 in Canandaigua, New York. The judge ordered the all-male jury to return a guilty verdict. In her comments to the court, Anthony exposed the trial for the travesty it was. She was fined $100 but refused to pay.

> **Source:** Ken Burns and Paul Barnes, *"Not For Ourselves Alone"*: The Story of Elizabeth Cady Stanton and Susan B. Anthony.
> http://www.pbs.org/stantonanthony/resources/index.html?body=04activity.html

Friends and Fellow-citizens: I stand before you to-night, under indictment for the alleged crime of having voted at the last Presidential election, without having a lawful right to vote. It shall be my work this evening to prove to you that in thus voting, I not only committed no crime, but, instead, simply exercised my citizen's right, guaranteed to me and all United States citizens by the National Constitution, beyond the power of any State to deny.

Our democratic-republican government is based on the idea of the natural right of every individual member thereof to a voice and a vote in making and executing the laws. We assert the province of government to be to secure the people in the enjoyment of their unalienable rights. We throw to the winds the old dogma that governments can give rights. Before governments were organized, no one denies that each individual possessed the right to protect his own life, liberty and property. And when 100 or 1,000,000 people enter into a free government, they do not barter away their natural rights; they simply pledge themselves to protect each other in the enjoyment of them, through prescribed judicial and legislative tribunals. They agree to abandon the methods of brute force in the adjustment of their differences, and adopt those of civilization.

Nor can you find a word in any of the grand documents left us by the fathers that assumes for government the power to create or to confer rights. The Declaration of Independence, the United States Constitution, the constitutions of the several states and the organic laws of the territories, all alike propose to protect the people in the exercise of their God-given rights. Not one of them pretends to bestow rights.

"All men are created equal, and endowed by their Creator with certain unalienable rights. Among these are life, liberty and the pursuit of happiness. That to secure these, governments are instituted among men, deriving their just powers from the consent of the governed."

Here is no shadow of government authority over rights, nor exclusion of any from their full and equal enjoyment. Here is pronounced the right of all men, and "consequently," as the Quaker preacher said, "of all women," to a voice in the government. And here, in this very first paragraph of the declaration, is the assertion of the natural right of all to the ballot; for, how can "the consent of the governed" be given, if the right to vote be denied. Again:

"That whenever any form of government becomes destructive of these ends, it is the right of the people to alter or abolish it, and to institute a new government, laying its foundations on such principles, and organizing its powers in such forms as to them shall seem most likely to effect their safety and happiness."

Surely, the right of the whole people to vote is here clearly implied, for however destructive in their happiness this government might become, a disfranchised class could neither alter nor abolish it, nor institute a new one, except by the old brute force method of insurrection and rebellion. One-half of the people of this nation to-day are utterly powerless to blot from the statute books an unjust law, or to write there a new and a just one. The women, dissatisfied as they are with this form of government, that enforces taxation without representation,—that compels them to obey laws to which they have never given their consent,—that imprisons and hangs them without a trial by a jury of their peers, that robs them, in marriage, of the custody of their own persons, wages and children,—are this half of the people left wholly at the mercy of the other half, in direct violation of the spirit and letter of the declarations of the framers of this government, every one of which was based on the immutable principle of equal rights to all. By those declarations, kings, priests, popes, aristocrats, were all alike dethroned, and placed on a common level politically, with the lowliest born subject or serf. By them, too, me, as such, were deprived of their divine right to rule, and placed on a political level with women. By the practice of those declarations all class and caste distinction will be abolished; and slave, serf, plebeian, wife, woman, all alike, bound from their subject position to the proud platform of equality. . . .

The preamble of the federal constitution says:

"We, the people of the United States, in order to form a more perfect union, establish justice, insure domestic tranquility, provide for the common defense, promote the general welfare and secure the blessings of liberty to ourselves and our posterity, do ordain and established this constitution for the United States of America."

It was we, the people, not we, the white male citizens, nor yet we, the male citizens; but we, the whole people, who formed this Union. And we formed it, not to give the blessings of liberty, but to secure them; not to the half of ourselves and the half of our posterity, but to the whole people-women as well as men. And it is downright mockery to talk to women of their enjoyment of the blessings of liberty while they are denied the use of the only means of securing them provided by this democratic-republican government-the ballot. . . .

For any State to make sex a qualification that must ever result in the disfranchisement of one entire half of the people, is to pass a bill of attainder, or an ex post facto law, and is therefore a violation of the supreme law of the land. By it, the blessings of liberty are forever withheld from women and their female posterity. . . .

There is no she, or her, or hers, in the tax laws. . . .

The same is true of all the criminal laws. . . .

The only question left to be settled, now, is: Are women persons? And I hardly believe any of our opponents will have the hardihood to say they are not. Being persons, then, women are citizens, and no state has a right to make any new law, or to enforce any old law, that shall abridge their privileges or immunities. Hence, every discrimination against women in the constitutions and laws of the several states, is to-day null and void, precisely as is every one against negroes.

Is the right to vote one of the privileges or immunities of citizens? I think the disfranchised ex-rebels, and the ex-state prisoners will agree with me, that it is not only one of the them, but the one without which all the others are nothing. Seek the first kingdom of the ballot, and all things else shall be given thee, is the political injunction.

Webster, Worcester and Bouvier all define citizen to be a person, in the United States, entitled to vote and hold office. . . .

Prior to the adoption of the thirteenth amendment, by which slavery was forever abolished, and black men transformed from property to persons, the judicial opinions of the country had always been in harmony with these definitions. To be a person was to be a citizen, and to be a citizen was to be a voter. . . .

If the fourteenth amendment does not secure to all citizens the right to vote, for what purpose was the grand old charter of the fathers lumbered with its unwieldy proportions? The republican party, and Judges Howard and Bingham, who drafted the document, pretended it was to do something for black men; and if that something was not to secure them in their right to vote and hold office, what could it have been? For, by the thirteenth amendment, black men had become people, and hence were entitled to all the privileges and immunities of the government, precisely as were the women of the country, and foreign men not naturalized. According to Associate Justice Washington, they already had the "Protection of the government, the enjoyment of life and liberty, with the right to acquire and possess property of every kind, and to pursue and obtain happiness and safety, subject to such restraints as the government may justly prescribe for the general welfare of the whole; the right of a citizen of one state to pass through or to reside in any other state for the purpose of trade, agriculture, professional pursuit, or otherwise; to claim the benefit of the writ of habeas corpus, to institute and maintain actions of any kind in the courts of the state; to take, hold, and dispose of property, either real or personal, and an exemption from higher taxes or impositions than are paid by the other citizens of the state."

Thus, you see, those newly freed men were in possession of every possible right, privilege and immunity of the government, except that of suffrage, and hence, needed no constitutional amendment for any other purpose. What right, I ask you, has the Irishman the day after he receives his naturalization papers that he did not possess the day before, save the right to vote and hold office? And the Chinamen, now crowding our Pacific coast, are in precisely the same position. What privilege or immunity has California or Oregon the constitutional right to deny them, save that of the ballot? Clearly, then if the fourteenth amendment was not to secure to black men their right to vote, it did nothing for them, since they possessed everything else before. But, if it was meant to be a prohibition of the states, to deny or abridge their right to vote-which I fully believe-then it did the same for all persons, white women included, born or naturalized in the United States; for the amendment does not say all male persons of African descent, but all persons are citizens. . . .

Clearly, then, the national government must not only define the rights of citizens, but it must stretch out its powerful hand and protect them in every state in this Union. . . .

But if you will insist that the fifteenth amendment's emphatic interdiction against robbing United States citizens of their right to vote," on account of race, color, or previous condition of servitude," is a recognition of the right, either of the United States, or any state, to rob citizens of that right, for any or all other reason, I will prove to you that the class of citizens for which I now plead, and to which I belong, may be, and sure, by all the principles of our government, and many of the laws of the states, included under the term "previous condition of servitude."

First, the married women and their legal status. What is servitude? "The condition of a slave," What is a slave? "A person who is robbed of the proceeds of his labor; a person who is subject to the will of another."

By the law of Georgia, South Carolina, and all the states of the South, the negro had no right to the custody and control of his person. He belonged to his master. If he was disobedient, the master had the right to use correction. If the negro didn't like the correction, and attempted to run away, the master had a right to use coercion to bring him back.

By the law of every state in this Union to-day, North as well as South, the married woman has no right to the custody and control of her person. The wife belongs to her husband; and if she refuses obedience to his will, he may use moderate correction, and if she doesn't like his moderate correction, and attempts to leave his "bed and board," the husband may use moderate coercion to bring her back. The little word "moderate," you see, is the saving clause for the wife, and would doubtless be overstepped should offended husband administer his correction with the "cat-o'-nine-tails," or accomplish his coercion with blood-hounds.

Again, the slave had no right to the earnings of his hands, they belonged to his master; no right to the custody of his children, they belonged to his master; no right to sue or be sued, or testify in the courts. If he committed a crime, it was the master who must sue or be sued.

In many of the states there has been special legislation, giving to married women the right to property inherited, or received by bequest, or earned by the pursuit of any avocation outside of the home; also, giving her the right to sue and be sued in matters pertaining to such separate property; but not a single state of this Union has ever secured the wife in the enjoyment of her right to the joint ownership of the joint earnings of the marriage copartnership. And since, in the nature of things, the vast majority of married women never earn a dollar, by work outside of their families, nor inherit a dollar from their fathers, it follows that from the day of their marriage to the day of the death of their husbands, not one of them ever has a dollar, except it shall please her husband to let her have it.

Is anything further needed to prove woman's condition of servitude sufficiently orthodox to entitle her to the guaranties of the fifteenth amendment?

Is there a man who will not agree with me, that to talk of freedom without the ballot, is mockery-is slavery-to the women of this Republic, precisely as New England's orator Wendell Phillips, at the close of the late war, declared it to be to the newly emancipated black men?

I admit that prior to the rebellion, by common consent, the right to enslave, as well as to disfranchise both native and foreign born citizens, was conceded to the States. But the one grand principle, settled by the war and the reconstruction legislation, is the supremacy of national power to protect the citizens of the United States in their right to freedom and the elective franchise, against any and every interference on the part of the several States. And again and again, have the American people asserted the triumph of this principle, by their overwhelming majorities for Lincoln and Grant.

The one issue of the last two Presidential elections was, whether the fourteenth and fifteenth amendments should be considered the irrevocable will of the people; and the decision was, they shall be—and that it is only the right, but the duty of the National Government to protect all United States citizens in the full enjoyment and free exercise of all their privileges and immunities against any attempt of any State to deny or abridge.

And in this conclusion Republican and Democrats alike agree.

Senator Frelinghuysen said:

"The heresy of State rights has been completely buried in these amendments, that as amended, the constitution confers not only national but State citizenship upon all persons born or naturalized within our limits."

The Call for the national Republican convention said:

"Equal suffrage has been engrafted on the national constitution; the privileges and immunities of American citizenship have become a part of the organic law."

The national Republican platform said:

"Complete liberty and exact quality in the enjoyment of all civil, political and public rights, should be established and maintained throughout the union by efficient and appropriate State and federal legislation."

If that means anything, it is that Congress should pass a law to require the States to protect women in their equal political rights, and that the States should enact laws making it the duty of inspectors of elections to receive women's votes on precisely the same conditions they do those of men.

Judge Stanley Mathews—a substantial Ohio democrat—in his preliminary speech at the Cincinnati convention, said most emphatically.

"The constitutional amendments have established the political equality of all citizens before the law."

President Grant, in his message to Congress March 30th 1870, on the adoption of the fifteenth amendment, said:

"A measure which makes at once four millions of people voters, is indeed a measure of greater importance than any act of the kind from the foundation of the Government to the present time."

How could four million negroes be made voter if two million were not included?

The California State Republican convention said:

"Among the many practical and substantial triumphs of the principles achieved by the Republican party during the past twelve years, it enumerated with pride and pleasure, the prohibiting of any State from abridging the privileges of any citizen of the Republic, the declaring the civil and political equality of every citizen, and the establishing all these principles in the federal constitution by amendments thereto, as the permanent law."

Benjamin F. Butler, in a recent letter to me, said:

"I do not believe anybody in Congress doubts that the Constitution authorizes the right of women to vote, precisely as it authorizes trial by jury and many other like rights guaranteed to citizens."

And again, General Butler said:

"It is not laws we want; there are plenty of laws—good enough, too. Administrative ability to enforce law is the great want of the age, in this country especially. Everybody talks of law, law. If everybody would insist on the enforcement of law, the government would stand on a firmer basis, and question would settle themselves."

And it is upon this just interpretation of the United States Constitution that our National Woman Suffrage Association which celebrates the twenty-fifth anniversary of the woman's rights movement in New York on the 6th of May next, has based all its arguments and action the past five years.

We no longer petition Legislature or Congress to give us the right to vote. We appeal to the women everywhere to exercise their too long neglected "citizen's right to vote." We appeal to the inspectors of election everywhere to receive the votes of all United States citizens as it is their duty to do. We appeal to United States commissioners and marshals to arrest the inspectors who reject the names and votes of United States citizens, as it is their duty to do, and leave those alone who, like our eighth ward inspectors, perform their duties faithfully and well.

We ask the juries to fail to return verdicts of "guilty" against honest, law-abiding, tax-paying United States citizens for offering their votes at our elections. Or against intelligent, worthy young men, inspectors of elections, for receiving and counting such citizens votes.

We ask the judges to render true and unprejudiced opinions of the law, and wherever there is room for a doubt to give its benefit on the side of liberty and equal rights to women, remembering that "the true rule of interpretation under our national constitution, especially since its amendments, is that anything for human rights is constitutional, everything against human right unconstitutional."

And it is on this line that we propose to fight our battle for the ballot-all peaceably, but nevertheless persistently through to complete triumph, when all United States citizens shall be recognized as equals before the law.

1. According to Anthony, what is the connection between citizenship and the right to vote? What example(s) did she use to prove her point?
2. According to Anthony, how do the Fourteenth and Fifteenth Amendments address the rights of women? How does she support her assertions?

16-11 James T. Rapier, Testimony Before U.S. Senate Regarding the Agricultural Labor Force in the South (1880)

An essential freedom African Americans gained in the post-Civil War era was the ability to move freely around the country. Seeking improvement of their situation, many African Americans emigrated to other states. As this excerpt shows, a variety of forces combined to push African Americans to emigrate.

A. Well, sir, there are several reasons why the colored people desire to emigrate from Alabama; one among them is the poverty of the South. On a large part of it a man cannot make a decent living. Another is their want of school privileges in the State: and there is a majority of the people who believe that they cannot any longer get justice in the courts; and another and the greatest reason is found in the local laws that we have, and which are very oppressive to that class of people in the black belt.

Q. State what some of them are.

A. First, we have only schools about three months in the year, and I suppose I need not say anything more on that head. In reference to the poverty of the soil, 33 to 40 per cent of the lands in Alabama is about all on which a man can make a living.

Q. Do you mean the parts that are subdued?

A. Yes, sir; the arable land. The average is one-third of a bale of cotton to the acre, not making three bales to the hand; and a hundred bushels of corn to the hand, on an average. Then take the price of cotton for the last two years; it has not netted more than $45 to $47.50 to the bale; and I suppose it would not be amiss for me to state something of the plans of working the land in Alabama.

Mr. Vance. It will be very proper.

The Witness. The general plan is that the landlord furnishes the land and the teams and feed for the teams and the implements, for which he draws one half of the crop. I remarked that the three bales of cotton and a hundred bushels of corn is about all that you can make to a hand. We allow in Alabama that much, for that is as much as a man can get out of it, and that is not enough to support his family, including himself and the feed of his family; $95 to $100 is as much as a hand can make, and that is not enough to feed any man in a Christian country. . . .

A. . . . Now, it is very clear that a man cannot live on such terms, and hence the conclusion of many of these people, that there is not a decent living for them in that State. They are like the white people, and their living no better. Numbers of them, probably not less than 20,000 whites, have left Alabama since the war and gone to Texas to better their condition, and the blacks are doing the same thing, and that is the whole there is of it. So far as the negroes are concerned now they have a high desire to submit their fate to their own keeping in another country. Now here is one of the laws which also affects us, to which I will call attention. It is found in the acts of Alabama for 1878-'79, page 63, act No. 57, section 1.

Section 1. *Be it enacted by the general assembly of Alabama*, That section 4369 of the Code be, and the same is hereby, amended so as to read as follows: Any person who shall buy, sell, receive, barter, or dispose of any cotton, corn, wheat, oats, pease, or potatoes after the hour of sunset and before the hour of sunrise of the next succeeding day, and any person who shall in any manner move, carry, convey, or transport, except within the limits of the farm or plantation on which it is raised or grown, any seed cotton between the hours of sunset and sunrise of the next succeeding day, shall be guilty of a misdemeanor, and, on conviction, shall be fined not less than ten nor more five hundred dollars, and may also be imprisoned in the county jail, or put to hard labor for the county, for not more than twelve months. But this section shall not effect the right of municipal corporations to establish and regulate under their charters public markets within their limits for the sale of commodities for culinary purposes, nor the right of any proprietor or owner of any plantation or premises to sell on such plantation or premises the necessary grain and provisions for the subsistence of man and beast for the night to traveling or transient persons, or for the use of agricultural laborers in his own employment on such plantation or premises: *Provided*, That the provisions of such section shall not apply to any person carrying seed cotton to a gin for the purpose of having the same ginned.

Now, the effect of this upon the labor of the South is this: A great many laborers work by the month, but all of them are under contract. If I live three miles from a store, and I must work from sunup to sundown, I cannot go where I can do my trading to the best advantage. A man is prevented, no matter whether his family is sick from sundown to sunrise, from going and selling anything that he has, as the landlord will not give them time between sunrise and sundown.

Q. What was the purpose of this law?

A. It was, as appears from the debates, to keep the negroes from going to stores and taking off seed cotton from the plantation. Certainly it was to have that effect, but it goes further and prevents a man from selling what he has raised and has a right to sell. If a man commits a crime he ought to be punished, but every man ought to have a right to dispose of his own property.

Q. Is there any particular limitation of time to which this law applies?

A. No, sir.

Q. It runs all the year round?

A. Yes, sir.

Q. After the division of the crops as well as before?

A. Yes, sir; it operates so that a man cannot sell his crop at all in many cases.

Q. Do you say that the landlord will not let him sell his crop or that he can prevent it?

A. I say he will not let him do it, because the landlord will not let him take two or three hours out of the time due him in the day to sell it, and the law prevents him from selling at night.

Q. You say the effect of it is not to let him sell his crop at all?

A. I do; for if a man agrees to work from sunup to sundown he is made to do it. I work them that way myself, and I believe all the rest do. . . .

Q. It shall not be lawful to buy or sell seed cotton?

A. Yes, sir.

Q. At any time?

A. Yes, sir; night or day.

Q. From nobody?

A. From nobody.

Q. White or black?—A. White or black; but you see it applies wholly to black counties.

Q. But there are some white people there, are there not?

A. Yes, sir; but I do not know many who raise seed cotton.

Q. I thought something, may be, was left out of that act?

A. No, sir; that is to say, the gist of the matter is this: I may raise as much cotton as I please in the seed, but I am prohibited by law from selling it to anybody but the landlord, who can buy it because he has advanced to me on the crop. One of the rules is this: I have people working for me to day, but I give them an outside patch. If a man makes outside 1,200 pounds of seed cotton, which is worth $2.50 per 100 pounds, he cannot sell it unless to me. I may say I will give him $1.50 per 100 pounds for it, and he will be forced to take it; but I cannot sell it again unless I have a merchantable bale, which is 500 pounds, or 450 pounds by the cotton congress.

Q. Then the effect of that law is to place all the seed cotton into the hands of the landlord?

A. Yes, sir.

Q. He is the only purchaser who is allowed by law to buy it?

A. Yes, sir; nobody else can buy it. . . .

Q. I thought the law said that grand larceny should consist of as much as $235 worth?

A. No, sir; you have not got it right yet. Two ears or a stalk of corn is a part of an outstanding crop, and any man who sells any part of an outstanding crop can be prosecuted and convicted of grand larceny. . . .

The Witness. The point is this: Under the laws of Alabama the probate judge, the clerk, and the sheriff have had the drawing of jurors, and have had since Alabama was admitted as a State; but this bill comes in and covers those counties where the Republicans are likely to have a majority, and where they would draw the jurors. The proper heading of the law might have been, "An act to keep negroes off the juries." I want to state that it is the general opinion of the colored people in Alabama, and I will say of some of the judges, that it is a difficult matter for a colored man to get justice when there is a case between him and a white man. I will cite one of those cases: There was a case in Montgomery in which Judge J.

Q. Smith presided. It was a civil suit. A white man had a black man's crop attached, and he had lost it. The colored man sued him on the attachment bond, and employed Judge Gardiner to defend or prosecute it for him. Soon after the case was given to the jury they brought in a verdict for the defendant. Judge Gardiner moved for a new trial, on the ground that the verdict was not in accordance with the facts; and the judge said, "I have observed that where an issue is between a white and a black man before a jury the verdict is almost invariably against the black man. The grounds on which the judge said he would not grant a new trial would be because he thinks the next verdict would not be different from that rendered, and as I do not think there would be a different verdict, I decline to give the new trial."

1. *What is the plight of the free southern black farmer according to this testimony? What particular challenges face the black farmer in this account?*
2. *In what ways is a black farmer in the south barely better off than he was under slavery?*
3. *What prejudices against blacks in the legal system are revealed by this testimony?*

16-12   A Sharecrop Contract (1882)

During the Reconstruction era, sharecropping emerged as the most common method of organizing and financing southern agriculture. Large plantations, no longer worked by gangs of slaves, were broken up into small plots worked by individual families. the following contract typifies the sort of formal arrangements that many thousands of poor black and white farmers made with local landowners

To every one applying to rent land upon shares, the following conditions must be read, and agreed to.

To every 30 and 35 acres, I agree to furnish the team, plow, and farming implements, except cotton planters, and I do not agree to furnish a cart to every cropper. The croppers are to have half of the cotton, corn, and fodder (and peas and pumpkins and potatoes if any are planted) if the following conditions are complied with, but-if not-they are to have only two-fifths ($^2/^5$). Croppers are to have no part or interest in the cotton seed raised from the crop planted and worked by them. No vine crops of any description, that is, no watermelons, muskmelons, . . . squashes or anything of that kind, except peas and pumpkins, and potatoes, are to be planted in the cotton or corn. All must work under my direction. All plantation work to be done by the croppers. My part of the crop to be housed by them, and the fodder and oats to be hauled and put in the house. All the cotton must be topped about 1st August. If any cropper fails from any cause to save all the fodder from his crop, I am to have enough fodder to make it equal to one-half of the whole if the whole amount of fodder had been saved.

For every mule or horse furnished by me there must be 1000 good sized rails. . . hauled, and the fence repaired as far as they will go, the fence to be torn down and put up from the bottom if I so direct. All croppers to haul rails and work on fence whenever I may order. Rails to be split when I may say. Each cropper to clean out every ditch in his crop, and where a ditch runs between two croppers, the cleaning out of that ditch is to be divided equally between them. Every ditch bank in the crop must be shrubbed down and cleaned off before the crop is planted and must be cut down every time the land is worked with his hoe and when the crop is "laid by," the ditch banks must be left clean of bushes, weeds, and seeds. The cleaning out of all ditches must be done by the first of October. The rails must be split and the fence repaired before corn is planted.

Each cropper must keep in good repair all bridges in his crop or over ditches that he has to clean out and when a bridge needs repairing that is outside of all their crops, then any one that I call on must repair it.

Fence jams to be done as ditch banks. If any cotton is planted on the land outside of the plantation fence, I am to have three-fourths of all the cotton made in those patches, that is to say, no cotton must be planted by croppers in their home patches.

All croppers must clean out stable and fill them with straw, and haul straw in front of stable whenever I direct. All the cotton must be manured, and enough fertilizer must be brought to manure each crop highly, the croppers to pay for one-half of all manure bought, the quantity to be purchased for each crop must be left to me.

No cropper is to work off the plantation when there is any work to be done on the land he has rented, or when his work is needed by me or other croppers. Trees to be cut down on Orchard, house field, & Evanson fences, leaving such as I may designate.

Road field is to be planted from the very edge of the ditch to the fence, and all the land to be planted close up to the ditches and fences. No stock of any kind belonging to croppers to run in the plantation after crops are gathered.

If the fence should be blown down, or if trees should fall on the fence outside of the land planted by any of the croppers, any one or all that I may call upon must put it up and repair it. Every cropper must feed or have fed, the team he works, Saturday nights, Sundays, and every morning before going to work, beginning to feed his team (morning, noon, and night every day in the week) on the day he rents and feeding it to including the 31st day of December. If any cropper shall from any cause fail to repair his fence as far as 1000 rails will go, or shall fail to clean out any part of his ditches, or shall fail to leave his ditch banks, any part of them, well shrubbed and clean when his crop is laid by, or shall fail to clean out stables, fill them up and haul straw in front of them whenever he is told, he shall have only two-fifths ($^2/_5$) of the cotton, corn, fodder, peas, and pumpkins made on the land he cultivates.

If any cropper shall fail to feed his team Saturday nights, all day Sunday and all the rest of the week, morning/noon, and night, for every time he so fails he must pay me five cents.

No corn or cotton stalks must be burned, but must be cut down, cut up and plowed in. Nothing must be burned off the land except when it is impossible to plow it in.

Every cropper must be responsible for all gear and farming implements placed in his hands, and if not returned must be paid for unless it is worn out by use.

Croppers must sow & plow in oats and haul them to the crib, but must have no part of them. Nothing to be sold from their crops, nor fodder nor corn to be carried out of the fields until my rent is all paid, and all amounts they owe me and for which I am responsible are paid in full.

I am to gin & pack all the cotton and charge every cropper an eighteenth of his part, the cropper to furnish his part of the bagging, ties, & twine. The sale of every cropper's part of the cotton to be made by me when and where I choose to sell, and after deducting all they owe me and all sums that I may be responsible for on their accounts, to pay them their half of the net proceeds. Work of every description, particularly the work on fences and ditches, to be done to my satisfaction, and must be done over until I am satisfied that it is done as it should be.

No wood to burn, nor light wood, nor poles, nor timber for boards, nor wood for any purpose whatever must be gotten above the house occupied by Henry Beasley-nor must any trees be cut down nor any wood used for any purpose, except for firewood, without my permission.

1. Identify and explain the stipulations of this contract that result in virtual slavery for the sharecropper.

PART SEVENTEEN
NEW SOUTH, EXPANDING WEST

17-1 Edward Gould Buffum, Six Months in the Gold Mines (1850)

Part of the California Gold Rush phenomenon was the rapid setting up of small, often temporary communities. These mining towns often had no official officers of the law, dispensing justice through citizen vigilante groups as occurred in the excerpt below.

A scene occurred about this time that exhibits in a striking light, the summary manner in which "justice" is dispensed in a community where there are no legal tribunals. We received a report on the afternoon of January 20th, that five men had been arrested at the dry diggings, and were under trial for a robbery. The circumstances were these:-A Mexican gambler, named Lopez, having in his possession a large amount of money, retired to his room at night, and was surprised about midnight by five men rushing into his apartment, one of whom applied a pistol to his head, while the others barred the door and proceeded to rifle his trunk. An alarm being given, some of the citizens rushed in, and arrested the whole party. Next day they were tried by a jury chosen from among the citizens, and sentenced to receive thirty-nine lashes each, on the following morning. Never having witnessed a punishment inflicted by Lynch-law, I went over to the dry diggings on a clear Sunday morning, and on my arrival, found a large crowd collected around an oak tree, to which was lashed a man with a bared back, while another was applying a raw cowhide to his already gored flesh. A guard of a dozen men, with loaded rifles pointed at the prisoners, stood ready to fire in case of an attempt being made to escape. After the whole had been flogged, some fresh charges were preferred against three of the men-two Frenchmen, named Garcia and Bissi, and a Chileno, named Manuel. These were charged with a robbery and attempt to murder, on the Stanislaus River, during the previous fall. The unhappy men were removed to a neighbouring house, and being so weak from their punishment as to be unable to stand, were laid stretched upon the floor. As it was not possible for them to attend, they were tried in the open air, in their absence, by a crowd of some two hundred men, who had organized themselves into a jury, and appointed a *pro tempore* judge. The charges against them were well substantiated, but amounted to nothing more than an attempt at robbery and murder; no overt act being even alleged. They were known to be bad men, however, and a general sentiment seemed to prevail in the crowd that they ought to be got rid of. At the close of the trial, which lasted some thirty minutes, the Judge put to vote the question whether they had been proved guilty. A universal affirmative was the response; and then the question "What punishment shall be inflicted?" was asked. A brutal-looking fellow in the crowd, cried out, "Hang them." The proposition was seconded, and met with almost universal approbation. I mounted a stump, and in the name of God, humanity, and law, protested against such a course of proceeding; but the crowd, by this time excited by frequent and deep potations of liquor from a neighbouring groggery, would listen to nothing contrary to their brutal desires, and even threatened to hang me if I did not immediately desist from any further remarks. Somewhat fearful that such might be my fate, and seeing the utter uselessness of further argument with them, I ceased, and prepared to witness the horrible tragedy. Thirty minutes only were allowed the unhappy victims to prepare themselves to enter on the scenes of eternity. Three ropes were procured, and attached to the limb of a tree. The prisoners were marched out, placed upon a wagon, and the ropes put round their necks. No time was given them for explanation. They vainly tried to speak, but none of them understanding English, there were obliged to employ their native tongues, which but few of those assembled understood. Vainly they called for an interpreter, for their cries were drowned by the yells of a now infuriated mob. A black handkerchief was bound around the eyes of each; their arms were pinioned, and at a given signal, without priest or prayer-book, the wagon was drawn from under them, and they were launched into eternity. Their graves were dug ready to receive them, and when life was entirely extinct, they were cut down and buried in their blankets. This was the first execution I ever witnessed.-God grant that it may be the last!

1. *Characterize the perspective of mining towns that is inferred from this account. What seem to be the laws and principles governing the behavior of the residents of this town?*
2. *What does this account suggest about the sense of autonomy that may have existed in mining towns far from any other established institutions of law or government? What factors might have contributed to this feeling?*

17-2 Lydia Allen Rudd, Diary of Westward Travel (1852)

The overland wagon trains of the 1840s and 1850s brought thousands of American families across the trans-Mississippi West to Oregon, California, or Utah. As this diary shows, the trip involved people leaving their homes, families, and most of the trappings of their "civilized" life for months traveling across a rugged natural environment populated by Native Americans.

May 6 1852 Left the Missouri river for our long journey across the wild uncultivated plains and unhabitated except by the red man. As we left the river bottom and ascended the bluffs the view from them was handsome! In front of us as far as vision could reach extended the green hills covered with fine grass. . . . Behind us lay the Missouri with its muddy water hurrying past as if in great haste to reach some destined point ahead all unheeding the impatient emigrants on the opposite shore at the ferrying which arrived faster than they could be conveyed over. About half a miles down the river lay a steamboat stuck fast on a sandbar. Still farther down lay the busy village of St. Joseph looking us a good bye and reminding us that we were leaving all signs of civilised life for the present. But with good courage and not one sigh of regret I mounted my pony (whose name by the way is Samy) and rode slowly on. In going some two miles, the scene changed from bright sunshine to drenching showers of rain this was not quite agreeable for in spite of our good blankets and intentions otherwise we got some wet. The rain detained us so that we have not made but ten miles today. . . .

May 7 I found myself this morning with a severe headache from the effects of yesterday's rain. . . .

There is a toll bridge across this stream kept by the Indians. The toll for our team in total was six bits. We have had some calls this evening from the Indians. We gave them something to eat and they left. Some of them [had] on no shirt only a blanket, whiles others were ornamented in Indian style with their faces painted in spots and stripes feathers and fur on their heads beeds on their neck brass rings on their wrists and arms and in their ears armed with rifles and spears.

May 8 . . . We have come about 12 miles and were obliged to camp in the open prairie without any wood. Mary and myself collected some dry weeds and grass and made a little fire and cooked some meat and the last of our supply of eggs with these and some hard bread with water we made our supper.

May 9 . . . We passed a new made grave today . . . a man from Ohio We also met a man that was going back: he had buried his Wife this morning She died from the effects of measels we have come ten miles today encamped on a small stream called Vermillion creek Wood and water plenty Their are as many as fifty waggons on this stream and some thousand head of stock It looks like a village the tents and waggons extend as much as a mile. . . .

Some are singing some talking and some laughing and the cattle are adding their mite by shaking their bells and grunt[ing]. Mosquitoes are intruding their unwelcome presence. Harry says that I must not sit here any longer writing but go to bed for I will not want to get up early in the morning to get breakfast.

May 10 I got up this morning and got breakfast and before sunrise we had eat in spite of Harry's prophecies to the contrary. . . .

May 11 We had a very heavy fog this morning which cleared up about noon. Our men are not any of them very well this morning. We passed another grave to day which was made this morning. The board stated that he died of cholera. He was from Indiana. We met several that had taken the back track for the states homesick I presume let them go. We have passed through a handsome country and have encamped on the Nimehaw river, the most beautiful spot that ever I saw in my life. I would like to live here. As far as the eye can reach either way lay handsome rolling prairies, not a stone a tree nor a bush even nothing but grass and flowers meets the eye until you reach the valley of the river which is as level as the house floor and about half a mile wide, where on the bank of the stream for two or three rods wide is one of the heaviest belts of timber I ever saw covered with thick foliage so thick that you could not get a glimpse of the stream through it. You can see this belt of timber for three or four miles from the hills on both sides winding through the prairie like some huge snake. We have traveled twelve miles. . . .

May 12 . . . Our men not much better.

May 13 . . . Henry has been no better to day. Soon after we stopped to night a man came along with a wheel barrow going to California: he is a dutchmann. He wheels his provisions and clothing all day and then stops where night overtakes him sleeps on the ground in the open air. He eats raw meat and bread for his supper. I think that he will get tired wheeling his way through the world by the time he gets to California.

May 14 Just after we started this morning we passed four men dig[g]ing a grave. They were packers. The man that had died was taken sick yesterday noon and died last night. They called it cholera morbus. The corpse lay on the ground a few feet from where they were dig[g]ing. The grave it was a sad sight. . . .

On the bank of the stream waiting to cross, stood a dray with five men harnessed to it bound for California. They must be some of the persevering kind I think. Wanting to go to California more than I do. . . . We passed three more graves this afternoon. . . .

Sept. 5 Traveled eighteen miles today encamped on a slough of powder river poor camp not much grass water nor wood. I am almost dead tonight. I have been sick two or three days with the bowel complaint and am much worse tonight.

Sept. 6 We have not been able to leave this miserable place today. I am not as well as yesterday and no physician to be had. We got a little medicine from a train tonight that has checked the disease some, the first thing that has done me any good.

Sept. 7 . . . I am some better today so much so that they ventured to move me this for the sake of a better camp. Mrs. Girtman is also sick with the same disease. Our cattle are most all of them ailing-there are two more that we expect will die every day. . . .

Oct. 8 started early this morning without any breakfast for the very good reason that we had nothing to eat still three miles from the falls safely landed about eight o'clock tired hungry and with a severe cold from last nights exposure something like civilization here in the shape of three or four houses there is an excuse here for a railroad of a mile and half on which to convey bag[g]age below the falls where they can again take water for the steamboat landing. Harry packed our bag[g]age down the railroad and the rest of us walked the car is drawn across the railroad by a mule and they will car[r]y no persons but sick. We again hired an Indian with his canoe to take us from the falls to the steamboat landing ar[r]ived about sundown a great many emigrants waiting for a chance to leave the steamboat and several flat boats lying ready to start out in the morning encamped on the shore for the night.

October 9-October 13 . . .

October 14 . . . I am so anxious to get some place to stop and settle that my patience is not worth much.

October 15-18 . . .

October 19 . . . We have had a very bad day today for traveling it has rained nearly all the time and it has rained very hard some of the time and we have had a miserable road the rain has made the hills very slippery and had to get up and down we have made but eleven miles of travel encamped on the prairie no water for our stock and not much for ourselves.

October 21 . . .

October 22 . . . Traveled three miles this morning and reached the village of Salem it is quite a pretty town a much handsomer place than Oregon City and larger. . . .

I am afraid that we shall be obliged to pack from here the rest of our journey and it will be a wet job another wet rainy day I am afraid that the rain will make us all sick. I am already begin to feel the affects of it by a bad cold.

October 23 . . . We cannot get any wagon to take us on our journey and are obliged to pack the rest of the way Mr. Clark and wife have found a house to live in and employment for the winter and they will stop here in Salem It took us until nearly noon to get our packs fixed for packing went about two miles and it rained so fast that we were obliged to stop got our dinner and supper in one meal cooked in a small cabin ignorant people but kind started again just

October 24-25 . . .

October 26 . . . we reached Burlington about two o'clock. There is one store one blacksmith shop and three or four dwelling houses. We encamped close by found Mr. Donals in his store an old acquaintance of my husband's. I do not know what we shall yet conclude on doing for the winter. There is no house in town that we can get to winter in. We shall probably stay here tomorrow and by the time know what we are to do for a while at least.

October 27 . . . Our men have been looking around for a house and employment and have been successful for which I feel very thankful. Harry has gone into copartnership with Mr. Donals in the mercantile business and we are to live in the back part of the store for this winter. Henry and Mary are going into Mr. D——house on his farm for the winter one mile from here. Mr. D——will also find him employment if he wants. I expect that we shall not make a claim after all our trouble in getting here on purpose for one. I shall have to be poor and dependent on a man my life time.

1. *Compare and contrast the diarist's hopes and first impressions regarding the westward journey with her resignation after they have reached their winter home.*
2. *Describe and summarize the various experiences depicted by the author along the journey that present significant obstacles for westward travelers.*

17-3   Horace Greeley, An Overland Journey (1860)

The expansion of the United State across the continent created issues regarding speedy and effective communication and transportation. The railroad appeared as a solution to these issues as the excerpt below indicates.

The social, moral, and intellectual blessings of a Pacific railroad can hardly be glanced at within the limits of an article. Suffice it for the present that I merely suggest them.

1. Our mails are now carried to and from California by steamships, via Panama, in twenty to thirty days, starting once a fortnight. The average time of transit from writers throughout the Atlantic states to their correspondents on the Pacific exceeds thirty days. With a Pacific railroad, this would be reduced to ten; for the letters written in Illinois or Michigan would reach their destinations in the mining counties of California quicker than letters sent from New York or Philadelphia would reach San Francisco. With a daily mail by railroad from each of our Atlantic cities to and from California, it is hardly possible that the amount of both letters and printed matter transmitted, and consequently of postage, should not be speedily quadrupled.
2. The first need of California to-day is a large influx of intelligent, capable, virtuous women. With a railroad to the Pacific, avoiding the miseries and perils of six thousand miles of ocean transportation, and making the transit a pleasant and interesting overland journey of ten days, at a reduced cost, the migration of this class would be immensely accelerated and increased. With wages for all kinds of women's work at least thrice as high on the Pacific as in this quarter, and with larger opportunities for honorable and fit settlement in life, I cannot doubt that tens of thousands would annually cross the Plains, to the signal benefit of California and of the whole country, as well as the improvement of their own fortunes and the profit of the railroad.
3. Thousands now staying in California, expecting to "go home" so soon as they shall have somewhat improved their circumstances, would send or come for their families and settle on the Pacific for life, if a railroad were opened. Tens of thousands who have been to California and come back, unwilling either to live away from their families or to expose them to the present hardships of migration thither, would return with all they have, prepared to spend their remaining days in the land of gold, if there were a Pacific railroad.
4. Education is the vital want of California, second to its need of true women. School-books, and all the material of education, are now scarce and dear there. Almost all books sell there twice as high as here, and many of the best are scarcely attainable at any rate. With the Pacific railroad, all this would be changed for the better. The proportion of school-houses to grogshops would rapidly increase. All the elements of moral and religious melioration would be multiplied. Tens of thousands of our best citizens would visit the Pacific coast, receiving novel ideas and impressions, to their own profit and that of the people thus visited. Civilization, intelligence, refinement, on both sides of the mountain-still more, in the Great Basin inclosed by them-would receive a new and immense impulse, and the Union would acquire a greater accession of strength, power, endurance, and true glory, than it would from the acquisition of the whole continent down to Cape Horn.

The only points of view in which a railroad from the Missouri to the Pacific remains to be considered are those of its practicability, cost, location, and the ways and means. Let us look at them:

I. As to practicability, there is no room for hesitation or doubt. The Massachusetts Western, the Erie, the Pennsylvania, and the Baltimore and Ohio, have each encountered difficulties as formidable as any to be overcome by a Pacific railroad this side of the Sierra Nevada. Were the railroad simply to follow the principal emigrant trail up the Platte and down the Snake and Columbia to Oregon, or south-westwardly from the South Pass to the foot of the Sierra, it would encounter no serious obstacle. . . .

But let that government simply resolve that the Pacific road shall be built-let Congress enact that sealed proposals for its construction shall be invited, and that whichever responsible company or corporation shall offer adequate security for that construction, to be completed within ten years, on the lowest terms, shall have public aid, provided the amount required do not exceed fifty millions of dollars, and the work will be done, certainly for fifty millions' bonus, probably for much less. The government on its part should concede to the company a mile in width, according to the section lines, of the public lands on either side of the road as built, with the right to take timber, stone and earth from any public lands without charge; and should require of said company that it carry a daily through-mail each way at the price paid other roads for conveying mails on first-class routes; and should moreover stipulate for the conveyance at all times of troops, arms, munitions, provisions, etc., for the public service, at the lowest rates, with a right to the exclusive possession and use of the road whenever a national exigency shall seem to require it. The government should leave the choice of route entirely to the company, only stipulating that it shall connect the navigable waters of the Mississippi with those of the Pacific Ocean, and that it shall be constructed wholly through our own territory. . . .

By adopting this plan, the rivalries of routes will be made to work for, instead of working against, the construction of the road. Strenuous efforts will be made by the friends of each to put themselves in position to bid low enough to secure the location; and the lowest rate at which the work can safely be undertaken will unquestionably be bid. The road will be the property of the company constructing it, subject only to the rights of use, stipulated and paid for by the government. And, even were it to cost the latter a bonus of fully fifty millions, I feel certain that every farthing of that large sum will have been reimbursed to the treasury within five years after the completion of the work in the proceeds of land sales, in increased postages, and in duties on goods imported, sold, and consumed because of this railroad-not to speak of the annual saving of millions in the cost of transporting and supplying troops.

Men and brethen! let us resolve to have a railroad to the Pacific-to have it soon. It will add more to the strength and wealth of our country than would the acquisition of a dozen Cubas. It will prove a bond of union not easily broken, and a new spring to our national industry, prosperity and wealth. It will call new manufactures into existence, and increase the demand for the products of those already existing. It will open new vistas to national and to individual aspiration, and crush out filibusterism by giving a new and wholesome direction to the public mind. My long, fatiguing journey was undertaken in the hope that I might do something toward the early construction of the Pacific Railroad; and I trust that it has not been made wholly in vain.

1. *What social, moral, and intellectual blessings would accompany the construction of a transcontinental railroad?*
2. *What obstacles to the construction of the railway are considered, and how are these obstacles overcome in this argument?*

17-4 Joseph G. McCoy, Historic Sketches of the Cattle Trade of the West and Southwest (1874)

In the post-Civil War era, the southern market for Texas cattle largely collapsed. Ranchers faced ruin and sought to connect to the burgeoning northern market by long cattle drives north to towns served by the railroads. This except describes on of those cattle drive along the famous Chisholm trial.

We left the herd fairly started upon the trail for the northern market. Of these trails there are several: one leading to Baxter Springs and Chetopa; another called the "Old Shawnee trail," leaving Red river and running eastward, crossing the Arkansas not far above Fort Gibson, thence bending westward up the Arkansas river. But the principal trail now traveled is more direct and is known as "Chisholm trail," so named from a semicivilized Indian who is said to have traveled it first. It is more direct, has more prairie, less timber, more small streams and less large ones, and altogether better grass and fewer flies (no civilized Indian tax or wild Indian disturbances) than any other route yet driven over, and is also much shorter in distance because direct from Red river to Kansas. Twenty-five to thirty-five days is the usual time required to bring a drove from Red river to the southern line of Kansas, a distance of between two hundred and fifty and three hundred miles, and an excellent country to drive over. So many cattle have been driven over the trail in the last few years that a broad highway is tread out, looking much like a national highway; so plain, a fool could not fail to keep in it. . . .

Few occupations are more cheerful, lively, and pleasant than that of the cowboy on a fine day or night; but when the storm comes, then is his manhood and often his skill and bravery put to test. When the night is inky dark and the lurid lightning flashes its zigzag course athwart the heavens, and the coarse thunder jars the earth, the winds moan fresh and lively over the prairie, the electric balls dance from tip to tip of the cattle's horns-then the position of the cowboy on duty is trying, far more than romantic. When the storm breaks over his head, the least occurrence unusual, such as the breaking of a dry weed or stick, or a sudden and near flash of lightning, will start the herd as if by magic, all at an instant, upon a wild rush, and woe to the horse or man or camp that may be in their path. The only possible show for safety is to mount and ride with them until you can get outside the stampeding column. It is customary to train cattle to listen to the noise of the herder, who sings in a voice more sonorous than musical a lullaby consisting of a few short monosyllables. A stranger to the business of stock driving will scarce credit the statement that the wildest herd will not run, so long as they can hear distinctly the voice of the herder above the din of the storm.

But if by any mishap the herd gets off on a real stampede, it is by bold, dashing, reckless riding in the darkest of nights, and by adroit, skillful management that it is checked and brought under control. The moment the herd is off, the cowboy turns his horse at full speed down the retreating column and seeks to get up beside the leaders, which he does not attempt to stop suddenly, for such an effort would be futile, but turns them to the left or right hand and gradually curves them into a circle, the circumference of which is narrowed down as fast as possible until the whole herd is rushing wildly round and round on as small a piece of ground as possible for them to occupy. Then the cowboy begins his lullaby note in a loud voice, which has a great effect in quieting the herd. When all is still and the herd well over its scare, they are returned to their bed ground, or held where stopped until daylight. . . .

After a drive of twenty-five to one hundred days the herd arrives in western Kansas, whither, in advance, its owner has come, and decided what point at which he will make his headquarters. Straightway a good herding place is sought out, and the herd, upon its arrival, placed thereon, to remain until a buyer is found, who is dilligently sought after; but if not found as soon as the cattle are fat, they are shipped to market. But the drover has a decided preference for selling on the prairie, for there he feels at home and self-possessed; but when he goes on the cars he is out of his element and doing something he doesn't understand much about and doesn't wish to learn, especially at the price it has cost many cattle shippers. . . .

We have in a former paper said that Texan drovers, as a class, were clannish, and easily gulled by promises of high prices for their stock. As an illustration of these statements we cite a certain secret meeting of the drovers held at one of the camps in 1867, whereat they all, after talking the matter over, pledged themselves to hold their cattle for 3 cents per pound gross and to sell none for less. One of the principal arguments used was that their cattle must be worth that price or those Illinoisans would not be expending so much money and labor in preparing facilities for shipping them. To this resolution they adhered persistently, refusing $2.75 per 100 pounds for fully 10,000 head; and afterwards, failing to get their 3 cents on the prairie for their cattle, shipped them to Chicago on their own account and sold them there at $2.25 to $2.50 per 100 pounds; and out of that paid a freight of $150 per car, realizing from $10 to $15 per head less than they had haughtily refused upon the prairie. Some of them refused to accept these prices and packed their cattle upon their own account. Their disappointment and chagrin at their failure to force a buyer to pay 3 cents per pound for their cattle was great and bitter, but their refusal to accept the offer of 23/4 cents per pound was great good fortune to the would-be buyers, for at that price $100,000 would have been lost on 10,000 head of cattle. An attempt was made the following year to form a combination to put up prices; but a burnt child dreads the fire, and the attempted combination failed, and every drover looked out sharply for himself.

Now one instance touching their susceptibility to being gulled by fine promises. In the fall of 1867, when Texan cattle were selling at from $24 to $28 per head in Chicago, a well-dressed, smooth-tongued individual put in an appearance at Abilene and claimed to be the representative of a certain (bogus) packing company of Chicago, and was desirous of purchasing several thousand head of cattle. He would pay Chicago prices at Abilene or, rather than be particular, $5 or $10 per head more than the same cattle would sell for in Chicago. It was astonishing to see how eagerly certain drovers fell into his trap and bargained their cattle off to him at $35 per head at Abilene, fully $15 more than they would pay out. But, mark you, the buyer, so "childlike and bland," could only pay the little sum of $25 down on 400 to 800 head, but would pay the balance when he got to Leavenworth with the cattle, he being afraid to bring his wealth up in that wild country. In the meantime they would load the cattle on the cars, bill them in the name of the buyer, and of course everything would be all right. Strange as it may appear, several of the hitherto most suspicious drovers of 1867 fell in with this swindler's scheme; and were actually about to let him ship their herds off on a mere verbal promise, when the parties in charge of the yards, seeing that the drovers were about to be defrauded out of their stock, posted them to have the cattle billed in their own name, and then, if the pay was not forthcoming, they would have possession of their own stock without troublesome litigation, as every man of sense anticipated they would have. When the swindler, after various excuses for his failures to pay at Leavenworth, Quincy, and Chicago (all the while trying to get the cattle into his own hands) found that he must come down with the cash, he very plainly told the Texan to go to Hades with his cattle. Instead of obeying this warm parting injunction of his newfound, high-priced buyer, he turned his cattle over to a regular commission man and received about $26 per head at Chicago less freight charges, or almost $18 per head at Abilene instead of $35 per head.

1. Summarize the author's account of the joys and dangers and physical risks of cattle herding.
2. Identify and describe the potential pitfalls for the cow herder as he attempted to do business with packing companies. What does this account reveal regarding the high financial risks of the cattle industry?

17-5   Helen Hunt Jackson, from *A Century of Dishonor* (1881)

Helen Hunt Jacksons A Century of Dishonor brought national attention to the plight of Native Americans when it was published in 1881. Jackson, a Massachusetts native who had traveled to California, describes in particular the plight of the California Indians, who had seen 90 percent of their population die from war and disease in the years after the gold rush.

There are within the limits of the United States between two hundred and fifty and three hundred thousand Indians, exclusive of those in Alaska. The names of the different tribes and bands, as entered in the statistical table so the Indian Office Reports, number nearly three hundred. One of the most careful estimates which have been made of their numbers and localities gives them as follows: "In Minnesota and States east of the Mississippi, about 32,500; in Nebraska, Kansas, and the Indian Territory, 70,650; in the Territories of Dakota, Montana, Wyoming, and Idaho, 65,000; in Nevada and the Territories of Colorado, New Mexico, Utah, and Arizona, 84,000; and on the Pacific slope, 48,000."

Of these, 130,000 are self-supporting on their own reservations, "receiving nothing from the Government except interest on their own moneys, or annuities granted them in consideration of the cession of their lands to the United States."

. . . Of the remainder, 84,000 are partially supported by the Government-the interest money due them and their annuities, as provided by treaty, being inadequate to their subsistence on the reservations where they are confined. . . .

There are about 55,000 who never visit an agency, over whom the Government does not pretend to have either control or care. These 55,000 "subsist by hunting, fishing, on roots, nuts, berries, etc., and by begging and stealing"; and this also seems to dispose of the accusation that the Indian will not "work for a living." There remains a small portion, about 31,000, that are entirely subsisted by the Government.

There is not among these three hundred bands of Indians one which has not suffered cruelly at the hands either of the Government or of white settlers. The poorer, the more insignificant, the more helpless the band, the more certain the cruelty and outrage to which they have been subjected. This is especially true of the bands on the Pacific slope. These Indians found themselves of a sudden surrounded by and caught up in the great influx of gold-seeking settlers, as helpless creatures on a shore are caught up in a tidal wave. There was not time for the Government to make treaties; not even time for communities to make laws. The tale of the wrongs, the oppressions, the murders of the Pacific-slope Indians in the last thirty years would be a volume by itself, and is too monstrous to be believed.

It makes little difference, however, where one opens the record of the history of the Indians; every page and every year has its dark stain. The story of one tribe is the story of all, varied only differences of time and place; but neither time nor place makes any difference in the main facts. Colorado is as greedy and unjust in 1880 as was Georgia in 1830, and Ohio in 1795; and the United States Government breaks promises now as deftly as then, and with an added ingenuity from long practice.

One of its strongest supports in so doing is the wide-spread sentiment among the people of dislike to the Indian, of impatience with his presence as a "barrier to civilization" and distrust of it as a possible danger. The old tales of the frontier life, with its horrors of Indian warfare, have gradually, by two or three generations' telling, produced in the average mind something like an hereditary instinct of questioning and unreasoning aversion which it is almost impossible to dislodge or soften. . . .

President after president has appointed commission after commission to inquire into and report upon Indian affairs, and to make suggestions as to the best methods of managing them. The reports are filled with eloquent statements of wrongs done to the Indians, of perfidies on the part of the Government; they counsel, as earnestly as words can, a trial of the simple and unperplexing expedients of telling truth, keeping promises, making fair bargains, dealing justly in all ways and all things. These reports are bound up with the Government's Annual Reports, and that is the end of them. . . .

The history of the Government connections with the Indians is a shameful record of broken treaties and unfulfilled promises. The history of the border white man's connection with the Indians is a sickening record of murder, outrage, robbery, and wrongs committed by the former, as the rule, and occasional savage outbreaks and unspeakably barbarous deeds of retaliation by the latter, as the exception.

Taught by the Government that they had rights entitled to respect, when those rights have been assailed by the rapacity of the white man, the arm which should have been raised to protect them has ever been ready to sustain the aggressor.

The testimony of some of the highest military officers of the United States is on record to the effect that, in our Indian wars, almost without exception, the first aggressions have been made by the white man. . . . Every crime committed by a white man against an Indian is concealed and palliated. Every offense committed by an Indian against a white man is borne on the wings of the post or the telegraph to the remotest corner of the land, clothed with all the horrors which the reality or imagination can throw around it. Against such influences as these are the people of the United States need to be warned.

To assume that it would be easy, or by any one sudden stroke of legislative policy possible, to undo the mischief and hurt of the long past, set the Indian policy of the country right for the future, and make the Indians at once safe and happy, is the blunder of a hasty and uninformed judgment. The notion which seems to be growing more prevalent, that simply to make all Indians at once citizens of the United States would be a sovereign and instantaneous panacea for all their ills and all the Government's perplexities, is a very inconsiderate one. To administer complete citizenship of a sudden, all round, to all Indians, barbarous and civilized alike, would be as grotesque a blunder as to dose them all round with any one medicine, irrespective of the symptoms and needs of their diseases. It would kill more than it would cure. Nevertheless, it is true, as was well stated by one of the superintendents of Indian Affairs in 1857, that, "so long as they are not citizens of the United States, their rights of property must remain insecure against invasion. The doors of the federal tribunals being barred against them while wards and dependents, they can only partially exercise the rights of free government, or give to those who make, execute, and construe the few laws they are allowed to enact, dignity sufficient to make them respectable. While they continue individually to gather the crumbs that fall from the table of the United States, idleness, improvidence, and indebtedness will be the rule, and industry, thrift, and freedom from debt the exception. The utter absence of individual title to particular lands deprives every one among them of the chief incentive to labor and exertion-the very mainspring on which the prosperity of a people depends."

All judicious plans and measures for their safety and salvation must embody provisions for their becoming citizens as fast as they are fit, and must protect them till then in every right and particular in which our laws protect other "persons" who are not citizens. . . .

However great perplexity and difficulty there may be in the details of any and every plan possible for doing at this late day anything like justice to the Indian, however, hard it may be for good statesmen and good men to agree upon the things that ought to be done, there certainly is, or ought to be, no perplexity whatever, on difficulty whatever, in agreeing upon certain things that ought not to be done, and which must cease to be done before the first steps can be taken toward righting the wrongs, curing the ills, and wiping out the disgrace to us of the present conditions of our Indians.

Cheating, robbing, breaking promises-these three are clearly things which must cease to be done. One more thing, also, and that is the refusal of the protection of the law to the Indian's rights of property, "of life, liberty, and the pursuit of happiness."

When these four things have ceased to be done, time, statesmanship, philanthropy, and Christianity can slowly and surely do the rest. Till these four things have ceased to be done, statesmanship and philanthropy alike must work in vain, and even Christianity can reap but small harvest.

1. *How does this document contradict the romantic perceptions the Americans may have had toward the relationship between Americans and the Indians? What attitudes toward Indian culture does this text target in its criticism?*
2. *What, according to this text, has been the American influence upon the Indian population?*

17-6 Congressional Report on Indian Affairs (1887)

In the 1880s, the federal government supported a program of assimilation for Native Americans. This program aimed at transforming the traditional Native American cultures and ways of life into those more in tune with mainstream America, stressing using the English language and dividing tribal lands into farming homesteads.

Longer and closer consideration of the subject has only deepened my conviction that it is a matter not only of importance, but of necessity that the Indians acquire the English language as rapidly as possible. The Government has entered upon the great work of educating and citizenizing the Indians and establishing them upon homesteads. The adults are expected to assume the role of citizens, and of course the rising generation will be expected and required more nearly to fill the measure of citizenship, and the main purpose of educating them is to enable them to read, write, and speak the English language and to transact business with English-speaking people. When they take upon themselves the responsibilities and privileges of citizenship their vernacular will be of no advantage. Only through the medium of the English tongue can they acquire a knowledge of the Constitution of the country and their rights and duties thereunder.

Every nation is jealous of its own language, and no nation ought to be more so than ours, which approaches nearer than any other nationality to the perfect protection of its people. True Americans all feel that the Constitution, laws, and institutions of the United States, in their adaptation to the wants and requirements of man, are superior to those of any other country; and they should understand that by the spread of the English language will these laws and institutions be more firmly established and widely disseminated. Nothing so surely and perfectly stamps upon an individual a national characteristic as language. So manifest and important is this that nations the world over, in both ancient and modern times, have ever imposed the strictest requirements upon their public schools as to the teaching of the national tongue. Only English has been allowed to be taught in the public schools in the territory acquired by this country from Spain, Mexico, and Russia, although the native populations spoke another tongue. All are familiar with the recent prohibitory order of the German Empire forbidding the teaching of the French language in either public or private schools in Alsace and Lorraine. Although the population is almost universally opposed to German rule, they are firmly held to German political allegiance by the military hand of the Iron Chancellor. If the Indians were in Germany or France or any other civilized country, they should be instructed in the language there used. As they are in an English-speaking country, they must be taught the language which they must use in transacting business with the people of this country. No unity or community of feeling can be established among different people unless they are brought to speak the same language, and thus become imbued with the like ideas of duty.

Deeming it for the very best interest of the Indian, both as an individual and as an embryo citizen, to have this policy strictly enforced among the various schools on Indian reservations, orders have been issued accordingly to Indian agents. . . .

It is believed that if any Indian vernacular is allowed to be taught by the missionaries in schools on Indian reservations, it will prejudice the youthful pupil as well as his untutored and uncivilized or semicivilized parent against the English language, and, to some extent at least, against Government schools in which the English language exclusively has always been taught. To teach Indian school children their native tongue is practically to exclude English, and to prevent them from acquiring it. This language, which is good enough for a white man and a black man, ought to be good enough for the red man. It is also believed that teaching an Indian youth in his own barbarous dialect is a positive detriment to him. The first step to be taken toward civilization, toward teaching the Indians the mischief and folly of continuing in their barbarous practices, is to teach them the English language. The impracticability, if not impossibility, of civilizing the Indians of this country in any other tongue than our own would seem to be obvious, especially in view of the fact that the number of Indian vernaculars is even greater than the number of tribes. Bands of the same tribes inhabiting different localities have different dialects, and sometimes can not communicate with each other except by the sign language. If we expect to infuse into the rising generation the leaven of American citizenship, we must remove the stumbling blocks of hereditary customs and manners, and of these language is one of the most important elements. . . .

But it has been suggested that this order, being mandatory, gives a cruel blow to the sacred rights of the Indians. Is it cruelty to the Indian to force him to give up his scalping-knife and tomahawk? Is it cruelty to force him to abandon the vicious and barbarous sun dance, where he lacerates his flesh, and dances and tortures himself even unto death? Is it cruelty to the Indian to force him to have his daughters educated and married under the laws of the land, instead of selling them at a tender age for a stipulated price into concubinage to gratify the brutal lusts of ignorance and barbarism?

Having been governed in my action solely by what I believed to be the real interests of the Indians, I have been gratified to receive from eminent educators and missionaries the strongest assurance of their hearty and full concurrence in the propriety and necessity of the order.

1. *Summarize the author's argument in support of the encouragement of the English language among the Indian peoples? What advantages does the English language give to the Indians?*
2. *Analyze the author's attitudes toward Indian culture and American society. How does the author's argument regarding language coincide with and encourage the American desire to conquer and civilize the Western territories?*

17-7 Tragedy at Wounded Knee (1890)

In the aftermath of the massacre at Wounded Knee, the Lakota chief Red Cloud summed up the reasons for Native American discontent. He stressed the disappearance of the Native American lifestyle and the failure of the federal government to keep their promises.

RED CLOUD'S SPEECH

I will tell you the reason for the trouble. When we first made treaties with the Government, our old life and our old customs were about to end; the game on which we lived was disappearing; the whites were closing around us, and nothing remained for us but to adopt their ways,-the Government promised us all the means necessary to make our living out of the land, and to instruct us how to do it, and with abundant food to support us until we could take care of ourselves. We looked forward with hope to the time we could be as independent as the whites, and have a voice in the Government.

The army officers could have helped better than anyone else but we were not left to them. An Indian Department was made with a large number of agents and other officials drawing large salaries-then came the beginning of trouble; these men took care of themselves but not of us. It was very hard to deal with the government through them-they could make more for themselves by keeping us back than by helping us forward.

We did not get the means for working our lands; the few things they gave us did little good.

Our rations began to be reduced; they said we were lazy. That is false. How does any man of sense suppose that so great a number of people could get work at once unless they were at once supplied with the means to work and instructors enough to teach them?

Our ponies were taken away from us under the promise that they would be replaced by oxen and large horses; it was long before we saw any, and then we got very few. We tried with the means we had, but on one pretext or another, we were shifted from one place to another, or were told that such a transfer was coming. Great efforts were made to break up our customs, but nothing was done to introduce us to customs of the whites. Everything was done to break up the power of the real chiefs.

Those old men really wished their people to improve, but little men, so-called chiefs, were made to act as disturbers and agitators. Spotted Tail wanted the ways of the whites, but an assassin was found to remove him. This was charged to the Indians because an Indian did it, but who set on the Indian? I was abused and slandered, to weaken my influence for good. This was done by men paid by the government to teach us the ways of the whites. I have visited many other tribes and found that the same things were done amongst them; all was done to discourage us and nothing to encourage us. I saw men paid by the government to help us, all very busy making money for themselves, but doing nothing for us. . . .

The men who counted (census) told all around that we were feasting and wasting food. Where did he see it? How could we waste what we did not have? We felt we were mocked in our misery; we had no newspaper and no one to speak for us. Our rations were again reduced.

You who eat three times a day and see your children well and happy around you cannot understand what a starving Indian feels! We were faint with hunger and maddened by despair. We held our dying children and felt their little bodies tremble as their soul went out and left only a dead weight in our hands. They were not very heavy but we were faint and the dead weighed us down. There was no hope on earth. God seemed to have forgotten.

Some one had been talking of the Son of God and said He had come. The people did not know; they did not care; they snatched at hope; they screamed like crazy people to Him for mercy they caught at the promise they heard He had made.

The white men were frightened and called for soldiers. We begged for life and the white men thought we wanted theirs; we heard the soldiers were coming. We did not fear. We hoped we could tell them our suffering and could get help. The white men told us the soldiers meant to kill us; we did not believe it but some were frightened and ran away to the Bad Lands. The soldiers came. They said: "don't be afraid-we come to make peace, not war." It was true; they brought us food. But the hunger-crazed who had taken fright at the soldiers' coming and went to the Bad Lands could not be induced to return to the horrors of reservation life. They were called Hostiles and the Government sent the army to force them back to their reservation prison.

FLYING HAWK'S RECOLLECTIONS OF WOUNDED KNEE (1936)

This was the last big trouble with the Indians and soldiers and was in the winter in 1890. When the Indians would not come in from the Bad Lands, they got a big army together with plenty of clothing and supplies and camp-and-wagon equipment for a big campaign; they had enough soldiers to make a round-up of all the Indians they called hostiles.

The Government army, after many fights and loss of lives, succeeded in driving these starving Indians, with their families of women and gaunt-faced children, into a trap, where they could be forced to surrender their arms. This was on Wounded Knee creek, northeast of Pine Ridge, and here the Indians were surrounded by the soldiers, who had Hotchkiss machine guns along with them. There were about four thousand Indians in this big camp, and the soldiers had the machine guns pointed at them from all around the village as the soldiers formed a ring about the tepees so that Indians could not escape.

The Indians were hungry and weak and they suffered from lack of clothing and furs because the whites had driven away all the game. When the soldiers had them all surrounded and they had their tepees set up, the officers sent troopers to each of them to search for guns and take them from the owners. If the Indians in the tepees did not at once hand over a gun, the soldier tore open their parfleech trunks and bundles and bags of robes or clothes,-looking for pistols and knives and ammunition. It was an ugly business, and brutal; they treated the Indians like they would torment a wolf with one foot in a strong trap; they could do this because the Indians were now in the white man's trap,-and they were helpless.

Then a shot was heard from among the Indian tepees. An Indian was blamed; the excitement began; soldiers ran to their stations; officers gave orders to open fire with the machine guns into the crowds of innocent men, women and children, and in a few minutes more than two hundred and twenty of them lay in the snow dead and dying. A terrible blizzard

377

raged for two days covering the bodies with Nature's great white blanket; some lay in piles of four or five; others in twos or threes or singly, where they fell until the storm subsided. When a trench had been dug of sufficient length and depth to contain the frozen corpses, they were collected and piled, like cord-wood, in one vast icy tomb. While separating several stiffened forms which had fallen in a heap, two of them proved to be women, and hugged closely to their breasts were infant babes still alive after lying in the storm for two days in 20° below zero weather.

I was there and saw the trouble,-but after the shooting was over; it was all bad.

1. Summarize the American government's treatment of the Indians according to Red Cloud.
2. What things in Flying Hawk's recollection stand out as particularly cruel and barbaric?

17-8 Benjamin Harrison, Report on Wounded Knee Massacre and the Decrease in Indian Land Acreage (1891)

The following is an excerpt from President Benjamin Harrison's annual message, delivered December 9, 1891, in which he describes the Wounded Knee Massacre and the progress of the program to decrease Native American land acreage

The outbreak among the Sioux which occurred in December last is as to its causes and incidents fully reported upon by the War Department and the Department of the Interior. That these Indians had some just complaints, especially in the matter of the reduction of the appropriation for rations and in the delays attending the enactment of laws to enable the Department to perform the engagements entered into with them, is probably true; but the Sioux tribes are naturally warlike and turbulent, and their warriors were excited by their medicine men and chiefs, who preached the coming of an Indian messiah who was to give them power to destroy their enemies. In view of the alarm that prevailed among the white settlers near the reservation and of the fatal consequences that would have resulted from an Indian incursion, I placed at the disposal of General Miles, commanding the Division of the Missouri, all such forces as we thought by him to be required. He is entitled to the credit of having given thorough protection to the settlers and of bringing the hostiles into subjection with the least possible loss of life. . . .

Since March 4, 1889, about 23,000,000 acres have been separated from Indian reservations and added to the public domain for the use of those who desired to secure free homes under our beneficent laws. It is difficult to estimate the increase of wealth which will result from the conversion of these waste lands into farms, but it is more difficult to estimate the betterment which will result to the families that have found renewed hope and courage in the ownership of a home and the assurance of a comfortable subsistence under free and healthful conditions. It is also gratifying to be able to feel, as we may, that this work has proceeded upon lines of justice toward the Indian, and that he may now, if he will, secure to himself the good influences of a settled habitation, the fruits of industry, and the security of citizenship.

1. Upon what grounds does Harrison justify the military actions at Wounded Knee? What is Harrison's attitude toward the Indians as it is expressed in this report?
2. What justification is given for the seizure of land formerly granted to the Indians? How does Harrison explain this seizure as beneficial to all, including the Indians who lost the land?

17-9 The Omaha Platform of the Populist Party (1892)

Farmer discontent had fueled the emergence of the Farmers' Alliance to mobilize support for agrarian issues. In 1892, a combination of farm and labor organizations formed the Peoples Party. The Omaha Platform summarized their complaints and solutions, many of which later were implemented.

Preamble

The conditions which surround us best justify our cooperation; we meet in the midst of a nation brought to the verge of moral, political, and material ruin. Corruption dominates the ballot-box, the Legislatures, the Congress, and touches even the ermine of the bench. The people are demoralized; most of the States have been compelled to isolate the voters at the polling places to prevent universal intimidation and bribery. The newspapers are largely subsidized or muzzled, public opinion silenced, business prostrated, homes covered with mortgages, labor impoverished, and the land concentrating in the hands of capitalists. The urban workmen are denied the right to organize for self-protection, imported pauperized labor beats down their wages, a hireling standing army, unrecognized by our laws, is established to shoot them down, and they are rapidly degenerating into European conditions. The fruits of the toil of millions are boldly stolen to build up colossal fortunes for a few, unprecedented in the history of mankind and the possessors of these, in turn, despise the Republic and endanger liberty. From the same prolific womb of governmental injustice we breed the two great classes-tramps and millionaires. . . .

Assembled on the anniversary of the birthday of the nation, and filled with the spirit of the grand general and chief who established our independence, we seek to restore the government of the Republic to the hands of the "plain people," with which class it originated. We assert our purposes to be identical with the purposes of the National Constitution; to form a more perfect union and establish justice, insure domestic tranquillity, provide for the common defense, promote the general welfare, and secure the blessings of liberty for ourselves and our posterity. . . .

Platform

We declare, therefore-

First.-That the union of the labor forces of the United States this day consummated shall be permanent and perpetual; may its spirit enter into all hearts for the salvation of the Republic and the uplifting of mankind.

Second.-Wealth belongs to him who creates it, and every dollar taken from industry without an equivalent is robbery. "If any will not work, neither shall he eat." The interests of rural and civil labor are the same; their enemies are identical.

Third.-We believe that the time has come when the railroad corporations will either own the people or the people must own the railroads. . . .

FINANCE.-We demand a national currency, safe, sound, and flexible issued by the general government only, a full legal tender for all debts, public and private. . . .

1. We demand free and unlimited coinage of silver and gold at the present legal ratio of 16 to 1.
2. We demand that the amount of circulating medium be speedily increased to not less than $50 per capita.
3. We demand a graduated income tax.
4. We believe that the money of the country should be kept as much as possible in the hands of the people, and hence we demand that all State and national revenues shall be limited to the necessary expenses of the government, economically and honestly administered.
5. We demand that postal savings banks be established by the government for the safe deposit of the earnings of the people and to facilitate exchange.

TRANSPORTATION. -Transportation being a means of exchange and a public necessity, the government should own and operate the railroads in the interest of the people. The telegraph and telephone, like the post-office system, being a necessity for the transmission of news, should be owned and operated by the government in the interest of the people.

LAND. -The land, including all the natural sources of wealth, is the heritage of the people, and should not be monopolized for speculative purposes, and alien ownership of land should be prohibited. All land now held by railroads and other corporations in excess of their actual needs, and all lands now owned by aliens should be reclaimed by the government and held for actual settlers only.

Expressions of Sentiments

1. RESOLVED, That we demand a free ballot, and a fair count of all elections, and pledge ourselves to secure it to every legal voter without Federal intervention, through the adoption by the States of the unperverted Australian or secret ballot system.
2. RESOLVED, That the revenue derived from a graduated income tax should be applied to the reduction of the burden of taxation now levied upon the domestic industries of this country.
3. RESOLVED, That we pledge our support to fair and liberal pensions to ex-Union soldiers and sailors.

4. RESOLVED, That we condemn the fallacy of protecting American labor under the present system, which opens our ports to the pauper and criminal classes of the world and crowds out our wage-earners; and we denounce the present ineffective laws against contract labor, and demand the further restriction of undesirable emigration.

5. RESOLVED, That we cordially sympathize with the efforts of organized workingmen to shorten the hours of labor, and demand a rigid enforcement of the existing eight-hour law on Government work, and ask that a penalty clause be added to the said law.

6. RESOLVED, That we regard the maintenance of a large standing army of mercenaries, known as the Pinkerton system, as a menace to our liberties, and we demand its abolition. . . .

7. RESOLVED, That we commend to the favorable consideration of the people and the reform press the legislative system known as the initiative and referendum.

8. RESOLVED, That we favor a constitutional provision limiting the office of President and Vice-President to one term, and providing for the election of Senators of the United States by a direct vote of the people.

9. RESOLVED, That we oppose any subsidy or national aid to any private corporation for any purpose.

1. What political situation has lead the proponents of this party to proclaim this platform?
2. Summarize the key economic, social, and political planks of this platform.

17-10   From *Plessy v. Ferguson* (1896)

Homer C. Plessy sued a railroad claiming that the separate railroad cars for whites and black violated his rights under the Thirteenth and Fourteenth amendments. This landmark 1896 Supreme Court case basically legalized racial segregation for fifty years, claiming separate but equal conditions did not violate the Constitution.

This case turns upon the constitutionality of an act of the general assembly of the state of Louisiana, passed in 1890, providing for separate railway carriages for the white and colored races. . . .

The constitutionality of this act is attacked upon the ground that it conflicts both with the 13th Amendment of the Constitution, abolishing slavery, and the 14th Amendment, which prohibits certain restrictive legislation on the part of the states.

1. That it does not conflict with the 13th Amendment, which abolished slavery and involuntary servitude, except as a punishment for crime, is too clear for argument. . . . Indeed, we do not understand that the 13th Amendment is strenuously relied upon by the plaintiff. . . .

The object of the [14th] amendment was undoubtedly to enforce the absolute equality of the two races before the law, but in the nature of things it could not have been intended to abolish distinctions based upon color, or to enforce social, as distinguished from political, equality, or a commingling of the two races upon terms unsatisfactory to either. Laws permitting, and even requiring their separation in places where they are liable to be brought into contact do not necessarily imply the inferiority of either race to the other, and have been generally, if not universally, recognized as within the competency of the state legislatures in the exercise of their police power. . . .

We consider the underlying fallacy of the plaintiff's argument to consist in the assumption that the enforced separation of the two races stamps the colored race with a badge of inferiority. If this be so, it is not by reason of anything found in the act, but solely because the colored race chooses to put that construction upon it. . . .

The argument also assumes that social prejudice may be overcome by legislation, and that equal rights cannot be secured to the Negro except by an enforced commingling of the two races. We cannot accept this proposition. If the two races are to meet on terms of social equality, it must be the result of natural affinities, a mutual appreciation of each other's merits and a voluntary consent of individuals. . . . Legislation is powerless to eradicate racial instincts or abolish distinctions based upon physical differences and the attempt to do so can only result in accentuating the difficulties of the present situation. If the civil and political right of both races be equal, one cannot be inferior to the other civilly or politically. If one race be inferior to the other socially, the Constitution of the United States cannot put them upon the same plane.

1. Explain the reasoning for the Supreme Court's decision in this case.
2. Explain what this document contends in regard to the law's ability to enforce social integration.

17-11   W. E. B. Du Bois, from "Of Mr. Booker T. Washington and Others" (1903)

Two different African American approaches to race relations arose in the late nineteenth and early twentieth centuries. A leader of the movement to actively integration and equal rights, W. E. B. DuBois criticizes the accommodationist policies of Booker T. Washington.

Easily the most striking thing in the history of the American Negro since 1876 is the ascendancy of Mr. Booker T. Washington. . . . His programme of industrial education, conciliation of the South, and submission and silence as to civil and political rights was not wholly original. . . . But Mr. Washington first indissolubly linked these things; he . . . changed it from a by-path into a veritable Way of Life. . . .

　　Mr. Washington represents in Negro thought the old attitude of adjustment and submission; but adjustment at such a peculiar time as to make his programme unique. This is an age of unusual economic development, and Mr. Washington's programme naturally takes an economic cast, becoming a gospel of Work and Money to such an extent as apparently almost completely to overshadow the higher aims of life. . . . Mr. Washington's programme practically accepts the alleged inferiority of the Negro races. . . . In the history of nearly all other races and peoples the doctrine preached at such crises has been that manly self-respect is worth more than lands and houses, and that a people who voluntarily surrender such respect, or cease striving for it, are not worth civilizing.

　　. . . Mr. Washington distinctly asks that black people give up, at least for the present, three things,-

First, political power.

Second, insistence on civil rights.

Third, higher education of Negro youth,

. . . The question then comes: Is it possible, and probable, that nine millions of men can make effective progress in economic lines if they are deprived of political rights, made a servile caste, and allowed only the most meagre chance for developing their exceptional men? If history and reason give any distinct answer to these questions, it is an emphatic No. . . .

　　. . . while it is a great truth to say that the Negro must strive and strive mightily to help himself, it is equally true that unless his striving be not simply seconded, but rather aroused and encouraged, by the initiative of the richer and wiser environing group, he cannot hope for great success.

　　. . . So far as Mr. Washington preaches Thrift, Patience, and Industrial Training for the masses, we must hold up his hands and strive with him, rejoicing in his honors and glorying in the strength of this Joshua called of God and of man to lead the headless host. But so far as Mr. Washington apologizes for injustice, North or South, does not rightly value the privilege and duty of voting, belittles the emasculating effects of caste distinctions, and opposes the higher training and ambition of our brighter minds,-so far as he, the South, or the Nation, does this, we must unceasingly and firmly oppose them.

1. Summarize Du Bois' characterization of Washington's beliefs and "programme."
2. Identify and explain Du Bois' response to Washington's approach to the struggle for racial equality.

PART EIGHTEEN
INDUSTRIALIZING AMERICA

18-1 Charles Loring Brace, "The Life of the Street Rats" (1872)

The rapid increase in European immigration to American cities created a juvenile delinquency problem of the children of these immigrants. As this document shows, poverty influenced the rise of a violent class of young people in the poor sections of New York City.

. . . The intensity of the American temperament is felt in every fibre of these children of poverty and vice. Their crimes have the unrestrained and sanguinary character of a race accustomed to overcome all obstacles. They rifle a bank, where English thieves pick a pocket; they murder, where European proletaires cudgel or fight with fists; in a riot, they begin what seems about to be the sacking of a city, where English rioters would merely batter policemen, or smash lamps. The "dangerous classes" of New York are mainly American-born, but the children of Irish and German immigrants. . . . .

There are thousands on thousands in New York who have no assignable home, and "flirt" from attic to attic, and cellar to cellar; there are other thousands more or less connected with criminal enterprises; and still other tens of thousands, poor, hard-pressed, and depending for daily bread on the day's earnings, swarming in tenement-houses, who behold the gilded rewards of toil all about them, but are never permitted to touch them.

All these great masses of destitute, miserable, and criminal persons believe that for ages the rich have had all the good things of life, while to them have been left the evil things. Capital to them is the tyrant.

Let but Law lift its hand from them for a season, or let the civilizing influences of American life fail to reach them, and, if the opportunity offered, we should see an explosion from this class which might leave this city in ashes and blood.

Seventeen years ago, my attention had been called to the extraordinarily degraded condition of the children in a district lying on the west side of the city, between Seventeenth and Nineteenth Streets, and the Seventh and Tenth Avenues. A certain block, called "Misery Row," in Tenth Avenue, was the main seed-bed of crime and poverty in the quarter, and was also invariably a "fever-nest." Here the poor obtained wretched rooms at a comparatively low rent; these they sub-let, and thus, in little, crowded, close tenements, were herded men, women and children of all ages. The parents were invariably given to hard drinking, and the children were sent out to beg or to steal. Besides them, other children, who were orphans, or who had run away from drunkards' homes, or had been working on the canal-boats that discharged on the docks near by, drifted into the quarter, as if attracted by the atmosphere of crime and laziness that prevailed in the neighborhood. These slept around the breweries of the ward, or on the hay-barges, or in the old sheds of Eighteenth and Nineteenth Streets. They were mere children, and kept life together by all sorts of street-jobs-helping the brewery laborers, blackening boots, sweeping sidewalks, "smashing baggages" (as they called it), and the like. Herding together, they soon began to form an unconscious society for vagrancy and idleness. Finding that work brought but poor pay, they tried shorter roads to getting money by petty [sic] thefts, in which they were very adroit. Even if they earned a considerable sum by a lucky day's job, they quickly spent it in gambling, or for some folly.

The police soon knew them as "street-rats"; but, like the rats, they were too quick and cunning to be often caught in their petty plunderings, so they gnawed away at the foundations of society undisturbed.

1. *Describe the conditions under which the "street rats" live according to this account.*
2. *What potential threat do the "street rats" pose to society and what must be done to prevent this threat?*

18-2 Progress and Poverty (1879)

Henry George could not reconcile the tremendous disproportion in wealth in the United States. He tried to explain why such wide chasms between rich and poor existed in Progress and Poverty. He was able to understand the gross disparity by dividing society into two broad categories: producers and predators. He believed that the best way to narrow the gap between the haves and the have nots was to create a harmony of capital and labor.

Source: Henry George, *Progress and Poverty* (New York: Doubleday & McClure, 1879), pp. 544–552.

In the short space to which this latter part of our inquiry is necessarily confined, I have been obliged to omit much that I would like to say, and to touch briefly where an exhaustive consideration would not be out of place.

Nevertheless, this, at least, is evident, that the truth to which we were led in the politico-economic branch of our inquiry is as clearly apparent in the rise and fall of nations and the growth and decay of civilizations, and that it accords with those deep-seated recognitions of relation and sequence that we denominate moral perceptions. Thus have been given to our conclusions the greatest certitude and highest sanction.

This truth involves both a menace and a promise. It shows that the evils arising from the unjust and unequal distribution of wealth, which are becoming more and more apparent as modern civilization goes on, are not incidents of progress, but tendencies which must bring progress to a halt; that they will not cure themselves, but, on the contrary, must, unless their cause is removed, grow greater and greater, until they sweep us back into barbarism by the road every previous civilization has trod. But it also shows that these evils are not imposed by natural laws; that they spring solely from social maladjustments which ignore natural laws, and that in removing their cause we shall be giving an enormous impetus to progress.

The poverty which in the midst of abundance pinches and embrutes men, and all the manifold evils which flow from it, spring from a denial of justice. In permitting the monopolization of the opportunities which nature freely offers to all, we have ignored the fundamental law of justice—for, so far as we can see, when we view things upon a large scale, justice seems to be the supreme law of the universe. But by sweeping away this injustice and asserting the rights of all men to natural opportunities, we shall conform ourselves to the law—we shall remove the great cause of unnatural inequality in the distribution of wealth and power; we shall abolish poverty; tame the ruthless passions of greed; dry up the springs of vice and misery; light in dark places the lamp of knowledge; give new vigor to invention and a fresh impulse to discovery; substitute political strength for political weakness; and make tyranny and anarchy impossible.

The reform I have proposed accords with all that is politically, socially, or morally desirable. It has the qualities of a true reform, for it will make all other reforms easier. What is it but the carrying out in letter and spirit of the truth enunciated in the Declaration of Independence—the "self-evident" truth that is the heart and soul of the Declaration—*"That all men are created equal; that they are endowed by their Creator with certain unalienable rights; that among these are life, liberty, and the pursuit of happiness!"*

These rights are denied when the equal right to land—on which and by which men alone can live—is denied. Equality of political rights will not compensate for the denial of the equal right to the bounty of nature. Political liberty, when the equal right to land is denied, becomes, as population increases and invention goes on, merely the liberty to compete for employment at starvation wages. This is the truth that we have ignored. And so there come beggars in our streets and tramps on our roads; and poverty enslaves men whom we boast are political sovereigns; and want breeds ignorance that our schools cannot enlighten; and citizens vote as their masters dictate; and the demagogue usurps the part of the statesman; and gold weighs in the scales of justice; and in high places sit those who do not pay to civic virtue even the compliment of hypocrisy; and the pillars of the republic that we thought so strong already bend under an increasing strain.

We honor Liberty in name and in form. We set up her statues and sound her praises. But we have not fully trusted her. And with our growth so grow her demands. She will have no half service!

Liberty! it is a word to conjure with, not to vex the ear in empty boastings. For Liberty means Justice, and Justice is the natural law—the law of health and symmetry and strength, of fraternity and co-operation.

They who look upon Liberty as having accomplished her mission when she has abolished hereditary privileges and given men the ballot, who think of her as having no further relations to the everyday affairs of life, have not seen her real grandeur—to them the poets who have sung of her must seem rhapsodists, and her martyrs fools! As the sun is the lord of life, as well as of light; as his beams not merely pierce the clouds, but support all growth, supply all motion, and call forth from what would otherwise be a cold and inert mass all the infinite diversities of being and beauty, so is liberty to mankind. It is not for an abstraction that men have toiled and died; that in every age the witnesses of Liberty have stood forth, and the martyrs of Liberty have suffered.

We speak of Liberty as one thing, and of virtue, wealth, knowledge, invention, national strength and national independence as other things. But, of all these, Liberty is the source, the mother, the necessary condition. She is to virtue what light is to color; to wealth what sunshine is to grain; to knowledge what eyes are to sight. She is the genius of invention, the brawn of national strength, the spirit of national independence. Where Liberty rises, there virtue grows, wealth increases, knowledge expands, invention multiplies human powers, and in strength and spirit the freer nation rises among her neighbors as Saul amid his brethren—taller and fairer. Where Liberty sinks, there virtue fades, wealth diminishes, knowledge is forgotten, invention ceases, and empires once mighty in arms and arts become a helpless prey to freer barbarians!

Only in broken gleams and partial light has the sun of Liberty yet beamed among men, but all progress hath she called forth.

Liberty came to a race of slaves crouching under Egyptian whips, and led them forth from the House of Bondage. She hardened them in the desert and made of them a race of conquerors. The free spirit of the Mosaic law took their thinkers up to heights where they beheld the unit of God, and inspired their poets with strains that yet phrase the highest exaltations of thought. Liberty dawned on the Phoenician coast, and ships passed the Pillars of Hercules to plow the unknown sea. She shed a partial light on Greece, and marble grew to shapes of ideal beauty, words became the instruments of subtlest thought, and against the scanty militia of free cities the countless hosts of the Great Kind broke like surges against a rock. She cast her beams on the four-acre farms of Italian husbandmen, and born of her strength a power came forth that conquered the world. They glinted from shields of German warriors, and Augustus wept his legions. Out of the night that followed her eclipse, her slanting rays fell again on free cities, and a lost learning revived, modern civilization began, a new world was unveiled; and as Liberty grew, so grew art, wealth, power, knowledge, and refinement. In the history of every nation we may read the same truth. It was the strength born of Magna Charta that won Crecy and Agincourt. It was the revival of Liberty from the despotism of the Tudors that glorified the Elizabethan age. It was the spirit that brought a crowned tyrant to the block that planted here the seed of a mighty tree. It was the energy of ancient freedom that, the moment it had gained unity, made Spain the mightiest power of the world, only to fall to the lowest depth of weakness when tyranny succeeded liberty. See, in France, all intellectual vigor dying under the tyranny of the Seventeenth Century to revive in splendor as Liberty awoke in the Eighteenth, and on the enfranchisement of French peasants in the Great Revolution, basing the wonderful strength that has in our time defied defeat.

Shall we not trust her?

In our time, as in times before, creep on the insidious forces that, producing inequality, destroy Liberty. On the horizon the clouds begin to lower. Liberty calls to us again. We must follow her further; we must trust her fully. Either we must wholly accept her or she will not stay. It is not enough that men should vote; it is not enough that they should be theoretically equal before the law. They must have liberty to avail themselves of the opportunities and means of life; they must stand on equal terms with reference to the bounty of nature. Either this, or Liberty withdraws her light! Either this, or darkness comes on, and the very forces that progress has evolved turn to powers that work destruction. This is the universal law. This is the lesson of the centuries. Unless its foundations be laid in justice the social structure cannot stand.

Our primary social adjustment is a denial of justice. In allowing one man to own the land on which and from which other men must live, we have made them his bondsmen in a degree which increases as material progress goes on. This is the subtle alchemy that in ways they do not realize is extracting from the masses in every civilized country the fruits of their weary toil; that is instituting a harder and more hopeless slavery in place of that which has been destroyed; that is bringing political despotism out of political freedom, and must soon transmute democratic institutions into anarchy.

It is this that turns the blessings of material progress into a curse. It is this that crowds human beings into noisome cellars and squalid tenement houses; that fills prisons and brothels; that goads men with want and consumes them with greed; that robs women of the grace and beauty of perfect womanhood; that takes from little children the joy and innocence of life's morning.

Civilization so based cannot continue. The eternal laws of the universe forbid it. Ruins of dead empires testify, and the witness that is in every soul answers, that it cannot be. It is something grander than Benevolence, something more august than Charity—it is Justice herself that demands of us to right this wrong. Justice that will not be denied; that cannot be put off—Justice that with the scales carries the sword. Shall we ward the stroke with liturgies and prayers? Shall we avert the decrees of immutable law by raising churches when hungry infants moan and weary mothers weep?

Though it may take the language of prayer, it is blasphemy that attributes to the inscrutable decrees of Providence the suffering and brutishness that come of poverty; that turns with folded hands to the All-Father and lays on Him the responsibility for the want and crime of our great cities. We degrade the Everlasting. We slander the Just One. A merciful man would have better ordered the world; a just man would crush with his foot such an ulcerous ant-hill! It is not the Almighty, but we who are responsible for the vice and misery that fester amid our civilization. The Creator showers upon us his gifts—more than enough for all. But like swine scrambling for food, we tread them in the mire—tread them in the mire, while we tear and rend each other!

In the very centers of our civilization to-day are want and suffering enough to make sick at heart whoever does not close his eyes and steel his nerves. Dare we turn to the Creator and ask Him to relieve it? Supposing the prayer were heard, and at the behest with which the universe sprang into being there should glow in the sun a greater power; new virtue fill the air; fresh vigor the soil; that for every blade of grass that now grows two should spring up, and the seed that now increases fifty-fold should increase a hundred-fold! Would poverty be abated or want relieved? Manifestly no! Whatever benefit would accrue would be but temporary. The new powers streaming through the material universe could be utilized only through land. And land, being private property, the classes that now monopolize the bounty of the Creator would monopolize all the new bounty. Land owners would alone be benefited. Rents would increase, but wages would still tend to the starvation point!

This is not merely a deduction of political economy; it is a fact of experience. We know it because we have seen it. Within our own times, under our very eyes, that Power which is above all, and in all, and through all; that Power of which the whole universe is but the manifestation; that Power which maketh all things, and without which is not anything made that is made, has increased the bounty which men may enjoy, as truly as though the fertility of nature had been increased. Into the mind of one came the thought that harnessed steam for the service of mankind. To the inner ear of another was whispered the secret that compels the lightning to bear a message round the globe. In every direction have the laws of matter been revealed; in every department of industry have arisen arms of iron and fingers of steel, whose effect upon the production of wealth has been precisely the same as an increase in the fertility of nature. What has been the result? Simply that land owners get all the gain. The wonderful discoveries and inventions of our century have neither increased wages nor lightened toil. The effect has simply been to make the few richer; the many more helpless!

Can it be that the gifts of the Creator may be thus misappropriated with impunity? Is it a light thing that labor should be robbed of its earnings while greed rolls in wealth—that the many should want while the few are surfeited? Turn to history, and on every page may be read the lesson that such wrong never goes unpunished; that the Nemesis that follows injustice never falters nor sleeps! Look around to-day. Can this state of things continue? May we even say, "After us the deluge!" Nay; the pillars of the state are trembling even now, and the very foundations of society begin to quiver with pent-up forces that glow underneath. The struggle that must either revivify, or convulse in ruin, is near at hand, if it be not already begun.

The fiat has gone forth! With steam and electricity, and the new powers born of progress, forces have entered the world that will either compel us to a higher plane or overwhelm us, as nation after nation, as civilization after civilization, have been overwhelmed before. It is the delusion which precedes destruction that sees in the popular unrest with which the civilized world is feverishly pulsing only the passing effect of ephemeral causes. Between democratic ideas and the aristocratic adjustments of society there is an irreconcilable conflict. Here in the United States, as there in Europe, it may be seen arising. We cannot go on permitting men to vote and forcing them to tramp. We cannot go on educating boys and girls in our public schools and then refusing them the right to earn an honest living. We cannot go on prating of the inalienable rights of man and then denying the inalienable right to the bounty of the Creator. Even now, in old bottles the new wine begins to ferment, and elemental forces gather for the strife!

But if, while there is yet time, we turn to Justice and obey her, if we trust Liberty and follow her, the dangers that now threaten must disappear, the forces that now menace will turn to agencies of elevation. Think of the powers now wasted; of the infinite fields of knowledge yet to be explored; of the possibilities of which the wondrous inventions of this century give us but a hint. With want destroyed; with greed changed to noble passions; with the fraternity that is born of equality taking the place of the jealousy and fear that now array men against each other; with mental power loosed by conditions that give to the humblest comfort and leisure; and who shall measure the heights to which our civilization may soar? Words fail the thought! It is the Golden Age of which poets have sung and high-raised seers have told in metaphor! It is the glorious vision which has always haunted man with gleams of fitful splendor. It is what he saw whose eyes at Patmos were closed in a trance. It is the culmination of Christianity—the City of God on earth, with its walls of jasper and its gates of pearl! It is the reign of the Prince of Peace!

1. *Why are political rights not sufficient to guarantee a comfortable standard of living for all people, especially those of the lower classes?*
2. *How does land ownership figure prominently in the explanation have why some people were financially fortunate and others were not?*
3. *Is wealth a measure of success? Compare George's thought on this with Carnegie's.*

18-3 The Gilded Age (1880)

The Gilded Age, a satirical novel by Mark Twain and Charles Dudley Warner, gave its name to the political era of the late nineteenth century. In this novel, Twain and Warner assailed corrupt politicians and a lackluster government. Prominent themes in the novel include trading political favors, profiteering, and special interests.

Source: Mark Twain and Charles Dudley Warner, *The Gilded Age* (Connecticut: American Publishing Company, 1880), pp. 217–227.

Cante-teca. Iapi-Waxte otonwe kin he cajeyatapi nawahon; otonwe wijice hinca keyape se wacanmi.
Toketu-kaxta. Han, hecetu; takuwicawaye wijicapi ota hen tipi.

Mahp. Ekta Oicim. ya.

The capital of the Great Republic was a new world to country-bred Washington Hawkins. St. Louis was a greater city, but its floating population did not hail from great distances, and so it had the general family aspect of the permanent population; but Washington gathered its people from the four winds of heaven, and so the manners, the faces and the fashions there, presented a variety that was infinite. Washington had never been in "society" in St. Louis, and he knew nothing of the ways of its wealthier citizens and had never inspected one of their dwellings. Consequently, everything in the nature of modern fashion and grandeur was a new and wonderful revelation to him.

Washington is an interesting city to any of us. It seems to become more and more interesting the oftener we visit it. Perhaps the reader has never been there? Very well. You arrive either at night, rather too late to do anything or see anything until morning, or you arrive so early in the morning that you consider it best to go to your hotel and sleep an hour or two while the sun bothers along over the Atlantic. You cannot well arrive at a pleasant intermediate hour, because the railway corporation that keeps the keys of the only door that leads into the town or out of it take care of that. You arrive in tolerably good spirits, because it is only thirty-eight miles from Baltimore to the capital, and so you have only been insulted three times (provided you are not in a sleeping car—the average is higher, there); once when you renewed your ticket after stopping over in Baltimore, once when you were about to enter the "ladies' car" without knowing it *was* a lady's car, and once when you asked the conductor at what hour you would reach Washington.

You are assailed by a long rank of hackmen who shake their whips in your face as you step out upon the sidewalk; you enter what they regard as a "carriage," in the capital, and you wonder why they do not take it out of service and put it in the museum, we have few enough antiquities, and it is little to our credit that we make scarcely any effort to preserve the few we have. You reach your hotel, presently—and here let us draw the curtain of charity—because of course you have gone to the wrong one. You being a stranger, how could you do otherwise? There are a hundred and eighteen bad hotels, and only one good one. The most renowned and popular hotel of them all is perhaps the worst one known to history.

It is winter, and night. When you arrived, it was snowing. When you reached the hotel, it was sleeting. When you went to bed, it was raining. During the night it froze hard, and the wind blew some chimneys down. When you got up in the morning, it was foggy. When you finished your breakfast at ten o'clock and went out, the sunshine was brilliant, the weather balmy and delicious, and the mud and slush deep and all-pervading. You will like the climate—when you get used to it.

You naturally wish to view the city; so you take an umbrella, an overcoat, and a fan, and go forth. The prominent features you soon locate and get familiar with; first you glimpse the ornamental upper works of a long, snowy palace projecting above a grove of trees, and a tall, graceful white dome with a statue on it surmounting the palace and pleasantly contrasting with the back-ground of blue sky. That building is the capitol; gossips will tell you that by the original estimates it was to cost $12,000,000, and that the government did come within $27,200,000 of building it for that sum.

You stand at the back of the capitol to treat yourself to a view, and it is a very noble one. You understand, the capitol stands upon the verge of a high piece of table land, a fine commanding position, and its front looks out over this noble situation for a city—but it don't see it, for the reason that when the capitol extension was decided upon, the property owners at once advanced their prices to such inhuman figures that the people went down and built the city in the muddy low marsh *behind* the temple of liberty; so now the lordly front of the building, with its imposing colonades, its projecting, graceful wings, its picturesque groups of statuary, and its long terraced ranges of steps, flowing down in white marble waves to the ground, merely looks out upon a sorrowful little desert of cheap boarding houses.

So you observe, that you take your view from the back of the capitol. And yet not from the airy outlooks of the dome, by the way, because to get there you must pass through the great rotunda; and to do that, you would have to see the marvelous Historical Paintings that hang there, and the bas-reliefs—and what have you done that you should suffer thus! And besides, you might have to pass through the old part of the building, and you could not help seeing Mr. Lincoln, as petrified by a young lady artist for $10,000—and you might take his marble emancipation proclamation, which he holds out in his hand and contemplates, for a folded napkin; and you might conceive from his expression and his attitude, that he is finding fault with the washing. Which is not the case. Nobody knows what *is* the matter with him; but everybody feels for him. Well, you ought not to go into the dome any how, because it would be utterly impossible to go up there without seeing the frescoes in it—and why should you be interested in the delirium tremens of art?

The capitol is a very noble and a very beautiful building, both within and without, but you need not examine it now. Still, if you greatly prefer going into the dome, go. Now your general glance gives you picturesque stretches of gleaming water, on your left, with a sail here and there and a lunatic asylum on shore; over beyond the water, on a distant elevation, you see a squat yellow temple which your eye dwells upon lovingly through a blur of unmanly moisture, for it recalls your lost boyhood and the Parthenons done in molasses candy which made it blest and beautiful. Still in the distance, but on this side of the water and close to its edge, the Monument to the Father of his Country towers out of the mud— sacred soil is the customary term. It has the aspect of a factory chimney with the top broken off. The skeleton of a decaying scaffolding lingers about its summit, and tradition says that the spirit of Washington often comes down and sits on those rafters to enjoy this tribute of respect which the nation has reared as the symbol of its unappeasable gratitude. The Monument is to be finished, some day, and at that time our Washington will have risen still higher in the nation's veneration, and will be known as the Great-Great-Grandfather of his Country. The memorial Chimney stands in a quiet pastoral locality that is full of reposeful expression. With a glass you can see the cow-sheds about its base, and the contented sheep nimbling pebbles in the desert solitudes that surround it, and the tired pigs dozing in the holy calm of its protecting shadow.

Now you wrench your gaze loose and you look down in front of you and see the broad Pennsylvania Avenue stretching straight ahead for a mile or more till it brings up against the iron fence in front of a pillared granite pile, the Treasury building—an edifice that would command respect in any capital. The stores and hotels that wall in this broad avenue are mean, and cheap, and dingy, and are better left without comment. Beyond the Treasury is a fine large white barn, with wide unhandsome grounds about it. The President lives there. It is ugly enough outside, but that is nothing to what it is inside. Dreariness, flimsiness, bad taste reduced to mathematical completeness is what the inside offers to the eye, if it remains yet what it always has been.

The front and right hand views give you the city at large. It is a wide stretch of cheap little brick houses, with here and there a noble architectural pile lifting itself out of the midst—government buildings, these. If the thaw is still going on when you come down and go about town, you will wonder at the short-sightedness of the city fathers, when you come to inspect the streets, in that they do not dilute the mud a little more and use them for canals.

If you inquire around a little, you will find that there are more boarding houses to the square acre in Washington than there are in any other city in the land, perhaps. If you apply for a home in one of them, it will seem odd to you to have the landlady inspect you with a severe eye and then ask you if you are a member of Congress. Perhaps, just as a pleasantry, you will say yes. And then she will tell you that she is "full." Then you show her her advertisement in the morning paper, and there she stands, convicted and ashamed. She will try to blush, and it will be only polite in you to take the effort for the deed. She shows you her rooms, now, and lets you take one—but she makes you pay in advance for it. That is what you will get for pretending to be a member of Congress. If you had been content to be merely a private citizen, your trunk would have been sufficient security for your board. If you are curious and inquire into this thing, the chances are that your landlady will be ill-natured enough to say that the person and property of a Congressman are exempt from arrest or detention, and that with the tears in her eyes she has seen several of the people's representatives walk off to their several States and Territories carrying her unreceipted board bills in their pockets for keepsakes. And before you have been in Washington many weeks you will be mean enough to believe her, too.

Of course you contrive to see everything and find out everything. And one of the first and most startling things you find out is, that every individual you encounter in the City of Washington almost—and certainly every separate and distinct individual in the public employment, from the highest bureau chief, clear down to the maid who scrubs Department halls, the night watchmen of the public buildings and the darkey boy who purifies the Department spittoons—represents Political Influence. Unless you can get the ear of a Senator, or a Congressman, or a Chief of a Bureau or Department, and persuade him to use his "influence" in your behalf, you cannot get an employment of the most trivial nature in Washington. Mere merit, fitness and capability, are useless baggage to you without "influence." The population of Washington consists pretty much entirely of government employés and the people who board them. There are thousands of these employés, and they have gathered there from every corner of the Union and got their berths through the intercession (command is nearer the word) of the Senators and Representatives of their respective States. It would be an odd circumstance to see a girl get employment at three or four dollars a week in one of the great public cribs without any political grandee to back her, but merely because she was worthy, and competent, and a good citizen of a free country that "treats all persons alike." Washington would be mildly thunderstruck at such a thing as that. If you are a member of Congress, (no offence,) and one of your constituents who doesn't know anything, and does not want to go into the bother of learning something, and has no money, and no employment, and can't earn a living, comes besieging you for help, do you say, "come, my friend, if your services were valuable you could get employment elsewhere—don't want you here?" Oh, no. You take him to a Department and say, "Here, give this person something to pass away the time at—and a salary"—and the thing is done. You throw him on his country. He is his country's child, let his country support him. There is something good and motherly about Washington, the grand old benevolent National Asylum for the Helpless.

The wages received by this great hive of employés are placed at the liberal figure meet and just for skilled and competent labor. Such of them as are immediately employed about the two Houses of Congress, are not only liberally paid also, but are remembered in the customary Extra Compensation bill which slides neatly through, annually, with the general grab that signalizes the last night of a session, and thus twenty per cent is added to their wages, for—for fun, no doubt.

Washington Hawkins' new life was an unceasing delight to him. Senator Dilworthy lived sumptuously, and Washington's quarters were charming—gas; running water, hot and cold; bath-room, coal fires, rich carpets, beautiful pictures on the walls; books on religion, temperance, public charities and financial schemes; trim colored servants, dainty food—everything a body could wish for. And as for stationery, there was no end to it; the government furnished; postage stamps were not needed—the Senator's frank could convey a horse through the mails, if necessary.

And then he saw such dazzling company. Renowned generals and admirals who had seemed but colossal myths when he was in the far west, went in and out before him or sat at the Senator's table, solidified into palpable flesh and blood; famous statesmen crossed his path daily, that once rare and awe-inspiring being, a congressman, was become a common spectacle—a spectacle so common, indeed, that he could contemplate it without excitement, even without embarrassment; foreign ministers were visible to the naked eye at happy intervals; he had looked upon the President himself, and lived. And more, this world of enchantment teemed with speculation—the whole atmosphere was thick with it—and that indeed was Washington Hawkins' native air; none other refreshed his lungs so gratefully. He had found paradise at last.

The more he saw of his chief the Senator, the more he honored him, and the more conspicuously the moral grandeur of his character appeared to stand out. To possess the friendship and the kindly interest of such a man, Washington said in a letter to Louise, was a happy fortune for a young man whose career had been so impeded and so clouded as his.

The weeks drifted by; Harry Brierly flirted, danced, added lustre to the brilliant Senatorial receptions, and diligently "buzzed" and "button-holed" Congressmen in the interest of the Columbus River scheme; meantime Senator Dilworthy labored hard in the same interest—and in others of equal national importance. Harry wrote frequently to Sellers, and always encouragingly; and from these letters it was easy to see that Harry was a pet with all Washington, and was likely to carry the thing through; that the assistance rendered him by "old Dilworthy" was pretty fair—pretty fair; "and every little helps, you know," said Harry.

Washington wrote Sellers officially, now and then. In one of his letters it appeared that whereas no member of the House committee favored the scheme at first, there was now needed but one more vote to compass a majority report. Closing sentence:

"Providence seems to further our efforts."

(Signed,) "ABNER DILWORTHY, U. S. S.
PER WASHINGTON HAWKINS, P. S."

At the end of a week, Washington was able to send the happy news,—officially, as usual,—that the needed vote had been added and the bill favorably reported from the Committee. Other letters recorded its perils in Committee of the whole, and by and by its victory, by just the skin of its teeth, on third reading and final passage. Then came letters telling of Mr. Dilworthy's struggles with a stubborn majority in his own committee in the Senate; of how these gentlemen succumbed, one by one, till a majority was secured.

Then there was a hiatus. Washington watched every move on the board, and he was in a good position to do this, for he was clerk of this committee, and also one other. He received no salary as private secretary, but these two clerkships, procured by his benefactor, paid him an aggregate of twelve dollars a day, without counting the twenty per cent, extra compensation which would of course be voted to him on the last night of the session.

He saw the bill go into Committee of the whole and struggle for its life again, and finally worry through. In the fullness of time he noted its second reading, and by and by the day arrived when the grand ordeal came, and it was put upon its final passage. Washington listened with bated breath to the "Aye!" "No!" "No!" "Aye!" of the voters, for a few dread minutes, and then could bear the suspense no longer. He ran down from the gallery and hurried home to wait.

At the end of two or three hours the Senator arrived in the bosom of his family, and dinner was waiting. Washington sprang forward, with the eager question on his lips, and the Senator said:

"We may rejoice freely, now, my son—Providence has crowned our efforts with success."

1. *What is the basis for calling Washington, D.C., the "grand old benevolent National Asylum for the Helpless"?*
2. *What are the worst features of Washington?*
3. *How are politicians typically portrayed in terms of their character?*

18-4 Richard K. Fox, from *Coney Island Frolics* (1883)

An important development of late nineteenth century America was the rise of leisure as an integral part of daily life. One of the more commercial and popular venues was the amusement park. Coney Island was the most famous amusement park in the nation.

There are various ways of bathing at Coney Island. You can go in at the West End, where they give you a tumbledown closet like a sentry box stuck up in the sand, or at the great hotels where more or less approach to genuine comfort is afforded. The pier, too, is fitted up with extensive bathing houses, and altogether no one who wants a dip in the briny and has a quarter to pay for it need to go without it.

If a man is troubled with illusions concerning the female form divine and wishes to be rid of those illusions he should go to Coney Island and closely watch the thousands of women who bathe there every Sunday.

A woman, or at least most women, in bathing undergoes a transformation that is really wonderful. They waltz into the bathing-rooms clad in all the paraphernalia that most gladdens the feminine heart. The hair is gracefully dressed, and appears most abundant; the face is decorated with all that elaborate detail which defies description by one uninitiated in the mysteries of the boudoir; the form is moulded by the milliner to distracting elegance of proportion, and the feet appear aristocratically slender and are arched in French boots.

Thus they appear as they sail past the gaping crowds of men, who make Coney Island a loafing place on Sundays. They seek out their individual dressing-rooms and disappear. Somewhere inside of an hour, they make their appearance ready for the briny surf. If it were not for the men who accompany them it would be impossible to recognize them as the same persons who but a little while ago entered those diminutive rooms. . . .

The broad amphitheatre at Manhattan Beach built at the water's edge is often filled with spectators. Many pay admission fees to witness the feats of swimmers, the clumsiness of beginners and the ludicrous mishaps of the never-absent stout persons. Under the bathinghouse is a sixty horse-power engine. It rinses and washes the suits for the bathers, and its steady puffing is an odd accompaniment to the merry shouts of the bathers and the noise of the shifting crowd ashore. . . .

A person who intends to bathe at Manhattan or Brighton Beach first buys a ticket and deposits it in a box such as is placed in every elevated railroad station. If he carries valuables he may have them deposited without extra charge in a safe that weighs seven tons and has one thousand compartments. He encloses them in an envelope and seals it. Then he writes his name partly on the flap of the envelope and partly on the envelope itself. For this envelope he receives a metal check attached to an elastic string, in order that he may wear it about his neck while bathing. This check has been taken from one of the compartments of the safe which bears the same number as the check. Into the same compartment the sealed envelope is put. When the bather returns from the surf he must return the check and must write his name on a piece of paper. This signature is compared with the one on the envelope. Should the bather report that his check has been lost or stolen his signature is deemed a sufficient warrant for the return of the valuables. The safe has double doors in front and behind. Each drawer may be drawn out from either side. When the throng presses six men may be employed at this safe.

1. **How does this piece capture the spirit of leisure enjoyed at Coney Island and other places of recreation?**

18-5 Address by George Engel, Condemned Haymarket Anarchist (1886)

European immigrants came to the United States seeking a better way of life. The factory condition they experienced contrasted with the promise of liberty that had attracted them to America. These conditions stimulated a radical labor response that erupted into violence at Chicago's Haymarket Square in 1886, as George Engel explains.

When, in the year 1872, I left Germany because it had become impossible for me to gain there, by the labor of my hands, a livelihood such as man is worthy to enjoy-the introduction of machinery having ruined the smaller craftsmen and made the outlook for the future appear very dark to them-I concluded to fare with my family to the land of America, the land that had been praised to me by so many as the land of liberty.

On the occasion of my arrival at Philadelphia, on the 8th of January, 1873, my heart swelled with joy in the hope and in the belief that in the future I would live among free men and in a free country. I made up my mind to become a good citizen of this country, and congratulated myself on having left Germany, and landed in this glorious republic. And I believe my past history will bear witness that I have ever striven to be a good citizen of this country. This is the first occasion of my standing before an American court, and on this occasion it is murder of which I am accused. And for what reasons do I stand here? For what reasons am I accused of murder? The same that caused me to leave Germany-the poverty-the misery of the working classes.

And here, too, in this "free republic," in the richest country of the world, there are numerous proletarians for whom no table is set; who, as outcasts of society, stray joylessly through life. I have seen human beings gather their daily food from the garbage heaps of the streets, to quiet therewith their knawing hunger. . . .

When in 1878, I came here from Philadelphia, I strove to better my condition, believing it would be less difficult to establish a means of livelihood here than in Philadelphia, where I had tried in vain to make a living. But here, too, I found myself disappointed. I began to understand that it made no difference to the proletarian, whether he lived in New York, Philadelphia, or Chicago. In the factory in which I worked, I became acquainted with a man who pointed out to me the causes that brought about the difficult and fruitless battles of the workingmen for the means of existence. He explained to me, by the logic of scientific Socialism, how mistaken I was in believing that I could make an independent living by the toil of my hands, so long as machinery, raw material, etc., were guaranteed to the capitalists as private property by the State. . . .

I took part in politics with the earnestness of a good citizen; but I was soon to find that the teachings of a "free ballot box" are a myth and that I had again been duped. I came to the opinion that as long as workingmen are economically enslaved they cannot be politically free. It became clear to me that the working classes would never bring about a form of society guaranteeing work, bread, and a happy life by means of the ballot. . . .

I . . . joined the International Working People's Association, that was just being organized. The members of that body have the firm conviction, that the workingman can free himself from the tyranny of capitalism only through force; just as all advances of which history speaks, have been brought about through force alone. We see from the history of this country that the first colonists won their liberty only through force that through force slavery was abolished, and just as the man who agitated against slavery in this country, had to ascend the gallows, so also must we. He who speaks for the workingman today must hang. And why? Because this Republic is not governed by people who have obtained their office honestly.

Who are the leaders at Washington that are to guard the interests of this nation? Have they been elected by the people, or by the aid of their money? They have no right to make laws for us, because they were not elected by the people. These are the reasons why I have lost all respect for American laws.

The fact that through the improvement of machinery so many men are thrown out of employment, or at best, working but half the time, brings them to reflection. They have leisure, and they consider how their conditions can be changed. Reading matter that has been written in their interest gets into their hands, and, faulty though their education may be, they can nevertheless cull the truths contained in those writings. This, of course, is not pleasant for the capitalistic class, but they cannot prevent it. And it is my firm conviction that in a comparatively short time the great mass of proletarians will understand that they can be freed from their bonds only through Socialism. One must consider what Carl Schurs said scarcely eight years ago: That, "in this country there is no space for Socialism;" and yet today Socialism stands before the bars of the court. For this reason it is my firm conviction that if these few years sufficed to make Socialism one of the burning questions of the day, it will require but a short time more to put it in practical operation.

All that I have to say in regard to my conviction is, that I was not at all surprised; for it has ever been that the men who have endeavored to enlighten their fellow man have been thrown into prison or put to death, as was the case with John Brown. I have found, long ago, that the workingman has no more rights here than any where else in the world. The State's Attorney has stated that we were not citizens. I have been a citizen this long time; but it does not occur to me to appeal for my rights as a citizen, knowing as well as I do that this does not make a particle of difference. Citizen or not-as a workingman I am without rights, and therefore I respect neither your rights nor your laws, which are made and directed by one class against the other; the working class.

Of what does my crime consist?

That I have labored to bring about a system of society by which it is impossible for one to hoard millions, through the improvements in machinery, while the great masses sink to degradation and misery. As water and air are free to all, so should the inventions of scientific men be applied for the benefit of all. The statute laws we have are in opposition to the laws of nature, in that they rob the great masses of their rights "to life, liberty, and the pursuit of happiness."

I am too much a man of feeling not to battle against the societary conditions of today. Every considerate person must combat a system which makes it possible for the individual to rake and hoard millions in a few years, while, on the other side, thousands become tramps and beggars.

Is it to be wondered at that under such circumstances men arise, who strive and struggle to create other conditions, where the humane humanity shall take precedence of all other considerations. This is the aim of Socialism, and to this I joyfully subscribe.

The States Attorney said here that "Anarchy" was "on trial."

Anarchism and Socialism are as much alike, in my opinion, as one egg is to another. They differ only in their tactics. The Anarchists have abandoned the way of liberating humanity which Socialists would take to accomplish this. I say: Believe no more in the ballot, and use all other means at your command. Because we have done so we stand arraigned here today-because we have pointed out to the people the proper way. The Anarchists are being hunted and persecuted for this in every clime, but in the face of it all Anarchism is gaining more and more adherents, and if you cut off our opportunities of open agitation, then will the work be done secretly. If the State's Attorney thinks he can root out Socialism by hanging seven of our men and condemning the other to fifteen years servitude, he is laboring under a very wrong impression. The tactics simply will be changed-that is all. No power on earth can rob the workingman of his knowledge of how to make bombs-and that knowledge he possesses. . . .

If Anarchism could be rooted out, it would have been accomplished long ago in other countries. On the night on which the first bomb in this country was thrown, I was in my apartments at home. I knew nothing of the conspiracy which the States Attorney pretends to have discovered.

It is true I am acquainted with several of my fellow-defendants with most of them, however, but slightly, through seeing them at meetings, and hearing them speak. Nor do I deny, that I too, have spoken at meetings, saying that, if every workingman had a bomb in his pocket, capitalistic rule would soon come to an end.

That is my opinion, and my wish; it became my conviction, when I mentioned the wickedness of the capitalistic conditions of the day.

When hundreds of workingmen have been destroyed in mines in consequence of faulty preparations, for the repairing of which the owners were too stingy, the capitalistic papers have scarcely noticed it. As with what satisfaction and cruelty they make their report, when here and there workingmen have been fired upon, while striking for a few cents increase in their wages, that they might earn only a scanty subsistence.

Can any one feel any respect for a government that accords rights only to the privileged classes, and none to the workers? We have seen but recently how the coal barons combined to form a conspiracy to raise the price of coal, while at the same time reducing the already low wages of their men. Are they accused of conspiracy on that account? But when working men dare ask an increase in their wages, the militia and the police are sent out to shoot them down.

For such a government as this I can feel no respect, and will combat them, despite their power, despite their police, despite their spies.

I hate and combat, not the individual capitalist, but the system that gives him those privileges. My greatest wish is that workingmen may recognize who are their friends and who are their enemies.

As to my conviction, brought about as it was, through capitalistic influence, I have not one word to say.

1. *Compare/contrasts Engel's hopes and expectations in coming to America and the reality with which he was faced.*
2. *Why, according to Engel, is it impossible for the working man to gain enough money to make an independent living? What factors are involved in the disenfranchisement and oppression of the working man?*
3. *Examine and explain Engel's opinion regarding what the working class must do to gain fair treatment and a chance for success? What historical precedents does Engel cite to support this conclusion? What obstacles stand in the way of the working class? What must be done to overcome these obstacles?*

18-6 Edward Bellamy, from *Looking Backward* (1888)

The rapid changes of the late nineteenth century led to contrasting visions of the future. The violence, poverty, and conflict promised a bleak times ahead while technology and other advances indicated bright, prosperous, and peaceful times ahead. Edward Bellamy's novel depicting a utopian future captured the popular imagination.

I myself was rich and also educated, and possessed, therefore, all the elements of happiness enjoyed by the most fortunate in that age. Living in luxury, and occupied only with the pursuit of the pleasures and refinements of life, I derived the means of my support from the labor of others, rendering no sort of service in return. My parents and grand-parents lived in the same way, and I expected that my descendants, if I had any, would enjoy a like easy existence.

. . . This mystery of use without consumption, of warmth without combustion, seems like magic, but was merely an ingenious application of the art now happily lost but carried to a great perfection by your ancestors, of shifting the burden of one's support on the shoulders of others. The man who had accomplished this, and it was the end all sought, was said to live on the income of his investments. . . . I shall only stop now to say that interest on investments was a species of tax in perpetuity upon the product of those engaged in industry which a person possessing or inheriting money was able to levy. . . .

* * * * *

"I would give a great deal for just one glimpse of the Boston of your day," replied Dr. Leete. "No doubt, as you imply, the cities of that period were rather shabby affairs. If you had the taste to make them splendid, which I would not be so rude as to question, the general poverty resulting from your extraordinary industrial system would not have given you the means. Moreover, the excessive individualism which then prevailed was inconsistent with much public spirit. What little wealth you had seems almost wholly to have been lavished in private luxury. Nowadays, on the contrary, there is no destination of the surplus wealth so popular as the adornment of the city, which all enjoy in equal degree." . . .

* * * * *

"As no such thing as the labor question is known nowadays," replied Dr. Leete, "and there is no way in which it could arise, I suppose we may claim to have solved it. . . . The solution came as the result of a process of industrial evolution which could not have terminated otherwise. All that society had to do was to recognize and cooperate with that evolution, when its tendency had become unmistakable." . . .

"Meanwhile, without being in the smallest degree checked by the clamor against it, the absorption of business by ever larger monopolies continued. In the United States there was not, after the beginning of the last quarter of the century, any opportunity whatever for individual enterprise in any important field of industry, unless backed by great capital. During the last decade of the century, such small businesses as still remained were fast-failing survivals of a past epoch. . . . The railroads had gone on combining till a few great syndicates controlled every rail in the land. In manufactories, every important staple was controlled by a syndicate. These syndicates, pools, trusts, or whatever their name, fixed prices and crushed all competition except when combinations as vast as themselves arose. Then a struggle, resulting in still greater consolidation, ensued.

" . . . The movement toward the conduct of business by larger and larger aggregations of capital, the tendency toward monopolies, which had been so desperately and vainly resisted, was recognized at last, in its true significance, as a process which only needed to complete its logical evolution to open a golden future to humanity.

"Early in the last century the evolution was completed by the final consolidation of the entire capital of the nation. The industry and commerce of the country, ceasing to be conducted by a set of irresponsible corporations and syndicates of private persons at their caprice and for their profit, were intrusted to a single syndicate representing the people, to be conducted in the common interest for the common profit. The nation, that is to say, organized as the one great business corporation in which all other corporations were absorbed. . . ."

1. *Summarize the process and effect of industrialization and monopoly that is described in this document.*

18-7   The Assassination of President Garfield

A disappointed and deranged office seeker named Charles Guiteau assassinated President James A. Garfield. After shooting Garfield in the back, Guiteau identified himself as a Stalwart; a faction within the Republican Party that supported General Grant, a radical southern policy, and the patronage system. Guiteau believed the crime he committed was essential for the good of the government and the nation. When he was brought to trial, the defense tried to prove that Guiteau was insane, but the jury convicted him and he was summarily executed.

Source: William W. Ireland, *Through the Ivory Gate: Studies in Psychology and History* (New York: Putnam's, 1889), pp. 179–180.

Guiteau himself first demanded the Austrian Mission, and then the consulship to France, as the reward of his services during the election campaign. He stated in a letter to the President that he was going to get married to a wealthy and accomplished heiress, and that together they might represent the nation with dignity and grace. Getting importunate and troublesome, the Secretary, Mr. Blaine, told him never to speak about the Paris consulship again to him, and the President refused to see him, and took no notice of his letters. Guiteau could neither speak French nor German, and was quite unfitted for these posts. He had rejected with disdain the advice to petition for a humbler place, but there is no proof that he would ever have got any employment whatever from the party now in office. Under these circumstances, the idea of improving the situation by killing the President entered Guiteau's mind like an inspiration, and dwelt there with the persistence of a fixed idea. It was singular that he did not know how to use firearms. He went to a shop to buy a pistol, and somebody coming in showed him how to load it. This was in Washington, where he had gone on the day of the President's inauguration. He went to an open space in the country, and practised with his pistol till he learned how to take aim. It was on the 8th of June that he bought the pistol. Guiteau himself said that he first conceived the idea of shooting the President about the middle of May. On the 12th of June he went to the little church which General Garfield attended, saw where he sat, and examined a window to see if a shot could be fired from that point. A week after, he came up with the President, who was going to the railway station. He was taking his sick wife to Long Branch. He went back to write in his notes that Mrs. Garfield looked so thin, and clung so tenderly to the President's arm, that his heart failed him, and he decided to take him alone. On the evening of the 1st July, he came up with the President walking with Mr. Blaine, and he might have shot them both in the dusk, and escaped. When cross-examined at the trial about this, he said that it was a very hot, sultry night, and he did not feel like it at the time. Whatever might be his motive, Guiteau intended that his crime should be done in public. He had prepared a number of documents and letters to the newspapers justifying his motives, and appealing for protection to his party, the Stalwarts. The danger which occupied his mind was the fear of being lynched by the mob. He had a cab ready to drive him to prison, and a letter to General Sherman asking him to send troops at once to guard the jail, and arrangements for a new issue of his book, "The Truth," which would now be sure to command a sale. The following is his appeal to the American people, dated Washington, D.C. 16th June, 1881 :—

"To the American People,—

"I conceived the idea of removing the President four weeks ago. Not a soul knew of my purpose. I conceived the idea myself, and kept it to myself. I read the newspapers carefully, for and against the administration, and gradually the conviction settled on me that the President's removal was a political necessity, because he proved a traitor to the men that made him, and thereby imperiled the life of the Republic. At the late Presidential election, the Republican party carried every Northern State. To-day, owing to the misconduct of the President and his Secretary of State, they could hardly carry ten Northern States. They certainly could not carry New York, and that is the pivotal State.

"Ingratitude is the basest of crimes. That the President, under the manipulation of his Secretary of State, has been guilty of the basest ingratitude to the Stalwarts admits of no denial. The expressed purpose of the President has been to crush General Grant and Senator Conkling, and thereby open the way for his renomination in 1884. In the President's madness he has wrecked the once grand old Republican party; and for this he dies.

"The men that saved the Republic must govern it, and not the men who sought its life.

"I had no ill-will to the President.

"This is not murder. It is a political necessity. It will make my friend Arthur President, and save the Republic. I have sacrificed only one. I shot the President as I would a rebel, if I saw him pulling down the American flag. I leave my justification to God and the American people.

"I expect President Arthur and Senator Conkling will give the nation the finest administration it has ever had. They are honest, and have plenty of brains and experience.   CHARLES GUITEAU."

The following document is even more characteristic of the mental peculiarities of the assassin. Though dated the day of the murder, it was said by Guiteau to have been written the day before :—

"WASHINGTON, *2nd July, 1881.*

"To the White House,—

"The President's tragic death was a sad necessity, but it will unite the Republican party and save the Republic. Life is a fleeting dream, and it matters little when one goes. A human life is of small value. During the war thousands of brave boys went down without a tear. I presume the President was a Christian, and that he will be happier in Paradise then here.

"It will be no worse for Mrs. Garfield, dear soul, to part with her husband this way than by natural death. He is liable to go at any time any way.

"I had no ill-will towards the President. His death was a political necessity. I am a lawyer, a theologian, a politician. I am a Stalwart of the Stalwarts. I was with General Grant and the rest of our men in New York during the canvass. I have some papers for the press, which I shall leave with Byron Andrews and his co-journalists at 1440 N.Y. Ave., where all the reporters can see them.

"I am going to jail.   CHARLES GUITEAU."

On the face of an envelope he had written :—

"I intend to place these papers, with my revolver, in the library of the State department. The reporters can copy them if they wish to in manifold.   CHARLES GUITEAU."

1. *Does Guiteau appear to be insane or disgruntled?*
2. *Guiteau claimed to have no ill will towards the president and that the assassination was a political necessity. How would he have come to this conclusion as a stalwart and as a rational person?*

18-8   Ida B. Wells-Barnett, from *A Red Record* (1895)

The rise of racial segregation was accompanied by racial violence that went punished by the law, including lynching. Journalist Ida B. Wells-Barnett emerged as the strongest voice against lynching.

A word as to the charge itself. In considering the third reason assigned by the Southern white people for the butchery of blacks, the question must be asked, what the white man means when he charges the black man with rape. Does he mean the crime which the statutes of the states describe as such? Not by any means. With the Southern white man, any misalliance existing between a white woman and a colored man is a sufficient foundation for the charge of rape. The southern white man says that it is impossible for a voluntary alliance to exist between a white woman and a colored man, and therefore, the fact of an alliance is a proof of force. In numerous instances where colored men have been lynched on the charge of rape, it was positively known at the time of lynching, and indisputably proven after the victim's death, that the relationship sustained between the man and the woman was voluntary and clandestine, and that in no court of law could even the charge of assault have been successfully maintained.

It was for the assertion of this fact, in the defense of her own race, that the writer hereof became an exile; her property destroyed and her return to her home forbidden under penalty of death, for writing the following editorial which was printed in her paper, the *Free Speech*, in Memphis, Tenn., May 21, 1892:

"Eight Negroes lynched since last issue of the *Free Speech:* one at Little Rock, Ark., last Saturday morning where the citizens broke (?) into the penitentiary and got their man; three near Anniston, Ala., one near New Orleans; and three at Clarksville, Ga.; the last three for killing a white man, and five on the same old racket-the new alarm about raping white women. The same programme of hanging, then shooting bullets into the lifeless bodies was carried out to the letter. Nobody in this section of the country believes in the old threadbare lie that Negro men rape white women. If Southern white men are not careful, they will overreach themselves and public sentiment will have a reaction; a conclusion will then be reached which will be very damaging to the moral reputation of their women."

But threats cannot suppress the truth, and while the Negro suffers the soul deformity, resultant from two and a half centuries of slavery, he is no more guilty of this vilest of all vile charges than the white man who would blacken his name.

During all the years of slavery, no such charge was ever made, not even during the dark days of the rebellion. . . . While the master was away fighting to forge the fetters upon the slave, he left his wife and children with no protectors save the Negroes themselves. . . .

Likewise during the period of alleged "insurrection," and alarming "race riots," it never occurred to the white man that his wife and children were in danger of assault. Nor in the Reconstruction era, when the hue and cry was against "Negro Domination," was there ever a thought that the domination would ever contaminate a fireside or strike toward the virtue of womanhood. . . .

It is not the purpose of this defense to say one word against the white women of the South. Such need not be said, but it is their misfortune that the . . . white men of that section . . . to justify their own barbarism . . . assume a chivalry which they do not possess. True chivalry respects all womanhood, and no one who reads the record, as it is written in the faces of the million mulattos in the South, will for a minute conceive that the southern white man had a very chivalrous regard for the honor due the women of his race, or respect for the womanhood which circumstances placed in his power. . . . Virtue knows no color line, and the chivalry which depends on complexion of skin and texture of hair can command no honest respect.

When emancipation came to the Negroes . . . from every nook and corner of the North, brave young white women . . . left their cultured homes, their happy associations and their lives of ease, and with heroic determination went to the South to carry light and truth to the benighted blacks. . . . They became the social outlaws in the South. The peculiar sensitiveness of the southern white men for women, never shed its protecting influence about them. No friendly word from their own race cheered them in their work; no hospitable doors gave them the companionship like that from which they had come. No chivalrous white man doffed his hat in honor or respect. They were "Nigger teachers"-unpardonable offenders in the social ethics of the South, and were insulted, persecuted and ostracized, not by Negroes, but by the white manhood which boasts of its chivalry toward women.

And yet these northern women worked on, year after year. . . . Threading their way through dense forests, working in schoolhouses, in the cabin and in the church, thrown at all times and in all places among the unfortunate and lowly Negroes, whom they had come to find and to serve, these northern women, thousands and thousands of them, have spent more than a quarter of a century in giving the colored people their splendid lessons for home and heart and soul. Without protection, save that which innocence gives to every good woman, they went about their work, fearing no assault and suffering none. Their chivalrous protectors were hundreds of miles away in their northern homes, and yet they never feared any "great dark-faced mobs." . . . They never complained of assaults, and no mob was ever called into existence to avenge crimes against them. Before the world adjudges the Negro a moral monster, a vicious assailant of womanhood and a menace to the sacred precincts of home, the colored people ask the consideration of the silent record of gratitude, respect, protection and devotion of the millions of the race in the South, to the thousands of northern white women who have served as teachers and missionaries since the war. . . .

These pages are written in no spirit of vindictiveness. . . . We plead not for the colored people alone, but for all victims of the terrible injustice which puts men and women to death without form of law. During the year 1894, there were

132 persons executed in the United States by due form of law, while in the same year, 197 persons were put to death by mobs, who gave the victims no opportunity to make a lawful defense. No comment need be made upon a condition of public sentiment responsible for such alarming results.

1. What does the author have to say regarding the charges of rape that are leveled against African Americans?

2. Explain the author's opinion of the "chivalry" of Southern men. What evidence does the author use to question it?

18-9 Booker T. Washington, Atlanta Exposition Address (1895)

With the rise of legalized racial segregation, African American leader Booker T. Washington made a famous speech at the Atlanta Exposition espousing a policy of self-help and accommodation to white society.

. . . Ignorant and inexperienced, it is not strange that in the first years of our new life we began at the top instead of at the bottom; that a seat in Congress or the state legislature was more sought than real estate or industrial skill; that the political convention or stump speaking had more attractions than starting a dairy farm or truck garden.

A ship lost at sea for many days suddenly sighted a friendly vessel. From the mast of the unfortunate vessel was seen a signal, "Water, water; we die of thirst!" The answer from the friendly vessel at once came back, "Cast down your bucket where you are." . . . The captain of the distressed vessel, at last heeding the injunction, cast down his bucket, and it came up full of fresh, sparkling water. . . . To those of my race who underestimate the importance of cultivating friendly relations with the southern white man, who is their next-door neighbor, I would say: "Cast down your bucket where you are"-cast it down in making friends in every manly way of the people of all races by whom we are surrounded.

Cast it down in agriculture, mechanics, in commerce, in domestic service, and in the professions. . . . Our greatest danger is that in the great leap from slavery to freedom we may overlook the fact that the masses of us are to live by the productions of our hands, and fail to keep in mind that we shall prosper in proportion as we learn to dignify and glorify common labour, and put brains and skill into the common occupations of life. . . . No race can prosper till it learns that there is as much dignity in tilling a field as in writing a poem. It is at the bottom of life we must begin, and not at the top.

To those of the white race who look to the incoming of those of foreign birth and strange tongue and habits for the prosperity of the South, were I permitted I would repeat what I say to my own race, "Cast down your bucket where you are." Cast it down among the eight millions of Negroes whose habits you know, whose fidelity and love you have tested in days when to have proved treacherous meant the ruin of your firesides. Cast down your bucket among these people who have, without strikes and labour wars, tilled your fields, cleared your forests, built your railroads and cities, and brought forth treasures from the bowels of the earth. . . . Casting down your bucket among my people . . . you will find that they will buy your surplus land, make blossom the waste places in your fields, and run your factories. While doing this, you can be sure in the future, as in the past, that you and your families will be surrounded by the most patient, faithful, law-abiding, and unresentful people that the world has seen. . . . In all things that are purely social we can be as separate as the finders, yet one as the hand in all things essential to mutual progress. . . .

The wisest among my race understand that the agitation of questions of social equality is the extremest folly, and that progress in the enjoyment of all the privileges that will come to us must be the result of severe and constant struggle rather than of artificial forcing. No race that has anything to contribute to the markets of the world is long in any degree ostracized. It is important and right that all privileges of the law be ours, but it is vastly more important that we be prepared for the exercise of these privileges. The opportunity to earn a dollar in a factory just now is worth infinitely more than the opportunity to spend a dollar in an opera-house.

1. Explain Booker T. Washington's theory on the most effective way for blacks to have an influence upon and rise in their society.

2. What does Washington mean when he exhorts his listeners to "cast down your buckets"? What does this mean to his black listeners? What does this mean to his white listeners?

18-10   United States Sanitary Commission, Sketch of Its Purposes (1864)

Rapid urban growth overtaxed meager municipal services creating unsanitary conditions in many cities. As this document shows, New York City residents faced many health perils in the streets. Such conditions eventually stimulated broad-based municipal reform.

I in a national life like our own,-a democracy, where the people universally take part in political affairs,-the government has no option in the case. The popular affections and sympathies will force themselves into the administration of army and all other affairs in times of deep national awakening. The practical question was not, Is it best to allow the army to depend in any degree upon the care of the people as distinguished from the government? Considered on administrative grounds alone, that question, we have no doubt, should be answered negatively. But no such question existed in a pure and simple form. It was this question rather, How shall this rising tide of popular sympathy, expressed in the form of sanitary supplies, and offers of personal service and advice, be rendered least hurtful to the army system, and most useful to the soldiers themselves? How shall it be kept from injuring the order, efficiency, and zeal of the regular bureau, and at the same time be left to do its intended work of succor and sympathy,-to act as a steady expression of the people's watchful care of their army, and as a true helper and supplementer of what the government may find it possible or convenient to do from its own resources? It was this mixed question the Sanitary Commission found itself called to answer, and its whole plan and working have been one steady reply to it. It could not be deemed wise, much less was it possible, to discourage and deaden the active sympathies of the people. They would follow their regiments to the field with home-comforts and provisions against wounds and sickness. The women would hurry to the hospitals and camps. For the first six months after the war began, the departments at Washington were fairly besieged by humane committees, masculine and feminine; business was interrupted, clogged, and snarled by the obtrusion of aid and comfort. Every regiment that went into the field had another regiment of anxious friends pushing into the camp to look after it, and supply its possible or real wants. State and local relief committees were named Legion; and it looked as if the Commissariat and Medical Departments were going to be swamped in popular ministrations. The beauty and glory of the affections which led to this self-sacrificing attendance and provision were not to be lost or dimmed by neglect. Nay, they were to be cherished with the utmost assiduity and the fullest sense of their national value.

On the other hand, the method, efficiency, and development of the governmental resources, the order and sway of the Medical Department, were not to be sacrificed or delayed by the allowance of an unregulated, superfluous, and sentimental beneficence. Scylla was to be shunned, and Charybdis not grazed. The people could not, let them try as hard as they would, do the government's work. They could neither build nor furnish nor work the hospitals. They could not even supply them with nurses; for men, as well as women, are absolutely necessary in that service, in military hospitals. On the other hand, a popular volunteer army could not live at all cut off from home sympathy, and from the demonstration of popular interest and watchfulness; nor could government fitly undertake certain services which the people were ready to render to the army, and which might, with extreme wisdom and pains, be permitted, and even encouraged, without injury to discipline and official responsibility.

Between these two important and indispensable interests, home feeling, and governmental responsibility and method, the Sanitary Commission steered its delicate and difficult way. It assigned to itself the task, requiring constant tact, of directing, without weakening or cooling, the warm and copious stream of popular beneficence toward the army. This owned its heat and fulness very much to its spontaneous and local character. Towns, cities, counties, States, were deeply interested in their own boys. To labor, night and day, for the very regiment that had rendezvoused in its square, or upon its common, to knit socks for feet that had crossed their own thresholds, and make garments to cover hearts that throbbed with their own blood, was not only easy for the people,-it was a necessity. And to send these by the hands of trusted townsmen, who should see these comforts put upon the very backs, or into the very mouths, they were designed for, was the most natural plan in the world, and seemingly the very best, as it certainly was the pleasantest. Why should not each State look after its own soldiers,-and each county, and each town, and each family? Certainly, this principle of local interest and personal affection could be depended on for longer and freer labors than any other. Was it safe to attempt to modify it, to mend it, to enlighten it, and to enlarge it? It was at least *necessary* to try to do this. Such a spontaneous, local liberality, however productive of materials and supplies of comfort, was absolutely unfurnished, as a very short experience proved, with the means and facilities for conveying, delivering, and applying its resources to the army. While our soldiers were mustering at a few near points, and drilling and disciplining for the contest, it was comparatively easy to reach particular regiments through special delegations, and with special supplies. But, after a few months, the armies of the Union left these convenient centres, and a very few miles of mud road between a corps and its base soon showed local committees the immense difficulties of *private* and *special* transportation. Moreover, when sickness began to appear, and anxiety for the well and strong was concentrated upon the feeble and ailing, the people soon began to discover that a soldier, after all, belonged more to the army than to his own regiment, and was ultimately thrown more on the care of the federal government and the general staff than upon his own surgeon and immediate officers. Slowly the nation learned that new thing in the experience of this generation, what a *General Hospital* is, and what the course taken with a sick soldier must be. They discovered that in the suddenness and unexpected character of army movements, men were very soon put far beyond the reach of the knowledge and following of any local protectors; that regiments were liable to be thrown from North to South, from East to West; from Alexandria to Port Hudson and Vicksburg; from Newbern to Nashville and Chattanooga; and that their own sons and brothers, if they were to be followed and watched over at all, must be looked after by a national and ubiquitous body, which was with the army everywhere, at home at all points, and with ends and objects that recognized neither State nor county nor regiment, but saw only the United States or Union soldier, and ministered to him impartially according to his need, with absolute indifference as to where he hailed from. To explain this state of things at the earliest moment became the urgent duty of the Sanitary Commission. Naturally, but unfortunately, so many State and local associations were already at work, and represented in or near the great camps, that a swarm of angry and jealous rivals gathered about the plan of the Sanitary Commission, and have never ceased to sting its agents with disparaging reports. So kind and worthy were the intentions of those whom these associations represented, and in many cases so honorable and laborious the efforts of these agents, so natural their prejudices and jealousies, that, while strongly disapproving the principle involved in them as radically subversive of what they were laboring to popularize, the Sanitary Commission could not find the heart to oppose them. It therefore simply strove to make its own plan widely understood, and, by doing the work in hand in the only thorough and satisfactory manner possible, to win by the degrees the confidence of the more distant and interior communities. On the whole, the intelligence with which the people have understood and appreciated its method is worthy of all admiration; and the mingled sense and magnanimity with which they have gradually substituted for their original motive the *federal* principle, which, though larger, nobler, and more patriotic, lacks personal incitement and local warmth and color, is a new proof of the capabilities of our people. . . .

The wonder is, that, in spite of them, there should have been so prodigious a triumph of the Federal principle in the humane work of ministering to the army. Local, personal, and religious prejudices have all yielded, more or less slowly, but steadily, to the self-vindicating claims of the Sanitary Commission. . . .

This is chiefly due to the wonderful spirit of nationality that beats in the breasts of American women. They, even more than the men of the country, from their utter withdrawal from partisan strifes and local politics, have felt the assault upon the life of the nation in its true national import. They are infinitely less *State-ish*, and more national in their pride and in their sympathies. They see the war in its broad, impersonal outlines; and while their particular and special affections are keener than men's, their general humanity and tender sensibility for unseen and distant sufferings is stronger and more constant. The women of the country, who are the actual creators, by the labor of their fingers, of the chief supplies and comforts needed by the soldiers, have been the first to understand, appreciate, and co-operate with the Sanitary Commission. . . .

1. *Examine and explain the circumstances necessitating a difficult balance on the part of the Sanitary Commision.*
2. *What are the aims of the Sanitary Commision and how are they both similar to and different from the desires and actions of local towns and their attempts to aid military personnel?*
3. *Identify and explain the distinction made in this document between how men and women view the war effort and the implementation of aid.*

18-11 Lincoln Steffens, from *The Shame of the Cities* (1904)

In the early twentieth century, muckraking journalists exposed many of the evils of American society, stimulating reforms. City political machines attracted many muckraking attacks, including this one by Lincoln Steffens.

The Philadelphia machine isn't the best. It isn't sound, and I doubt if it would stand in New York or Chicago. The enduring strength of the typical American political machine is that it is a natural growth-a sucker, but deep-rooted in the people. The New Yorkers vote for Tammany Hall. The Philadelphians do not vote; they are disfranchised, and their disfranchisement is one anchor of the foundation of the Philadelphia organization.

This is no figure of speech. The honest citizens of Philadelphia have no more rights at the polls than the negroes down South. Nor do they fight very hard for this basic privilege. You can arouse their Republican ire by talking about the black Republican votes lost in the Southern States by white Democratic intimidation, but if you remind the average Philadelphian that he is in the same position, he will look startled, then say, "That's so, that's literally true, only I never thought of it in just that way." And it is literally true.

The machine controls the whole process of voting, and practices fraud at every stage. The assessor's list is the voting list, and the assessor is the machine's man. . . . The assessor pads the list with the names of dead dogs, children, and non-existent persons. One newspaper printed the picture of a dog, another that of a little four-year-old negro boy, down on such a list. A ring orator in a speech resenting sneers at his ward as "low down" reminded his hearers that that was the ward of Independence Hall, and naming over signers of the Declaration of Independence, he closed his highest flight of eloquence with the statement that "these men, the fathers of American liberty, voted down here once. And," he added, with a catching grin, "they vote here yet." Rudolph Blankenburg, a persistent fighter for the right and the use of the right to vote (and, by the way, an immigrant), sent out just before one election a registered letter to each voter on the rolls of a certain selected division. Sixty-three per cent were returned marked "not at," "removed," "deceased," etc. From one four-story house where forty-four voters were addressed, eighteen letters came back undelivered; from another of forty-eight voters, came back forty-one letters; from another sixty-one out of sixty-two; from another, forty-four out of forty-seven. Six houses in one division were assessed at one hundred and seventy-two voters, more than the votes cast in the previous election in any one of two hundred entire divisions.

The repeating is done boldly, for the machine controls the election officers, often choosing them from among the fraudulent names; and when no one appears to serve, assigning the heeler ready for the expected vacancy. The police are forbidden by law to stand within thirty feet of the polls, but they are at the box and they are there to see that the machine's orders are obeyed and that repeaters whom they help to furnish are permitted to vote without "intimidation" on the names they, the police, have supplied. . . .

1. Summarize the power and effect of the political machine as it is described in this document.

18-12   Etiquette for the Upper Classes (1919)

As the ranks of the wealthy increased in the late nineteenth century, the upper classes determined new ways to define themselves. Expensive clothes and opulent homes were imposing physical expressions of wealth. Complex systems of etiquette were another method of discreetly identifying members of the privileged and moneyed classes. Visiting cards became necessary equipment of those in society, and the rules of their use became increasingly complicated. The method of presenting the card, folding certain corners of the card, the way the card was printed, all represented areas where the neophyte could commit an egregious faux pas. In a period so fraught with social pitfalls, comprehensive etiquette books abounded.

> **Source:** Emily Holt, *Encyclopaedia of Etiquette*, (New York 1919), pp. 45–47; Margaret Sangster, *Good Manners for All Occasions*, (New York 1904), p. 95.

VISITING CARDS FOR WOMEN

Their size varies but slightly from season to season. As a rule, the visiting cards used by married women are somewhat larger than those adopted by unmarried women. The material and quality of the card should be the very best. Pure white bristol board of medium weight, with the surface polished, not glazed, and with the name engraved thereon in black ink are the distinguishing features of the cards used in good society. Now and then very thin small slips of bristol board are seen, but these signify a passing fashion and cannot be commended for feminine use, though gentlemen frequently adopt the use of thin cards, in order to avoid any extra bulkiness in the waistcoat pocket.

Block, script, and old English lettering are all fashionable types for the engraving of the present *carte de visite;* and in size of card and style and wording of inscription the models on this page are reliable.

PROPER TITLES

Beveled or gilded edges, crests, or any decoration and engraving beyond the name, address, and day at home, do not evince taste or a knowledge of the nicest social customs. A lady's card in America never bears any other title than *Mrs. or Miss;* to dispense with these simple titles is to commit a solecism. A woman is not privileged to share on her card the dignities conferred upon her husband; the wife of the admiral is merely Mrs. George Dewey; the president's wife is Mrs. William McKinley, and even the woman, whether married or single, who has herself received the title of doctor should not affix it to her name on any but her business cards. A woman who practices medicine should use two kinds of cards. One should bear her name, thus, *Dr. Eleanor Baxter Brown,* or *Eleanor Baxter Brown, M.D.,* with her address in one corner and her office hours in another. This would be for professional uses only. Another—for social uses—should bear her name thus: *Miss Eleanor Baxter Brown,* or *Mrs. Thomas Russell Brown,* with only her house address in the corner.

<table>
<tr><td>MRS. DAVIS FLOYD WENDELL

125 WEST ELM STREET</td><td>MISS MARY WENDELL

125 WEST ELM STREET</td></tr>
</table>

Cards of the most approved type give the full Christian name or names, if there is more than one, as well as the surname. It is rather more modish, for example, to have the inscription read, *Mrs. Philip Hoffman Brown,* than *Mrs. Philip H. Brown; Miss Mary Ellsworth Brown,* than *Miss Mary E. Brown;* and unmarried women, as a rule, forbear the use of diminutives such as *Mamie, Maggie, Polly* and *Sadie* on their calling cards.

The senior matron of the oldest branch of a family may, if she pleases, drop her husband's Christian name from her cards, and let the card read simply, for example, *Mrs. Venables;* and her eldest unmarried daughter is entitled to omit her own Christian name, and use a card reading, for example, *Miss Venables.* Where, however, there are several families of the same name in a city or community, all mingling more or less in one circle of society, this is apt to create confusion in the minds of their friends and the safest course is not to omit the identifying Christian names.

THE DAY AT HOME SIGNIFIED

The name of a day of the week is engraved in the left-hand lower corner of the visiting card—*Fridays, Tuesdays, Thursdays* as the choice may be—without explanation or remark, if one wishes to signify to her friends and acquaintances that on a special afternoon of every week, after three and until six o'clock, she will be prepared to receive their calls. But if one wishes to set a particular limit to the term of receiving, the card should in some way specify that, as *Thursdays until Lent, Saturdays until April, First Mondays* (meaning, first in the month), or *First and Fourth Wednesdays* (meaning, first and fourth in the month).

* * *

Occasionally one receives a card on which the letters P. P. C. have been written. As everyone knows, these letters mean, To take leave—*Pour prendre congé.* A person going away for a long absence, going abroad, or about to change one's residence, leaves cards upon all her friends with these letters written thereon. Such cards are not used by people who are going away for only a short absence.

The letters P. F. on a card signify *Pour felicitation.* These letters are sometimes used when a person wishes to send congratulations after a wedding or after the birth of a child or any other happy event.

R. S. V. P., letters frequently appearing on invitations, are not usually written upon visiting cards. Their meaning is, "Answer, if you please," and whenever invitations bear these letters a reply is required, with the least possible delay.

1. Why do you think that so much attention was focused on a thing as seemingly simple as a visiting card?
2. Why were good manners elevated to the domain of the wealthy & privileged?

18-13   Scientific Management (1919)

Frederick Winslow Taylor, the "efficiency expert," introduced employers and employees to the concept of the Scientific Management of production. Popularly known as "Taylorization" these new principles emphasized streamlined organization, efficient factory arrangement, standardized tools, and planning departments. Employers were attracted to this because Taylorization promised efficiency and greater

399

profits. Labor was skeptical because scientific management also included "speed ups" that stretched the limits of human endurance.

Source: Frederick Winslow Taylor, *The Principles of Scientific Management* (New York: Harper, 1919), pp, 9–16.

The principal object of management should be to secure the maximum prosperity for the employer, coupled with the maximum prosperity for each employé.

The words "maximum prosperity" are used, in their broad sense, to mean not only large dividends for the company or owner, but the development of every branch of the business to its highest state of excellence, so that the prosperity may be permanent.

In the same way maximum prosperity for each employé means not only higher wages than are usually received by men of his class, but, of more importance still, it also means the development of each man to his state of maximum efficiency, so that he may be able to do, generally speaking, the highest grade of work for which his natural abilities fit him, and it further means giving him, when possible, this class of work to do.

It would seem to be so self-evident that maximum prosperity for the employer, coupled with maximum prosperity for the employé, ought to be the two leading objects of management, that even to state this fact should be unnecessary. And yet there is no question that, throughout the industrial world, a large part of the organization of employers, as well as employés, is for war rather than peace, and that perhaps the majority on either side do not believe that it is possible so to arrange their mutual relations that their interests become identical.

The majority of these men believe that the fundamental interest of employés and employers are necessarily antagonistic. Scientific management, on the contrary, has for its very foundation the firm conviction that the true interests of the two are one and the same; that prosperity for the employer cannot exist through a long term of years unless it is accompanied by prosperity for the employé, and *vice versa*; and that it is possible to give the workman what he most wants—high wages—and the employer what he wants—a low labor cost—for his manufactures.

It is hoped that some at least of those who do not sympathize with each of these objects may be led to modify their views; that some employers, whose attitude toward their workmen has been that of trying to get the largest amount of work out of them for the smallest possible wages, may be led to see that a more liberal policy toward their men will pay them better; and that some of those workmen who begrudge a fair and even a large profit to their employers, and who feel that all of the fruits of their labor should belong to them, and that those for whom they work and the capital invested in the business are entitled to little or nothing, may be led to modify these views.

No one can be found who will deny that in the case of any single individual the greatest prosperity can exist only when that individual has reached his highest state of efficiency; that is, when he is turning out his largest daily output.

The truth of this fact is also perfectly clear in the case of two men working together. To illustrate: if you and your workman have become so skilful that you and he together are making two pairs of shoes in a day, while your competitor and his workman are making only one pair, it is clear that after selling your two pairs of shoes you can pay your workman much higher wages than your competitor who produces only one pair of shoes is able to pay his man, and that there will still be enough money left over for you to have a larger profit than your competitor.

In the case of a more complicated manufacturing establishment, it should also be perfectly clear that the greatest permanent prosperity for the workman, coupled with the greatest prosperity for the employer, can be brought about only when the work of the establishment is done with the smallest combined expenditure of human effort, plus nature's resources, plus the cost for the use of capital in the shape of machines, buildings, etc. Or, to state the same thing in a different way: that the greatest prosperity can exist only as the result of the greatest possible productivity of the men and machines of the establishment—that is, when each man and each machine are turning out the largest possible output; because unless your men and your machines are daily turning out more work than others around you, it is clear that competition will prevent your paying higher wages to your workmen than are paid to those of your competitor. And what is true as to the possibility of paying high wages in the case of two companies competing close beside one another is also true as to whole districts of the country and even as to nations which are in competition. In a word, that maximum prosperity can exist only as the result of maximum productivity. Later in this paper illustrations will be given of several companies which are earning large dividends and at the same time paying from 30 per cent. to 100 per cent. higher wages to their men than are paid to similar men immediately around them, and with whose employers they are in competition. These illustrations will cover different types of work, from the most elementary to the most complicated.

If the above reasoning is correct, it follows that the most important object of both the workmen and the management should be the training and development of each individual in the establishment, so that he can do (at his fastest pace and with the maximum of efficiency) the highest class of work for which his natural abilities fit him.

These principles appear to be so self-evident that many men may think it almost childish to state them. Let us, however, turn to the facts, as they actually exist in this country and in England. The English and American peoples are the greatest sportsmen in the world. Whenever an American workman plays baseball, or an English workman plays cricket, it is safe to say that he strains every nerve to secure victory for his side. He does his very best to make the largest possible number of runs. The universal sentiment is so strong that any man who fails to give out all there is in him in sport is branded as a "quitter," and treated with contempt by those who are around him.

When the same workman returns to work on the following day, instead of using every effort to turn out the largest possible amount of work, in a majority of the cases this man deliberately plans to do as little as he safely can—to turn out far less work than he is well able to do—in many instances to do not more than one-third to one-half of a proper day's work. And in fact if he were to do his best to turn out his largest possible day's work, he would be abused by his fellow-workers for so doing, even more than if he had proved himself a "quitter" in sport. Underworking, that is, deliberately working slowly so as to avoid doing a full day's work, "soldiering," as it is called in this country.

It will be shown later in this paper that doing away with slow working and "soldiering" in all its forms and so arranging the relations between employer and employee that each workman will work to his very best advantage and at his best speed, accompanied by the intimate cooperation with the management and the help (which the workman should receive) from the management, would result on the average in nearly doubling the output of each man and each machine. What other reforms, among those which are being discussed by these two nations, could do as much toward promoting prosperity, toward the diminution of poverty, and the alleviation of suffering? America and England have been recently agitated over such subjects as the tariff, the control of the large corporations on the one hand, and of hereditary power on the other hand, and over various more or less socialistic proposals for taxation, etc. On these subjects both peoples have been profoundly stirred, and yet hardly a voice has been raised to call attention to this vastly greater and more important subject of "soldiering," which directly and powerfully affects the wages, the prosperity, and the life of almost every working-man, and also quite as much the prosperity of every industrial establishment in the nation.

The elimination of "soldiering" and of the several causes of slow working would so lower the cost of production that both our home and foreign markets would be greatly enlarged, and we could compete on more than even terms with our rivals. It would remove one of the fundamental causes for dull times, for lack of employment, and for poverty, and therefore would have a more permanent and far-reaching effect upon these misfortunes than any of the curative remedies that are now being used to soften their consequences. It would insure higher wages and make shorter working hours and better working and home conditions possible.

Why is it, then, in the face of the self-evident fact that maximum prosperity can exist only as the result of the determined effort of each workman to turn out each day his largest possible day's work, that the great majority of our men are deliberately doing just the opposite, and that even when the men have the best of intentions their work is in most cases far from efficient?

There are three causes for this condition, which may be briefly summarized as:

First. The fallacy, which has from time immemorial been almost universal among workmen, that a material increase in the output of each man or each machine in the trade would result in the end in throwing a large number of men out of work.

Second. The defective systems of management which are in common use, and which make it necessary for each workman to soldier, or work slowly, in order that he may protect his own best interests.

Third. The inefficient rule-of-thumb methods, which are still almost universal in all trades, and in practising which our workmen waste a large part of their effort.

This paper will attempt to show the enormous gains which would result from the substitution by our workmen of scientific for rule-of-thumb methods.

1. *What were the advantages of scientific management for employers and for workers? Would you feel more productive working according to these principles?*
2. *What is soldiering and how was it incompatible with scientific management?*
3. *Is it true, as Taylor argues, that the interests of employer and employee are the same?*

PART NINETEEN
IMMIGRANT AND URBAN NATION

19-1 Memorial of the Chinese Six Companies to U.S. Grant, President of the United States (1876)

Though Chinese laborers played a central role in the building of transcontinental railroads, American labor organizations and other groups lobbied to halt Chinese immigration. As this document shows, the Chinese business community opposed any exclusion of the Chinese from the United States. In 1882, the Chinese Exclusion Act was passed, halting immigration from that country.

TO HIS EXCELLENCY U. S. GRANT, PRESIDENT OF THE UNITED STATES OF AMERICA

Sir: In the absence of any Consular representative, we, the undersigned, in the name and in behalf of the Chinese people now in America, would most respectfully present for your consideration the following statements regarding the subject of Chinese emigration to this country:

We understand that it has always been the settled policy of your honorable Government to welcome emigration to your shores from all countries, without let or hindrance. The Chinese are not the only people who have crossed the ocean to seek a residence in this land. . . .

American steamers, subsidized by your honorable Government, have visited the ports of China, and invited our people to come to this country to find employment and improve their condition. Our people have been coming to this country for the last twenty-five years, but up to the present time there are only 150,000 Chinese in all these United States. 60,000 of whom are in California, and 30,000 in the city of San Francisco.

Our people in this country, for the most part, have been peaceable, law-abiding, and industrious. They performed the largest part of the unskilled labor in the construction of the Central Pacific Railroad, and also of all other railroads on this coast. They have found useful and remunerative employment in all the manufacturing establishments of this coast, in agricultural pursuits, and in family service. While benefiting themselves with the honest reward of their daily toil, they have given satisfaction to their employers and have left all the results of their industry to enrich the State. They have not displaced white laborers from these positions, but have simply multiplied the industrial enterprises of the country.

The Chinese have neither attempted nor desired to interfere with the established order of things in this country, either of politics or religion. They have opened no whiskey saloons for the purpose of dealing out poison and degrading their fellow-men. They have promptly paid their duties, their taxes, their rents, and their debts.

It has often occurred, about the time of the State and general elections, that political agitators have stirred up the minds of the people in hostility to the Chinese, but formerly the hostility has usually subsided after the elections were over.

At the present time an intense excitement and bitter hostility against the Chinese in this land, and against further Chinese emigration, has been created in the minds of the people, led on by His Honor the Mayor of San Francisco and his associates in office, and approved by His Excellency the Governor, and other great men of the State. These great men gathered some 20,000 of the people of this city together on the evening of April 5, and adopted an address and resolutions against Chinese emigration. They have since appointed three men (one of whom we understand to be the author of the address and resolutions) to carry that address and those resolutions to your Excellency, and to present further objections, if possible, against the emigration of the Chinese to this country.

It is charged against us that not one virtuous Chinawoman has been brought to this country, and that here we have no wives nor children. The fact is, that already a few hundred Chinese families have been brought here. These are all chaste, pure, keepers-at-home, not known on the public street. There are also among us a few hundred, perhaps a thousand, Chinese children born in America. The reason why so few of our families are brought to this country is because it is contrary to the custom and against the inclination of virtuous Chinese women to go so far from home, and because the frequent outbursts of popular indignation against our people have not encouraged us to bring our families with us against their will. . . .

It is charged against us that we have purchased no real estate. The general tone of public sentiment has not been such as to encourage us to invest in real estate, and yet our people have purchased and now own over $800,000 worth of real estate in San Francisco alone.

It is charged against us that we eat rice, fish, and vegetables. It is true that our diet is slightly different from the people of this honorable country; our tastes in these matters are not exactly alike, and cannot be forced. But is that a sin on our part of sufficient gravity to be brought before the President and Congress of the United States?

It is charged that the Chinese are no benefit to this country. Are the railroads built by Chinese labor no benefit to the country? Are the manufacturing establishments, largely worked by Chinese, no benefit to this country? Do not the results of the daily toil of a hundred thousand men increase the riches of this country? Is it no benefit to this country that the Chinese annually pay over $2,000,000 duties at the Custom house of San Francisco? Is not the $200,000 annual poll-tax paid by the Chinese any benefit? And are not the hundreds of thousands of dollars taxes on personal property, and the foreign miners' tax, annually paid to the revenues of this country, any benefit? . . .

It is charged that all Chinese laboring men are slaves. This is not true in a single instance. Chinamen labor for bread. They pursue all kinds of industries for a livelihood. Is it so then that every man laboring for his livelihood is a slave? If these men are slaves, then all men laboring for wages are slaves.

It is charged that the Chinese commerce brings no benefit to American bankers and importers. But the fact is that an immense trade is carried on between China and the United States by American merchants, and all the carrying business of both countries, whether by steamers, sailing vessels or railroads, is done by Americans. No China ships are engaged in the carrying traffic between the two countries. Is it a sin to be charged against us that the Chinese merchants are able to conduct their mercantile business on their own capital? And is not the exchange of millions of dollars annually by the Chinese with the banks of this city any benefit to the banks?

We respectfully ask a careful consideration of all the foregoing statements. The Chinese are not the only people, nor do they bring the only evils that now afflict this country.

1. *Summarize the accusations leveled against Chinese immigrants that are identified in this document.*
2. *What defense is made in this document against the charges that Chinese immigrants are detrimental to American society and business?*

19-2   Plain Facts for Old and Young (1884)

J. H. Kellogg insisted on a regime of physical and moral purity to insure proper standards of health and decorum. His concerns were shaped by anxiety that even good people could fall prey to a vast array of sins in the anonymity of large cities. The worst sin against God and nature, according to Kellogg was that of "self-abuse." He condemned masturbation for both men and women as an activity of debased human beings that resulted in underdeveloped, dyspeptic, drooling and idiotic men, and accounted for listlessness, pimples, and hysteria in women.

Source: J.H. Kellogg, *Plain Facts for Old and Young* (Iowa: I. F. Sengner, 1884), pp. 419–31; 471–83.

A CHAPTER FOR BOYS

Boys, this chapter is for you. It is written and printed purposely for you. If you do not read another word in the book, read these few pages if you are old enough to do so. Read each line carefully and thoughtfully. You may not find anything to make you laugh—possibly you may: but you will be certain to find something of almost inestimable value to you in every line.

Who are Boys?—Boys are scarce now-a-days. In the days of Methuselah, male human beings were still boys when nearly a century old; twenty-five years ago boys were still such until well out of their "teens"; now the interval between infancy and the age at which the boy becomes a young man is so brief that boyhood is almost a thing of the past. The happy period of care-free, joyous innocence which formerly intervened between childhood and early manhood is now almost unobservable. Boys grow old too fast. They learn to imitate the vices and the manners of their seniors before they reach their teens, and are impatient to be counted as men, no matter how great may be their deficiencies, their unfitness for the important duties and responsibilities of life. The consequence of this inordinate haste and impatience to be old, is premature decay. Unfortunately the general tendency of the young members of the rising generation is to copy the vices of their elders, rather than the virtues of true manliness. A strong evidence of this fact, if there were no other, is the unnaturally old-looking faces which so many of our boys present. At the present time the average boy of twelve knows more of vice and sin than the youth of twenty of the past generation.

It is not so much for these human mushrooms, which may be not inaptly compared to toadstools which grow up in a single night and almost as speedily decay, that we write, but for the old-fashioned boys, the few such there may be, those who have not yet learned to love sin, those whose minds are still pure and uncontaminated. Those who have already begun a course of vice and wickedness we have little hope of reforming; but we are anxious to offer a few words of counsel and warning which may possibly help to save as brands plucked from a blazing fire, those whose moral sense is yet alive, who have quick and tender consciences, who aspire to be truly noble and good.

What are Boys for?—This question was answered with exact truthfulness by a little boy, who, when contemptuously accosted by a man with the remark, "What are you good for?" replied, "Men are made of such as we." Boys are the beginnings of men. They sustain the same relation to men that the buds do to full-blown flowers. They are still more like the small green apples which first appear when the blossoms drop from the branches, compared with the ripe, luscious fruit which in autumn bends the heavy-laden boughs almost to breaking. Often, like the young apples, boys are green; but this is only natural, and should be considered no disgrace to the boys. If they grow up naturally they will ripen with age, like the fruit, developing at each successive stage of life additional attractions and excellent qualities.

Boys the Hope of the World.—A nation's most valuable property is its boys. A nation which has poor, weakly, vicious boys will have still weaker, more vicious and untrustworthy men. A country with noble, virtuous, vigorous boys, is equally sure of having noble, pious, brave, and energetic men. Whatever debases, contaminates, or in any way injures the boys of a country, saps and undermines the very foundation of the nation's strength and greatness. Save the boys from vice and crime, give them good training, physically, mentally, and morally, and the prosperity of the nation is assured.

Man the Masterpiece.—When a skillful artist perfects a work of art, a painting, a drawing, a statue, or some other work requiring great talent and exceeding all his other efforts, it is called his masterpiece. So man is the noblest work of God, the masterpiece of the Almighty. Numerous anecdotes are told of the sagacity of dogs, horses, elephants and other animals, of their intelligence and ingenious devices in overcoming obstacles, avoiding difficulties, etc. Our admiration and wonder are often excited by the scarcely less than human wisdom shown by these lowly brothers of the human race. We call them noble animals; but they are only noble brutes, at best. Compared with man, even in his most humble form, as seen in the wild savage that hunts and devours his prey like a wild beast, a lion or a tiger, they are immeasurably inferior. And in his highest development, man civilized, cultivated, Christianized, learned, generous, pious, certainly stands at the head of all created things.

Boys, do you love what is noble, what is pure, what is grand, what is good? You may each, if you will, become such yourselves. Let us consider for a moment.

How a Noble Character is Ruined.—A noble character is formed by the development of the good qualities of an individual. A bad character is formed by the development of bad traits, or evil propensities. In other words, sin is the cause of the demoralization of character, the debasing of the mind, the loss of nobility of which we see so much around us in the world. Sin is the transgression of some law. There are two kinds of sins: those which are transgressions of the moral law, and those which are transgressions of physical laws. Both classes of sins are followed by penalties. If a person violates the laws of health, he is just as certain to suffer as though he tells a "falsehood, steals, murders, or commits any other crime. Perfect obedience to all of nature's laws, including of course all moral laws, is necessary to perfect health and perfect nobleness of character. . . .

Self-Abuse.—Secret vice, masturbation, and self-pollution are other names applied to this same awful sin against nature and against God. We shall not explain here the exact nature of the sin, as very few boys are so ignorant or so innocent as to be unacquainted with it. To this sin and its awful consequences we now wish to call the attention of all who may read these lines.

A Dreadful Sin.—The sin of self-pollution is one of the vilest, the basest, and the most degrading that a human being can commit. It is worse than beastly. Those who commit it place themselves far below the meanest brute that breathes. The most loathsome reptile, rolling in the slush and slime of its stagnant pool, would not bemean itself thus. It is true that monkeys sometimes have the habit, but only when they have been taught it by vile men or boys. A boy who is thus guilty ought to be ashamed to look into the eyes of an honest dog. Such a boy naturally shuns the company of those who are pure and innocent. He cannot look with assurance into his mother's face. It is difficult for any one to catch his eye, even for a few seconds. He feels his guilt and acts it out, thus making it known to every one. Let such a boy think how he must appear in the eyes of the Almighty. Let him only think of the angels, pure, innocent, and holy, who are eye-witnesses of his shameful practices. Is not the thought appalling? Would he dare commit such a sin in the presence of his father, his mother, or his sisters? No, indeed. How, then, will he dare to defile himself in the presence of Him from whose all-seeing eye nothing is hid?

The Bible utters the most solemn warnings against sexual sins. The inhabitants of Sodom and Gomorrah were destroyed by fire and brimstone for such transgressions. Onan was struck dead in the act of committing a vileness of this sort. For similar vices the wicked inhabitants of Palestine were destroyed, and their lands given to the Hebrews. For a single violation of the seventh commandment, one of the most notable Bible characters, David, suffered to the day of his death. Those who imagine that this sin is not a transgression of the seventh commandment may be assured that this most heinous, revolting, and unnatural vice is in every respect more pernicious, more debasing, and more immoral than what is generally considered as violation of the commandment which says, "Thou shalt not commit adultery," and is itself a most flagrant violation of the same commandment.

Those who imagine that they "have a right to do as they please with themselves," so long as no one else is immediately affected, must learn that we are not our own masters; we belong to our Creator, and are accountable to God not only

404

for the manner in which we treat our fellow-men, but for how we treat ourselves, for the manner in which we use the bodies which he has given us. The man who commits suicide, who takes his own life, is a murderer as much as he who kills a fellow-man. So, also, he who pollutes himself in the manner we are considering, violates the seventh commandment, although the crime is in both cases committed against himself. Think of this, ye youth who defile yourselves in secret and seek to escape the punishment of sin. In Heaven a faithful record of your vile commandment-breaking is kept, and you must meet it by-and-by. You are fixing your fate for eternity; and each daily act in some degree determines what it shall be. Are you a victim of this fascinating vice, stop, repent, reform before you are forever ruined, a mental, moral, and physical wreck.

A CHAPTER FOR GIRLS

We have written this chapter especially for girls, and we sincerely hope that many will read it with an earnest desire to be benefited by so doing. The subject of which we have to write is a delicate one, and one which, we regret exceedingly, needs to be written about. But our experience as a physician has proven to us again and again that it is of the utmost importance that something be said, that words of warning should be addressed particularly to the girls and maidens just emerging into womanhood, on a subject which vitally concerns not only their own future health and happiness, but the prosperity and destiny of the race. Probably no one can be better fitted to speak on this subject than the physician. A physician who has given careful attention to the health and the causes of ill-health of ladies, and who has had opportunities for observing the baneful influence exerted upon the bodies and minds of girls and young women by the evil practices of which it is our purpose here to speak, can better appreciate than can others the magnitude of the evil, and is better prepared to speak upon the subject understandingly and authoritatively. Gladly would we shun the task which has been pressed upon us, but which we have long avoided, were it not for the sense of the urgent need of its performance of which our professional experience has thoroughly convinced us. We cannot keep our lips closed when our eyes are witnesses to the fact that thousands of the fairest and best of our girls and maidens are being beguiled into everlasting ruin by a soul-destroying vice which works unseen, and often so insidiously that its results are unperceived until the work of ruin is complete.

The nature of our subject necessitates that we should speak plainly, though delicately, and we shall endeavor to make our language comprehensible by any one old enough to be benefited by the perusal of this chapter. We desire that all who read these pages may receive lasting benefit by so doing. The subject is one upon which every girl ought to be informed, and to which she should give serious attention, at least sufficiently long to become intelligent concerning the evils and dangers to which girls are exposed from this source.

Girlhood.—Nothing is so suggestive of innocence and purity as the simple beauty of girlhood when seen in its natural freshness, though too seldom, now-a-days, is it possible to find in our young girls the natural grace and healthy beauty which were common among the little maidens of a quarter of a century ago. The ruddy cheeks and bright eyes and red lips which are indicative of a high degree of healthy vigor are not so often seen to-day among the small girls in our public schools and passing to and fro upon the streets. The pale cheeks, languid eyes, and almost colorless lips which we more often see, indicate weakly constitutions and delicate health, and prophesy a short and suffering life to many. Various causes are at work to produce this unfortunate decline; and while we hope that in the larger share of cases, bad diet, improper clothing, confinement in poorly ventilated rooms with too little exercise, and similar causes, are the active agents, we are obliged to recognize the fact that there is in far too many cases another cause, the very mention of which makes us blush with shame that its existence should be possible. But of this we shall speak again presently.

Real girls are like the just opening buds of beautiful flowers. The beauty and fragrance of the full-blossomed rose scarcely exceed the delicate loveliness of the swelling bud which shows between the sections of its bursting calyx the crimson petals tightly folded beneath. So the true girl possesses in her sphere as high a degree of attractive beauty as she can hope to attain in after-years, though of a different character. But genuine girls are scarce. Really natural little girls are almost as scarce as real boys. Too many girls begin at a very early age to attempt to imitate the pride and vanity manifested by older girls and young ladies. It is by many supposed that to be ladylike should be the height of the ambition of girls as soon as they are old enough to be taught respecting propriety of behavior, which is understood to mean that they must appear as unnatural as possible in attempting to act like grown-up ladies. Many mothers who wish their daughters to be models of perfection, but whose ideas of perfect deportment are exceedingly superficial in character, dress up their little daughters in fine clothing, beautiful to look at, but very far from what is required for health and comfort, and then continually admonish the little ones that they must keep very quiet and "act like little ladies." Such a course is a most pernicious one. It fosters pride and vanity, and inculcates an entirely wrong idea of what it is to be ladylike,—to be a true lady, to be true to nature as a girl. Such artificial training is damaging alike to mind and body; and it induces a condition of mind and of the physical system which is very conducive to the encouragement of dangerous tendencies.

How to Develop Beauty and Loveliness.—All little girls want to be beautiful. Girls in general care much more for their appearance than do boys. They have finer tastes, and greater love for whatever is lovely and beautiful. It is a natural desire, and should be encouraged. A pure, innocent, beautiful little girl is the most lovely of all God's creatures. All are not equally beautiful, however, and cannot be; but all may be beautiful to a degree that will render them attractive. Let all little girls who want to be pretty, handsome, or good looking, give attention and we will tell them how. Those who are homely should listen especially, for all may become good-looking, though all cannot become remarkably beautiful. First of all, it is necessary that the girl who wishes to be handsome, to be admired, should be good. She must learn to love what is right and true. She must be pure in mind and act. She must be simple in her manners, modest in her deportment, and kind in her ways.

Second in importance, though scarcely so, is the necessity of health. No girl can long be beautiful without health; and no girl who enjoys perfect health can be really ugly in appearance. A healthy countenance is always attractive. Disease wastes the rounded features, bleaches out the roses from the cheeks and the vermilion from the lips. It destroys the luster of the eye and the elasticity of the step. Health is essential to beauty. In fact, if we consider goodness as a state of moral health, then health is the one great requisite of beauty.

Health is obtained and preserved by the observance of those natural laws which the Creator has appointed for the government of our bodies. The structure of these bodies we may do well to study for a few moments.

The Human Form Devine.—Go with us to one of the large cities, and we will show you one of the most marvelous pieces of mechanism ever invented, a triumph of ingenuity, skill, and patient persevering labor for many years. This wonderful device is a clock which will run more than one hundred years. It is so constructed that it indicates not only the time of day, the day of the month and year, itself making all the necessary changes for leap year, but shows the motions of the earth around the sun, together with the movements and positions of all the other planets, and many other marvelous things. When it strikes at the end of each hour, groups of figures go through a variety of curious movements most closely resembling the appearance and actions of human beings.

The maker of this remarkable clock well deserves the almost endless praise which he receives for his skill and patience, for his work is certainly wonderful; but the great clock, with its curious and complicated mechanism, is a coarse and bungling affair when compared with the human body. The clock doubtless contains thousands of delicate wheels and springs, and is constructed with all the skill imaginable; and yet the structure of the human body is infinitely more delicate. The clock has no intelligence; but a human being can hear, see, feel, taste, touch, and think. The clock does only what its maker designed to have it do, and can do nothing else. The human machine is a living mechanism; it can control its own movements, can do as it will, within certain limits. What is very curious indeed, the human machine has the power to mend itself, so that when it needs repairs it is not necessary to send it to a shop for the purpose, but all that is required is to give nature an opportunity and the system repairs itself.

A Wonderful Process.—We have not space to describe all the wonderful mechanism of this human machine, but must notice particularly one of its most curious features, a provision by which other human beings, living machines like itself, are produced. All living creatures possess this power. A single potato placed in the ground becomes a dozen or more, by a process of multiplying. A little seed planted in the earth grows up to be a plant, produces flowers, and from the flowers come other seeds, not one, but often a great many, sometimes hundreds from a single seed. Insects, fishes, birds, and all other animals, thus multiply. So do human beings, and in a similar manner. The organs by which this most marvelous process is carried on in plants and animals, including also human beings, are called sexual organs. Flowers are the sexual organs of plants. And flowers are always the most fragrant and the most beautiful when they are engaged in this wonderful and curious work.

Human Buds.—A curious animal which lives near the seashore, in shallow water, attached to a rock like a water plant, puts out little buds which grow awhile and then drop off, and after a time become large individuals like the parent, each in turn producing buds like the one from which it grew. Human beings are formed by a similar process. Human buds are formed by an organ for the purpose possessed only by the female sex, and these, under proper circumstances, develop into infant human beings. The process, though so simply stated, is a marvelously complicated one, which cannot be full explained here; indeed, it is one of the mysteries which it is beyond the power of human wisdom fully to explain.

The production of these human buds is one of the most important and sacred duties of woman. It is through this means that she becomes a mother, which is one of the grandest and noblest functions of womanhood. It is the motherly instinct that causes little girls to show such fondness for dolls, a perfectly natural feeling which may be encouraged to a moderate degree without injury.

How Beauty is Marred.—As already remarked, mental, moral and physical health are the requisites for true beauty, and to secure these, obedience to all the laws of health is required. The most beautiful face is soon marred when disease begins its ravages in the body. The most beautiful character is as speedily spoiled by the touch of moral disease, or sin. The face is a mirror of the mind, the character; and a mind full of evil, impure thoughts is certain to show itself in the face in spite of rosy cheeks and dimples, ruby lips and bewitching smiles. The character is written on the face as plainly as the face may be pictured by an artist on canvas.

To be more explicit, the girl who disregards the laws of health, who eats bad food, eats at all hours or at unseasonable hours, sits up late at night, attends fashionable parties and indulges in the usual means of dissipation there afforded, dancing, wine, rich suppers, etc., who carefully follows the fashions in her dress, lacing her waist to attain the fashionable degree of slenderness, wearing thin, narrow-toed gaiters with French heels, and insufficiently clothing the limbs in cold weather, and who in like manner neglects to comply with the requirements of health in other important particulars, may be certain that sooner or later, certainly at no distant day, she will become as unattractive and homely as she can wish not to be. Girls and young ladies who eat largely of fat meat, rich cakes and pies, confectionery, iced creams, and other dietetic abominations, cannot avoid becoming sallow and hollow-eyed. The cheeks may be ever so plump and rosy, they will certainly lose their freshness and become hollow and thin. Chalk and rouge will not hide the defect, for everybody will discover the fraud, and will of course know the reason why it is practiced.

A Beauty-Destroying Vice.—But by far the worst enemy of beauty and health of body, mind, and soul, we have not yet mentioned. It is a sin concerning which we would gladly keep silence; but we cannot see so many of our most beautiful and promising girls and young ladies annually being ruined, often for this world and the next alike, without uttering the word of warning needed.

As before remarked, the function of maternity, which is the object of the sexual system in woman, when rightly exercised is the most sacred and elevated office which a woman can perform for the world. The woman who is a true mother has an opportunity of doing for the race more than all other human agencies combined. The mother's influence is the controlling influence in the world. The mother molds the character of her children. She can make of their plastic minds almost what she will if she is herself prepared for the work. On the other hand, misuse or abuse of the sexual organism is visited in girls and woman, as in boys and men, with the most fearful penalties. Nothing will sooner deprive a girl or young lady of the maidenly grace and freshness with which nature blesses woman in her early years than secret vice. We have the greatest difficulty in making ourself believe that it is possible for beings designed by nature to be pure and innocent, in all respects free from impurity of any sort, to become so depraved by sin as to be willing to devote themselves to so vile and filthy a practice. Yet the frequency with which cases have come under our observation which clearly indicate the alarming prevalence of the practice, even among girls and young women who would naturally be least suspected, compels us to recognize the fact. The testimony of many eminent physicians whose opportunities for observation have been very extensive shows that the evil is enormously greater than people generally are aware. Instructors of the youth, of large experience, assert the same. Nor is the evil greater in America than in some other countries. One writer declares that the vice is almost universal among the girls of Russia, which may be due to the low condition in which the women of that country are kept.

Terrible Effects of Secret Vice.—The awful effects of this sin against God and nature, this soul-and-body-destroying vice, become speedily visible in those who are guilty of it. The experienced eye needs no confession on the part of the victim to read the whole story of sinful indulgence and consequent disease. The vice stamps its insignia upon the countenance; it shows itself in the walk, in the changed disposition and the loss of healthy vigor. It is not only impossible for a victim of this sinful practice to hide from the all-seeing eye of God the vileness perpetrated in secret, but it is also useless to attempt to hide from human eyes the awful truth.

Headache, side-ache, back-ache, pains in the chest, and wandering pains in various parts of the body,—these are but a few of the painful ailments from which girls who are guilty of this sin suffer. Many of the tender spines which cause great solicitude on the part of parents and physicians, who fear that disease of the spine is threatening the life of a beloved daughter, not infrequently originate in this way. Much of the hysteria which renders wretched the lives of thousands of young ladies and the fond friends who are obliged to care for and attend them, arises from sexual transgression of the kind of which we are speaking. The blanched cheeks, hollow, expressionless eyes, and rough, pimply skins of many school-girls are due to this cause alone. We do not mean by this to intimate that every girl who has pimples upon her face is guilty of secret vice; but this sin is undoubtedly a very frequent cause of the unpleasant eruption which so often appears upon the foreheads of both sexes. It would be very unjust, however, to charge a person with the sin unless some further evidence than that of an eruption on the face was afforded.

The inability to study, to apply themselves in any way except when stimulated by something of a very exciting character, which many girls exhibit, is in a large proportion of cases due to the practice of which we are writing. Often enough the effects which are attributed to overstudy are properly due to this debasing habit. We have little faith in the great outcry made in certain quarters about the damaging effects of study upon the health of young ladies. A far less worthy cause is in many cases the true one, to which is attributable the decline in health at a critical period when all the vital forces of the system are necessarily called into action to introduce the activity of a new function.

Hundreds of girls break down in health just as they are entering womanhood. At from twelve to eighteen years of age the change naturally occurs which transforms the girl into a woman by the development of functions previously latent. This critical period is one through which every girl in health ought to pass with scarcely any noticeable disturbance; and if during the previous years of life the laws of health were observed, there would seldom be any unusual degree of suffering at this time. Those who have before this period been addicted to the vile habit of which we are writing, will almost invariably show at this time evidences of the injury which has been wrought. The unnatural excitement of the organs before the period of puberty, lays the foundation for life-long disease. When that critical epoch arrives, the organs are found in a state of congestion often bordering on inflammation. The increased congestion which naturally occurs at this time in many cases is sufficient to excite most serious disease. Here is the beginning of a great many of the special diseases which are the bane and shame of the sex. Displacements of various sorts, congestions, neuralgia of the ovaries, leucorrhoea, or whites, and a great variety of kindred maladies, are certain to make their appearance at this period or soon after in those who have previously been guilty of self-abuse. If the evil influences already at work are augmented by tight lacing, improper dressing of the extremities, hanging heavy skirts upon the hips, and fashionable dissipation generally, the worst results are sure to follow, and the individual is certain to be a subject for the doctors for a good portion of her life.

A talented writer some time since contributed to a popular magazine an article entitled, "The Little Health of Women," which contained many excellent hints respecting the influences at work to undermine the health and destroy the constitutions of American women; but he did not even hint at this potent cause, which, we firmly believe, is responsible for a far greater share of the local disease and general poor health of girls, young women, and married ladies, than has been generally recognized. These are startling facts, but we are prepared to substantiate them.

1. *Why was Kellogg obsessed with the "secret vice"?*
2. *Does he imply that passion and eroticism are suddenly incompatible with the demands of modern industrial culture?*
3. *How would Kellogg define the role and destiny of women? Of men?*

19-3 Anglo-Saxon Culture Under Siege (1885)

Josiah Strong believed that the Anglo-Saxon race was destined, if not duty-bound, to shape the future of the world. However, while clearly superior, Anglo-Saxon culture was besieged by threats on all sides. Perils such as immigration, Romanism, Mormonism, intemperance, socialism, wealth and the city all combined to undermine native white protestant American virtues. Strong's book, Our Country, was intended to place all Anglo-Saxons, the guardians of the culture, on alert.

> **Source:** Josiah Strong, *Our Country* (New York: Taylor and Baker for the American Home Missionary Society, 1885), pp. 40–46.

Consider briefly the moral and political influence of immigration. 1. Influence on morals. Let me hasten to recognize the high worth of many of our citizens of foreign birth, not a few of whom are eminent in the pulpit and in all the learned professions. Many come to us in full sympathy with our free institutions, and desiring to aid us in promoting a Christian civilization. But no one knows better than these same intelligent and Christian foreigners that they do not represent the mass of immigrants. The typical immigrant is a European peasant, whose horizon has been narrow, or false, and whose ideas of life are low. Not a few belong to the pauper and criminal classes. "From a late report of the Howard Society of London, it appears that 'seventy-four per cent of the Irish discharged convicts have found their way to the United States.'"[1] Moreover, immigration is demoralizing. No man is held upright simply by the strength of his own roots; his branches interlock with those of other men, and thus society is formed, with all its laws and customs and force of public opinion. Few men appreciate the extent to which they are indebted to their surroundings for the strength with which they resist, or do, or suffer. All this strength the emigrant leaves behind him. He is isolated in a strange land, perhaps doubly so by reason of a strange speech. He is transplanted from a forest to an open prairie, where, before he is rooted, he is smitten with the blasts of temptation.

We have a good deal of piety in our churches that will not bear transportation. It cannot endure even the slight change of climate involved in spending a few summer weeks at a watering place, and is commonly left at home. American travelers in Europe often grant themselves license, on which, if at home, they would frown. Very many church-members, when they go west, seem to think they have left their Christian obligations with their church-membership in the East. And a considerable element of our American-born population are apparently under the impression that the Ten Commandments are not binding west of the Missouri. Is it strange, then, that those who come from other lands, whose old associations are all broken and whose reputations are left behind, should sink to a lower moral level? Across the sea they suffered many restraints which are here removed. Better wages afford larger means of self-indulgence; often the back is not strong enough to bear prosperity, and liberty too often lapses into license. Our population of foreign extraction is sadly conspicuous in our criminal records. This element constituted in 1870 twenty per cent of the population of New England, and furnished seventy-five per cent of the crime. That is, it was twelve times as much disposed to crime as the native stock. The hoodlums and roughs of our cities are, most of them, American-born of foreign parentage. Of the 680 discharged convicts who applied to the Prison Association of New York for aid, during the year ending June 30th, 1882, 442 were born in the United States, against 238 foreign-born; while only 144 reported native parentage against 536 who reported foreign parentage.

The Rhode Island Work-house and House of Correction had received, to December 31st, 1882, 6,202 persons on commitment. Of this number, fifty-two per cent were native-born and seventy-six per cent were born of foreign parentage.[2] While in 1880 the foreign-born were only thirteen per cent of the entire population, they furnish nineteen per cent of the convicts in our penitentiaries, and forty-three per cent of the inmates of work-houses and houses of correction. And it must be borne in mind that a very large proportion of the native-born prisoners were of foreign parentage.

Moreover, immigration not only furnishes the greater portion of our criminals, it is also seriously affecting the morals of the native population. It is disease and not health which is contagious. Most foreigners bring with them continental ideas of the Sabbath, and the result is sadly manifest in all our cities, where it is being transformed from a holy day into a holiday. But by far the most effective instrumentality for debauching popular morals is the liquor traffic, and this is chiefly carried on by foreigners. In 1880, of the "Traders and dealers in liquors and wines,"[3] (I suppose this means wholesale dealers) sixty-three per cent were foreign-born, and of the brewers and maltsters seventy-five per cent, while a large proportion of the remainder were of foreign parentage. Of saloon-keepers about sixty per cent were foreign-born, while many of the remaining forty percent of these corrupters of youth, these western Arabs, whose hand is against every man, were of foreign extraction.

2. We can only glance at the political aspects of immigration. As we have already seen, it is immigration which has fed fat the liquor power; and there is a liquor vote. Immigration furnishes most of the victims of Mormonism; and there is a Mormon vote. Immigration is the strength of the Catholic church; and there is a Catholic vote. Immigration is the mother and nurse of American socialism; and there is to be a socialist vote. Immigration tends strongly to the cities, and gives to them their political complexion. And there is no more serious menace to our civilization than our rabble-ruled cities. These several perils, all of which are enhanced by immigration, will be considered in succeeding chapters.

Many American citizens are not Americanized. It is as unfortunate as it is natural, that foreigners in this country should cherish their own language and peculiar customs, and carry their nationality, as a distinct factor, into our politics. Immigration has created the "German vote" and the "Irish vote," for which politicians bid, and which have already been decisive of state elections, and might easily determine national. A mass of men but little acquainted with our institutions, who will act in concert and who are controlled largely by their appetites and prejudices, constitute a very paradise for demagogues.

We have seen that immigration is detrimental to popular morals. It has a like influence upon popular intelligence, for the percentage of illiteracy among the foreign-born population is thirty-eight per cent greater than among the native-born whites. Thus immigration complicates our moral and political problems by swelling our dangerous classes. And as immigration is to increase much more rapidly than the population, we may infer that the dangerous classes are to increase more rapidly than hitherto.[4] It goes without saying, that there is a dead-line of ignorance and vice in every republic, and when it is touched by the average citizen, free institutions perish; for intelligence and virtue are as essential to the life of a republic as are brain and heart to the life of a man.

A severe strain upon a bridge may be borne with safety if evenly distributed, which, if concentrated, would ruin the whole structure. There is among our population of alien birth an unhappy tendency toward aggregation, which concentrates the strain upon portions of our social and political fabric. Certain quarters of many of the cities are, in language, customs and costumes, essentially foreign. Many colonies have bought up lands and so set themselves apart from Americanizing influences. In 1845, New Glarus, in southern Wisconsin, was settled by a colony of 108 persons from one of the cantons of Switzerland. In 1880 they numbered 1,060 souls; and "No Yankee lives within a ring of six miles round the first built dug-out." This Helvetian settlement, founded three years before Wisconsin became a state, has preserved its race, its language, its worship, and its customs in their integrity. Similar colonies are now being planted in the West. In some cases 100,000 or 200,000 acres in one block, have been purchased by foreigners of one nationality and religion; thus building up states within a state, having different languages, different antecedents, different religions, different ideas and habits, preparing mutual jealousies, and perpetuating race antipathies. If our noble domain were tenfold larger than it is, it would still be too small to embrace with safety to our national future, little Germanies here, little Scandinavias there, and little Irelands yonder. A strong centralized government, like that of Rome under the Caesars, can control heterogenous populations, but local self-government implies close relations between man and man, a measure of sympathy, and, to a certain extent, community of ideas. Our safety demands the assimilation of these strange populations, and the process of assimilation will become slower and more difficult as the proportion of foreigners increases.

When we consider the influence of immigration, it is by no means reassuring to reflect that seventy-five per cent of it is pouring into the formative West. We have seen that in 1900 our foreign population, with their children of the first generation, will probably number not less than 43,000,000. If the movement westward continues, as it probably will, until the free farming lands are all taken, 25,000,000 of that foreign element will be west of the Mississippi. And this will be two-thirds of all the population of the West, even if that population should increase 350 per cent between 1880 and 1900. Already is the proportion of foreigners in the territories from two to three times greater than in the states east of the Mississippi. We may well ask—and with special reference to the West—whether this in-sweeping immigration is to foreignize us, or we are to Americanize it. Mr. Beecher hopefully says, when the lion eats an ox the ox becomes lion, not the lion ox. The illustration would be very neat if it only illustrated. The lion happily has an instinct controlled by an unfailing law which determines what, and when, and how much he shall eat. If that instinct should fail, and he should some day eat a badly diseased ox, or should very much over-eat, we might have on our hands a very sick lion. I can even conceive that under such conditions the ignoble ox might slay the king of beasts. Foreigners are not coming to the United States in answer to any appetite of ours, controlled by an unfailing moral or political instinct. They naturally consult their own interests in coming, not ours. The lion, without being consulted as to time, quantity or quality, is having the food thrust down his throat, and his only alternative is, digest or die.

1. How does Strong argue that immigration [as a process] would undermine the American character?
2. What evidence supports Strong's claims of the pernicious influence of immigration to America?

19-4   How the Other Half Lives (1890)

In the arresting exposé How the Other Half Lives, Jacob Riis served up disturbing images in prose and photographs of the lives of America's most destitute and vulnerable. The world Riis laid bare seemed incongruous with the veneer of American prosperity and advancement. The poor, as Riis understood them, were the hapless victims of the capitalistic avarice, which ironically also fueled the engines of American economic growth and expansion.

Source: Jacob Riis, *How the Other Half Lives* (New York: Penguin, 1890), pp. 135–140.

THE PROBLEM OF THE CHILDREN

The problem of the children becomes, in these swarms, to the last degree perplexing. Their very number makes one stand aghast. I have already given instances of the packing of the child population in East Side tenements. They might be continued indefinitely until the array would be enough to startle any community. For, be it remembered, these children with the training they receive—or do not receive—with the instincts they inherit and absorb in their growing up, are to be our future rulers, if our theory of government is worth anything. More than a working majority of our voters now register from the tenements. I counted the other day the little ones, up to ten years or so, in a Bayard Street tenement that for a yard has a triangular space in the centre with sides fourteen or fifteen feet long, just room enough for a row of ill-smelling closets at the base of the triangle and a hydrant at the apex. There was about as much light in this "yard" as in the average cellar. I gave up my self-imposed task in despair when I had counted one hundred and twenty-eight in forty families. Thirteen I had missed, or not found in. Applying the average for the forty to the whole fifty-three, the house contained one hundred and seventy children. It is not the only time I have had to give up such census work. I have in mind an alley—an inlet rather to a row of rear tenements—that is either two or four feet wide according as the wall of the crazy old building that gives on it bulges out or in. I tried to count the children that swarmed there, but could not. Sometimes I have doubted that anybody knows just how many there are about. Bodies of drowned children turn up in the rivers right along in summer whom no one seems to know anything about. When last spring some workmen, while moving a pile of lumber on a North River pier, found under the last plank the body of a little lad crushed to death, no one had missed a boy, though his parents afterward turned up. The truant officer assuredly does not know, though he spends his life trying to find out, somewhat illogically perhaps since the department that employs him admits that thousands of poor children are crowded out of the schools year by year for want of room. There was a big tenement in the Sixth Ward, now happily appropriated by the beneficent spirit of business that blots out so many foul spots in New York —it figured not long ago in the official reports as "an out-and-out hogpen"—that had a record of one hundred and two arrests in four years among its four hundred and seventy-eight tenants, fifty-seven of them for drunken and disorderly conduct. I do not know how many children there were in it, but the inspector reported that he found only seven in the whole house who owned that they went to school. The rest gathered all the instruction they received running for beer for their elders. Some of them claimed the "flat" as their home as a mere matter of form. They slept in the streets at night. the official came upon a little party of four drinking beer out of the cover of a milk-can in the hallway. They were of the seven good boys and proved their claim to the title by offering him some.

The old question, what to do with the boy, assumed a new and serious phase in the tenements. Under the best conditions found there, it is not easily answered. In nine cases out of ten he would make an excellent mechanic, if trained early to work at a trade, for he is neither dull nor slow, but the short-sighted depotism of the trades unions has practically closed that avenue to him. Trade-schools, however excellent, cannot supply the opportunity thus denied him, and at the outset the boy stands condemned by his own to low and ill-paid drudgery, held down by the hand that of all should labor to raise him. Home, the greatest factor of all in the training of the young, means nothing to him but a pigeon-hole in a coop along with so many other human animals. Its influence is scarcely of the elevating kind, if it have any. The very games at which he takes a hand in the street become polluting in its atmosphere. With no steady hand to guide him, the boy takes naturally to idle ways. Caught in the street by the truant officer, or by agents of the Children's Societies, peddling, perhaps, or begging, to help out the family resources, he runs the risk of being sent to a reformatory, where contact with vicious boys older than himself soon develops the latent possibilities for evil that lie hidden in him. The city has no Truant Home in which to keep him, and all efforts of the children's friends to enforce school attendance are paralyzed by this want. The risk of the reformatory is too great. What is done in the end is to let him take chances—with the chances all against him. The result is the rough young savage, familiar from the street. Rough as he is, if any one doubt that this child of common clay have in him the instinct of beauty, of love for the ideal of which his life has no embodiment, let him put the matter to the test. Let him take into a tenement block a handful of flowers from the fields and watch the brightened faces, the sudden abandonment of play and fight that go ever hand in hand where there is no elbow-room, the wild entreaty for "posies," the eager love with which the little messengers of peace are shielded, once possessed; then let him change his mind. I have seen an armful of daisies keep the peace of a block better than a policeman and his club, seen instincts awaken under their gentle appeal, whose very existence the soil in which they grew made seem a mockery. I have not forgotten the deputation of ragamuffins from a Mulberry Street alley that knocked at my office door one morning on a mysterious expedition for flowers, not for themselves, but for "a lady," and having obtained what they wanted, trooped off to bestow them, a ragged and dirty little band, with a solemnity that was quite unusual. It was not until an old man called the next day to thank me for the flowers that I found out they had decked the bier of a pauper, in the dark rear room when she lay waiting in her pine board coffin for the city's hearse. Yet, as I knew, that dismal alley with its barebrick walls, between which no sun ever rose or set, was the world of those children. It filled their young lives. Probably not one of them had ever been out of the sight of it. They were too dirty, too ragged, and too generally disreputable, too well hidden in their slum besides, to come into line with the Fresh Air summer boarders.

With such human instincts and cravings, forever unsatisfied, turned into a haunting curse; with appetite ground to keenest edge by a hunger that is never fed, the children of the poor grow up in joyless homes to lives of wearisome toil that claims them at an age when the play of their happier fellows has but just begun. Has a yard of turf been laid and a vine been coaxed to grow within their reach, they are banished and barred out from it as from a heaven that is not for such as they. I came upon a couple of youngsters in a Mulberry Street yard a while ago that were chalking on the fence their first lesson in "writin'." And this is what they wrote: "Keeb of te Grass." They had it by heart, for there was not, I verily believe, a green sod within a quarter of a mile. Home to them is an empty name. Pleasure? A gentleman once catechized a ragged class in a down-town public school on this point, and recorded the result: Out of forty-eight boys twenty had never seen the Brooklyn Bridge that was scarcely five minutes' walk away, three only had been in Central Park, fifteen had known the joy of a ride in a horse-car. The street, with its ash-barrels and its dirt, the river that runs foul with mud, are their domain. What training they receive is picked up there. And they are apt pupils. If the mud and the dirt are easily reflected in their lives, what wonder? Scarce half-grown, such lads as these confront the world with the challenge to give them their due, too long withheld, or ———. Our jails supply the answer to the alternative.

A little fellow who seemed clad in but a single rag was among the flotsam and jetsam stranded at Police Headquarters one day last summer. No one knew where he came from or where he belonged. The boy himself knew as little about it as anybody, and was the least anxious to have light shed on the subject after he had spent a night in the matron's nursery. The discovery that beds were provided for boys to sleep in there, and that he could have "a whole egg" and three slices of bread for breakfast put him on the best of terms with the world in general, and he decided that Headquarters was a "bully place." He sang "McGinty" all through, with Tenth Avenue variations, for the police, and then settled down to the serious business of giving an account of himself. The examination went on after this fashion:

"Where do you go to church, my boy?"

"We don't have no clothes to go to church." And indeed his appearance, as he was, in the door of any New York church would have caused a sensation.

"Well, where do you go to school, then?"

"I don't go to school," with a snort of contempt.

"Where do you buy your bread?"

"We don't buy no bread; we buy beer," said the boy, and it was eventually the saloon that led the police as a landmark to his "home." It was worthy of the boy. As he had said, his only bed was a heap of dirty straw on the floor, his daily diet a crust in the morning, nothing else.

Into the rooms of the Children's Aid Society were led two little girls whose father had "busted up the house" and put them on the street after their mother died. Another, who was turned out by her step-mother "because she had five of her own and could not afford to keep her," could not remember ever having been in church or Sunday-school, and only knew the name of Jesus through hearing people swear by it. She had no idea what they meant. These were specimens of the overflow from the tenements of our home-heathen that are growing up in New York's streets to-day, while tender hearted men and women are busying themselves with the socks and the hereafter of well-fed little Hottentots thousands of miles away. According to Canon Taylor, of York, one hundred and nine missionaries in the four fields of Persia, Palestine, Arabia, and Egypt spent one year and sixty thousand dollars in converting one little heathen girl. If there is nothing the matter with those missionaries, they might come to New York with a good deal better prospect of success.

By those who lay flattering unction to their souls in the knowledge that to-day New York has, at all events, no brood of the gutters of tender years that can be homeless long unheeded, let it be remembered well through what effort this judgment has been averted. In thirty-seven years the Children's Aid Society, that came into existence as an emphatic protest against the tenement corruption of the young, has sheltered quite three hundred thousand outcast, homeless, and orphaned children in its lodging-houses, and has found homes in the West for seventy thousand that had none. Doubtless, as a mere stroke of finance, the five millions and a half thus spent were a wiser investment than to have let them grow up thieves and thugs. In the last fifteen years of this tireless battle for the safety of the State the intervention of the Society for the Prevention of Cruelty to Children has been invoked for 138,891 little ones; it has thrown its protection around more than twenty-five thousand helpless children, and has convicted nearly sixteen thousand wretches of child-beating and abuse. Add to this the standing army of fifteen thousand dependent children in New York's asylums and institutions, and some idea is gained of the crop that is garnered day by day in the tenements, of the enormous force employed to check their inroads on our social life, and of the cause for apprehension that would exist did their efforts flag for ever so brief a time.

Nothing is now better understood than that the rescue of the children is the key to the problem of city poverty, as presented for our solution to-day; that a character may be formed where to reform it would be a hopeless task. The concurrent testimony of all who have to undertake it at a later stage: that the young are naturally neither vicious nor hardened, simply weak and undeveloped, except by the bad influences of the street, makes this duty all the more urgent as well as hopeful. Helping hands are held out on every side. To private charity the municipality leaves the entire care of its proletariat of tender years, lulling its conscience to sleep with liberal appropriations of money to foot the bills. Indeed, it is held by those whose opinions are entitled to weight that it is far too liberal a paymaster for its own best interests and those of its wards. It deals with the evil in the seed to a limited extent in gathering in the outcast babies from the streets. To the ripe fruit the gates of its prisons, its reformatories, and its workhouses are opened wide the year round. What the showing would be at this end of the line were it not for the barriers wise charity has thrown across the broad highway to ruin—is building day by day—may be measured by such results as those quoted above in the span of a single life.

1. How does Riis account for the miserable lives of the children in his report?

2. What connections does Riis make between poverty and vice? Does ethnicity or class figure more prominently?

19-5   The People's Party Platform (1892)

Feeling that neither major political party represented their interests, populists formed the People's Party in 1892 to pursue their political and economic agenda. Their party platform presented many reform ideas that were later implemented.

We have witnessed for more than a quarter of a century the struggles of the two great political parties for power and plunder, while grievous wrongs have been inflicted upon the suffering people. We charge that the controlling influences dominating both these parties have permitted the existing dreadful conditions to develop without serious effort to prevent or restrain them. Neither do they now promise us any substantial reform. They have agreed together to ignore in the coming campaign every issue but one. They propose to drown the outcries of a plundered people with the uproar of a sham battle over the tariff, so that capitalists, corporations, national banks, rings, trusts, watered stock, the demonetization of silver, and the oppressions of the usurers may all be lost sight of. They propose to sacrifice our homes, lives and children on the altar of mammon; to destroy the multitude in order to secure corruption funds from the millionaires. . . .

We declare, therefore,-

First. That the union of the labor forces of the United States this day consummated shall be permanent and perpetual; may its spirit enter all hearts for the salvation of the republic and the uplifting of mankind!

Second. Wealth belongs to him who creates it, and every dollar taken from industry without an equivalent is robbery. "If any will not work, neither shall he eat." The interests of rural and civic labor are the same; their enemies are identical.

Third. We believe that the time has come when the railroad corporations will either own the people or the people must own the railroads; and, should the government enter upon the work of owning and managing all railroads, we should favor an amendment to the Constitution by which all persons engaged in the government service shall be placed under a civil service regulation of the most rigid character, so as to prevent the increase of the power of the national administration by the use of such additional government employees.

First, *Money.* We demand a national currency, safe, sound, and flexible, issued by the general government only, a full legal tender for all debts, public and private, and that, without the use of banking corporations, a just, equitable, and efficient means of distribution direct to the people, at a tax not to exceed two per cent per annum, to be provided as set forth in the sub-treasury plan of the Farmers' Alliance, or a better system; also, by payments in discharge of its obligations for public improvements.

(a) We demand free and unlimited coinage of silver and gold at the present legal ratio of sixteen to one.

(b) We demand that the amount of circulating medium be speedily increased to not less than fifty dollars per capita.

(c) We demand a graduated income tax.

(d) We believe that the money of the country shall be kept as much as possible in the hands of the people, and hence we demand that all state and national revenues shall be limited to the necessary expenses of the government economically and honestly administered.

(e) We demand that postal savings banks be established by the government for the safe deposit of the earnings of the people and to facilitate exchange.

Second, *Transportation.* Transportation being a means of exchange and a public necessity, the government should own and operate the railroads in the interest of the people.

(a) The telegraph and telephone, like the post-office system, being a necessity for the transmission of news, should be owned and operated by the government in the interest of the people.

Third, *Land.* The land, including all the natural sources of wealth, is the heritage of the people, and should not be monopolized for speculative purposes, and alien ownership of land should be prohibited. All land now held by railroads and other corporations in excess of their actual needs, and all lands now owned by aliens, should be reclaimed by the government and held for actual settlers only.

RESOLUTIONS

Whereas, Other questions have been presented for our consideration, we hereby submit the following, not as a part of the platform of the People's party, but as resolutions expressive of the sentiment of this convention.

1. *Resolved,* That we demand a free ballot and a fair count in all elections, and pledge ourselves to secure it to every legal voter without federal intervention, through the adoption by the States of the unperverted Australian or secret ballot system.
2. *Resolved,* That the revenue derived from a graduated income tax should be applied to the reduction of the burden of taxation now resting upon the domestic industries of this country.
3. *Resolved,* That we pledge our support to fair and liberal pensions to ex-Union soldiers and sailors.
4. *Resolved,* That we condemn the fallacy of protecting American labor under the present system, which opens our ports to the pauper and criminal classes of the world, and crowds out our wage-earners; and we denounce the present ineffective laws against contract labor, and demand the further restriction of undesirable immigration.

5. *Resolved*, That we cordially sympathize with the efforts of organized workingmen to shorten the hours of labor, and demand a rigid enforcement of the existing eight-hour law on government work, and ask that a penalty clause be added to the said law.

6. *Resolved*, That we regard the maintenance of a large standing army of mercenaries, known as the Pinkerton system, as a menace to our liberties, and we demand its abolition; and we condemn the recent invasion of the Territory of Wyoming by the hired assassins of plutocracy, assisted by federal officials.

7. *Resolved*, That we commend to the favorable consideration of the people and the reform press the legislative system known as the initiative and referendum.

8. *Resolved*, That we favor a constitutional provision limiting the office of President and Vice-President to one term, and providing for the election of senators of the United States by a direct vote of the people.

9. *Resolved*, That we oppose any subsidy or national aid to any private corporation for any purpose.

10. *Resolved*, That this convention sympathizes with the Knights of Labor and their righteous contest with the tyrannical combine of clothing manufacturers of Rochester, and declares it to be the duty of all who hate tyranny and oppression to refuse to purchase the goods made by said manufacturers, or to patronize any merchants who sell such goods.

1. What political situation has lead the proponents of this party to proclaim this platform?
2. Summarize the key economic, social, and political planks of this platform.

19-6 The Secret Oath of the American Protective Association (1893)

European immigration in the late nineteenth century included many Eastern and southern European Roman Catholics. Opposition arose among American-born Protestants, stimulating the rise of nativist organizations that protested against Catholic influence.

I do most solemnly promise and swear that I will always, to the utmost of my ability, labor, plead, and wage a continuous warfare against ignorance and fanaticism; that I will use my utmost power to strike the shackles and chains of blind obedience to the Roman Catholic Church from the hampered and bound consciences of a priest-ridden and church-oppressed people; that I will never allow anyone, a member of the Roman Catholic Church, to become a member of this order, I knowing him to be such; that I will use my influence to promote the interest of all Protestants everywhere in the world that I may be; that I will not employ a Roman Catholic in any capacity, if I can procure the services of a Protestant.

I furthermore promise and swear that I will not aid in building or maintaining, by my resources, any Roman Catholic church or institution of their sect or creed whatsoever, but will do all in my power to retard and break down the power of the Pope, in this country or any other; that I will not enter into any controversy with a Roman Catholic upon the subject of this order, nor will I enter into any agreement with a Roman Catholic to strike or create a disturbance whereby the Catholic employees may undermine and substitute their Protestant co-workers; that in all grievances I will seek only Protestants, and counsel with them to the exclusion of all Roman Catholics, and will not make known to them anything of any nature matured at such conferences.

I furthermore promise and swear that I will not countenance the nomination, in any caucus or convention, of a Roman Catholic for any office in the gift of the American people, and that I will not vote for, or counsel others to vote for, any Roman Catholic, but will vote only for a Protestant, so far as may lie in my power (should there be two Roman Catholics in opposite tickets, I will erase the name on the ticket I vote); that I will at all times endeavor to place the political positions of this government in the hands of Protestants, to the entire exclusion of the Roman Catholic Church, of the members thereof, and the mandate of the Pope.

To all of which I do most solemnly promise and swear, so help me God.
Amen.

1. What is the stance of this document in relation to the Catholic Church? What seem to be the driving force and prevailing fears behind its stance?

19-7 Adna Weber, The Growth of Cities in the Nineteenth Century (1899)

Industrialization stimulated rapid urban growth. As this document indicates, the proliferation of cities was considered an essential part of the industrial process fulfilling important market functions.

In a new country the rapid growth of cities is both natural and necessary, for no efficient industrial organization of a new settlement is possible without industrial centres to carry on the necessary work of assembling and distributing goods. A Mississippi Valley empire rising suddenly into being without its Chicago and its smaller centres of distribution is almost inconceivable to the nineteenth century economist. That America is the "land of mushroom cities" is therefore not at all surprising.

But, on the other hand, it is astonishing that the development of the cities in a new country should outstrip that of the rural districts which they serve. The natural presumption would be that so long as land remains open to settlement, the superfluous population of the older States or of Europe would seek the fundamental, or food-producing, industry of agriculture, and build up cities only in a corresponding degree. Yet in the great cereal regions of the West, the cities have grown entirely out of proportion to the rural parts, resulting there, as in the East and in Europe, in an increasing concentration of the population. . . .

It is now clear that the growth of cities must be studied as a part of the question of distribution of population, which is always dependent upon the economic organization of society-upon the constant striving to maintain as many people as possible upon a given area. The ever-present problem is so to distribute and organize the masses of men that they can render such services as favor the maintenance of the nation and thereby accomplish their own preservation. Population follows the line of least resistance in its distribution, and will consequently be affected by changes in the methods of production. When the industrial organization demands the presence of laborers in particular localities in order to increase its efficiency, laborers will be found there; the means of attraction will have been "better living"-in other words, an appeal to the motive of self-interest. Economic forces are therefore the principal cause of concentration of population in cities. . . .

Now, without stretching the analogy, we may liken industrial society of to-day-embracing all countries within the circle of exchange of products-to a great organism composed of heterogeneous parts. This organism, however, is the product of ages of slow growth. Originally, in place of the one all-embracing social organism, there were myriads of small social units, each complete in itself and independent of the others, if not positively hostile to them. The history of civilization is simply the narrative description of the breaking down of the barriers that separated the primitive social units-the original family group, clan, patriarchal family, the enlarged village community or the manorial group. And the most conspicuous and influential role in the process was played by the trader, working upon men's desires for what they did not possess or produce. Neither war (conquest) nor religion has been of so vital and far-reaching influence in the integration and amalgamation of isolated social groups as trade and commerce.

When, therefore, it is pointed out that towns owe their origin to trade, that the commercial metropolis of to-day is the successor of the primitive market-place established beside the boundary stone between hostile but avaricious tribal groups, that the extension of the market means the enlargement of the market-centre-then one will readily perceive the connection of the growth of industrial society to its present world-wide dimensions with our problem of the concentration of population. . . .

If men were like other animals and had no further wants than bodily appetites and passions, there would be no large aggregations of people; for in order to produce food, men must live either in scattered habitations like American farmers, or in hamlets like the ancient family or tribal group, the village community, the Russian *mir*, and the modern agricultural village of Continental Europe. Even with a comparatively high grade of wants, men may live in these small groups, each of which is economically autonomous and self-sufficing, producing for itself and buying and selling little if anything. It is the period of the *Naturalwirthschaft*, in which all payments are in kind. The principle of division of labor finally led to the disruption of the village community, but its triumph was long delayed. The principle was of course grasped only imperfectly by primitive man. At first the only division was that based on sex, age, muscular power, or relation to the governing head of the group; in other respects there was no assignment of special tasks to particular individuals. Very gradually men discovered among themselves differences of natural aptitude. The members of a community at length realized that it was more economical to have their flour made in a village mill by one member who should give all his time to that particular work, than to have it made by bits in a score of individual mills. One by one other industries have followed the mill-have departed from the separate households and taken up their abode in a central establishment. Clothing ceased to be made at home; there arose a village weaver and a village shoemaker. To this process of development there is almost no conceivable end. Only a few years ago the American farmer not only raised his own food, but furnished his own fuel and sometimes made his own clothing. Now, however, he is a specialist, and thinks nothing of going to the market even for table supplies. Formerly, the farmer made his own tools; now he buys implements made in factories. But yesterday, and the men who reaped the fields of ripe grain were bound to the soil and compelled to dwell in isolated homes or small communities; to-day these men live in cities and make machinery to reap the grin.

Thus, it appears that agriculture, the industry that disperses men, has ever narrowed its scope. Formerly, when men's wants were few and simple, agriculture was the all-embracing occupation. The agriculturist produced the necessary sustenance, and in his idle moments made whatever else he needed. But human wants have greatly multiplied and can no longer be satiated with food-products alone. Moreover, the business of providing for the new wants has been separated from agriculture. The total result is that the proportion of people who must devote themselves to the satisfaction of the elementary wants of society has vastly diminished and is still diminishing.

And this result is attained not only by the diminishing importance of bread and butter in the realm of human wants, but also by the increased per capita product which a specialized body of workers can win from the soil. By the use of fertilizers, by highly scientific methods of cultivation, by labor-saving machinery, and by the construction of transportation systems to open up distant and virgin fields, the present century has immensely reduced the relative number of workers who must remain attached to the soil to provide society's food-supply.

These facts are of fundamental importance in seeking the causes of urban growth. For cities are made up of persons who do not cultivate the soil; their existence presupposes a surplus food-supply, which in turn premises either great fertility of the soil or an advanced stage of the agricultural arts, and in either case convenient means of transportation.

1. *What trend in the growth of cities is noted in this document, and what consideration does this trend require?*
2. *Summarize some of the key causes of urban growth identified in this document.The Currents of Progressivism.*

19-8   Lee Chew, *Life of a Chinese Immigrant* (1903)

The following selection is from a biography of a Chinese immigrant commissioned by the reformist journal The Independent. Note that Chew arrived in the United States before the Chinese Exclusion Act of 1882, and was therefore dictating this as a middle-aged man. Chew was involved in many of the jobs associated with Chinese immigrants during this period-mining, laundry, and railroad construction.

From *The Independent*, 54 (2818), February 19, 1903, 417-423.

The village where I was born is situated in the province of Canton, on one of the banks of the Si-Kiang River. It is called a village, altho it is really as big as a city, for there are about 5,000 men in it over eighteen years of age-women and children and even youths are not counted in our villages....

...I heard about the American foreign devils, that they were false, having made a treaty by which it was agreed that they could freely come to China, and the Chinese as freely go to their country. After this treaty was made China opened its doors to them and then they broke the treaty that they had asked for by shutting the Chinese out of their country....

The man had gone away from our village a poor boy. Now he returned with unlimited wealth, which he had obtained in the country of the American wizards. After many amazing adventures he had become a merchant in a city called Mott Street, so it was said....

Having made his wealth among the barbarians this man had faithfully returned to pour it out among his tribesmen, and he is living in our village now very happy, and a pillar of strength to the poor.

The wealth of this man filled my mind with the idea that I, too, would like to go to the country of the wizards and gain some of their wealth, and after a long time my father consented, and gave me his blessing, and my mother took leave of me with tears, while my grandfather laid his hand upon my head and told me to remember and live up to the admonitions of the Sages, to avoid gambling, bad women and men of evil minds, and so to govern my conduct that when I died my ancestors might rejoice to welcome me as a guest on high.

My father gave me $100, and I went to Hong Kong with five other boys from our place and we got steerage passage on a steamer, paying $50 each....

...Of the great power of these people I saw many signs. The engines that moved the ship were wonderful monsters, strong enough to lift mountains. When I got to San Francisco, which was before the passage of the Exclusion act, I was half starved, because I was afraid to eat the provisions of the barbarians, but a few days' living in the Chinese quarter made me happy again....

The Chinese laundryman does not learn his trade in China; there are no laundries in China.... All the Chinese laundrymen here were taught in the first place by American women just as I was taught.

When I went to work for that American family I could not speak a word of English, and I did not know anything about house work. The family consisted of husband, wife and two children. They were very good to me and paid me $3.50 a week, of which I could save $3....

In six months I had learned how to do the work of our house quite well, and I was getting $5 a week and board, and putting away about $4.25 a week. I had also learned some English, and by going to a Sunday school I learned more English and something about Jesus, who was a great Sage, and whose precepts are like those of Kong-foo-tsze.

It was twenty years ago when I came to this country, and I worked for two years as a servant, getting at least $35 a month. I sent money home to comfort my parents....

When I first opened a laundry it was in company with a partner, who had been in the business for some years. We went to a town about 500 miles inland, where a railroad was building. We got a board shanty and worked for the men employed by the railroads....

We were three years with the railroad, and then went to the mines, where we made plenty of money in gold dust, but had a hard time, for many of the miners were wild men who carried revolvers and after drinking would come into our place to shoot and steal shirts, for which we had to pay. One of these men hit his head hard against a flat iron and all the miners came and broke our laundry, chasing us out of town. They were going to hang us. We lost all our property and $365 in money, which a member of the mob must have found.

Luckily most of our money was in the hands of Chinese bankers in San Francisco. I drew $500 and went East to Chicago, where I had a laundry for three years, during which I increased my capital to $2,500. After that I was four years in Detroit. I went home to China in 1897, but returned in 1898, and began a laundry business in Buffalo.

The ordinary laundry shop is generally divided into three rooms. In front is the room where the customers are received, behind that a bedroom and in the back the work shop, which is also the dining room and kitchen. The stove and cooking utensils are the same as those of the Americans....

I have found out, during my residence in this country, that much of the Chinese prejudice against Americans is unfounded, and I no longer put faith in the wild tales that were told about them in our village, tho some of the Chinese, who have been here twenty years and who are learned men, still believe that there is no marriage in this country, that the land is infested with demons and that all the people are given over to general wickedness.

I know better. Americans are not all bad, nor are they wicked wizards. Still, they have their faults, and their treatment of us is outrageous....

The reason why so many Chinese go into the laundry business in this country is because it requires little capital and is one of the few opportunities that are open....

There is no reason for the prejudice against the Chinese. The cheap labor cry was always a falsehood. Their labor was never cheap, and is not cheap now. It has always commanded the highest market price. But the trouble is that the Chinese are such excellent and faithful workers that bosses will have no others when they can get them. If you look at men working on the street you will find an overseer for every four or five of them. That watching is not necessary for Chinese. They work as well when left to themselves as they do when some one is looking at them....

1. *What stories of America had the author been exposed to? What were the author's expectations upon coming to America? How did these expectations and preconceptions compare with the author's actual experience?*
2. *Describe the measure of success and difficulty experienced by the author. To what does the author attribute his success? his difficulty?*

19-9   Lincoln Steffens, from *The Shame of the Cities* (1904)

In the early twentieth century, muckraking journalists exposed many of the evils of American society, stimulating reforms. City political machines attracted many muckraking attacks, including this one by Lincoln Steffens.

The Philadelphia machine isn't the best. It isn't sound, and I doubt if it would stand in New York or Chicago. The enduring strength of the typical American political machine is that it is a natural growth-a sucker, but deep-rooted in the people. The New Yorkers vote for Tammany Hall. The Philadelphians do not vote; they are disfranchised, and their disfranchisement is one anchor of the foundation of the Philadelphia organization.

This is no figure of speech. The honest citizens of Philadelphia have no more rights at the polls than the negroes down South. Nor do they fight very hard for this basic privilege. You can arouse their Republican ire by talking about the black Republican votes lost in the Southern States by white Democratic intimidation, but if you remind the average Philadelphian that he is in the same position, he will look startled, then say, "That's so, that's literally true, only I never thought of it in just that way." And it is literally true.

The machine controls the whole process of voting, and practices fraud at every stage. The assessor's list is the voting list, and the assessor is the machine's man. . . . The assessor pads the list with the names of dead dogs, children, and non-existent persons. One newspaper printed the picture of a dog, another that of a little four-year-old negro boy, down on such a list. A ring orator in a speech resenting sneers at his ward as "low down" reminded his hearers that that was the ward of Independence Hall, and naming over signers of the Declaration of Independence, he closed his highest flight of eloquence with the statement that "these men, the fathers of American liberty, voted down here once. And," he added, with a catching grin, "they vote here yet." Rudolph Blankenburg, a persistent fighter for the right and the use of the right to vote (and, by the way, an immigrant), sent out just before one election a registered letter to each voter on the rolls of a certain selected division. Sixty-three per cent were returned marked "not at," "removed," "deceased," etc. From one four-story house where forty-four voters were addressed, eighteen letters came back undelivered; from another of forty-eight voters, came back forty-one letters; from another sixty-one out of sixty-two; from another, forty-four out of forty-seven. Six houses in one division were assessed at one hundred and seventy-two voters, more than the votes cast in the previous election in any one of two hundred entire divisions.

The repeating is done boldly, for the machine controls the election officers, often choosing them from among the fraudulent names; and when no one appears to serve, assigning the heeler ready for the expected vacancy. The police are forbidden by law to stand within thirty feet of the polls, but they are at the box and they are there to see that the machine's orders are obeyed and that repeaters whom they help to furnish are permitted to vote without "intimidation" on the names they, the police, have supplied. . . .

1. Summarize the power and effect of the political machine as it is described in this document.

19-10   William T. Riordon, from *Plunkitt of Tammany Hall* (1905)

The growth of cities and increasing immigration led to the rise of political machines that used graft and corruption to gain and keep power. One of the most famous machines was New York City's Tammany Hall. Plunkitt of Tammany Hall was a muckraking work of the Progressive era that exposed the corruption of political machines.

"Everybody is talkin' these days about Tammany men growin' rich on graft, but nobody thinks of drawin' the distinction between honest graft and dishonest graft. There's all the difference in the world between the two. Yes, many of our men have grown rich in politics. I have myself. I've made a big fortune out of the game, and I'm gettin' richer every day, but I've not gone in for dishonest graft-blackmailin' gamblers, saloon-keepers, disorderly people, etc.-and neither has any of the men who have made big fortunes in politics.

"There's an honest graft, and I'm an example of how it works. I might sum up the whole thing by sayin': 'I seen my opportunities and I took 'em.'

"Just let me explain my examples. My party's in power in the city, and it's goin' to undertake a lot of public improvements. Well, I'm tipped off, say, that they're going to lay out a new park at a certain place.

"I see my opportunity and I take it. I go to that place and I buy up all the land I can in the neighborhood. Then the board of this or that makes its plan public, and there is a rush to get my land, which nobody cared particular for before.

"Ain't it perfectly honest to charge a good price and make a profit on my investment and foresight? Of course it is. Well, that's honest graft. . . .

". . . It's just like lookin' ahead in Wall Street or in the coffee or cotton market.

". . . Now, let me tell you that most politicians who are accused of robbin the city get rich the same way.

"They didn't steal a dollar from the city treasury. They just seen their opportunities and took them. That is why, when a reform administration comes in and spends a half million dollars in tryin' to find the public robberies they talk about in the campaign, they don't find them.

"The books are always all right. The money in the city treasury is all right. Everything is all right All they can show is that the Tammany heads of departments looked after their friends, within the law, and gave them what opportunities they could to make honest graft. . . .

"I've been readin' a book by Lincoln Steffens on *The Shame of the Cities*. Steffens means well but, like all reformers, he don't know how to make distinctions. He can't see no difference between honest graft and dishonest graft and, consequent, he gets things all mixed up. There's the biggest kind of a difference between political looters and politicians who make a fortune out of politics by keepin' their eyes wide open. The looter goes in for himself alone without considerin' his organization or his city. The politician looks after his own interests, the organization's interests, and the city's interests all at the same time. . . ."

1. What, according to the speaker in this document, is the difference between honest graft and dishonest graft?

19-11   John Spargo, From *The Bitter Cry of Children* (1906)

This selection describes the plight of children working in coal mines. Children were often put to work by their parents as a way of keeping the family out of poverty, and for employers, child labor was inexpensive and children were often thought to be more adept at detailed work. They thus were widely used in the textile and mining industries. Child labor outraged middle-class native-born reformers who sentimentalized childhood.

From John Spargo, *The Bitter Cry of Children* (New York: Macmillan, 1906), 163-165.

Work in the coal breakers is exceedingly hard and dangerous. Crouched over the chutes, the boys sit hour after hour, picking out the pieces of slate and other refuse from the coal as it rushes past to the washers. From the cramped position they have to assume, most of them become more or less deformed and bent-backed like old men. When a boy has been working for some time and begins to get round-shouldered, his fellows say that "He's got his boy to carry around whenever he goes."

The coal is hard, and accidents to the hands, such as cut, broken, or crushed fingers, are common among the boys. Sometimes there is a worse accident: a terrified shriek is heard, and a boy is mangled and torn in the machinery, or disappears in the chute to be picked out later smothered and dead. Clouds of dust fill the breakers and are inhaled by the boys, laying the foundations for asthma and miners' consumption.

I once stood in a breaker for half an hour and tried to do the work a twelve-year-old boy was doing day after day, for ten hours at a stretch, for sixty cents a day. The gloom of the breaker appalled me. Outside the sun shone brightly, the air was pellucid, and the birds sang in chorus with the trees and the rivers. Within the breaker there was blackness, clouds of deadly dust enfolded everything, the harsh, grinding roar of the machinery and the ceaseless rushing of coal through the chutes filled the ears. I tried to pick out the pieces of slate from the hurrying stream of coal, often missing them; my hands were bruised and cut in a few minutes; I was covered from head to foot

with coal dust, and for many hours afterwards I was expectorating some of the small particles of anthracite I had swallowed.

I could not do that work and live, but there were boys of ten and twelve years of age doing it for fifty and sixty cents a day. Some of them had never been inside of a school; few of them could read a child's primer. True, some of them attended the night schools, but after working ten hours in the breaker the educational results from attending school were practically nil. "We goes fer a good time, an' we keeps de guys wot's dere hoppin' all de time," said little Owen Jones, whose work I had been trying to do....

As I stood in that breaker I thought of the reply of the small boy to Robert Owen [British social reformer]. Visiting an English coal mine one day, Owen asked a twelve-year-old if he knew God. The boy stared vacantly at his questioner: "God?" he said, "God? No, I don't. He must work in some other mine." It was hard to realize amid the danger and din and blackness of that Pennsylvania breaker that such a thing as belief in a great All-good God existed.

From the breakers the boys graduate to the mine depths, where they become door tenders, switch boys, or mule drivers. Here, far below the surface, work is still more dangerous. At fourteen and fifteen the boys assume the same risks as the men, and are surrounded by the same perils. Nor is it in Pennsylvania only that these conditions exist. In the bituminous mines of West Virginia, boys of nine or ten are frequently employed. I met one little fellow ten years old in Mt. Carbon, W. Va., last year, who was employed as a "trap boy." Think of what it means to be a trap boy at ten years of age. It means to sit alone in a dark mine passage hour after hour, with no human soul near; to see no living creature except the mules as they pass with their loads, or a rat or two seeking to share one's meal; to stand in water or mud that covers the ankles, chilled to the marrow by the cold draughts that rush in when you open the trap door for the mules to pass through; to work for fourteen hours-waiting-opening and shutting a door-then waiting again-for sixty cents; to reach the surface when all is wrapped in the mantle of night, and to fall to the earth exhausted and have to be carried away to the nearest "shack" to be revived before it is possible to walk to the farther shack called "home." Boys twelve years of age may be legally employed in the mines of West Virginia, by day or by night, and for as many hours as the employers care to make them toil or their bodies will stand the strain. Where the disregard of child life is such that this may be done openly and with legal sanction, it is easy to believe what miners have again and again told me-that there are hundreds of little boys of nine and ten years of age employed in the coal mines of this state.

1. Who were the breaker boys and under what conditions did they work?
2. What were the likely futures of the breaker boys?

19-12 Mary Antin, The Promised Land (1912)

For many European immigrants, the United States represented opportunity. For Mary Antin and her family opportunity meant assimilating into American culture. It also meant the ability to go to school and to found your own business. Though as Antin observed, this opportunity involved overcoming poverty.

In our flat we did not think of such a thing as storing the coal in the bathtub. There was no bathtub. So in the evening of the first day my father conducted us to the public baths. As we moved along in a little procession, I was delighted with the illumination of the streets. So many lamps, and they burned until morning, my father said, and so people did not need to carry lanterns. In America, then, everything was free, as we had heard in Russia. Light was free; the streets were as bright as a synagogue on a holy day. Music was free; we had been serenaded, to our gaping delight, by a brass band of many pieces, soon after our installation on Union Place.

Education was free. That subject my father had written about repeatedly, as comprising his chief hope for us children, the essence of American opportunity, the treasure that no thief could touch, not even misfortune or poverty. It was the one thing that he was able to promise us when he sent for us; surer, safer than bread or shelter. On our second day I was thrilled with the realization of what this freedom of education meant. A little girl from across the alley came and offered to conduct us to school. My father was out, but we five between us had a few words of English by this time. We knew the word school. We understood. This child, who had never seen us till yesterday, who could not pronounce our names, who was not much better dressed than we, was able to offer us the freedom of the schools of Boston! No application made, no questions asked, no examinations, rulings, exclusions; no machinations, no fees. The doors stood open for every one of us. The smallest child could show us the way.

This incident impressed me more than anything I had heard in advance of the freedom of education in America. It was a concrete proof-almost the thing itself. One had to experience it to understand it. . . .

The kind of people who assisted us in these important matters form a group by themselves in the gallery of my friends. If I had never seen them from those early days till now, I should still have remembered them with gratitude. When I enumerate the long list of my American teachers, I must begin with those who came to us on Wall Street and taught us our first steps. To my mother, in her perplexity over the cookstove, the woman who showed her how to make the fire was an angel of deliverance. A fairy godmother to us children was she who led us to a wonderful country called "uptown," where, in a dazzlingly beautiful palace called a "department store," we exchanged our hateful homemade European costumes, which pointed us out as "greenhorns" to the children on the street, for real American machine-made garments, and issued forth glorified in each other's eyes.

With our despised immigrant clothing we shed also our impossible Hebrew names. A committee of our friends, several years ahead of us in American experience, put their heads together and concocted American names for us all. Those of our real names that had no pleasing American equivalents they ruthlessly discarded, content if they retained the initials. My mother, possessing a name that was not easily translatable, was punished with the undignified nickname of Annie. Fetchke, Joseph, and Deborah issued as Frieda, Joseph, and Dora, respectively. As for poor me, I was simply cheated. The name they gave me was hardly new. My Hebrew name being Maryashe in full, Mashke for short, Russianized into Marya *(Mar-ya)*, my friends said that it would hold good in English as *Mary*; which was very disappointing, as I longed to possess a strange-sounding American name like the others. . . .

In Chelsea, as in Boston, we made our stand in the wrong end of the town. Arlington Street was inhabited by poor Jews, poor Negroes, and a sprinkling of poor Irish. The side streets leading from it were occupied by more poor Jews and Negroes. It was a proper locality for a man without capital to do business. My father rented a tenement with a store in the basement. He put in a few barrels of flour and of sugar, a few boxes of crackers, a few gallons of kerosene, an assortment of soap of the "save the coupon" brands; in the cellar, a few barrels of potatoes, and a pyramid of kindling-wood; in the showcase, an alluring display of penny candy. He put out his sign, with a gilt-lettered warning of "Strictly Cash," and proceeded to give credit indiscriminately. That was the regular way to do business on Arlington Street. My father, in this three years' apprenticeship, had learned the trick of many trades. He knew when and how to "bluff." The legend of "Strictly Cash" was a protection against notoriously irresponsible customers; while none of the "good" customers, who had a record for paying regularly on Saturday, hesitated to enter the store with empty purses.

If my father knew the tricks of the trade, my mother could be counted on to throw all her talent and tact into the business. Of course she had no English yet, but as she could perform the acts of weighing, measuring, and mental computation of fractions mechanically, she was able to give her whole attention to the dark mysteries of the language, as intercourse with her customers gave her opportunity. In this she made such rapid progress that she soon lost all sense of disadvantage, and conducted herself behind the counter very much as if she were back in her old store in Polotzk. It was far more cosey than Polotzk-at least, so it seemed to me; for behind the store was the kitchen, where, in the intervals of slack trade, she did her cooking and washing. Arlington Street customers were used to waiting while the storekeeper salted the soup or rescued a loaf from the oven.

Once more Fortune favored my family with a thin little smile, and my father, in reply to a friendly inquiry, would say, "One makes a living," with a shrug of the shoulders that added "but nothing to boast of." It was characteristic of my attitude toward bread-and-butter matters that this contented me, and I felt free to devote myself to the conquest of my new world. Looking back to those critical first years, I see myself always behaving like a child let loose in a garden to play and dig and chase the butterflies. Occasionally, indeed, I was stung by the wasp of family trouble; but I knew a healing ointment-my faith in America. My father had come to America to make a living. America, which was free and fair and kind, must presently yield him what he sought. I had come to America to see a new world, and I followed my own ends with the utmost assiduity; only, as I ran out to explore, I would look back to see if my house were in order behind me-if my family still kept its head above water.

In after years, when I passed as an American among Americans, if I was suddenly made aware of the past that lay forgotten,-if a letter from Russia, or a paragraph in the newspaper, or a conversation overheard in the street-car, suddenly reminded me of what I might have been,-I thought it miracle enough that I, Mashke, the granddaughter of Raphael the Russian, born to a humble destiny, should be at home in an American metropolis, be free to fashion my own life, and should dream my dreams in English phrases. But in the beginning my admiration was spent on more concrete embodiments of the splendors of America; such as fine houses, gay shops, electric engines and apparatus, public buildings, illuminations, and parades. My early letters to my Russian friends were filled with boastful descriptions of these glories of my new country. No native citizen of Chelsea took such pride and delight in its institutions as I did. It required no fife and drum corps, no Fourth of July procession, to set me tingling with patriotism. Even the common agents and instruments of municipal life, such as the letter carrier and the fire engine, I regarded with a measure of respect. I know what I thought of people who said that Chelsea was a very small, dull, unaspiring town, with no discernible excuse for a separate name or existence.

1. *Identify the luxuries and new opportunities that are available to the narrator of this document upon immigrating to New York.*
2. *In what ways does America represent a land of opportunity for the narrator and her family?*
3. *Identify signs of hardship of immigration and beginning a new life in New York that are included in this text.*

PART TWENTY
AMERICA AROUND THE GLOBE

20-1 Josiah Strong, from *Our Country* (1885)

Josiah Strong, an Ohio Congregationalist minister, became a prominent figure during America's Gilded Age when he published Our Country, *a critique on modern development. Often critical of large cities, which he felt posed a threat to morals and social order, Strong also condemned urban culture in general as contrary to Christian teachings.*

Every race which has deeply impressed itself on the human family has been the representative of some great idea-one or more-which had given direction to the nation's life and form to its civilization. Among the Egyptians this seminal idea was life, among the Persians it was light, among the Hebrews it was purity, among the Greeks it was beauty, among the Romans it was law. The Anglo-Saxon is the representative of two great ideas, which are closely related. One of them is that of civil liberty. Nearly all of the civil liberty in the world is enjoyed by Anglo-Saxons: the English, the British colonists, and the people of the United States. . . . The noblest races have always been lovers of liberty. That love ran strong in early German blood, and has profoundly influenced the institutions of all the branches of the great German family; but it was left for the Anglo-Saxon branch fully to recognize the right of the individual to himself, and formally to declare it the foundation stone of government.

The other great idea of which the Anglo-Saxon is the exponent is that of a pure spiritual Christianity. It was no accident that the great reformation of the sixteenth century originated among a Teutonic, rather than a Latin people. It was the fire of liberty burning in the Saxon heart that flamed up against the absolutism of the Pope. . . .

It is not necessary to argue to those for whom I write that the two great needs of mankind, that all men may be lifted up into the light of the highest Christian civilization, are, first, a pure, spiritual Christianity, and, second, civil liberty. Without controversy, these are the forces which, in the past, have contributed most to the elevation of the human race, and they must continue to be, in the future, the most efficient ministers to its progress. It follows, then, that the Anglo-Saxon, as the great representative of these two ideas, the depositary [*sic*] of these two greatest blessings, sustains peculiar relations to the world's future, is divinely commissioned to be, in a peculiar sense, his brother's keeper. . . .

There can be no reasonable doubt that North America is to be the great home of the Anglo-Saxon, the principal seat of his power, the center of his life and influence. Not only does it constitute seven-elevenths of his possessions, but this empire is unsevered, while the remaining four-elevenths are fragmentary and scattered over the earth. Australia will have a great population; but its disadvantages, as compared with North America, are too manifest to need mention. Our continent has room and resources and climate, it lies in the pathway of the nations, it belongs to the zone of power, and already, among Anglo-Saxons, do we lead in population and wealth.

Mr. Darwin is not only disposed to see, in the superior vigor of our people, an illustration of his favorite theory of natural selection, but even intimates that the world's history thus far has been simply preparatory for our future, and tributary to it. He says: "There is apparently much truth in the belief that the wonderful progress of the United States, as well as the character of the people, are the results of natural selection; for the more energetic, restless, and courageous men from all parts of Europe have emigrated during the last ten or twelve generations to that great country, and have there succeeded best. . . ."

. . . The time is coming when the pressure of population on the means of subsistence will be felt there as it is now felt in Europe and Asia. Then will the world enter upon a new stage of its history-the final competition of races, for which the Anglo-Saxon is being schooled. Long before the thousands millions are here, the mighty centrifugal tendency, inherent in this stock and strengthened in the United States, will assert itself. Then this race of unequaled energy, with all the majesty of numbers and the might of wealth behind it-the representative, let us hope, of the largest liberty, the purest Christianity, the highest civilization-having developed peculiarly aggressive traits calculated to impress its institutions upon mankind, will spread itself over the earth. If I read not amiss, this powerful race will move down upon Mexico, down upon Central and South America, out upon the islands of the sea, over upon Africa and beyond. And can anyone doubt that the result of this competition of races will be the "survival of the fittest"? . . .

In my own mind, there is no doubt that the Anglo-Saxon is to exercise the commanding influence in the world's future; but the exact nature of that influence is, as yet, undetermined. How far his civilization will be materialistic and atheistic, and how long it will take thoroughly to Christianize and sweeten it, how rapidly he will hasten the coming of the kingdom wherein dwelleth righteousness, or how many ages he may retard it, is still uncertain; but it is now being swiftly determined. . . .

Notwithstanding the great perils which threaten it, I cannot think our civilization will perish; but I believe it is fully in the hand of the Christians of the United States, during the next fifteen or twenty years, to hasten or retard the coming of Christ's kingdom in the world by hundreds, and perhaps thousands, of years. We of this generation and nation occupy the Gibraltar of the ages which command the world's future.

1. *According to Strong, which two great ideas have found their greatest representation in the Anglo-Saxons? Explain his support for this belief. What is the link between these two ideas?*
2. *What responsibility does Strong believe Anglo-Saxons must assume considering the riches they have to offer to the world?*
3. *How does Strong integrate Darwinian theory into his belief? What do these theories together mean in regard to the influence of the Anglo-Saxons upon the rest of the world?*

20-2 Henry Cabot Lodge, "The Business World vs. the Politicians" (1895)

Opponents of American expansion overseas in the late nineteenth century partially based their arguments on traditional American foreign policy that stressed neutrality and noninterference of Europe in the Americas. Supporters of imperial expansion, such as Massachusetts Senator Henry Cabot Lodge dismissed such arguments claiming Washington's counsel on neutrality and the Monroe Doctrine has nothing to do with United States expansion.

If the Democratic party has had one cardinal principle beyond all others, it has been that of pushing forward the boundaries of the United States. Under this Administration, governed as it is by free-trade influences, this great principle of the Democratic party during nearly a century of existence has been utterly abandoned. Thomas Jefferson, admitting that he violated the Constitution while he did it, effected the Louisiana purchase, but Mr. Cleveland has labored to overthrow American interests and American control in Hawaii. Andrew Jackson fought for Florida, but Mr. Cleveland is eager to abandon Samoa. . . . It is the melancholy outcome of the doctrine that there is no higher aim or purpose for men or for nations than to buy and sell, to trade jack-knives and make everything cheap. No one underrates the importance of the tariffs or the still greater importance of a sound currency. But of late years we have been so absorbed in these economic questions that we have grown unmindful of others. We have had something too much of these disciples of the Manchester school, who think the price of calico more important than a nation's honor, the duties on pig iron of more moment than the advance of a race.

It is time to recall what we have been tending to forget: that we have always had and that we have now a foreign policy which is of great importance to our national well-being. The foundation of that policy was Washington's doctrine of neutrality. To him and to Hamilton we owe the principle that it was not the business of the United States to meddle in the affairs of Europe. When this policy was declared, it fell with a shock upon the Americans of that day, for we were still colonists in habits of thought and could not realize that the struggles of Europe did not concern us. Yet the establishment of the neutrality policy was one of the greatest services which Washington and Hamilton rendered to the cause of American nationality. The corollary of Washington's policy was the Monroe doctrine, the work of John Quincy Adams, a much greater man than the President whose name it bears. Washington declared that it was not the business of the United States to meddle in the affairs of Europe, and John Quincy Adams added that Europe must not meddle in the Western hemisphere. As I have seen it solemnly stated recently that the annexation of Hawaii would be a violation of the Monroe doctrine, it is perhaps not out of place to say that the Monroe doctrine has no bearing on the extension of the United States, but simply holds that no European power shall establish itself in the Americas or interfere with American governments.

The neutrality policy and the Monroe doctrine are the two great principles established at the outset by far-seeing statesmen in regard to the foreign relations of the United States. But it would be a fatal mistake to suppose that our foreign policy stopped there, or that these fundamental propositions in any way fettered the march of the American people. Washington withdrew us from the affairs of Europe, but at the same time he pointed out that our true line of advance was to the West. He never for an instant thought that we were to remain stationary and cease to move forward. He saw, with prophetic vision, as did no other man of his time, the true course for the American people. He could not himself enter into the promised land, but he showed it to his people, stretching from the Blue Ridge to the Pacific Ocean. We have followed the teachings of Washington. We have taken the great valley of the Mississippi and pressed on beyond the Sierras. We have a record of conquest, colonization, and territorial expansion unequalled by any people in the nineteenth century. We are not to be curbed now by the doctrines of the Manchester school which have never been observed in England, and which as an importation are even more absurdly out of place here than in their native land. It is not the policy of the United States to enter, as England has done, upon the general acquisition of distant possession in all parts of the world. Our government is not adapted to such a policy, and we have no need of it, for we have an ample field at home; but at the same time it must be remembered that while in the United States themselves we hold the citadel of our power and greatness as a nation, there are outworks essential to the defence of that citadel which must neither be neglected nor abandoned.

There is a very definite policy for American statesmen to pursue in this respect if they would prove themselves worthy inheritors of the principles of Washington and Adams. We desire no extension to the south, for neither the population nor the lands of Central or South America would be desirable additions to the United States. But from the Rio Grande to the Arctic Ocean there should be but one flag and one country. Neither race nor climate forbids this extension, and every consideration of national growth and national welfare demands it. In the interests of our commerce and of our fullest development we should build the Nicaragua canal, and for the protection of that canal and for the sake of our commercial supremacy in the Pacific we should control the Hawaiian Islands and maintain our influence in Samoa. England has studded the West Indies with strong places which are a standing menace to our Atlantic seaboard. We should have among those islands at least one strong naval station, and when the Nicaragua canal is built, the island of Cuba, still sparsely settled and of almost unbounded fertility, will become to us a necessity. Commerce follows the flag, and we should build up a navy strong enough to give protection to Americans in every quarter of the globe and sufficiently powerful to put our coasts beyond the possibility of successful attack.

The tendency of modern times is toward consolidation. It is apparent in capital and labor alike, and it is also true of nations. Small States are of the past and have no future. The modern movement is all toward the concentration of people and territory into great nations and large dominions. The great nations are rapidly absorbing for their future expansion and their present defence all the waste places of the earth. It is a movement which makes for civilization and the advancement of the race. As one of the great nations of the world, the United States must not fall out of the line of march.

For more than thirty years we have been so much absorbed with grave domestic questions that we have lost sight of these vast interests which lie just outside our borders. They ought to be neglected no longer. They are not only of material importance, but they are matters which concern our greatness as a nation and our future as a great people. They appeal to our national honor and dignity and to the pride of country and of race. If the humiliating foreign policy of the present Administration has served to call attention to these questions and to remind us that they are quite as important at least as tariffs or currency, it will perhaps prove to have been a blessing in disguise. When we face a question of foreign relations it should never be forgotten that we meet something above and beyond party politics, something that rouses and appeals to the patriotism and the Americanism of which we never can have too much, and of which during the last two years our Government has shown altogether too little.

1. What is the relationship between America's policy of neutrality and the Monroe doctrine as it is described in this document?
2. What is the attitude of this author in regard to American expansion and imperialism?

20-3 Albert Beveridge, "The March of the Flag" (1898)

Albert Beveridge, a Republican senator from Indiana, was one of the leading spokesmen for a strongly expansionist foreign policy. In this address, which was widely read during the period, Beveridge merged prevalent opinions about America◊s civilizing mission with its economic destiny.

It is a noble land that God has given us; a land that can feed and clothe the world; a land whose coastlines would enclose half the countries of Europe; a land set like a sentinel between the two imperial oceans of the globe, a greater England with a nobler destiny.

It is a mighty people that He has planted on this soil; a people sprung from the most masterful blood of history; a people perpetually revitalized by the virile, man-producing working folk of all the earth; a people imperial by virtue of their power, by right of their institutions, by authority of their Heaven-directed purposes-the propagandists and not the misers of liberty.

It is a glorious history our God has bestowed upon His chosen people; a history heroic with faith in our mission and our future; a history of statesmen who flung the boundaries of the Republic out into unexplored lands and savage wilderness; a history of soldiers who carried the flag across blazing deserts and through the ranks of hostile mountains, even to the gates of sunset; a history of a multiplying people who overran a continent in half a century; a history of prophets who saw the consequences of evils inherited from the past and of martyrs who died to save us from them; a history divinely logical, in the process of whose tremendous seasoning we find ourselves to-day.

Therefore, in this campaign, the question is larger than a party question. It is an American question. It is a world question. Shall the American people continue their march toward the commercial supremacy of the world? Shall free institutions broaden their blessed reign as the children of liberty wax in strength, until the empire of our principles is established over the hearts of all mankind?

Have we no mission to perform, no duty to discharge to our fellowman? Has God endowed us with gifts beyond our deserts and marked us as the people of His peculiar favor, merely to rot in our own selfishness, as men and nations must, who take cowardice for their companion and self for their deity-as China has, as India has, as Egypt has?

Shall we be as the man who had one talent and hid it, or as he who had ten talents and use them until they grew to riches? And shall we reap the reward that waits on our discharge of our high duty; shall we occupy new markets for what our farmers raise, our factories make, our merchants sell-aye, and, please God, new markets for what our ships shall carry?

Hawaii is ours, Puerto Rico is to be ours; at the prayer of her people Cuba finally will be ours; in the islands of the East, even to the gates of Asia, coaling stations are to be ours at the very least; the flag of a liberal government is to float over the Philippines, and may it be the banner that Taylor unfurled in Texas and Frèmont carried to the coast.

The Opposition tells us that we ought not to govern a people without their consent. I answer, The rule of liberty that all just government derives its authority from the consent of the governed, applies only to those who are capable of self-government. We govern the Indians without their consent, we govern our territories without their consent, we govern our children without their consent. How do they know that our government would be without their consent? Would not the people of the Philippines prefer the just, human, civilizing government of this Republic to the savage, bloody rule of pillage and extortion from which we have rescued them?

And, regardless of this formula of words made only for enlightened, self-governing people, do we owe no duty to the world? Shall we turn these peoples back to the reeking hands from which we have taken them? Shall we abandon them, with Germany, England, Japan, hungering for them? Shall we save them from those nations, to give them a self-rule of tragedy? . . . Then, like men and not like children, let us on to our tasks, our mission, and our destiny.

Wonderfully has God guided us. Yonder at Bunker Hill and Yorktown His providence was above us. At New Orleans and on ensanguined seas His hand sustained us. Abraham Lincoln was His minister and His was the altar of freedom the Nation's soldiers set up on a hundred battle-fields. His power directed Dewey in the East and delivered the Spanish fleet into our hands, as He delivered the elder Armada into the hands of our English sires two centuries ago. The American people can not use a dishonest medium of exchange; it is ours to set the world its example of right and honor. We can not fly from our world duties; it is ours to execute the purpose of a fate that has driven us to be greater than our small intentions. we can not retreat from any soil where Providence has unfurled our banner; it is ours to save that soil for liberty and civilization.

1. *What is the author's opinion of the history of success enjoyed by America?*
2. *How does this document capture the sentiments and attitudes of "The Imperialism of Righteousness"?*

20-4 The Spanish-American War (1898)

American interests in Cuba revived in the late nineteenth century. Periodic Cuban rebellions against Spanish control and the relaxing of American isolationism combined to stimulate awareness in the Caribbean. Government and business desired a stable Caribbean, and sensational journalism attracted public attention to atrocities in Cuba. The timing of these attractions made Cuba independence an American cause celebré.

> **Source:** "The War with Spain and After," *Atlantic Monthly* (June 1898) vol. 18, pp. 722–25; reprinted in Alfred B. Hart, ed., *American History Told by Contemporaries* vol. IV (New York: MacMillan, 1898–1929), pp. 573–575.

REASONS FOR WAR (1898)

Anonymous

We have had a Cuban question for more than ninety years. At times it has disappeared from our politics, but it has always reappeared. Once we thought it wise to prevent the island from winning its independence from Spain, and thereby, perhaps, we entered into moral bonds to make sure that Spain governed it decently. Whether we definitely contracted such an obligation or not, the Cuban question has never ceased to annoy us. The controversies about it make a long series of chapters in one continuous story of diplomatic trouble. Many of our ablest statesmen have had to deal with it as secretaries of state and as ministers to Spain, and not one of them has been able to settle it. One President after another has taken it up, and every one has transmitted it to his successor. It has at various times been a "plank" in the platforms of all our political parties,—

as it was in both the party platforms of 1896,—and it has been the subject of messages of nearly all our Presidents, as it was of President Cleveland's message in December, 1896, in which he distinctly expressed the opinion that the United States might feel forced to recognize "higher obligations" than neutrality to Spain. In spite of periods of apparent quiet, the old trouble has always reappeared in an acute form, and it has never been settled; nor has there recently been any strong reason for hope that it could be settled merely by diplomatic negotiation with Spain. Our diplomats have long had an experience with Spanish character and methods such as the public can better understand since war has been in progress. The pathetic inefficiency and the continual indirection of the Spanish character are now apparent to the world; they were long ago apparent to those who have had our diplomatic duties to do.

Thus the negotiations dragged on. We were put to trouble and expense to prevent filibustering, and filibustering continued in spite of us. More than once heretofore has there been danger of international conflict, as for instance when American sailors on the Virginius were executed in Cuba in 1873. Propositions have been made to buy the island, and plans have been formed to annex it. All the while there have been American interests in Cuba. Our citizens have owned property and made investments there, and done much to develop its fertility. They have paid tribute, unlawful as well as lawful, both to insurgents and to Spanish officials. They have lost property, for much of which no indemnity has been paid. All the while we have had a trade with the island, important during periods of quiet, irritating during periods of unrest.

The Cuban trouble is, therefore, not a new trouble even in an acute form. It had been moving toward a crisis for a long time. Still, while our government suffered these diplomatic vexations, and our citizens these losses, and our merchants these annoyances, the mass of the American people gave little serious thought to it. The newspapers kept us reminded of an opera-bouffe war that was going on, and now and then there came information of delicate and troublesome diplomatic duties for our minister to Spain. If Cuba were within a hundred miles of the coast of one of our populous states and near one of our great ports, periods of acute interest in its condition would doubtless have come earlier and oftener, and we should long ago have had to deal with a crisis by warlike measures. Or if the insurgents had commanded respect instead of mere pity, we should have paid heed to their struggle sooner; for it is almost an American maxim that a people cannot govern itself till it can win its own independence.

When it began to be known that Weyler's method of extermination was producing want in the island, and when appeals were made to American charity, we became more interested. . . .

The American public was in this mood when the battleship Maine was blown up in the harbor of Havana. The masses think in events, and not in syllogisms, and this was an event. This event provoked suspicions in the public mind. The thought of the whole nation was instantly directed to Cuba. The fate of the sailors on the Virginius, twenty-five years ago, was recalled. The public curiosity about everything Cuban and Spanish became intense. The Weyler method of warfare became more generally known. The story of our long diplomatic trouble with Spain was recalled. . . .

There is no need to discuss minor and accidental causes that hastened the rush of events; but such causes were not lacking either in number or in influence. . . . But all these together could not have driven us to war if we had not been willing to be driven,—if the conviction had not become firm in the minds of the people that Spanish rule in Cuba was a blot on civilization that had now begun to bring reproach to us; and when the President, who favored peace, declared it "intolerable," the people were ready to accept his judgment.

. . . We rushed into war almost before we knew it, not because we desired war, but because we desired something to be done with the old problem that should be direct and definite and final. Let us end it once for all. . . .

Not only is there in the United States an unmistakable popular approval of war as the only effective means of restoring civilization in Cuba, but the judgment of the English people promptly approved it,—giving evidence of an instinctive race and institutional sympathy. If Anglo-Saxon institutions and methods stand for anything, the institutions and methods of Spanish rule in Cuba are an abomination and a reproach. And English sympathy is not more significant as an evidence of the necessity of the war and as a good omen for the future of free institutions than the equally instinctive sympathy with Spain that has been expressed by some of the decadent influences on the Continent; indeed, the real meaning of American civilization and ideals will henceforth be somewhat more clearly understood in several quarters of the world.

American character will be still better understood when the whole world clearly perceives that the purpose of the war is only to remove from our very doors this cruel and inefficient piece of mediaevalism which is one of the two great scandals of the closing years of the century; for it is not a war of conquest. . . .

1. Why did the author suggest that American intervention in Cuba represented an introduction of progress and uplift for the Cuban people?
2. What accounts for America's sudden interest in Cuba? What national interests did the United States need to protect in Cuba?

20-5 William McKinley, "Decision on the Philippines" (1900)

Following the U. S. victory in the Spanish-American War, the government had to decide on a policy towards the Philippines. A strong debate arose among imperialists and anti-imperialists. But as this document shows, the decision rested with President McKinley who decided to retain the Philippines as an American possession.

When next I realized that the Philippines had dropped into our laps, I confess I did not know what to do with them. I sought counsel from all sides-Democrats as well as Republicans-but got little help. I thought first we would take only Manila; then Luzon; then other islands, perhaps, also.

I walked the floor of the White House night after night until midnight; and I am not ashamed to tell you, gentlemen, that I went down on my knees and prayed to Almighty God for light and guidance more than one night. And one night late it came to me this way-I don't know how it was, but it came:

(1) That we could not give them back to Spain-that would be cowardly and dishonorable;

(2) That we could not turn them over to France or Germany, our commercial rivals in the Orient-that would be bad business and discreditable;

(3) That we could not leave them to themselves-they were unfit for self-government, and they would soon have anarchy and misrule worse then Spain's was; and

(4) That there was nothing left for us to do but to take them all, and to educate the Filipinos, and uplift and civilize and Christianize them and by God's grace do the very best we could by them, as our fellow men for whom Christ also died.

And then I went to bed and went to sleep, and slept soundly, and the next morning I sent for the chief engineer of the War Department (our map-maker), and I told him to put the Philippines on the map of the United States (pointing to a large map on the wall of his office), and there they are and there they will stay while I am President!

1. Summarize McKinley's reasons for wanting to occupy and influence the Philippines. Upon what basis does he justify American interests in the Philippines?

20-6 The Boxer Rebellion (1900)

The United States and other western industrial nations competed aggressively for a share of the tremendous market opportunities in China. Driven by the potential of huge profits, the western nations raced to carve out spheres of influence. Missionaries arrived in advance of the business establishment, and an indirect benefit of their work was learning the native language and culture, drawing maps and introducing the native population to western standards of life and religion. Mission work was in this way a tremendous help to the business communities there, although the assistance was unintentional and indirect. The onslaught of western religious, commercial, and political interests inflamed many Chinese to defend their culture by rejecting the "foreign devils." The Boxer Rebellion led by Chinese nationalists targeted mission settlements, foreign and diplomatic compounds.

> **Source:** Mrs. E. K. Lowery, "A Woman's Diary of the Siege of Pekin," *McClure's Magazine* (Nov. 1900) vol. 16, pp. 66–77; Reprinted in Alfred B. Hart, *American History Told by Contemporaries* vol. IV (New York: MacMillan, 1898–1929), pp. 619–622.

BESIEGED IN PEKIN (1900)

By Mrs. Katharine Mullikin Lowry

Mrs. Lowry resided for five years in China, where her husband was formerly connected with the United States embassy at Pekin. When the Boxer insurrection began, she was living at the Methodist Episcopal mission settlement in Pckin. The "Sir Claude" in the text was the British minister, Sir Claude MacDonald.

WEDNESDAY, June 13 [1900]: About 6.30 P.M. there is excitement and loud voices at the Ha-ta gate, and from the Woman's Foreign Missionary Society's upper windows soldiers can be seen on the wall looking into the street. Later, smoke and flame announce that our street chapel is being burned. All night long fires spring up in different parts of the city. (All the different mission compounds and Catholic churches were first looted and then burned, except the Pei-Tang, which was guarded). . . .

THURSDAY, June 14: To-day some of our number went to the Legation carrying the records, mission history, deeds, etc. . . .

FRIDAY, June 15: Last night for two hours awful sounds of raging heathen filled the air, and seemed to surge against the wall in the southern city, opposite our place. Some estimated there were 50,000 voices. "Kill the foreign devil! Kill, kill, kill!" they yelled till it seemed hell was let loose. . . .

WEDNESDAY, June 20: About nine A.M. . . . great excitement was caused by the word that Baron von Ketteler, The German Minister, had been shot on his way to the Tsungli Yamen, and his interpreter wounded. . . . Captain Hall thought as it would be impossible to hold the compound against soldiers, our only chance would be to abandon it immediately, while it is still possible for women and children to walk on the street. He therefore sends word to the Legation that he wishes to be relieved, and sets the time for leaving the compound at eleven A.M., with no baggage except what we can carry in our hands. . . . At eleven o'clock the melancholy file takes up its march, the seventy foreigners at the front, two and two, the gentlemen, with their guns, walking by the side of the ladies and children, while behind follow over 500 Chinese refugees who have been with us all these twelve mournful days, the twenty marines with Captain Myers bringing up the rear—656 persons in all. Sad, indeed, did we feel to thus march away from our homes, leaving them with all their contents to certain destruction. . . .

The nationalities represented here (British Legation) are American, Austrian, Belgian, Boer, British, Chinese, Danish, Dutch, French, Finn, German, Italian, Japanese, Norwegian, Portuguese, Russian, Spanish, Swedish. . . . They are divided into men, 245; women, 149; children, 79; total, 473; not including the marines, of whom there were 409. . . . The Chinese here number about 700 to 800 Protestants and 2,000 Catholics. . . .

THURSDAY, June 21 : To-day Sir Claude requests that Mr. Gamewell take full charge of fortifying this place, and that committees be appointed with full authority to control our defenses. This is done. Mr. Tewkesbury is made head of the general committees. Other committees are appointed for fire, food, fuel, Chinese labor, foreign labor, sanitation, and water, and in a remarkably short time this motley crowd of many nationalities is thoroughly organized for the best good of all. Mr. Gamewell suggests the use of sand-bags in the defense, and the making of them begins, the church being headquarters for this work. Large fires are seen raging in many parts of the city. . . .

SATURDAY, June 23 : To-day has been one of great excitement. Five big fires rage close about us, and bucket lines are formed several times. Some of the fires are started by the Chinese; some by our people, to burn out places which are dangerous to us, because the Chinese may burn them or can fire from them. After burning the Russian Bank the Chinese start a fire in the Han Lin College, with a wind blowing from the north, which makes it very dangerous for us. Hardly is the fire under way, however, when the wind providentially changes and we are saved from that danger, though much hard work is required in passing water. Sentiment and fear of antagonizing the Chinese caused our people to refrain from firing this Han Lin College, the very foundation of Chinese literature and culture. The intense hatred of the Chinese for us is shown by the fact that they themselves set fire to this relic of the ages. . . . It is said the destruction of this Han Lin Library is only paralleled by the burning of the Alexandrian Library.

SUNDAY, June 24 : To-day the Chinese do their first shelling. . . .

WEDNESDAY, June 27 : The usual nerve strain is endured all day from the bullets and shells. We shall forget how it feels to be without their sound. The nights are dreadful with the sound of shattering tiles and falling bricks, and there is so much echo in the courts that at night it is hard to locate where an attack is being made, and harder still to sleep at all. At eleven P.M. an alarm is rung at the bell tower for all to assemble there with their firearms. This is the second or third general alarm we have had, and they frighten us almost worse than the attacks. . . .

FRIDAY, June 29. . . . To-day many gentlemen are busy constructing bomb-proof houses, to which we may retreat if necessary. . . .

FRIDAY, July 6. . . . Another unsuccessful sortie is made from the Fu after the big gun to the northeast which does so much damage, the Japanese commander being killed and a Japanese and an Austrian wounded. . . .

TUESDAY, July 17: Last night, about six P.M., the . . . messenger . . . brought a letter and a telegram in cipher. The latter when translated read, "Washington, Conger, send tidings, bearer." Mr. Conger is puzzled, as the code can be none other than that of the State Department, yet it is incomplete, as there is no date nor signature. . . .

WEDNESDAY, July 18: Major Conger asks in his reply . . . to have his cablegram completed, as he does not know from whom it comes. They send back the whole thing. The first message proves to be included in a cablegram from Chinese Minister Wu to his Government, which accounts for the lack of date and signature. Complete message from Wu is as follows: "United States gladly assist China, but they are thinking of Major Conger. Inclosed is message inquiring for his health. Please deliver and forward reply." Major Conger sent in cipher cable the following: "Surrounded and fired upon by Chinese for a month. If not relieved soon, massacre will follow." This the Tsungli Yamen promises to send. . . .

FRIDAY, July 27. . . . To-day there was sent in with the compliments of the Tsungli Yamen 1,000 catties of flour, and over a hundred each of watermelons, cucumbers, egg plants, and squashes.

SATURDAY, July 28. . . . It is estimated that from July 10th to 25th 2,800 cannon-balls or shells came into these premises, between sixty and seventy striking Sir Claude's house alone. There have been as many as 400 in one day. . . .

TUESDAY, August 14 : Last night was certainly the most frightful we have had. Although they had fired all day yesterday, the Chinese began with renewed vigor about eight P.M., at the very moment that a terrific thunderstorm with lightning and torrents of rain set in. Shells, bullets, and fire-crackers vied with the noise of the elements, while our big guns, the Colt's automatic, the Nordenfeldt, the Austrian and Italian guns, and "Betsey" added to the noise; for our men were wild, and felt like doing their best, for it was now certain that the foreign troops could not be far distant. In fact, the boom of the distant cannon could easily be heard, and no one felt like sleeping, had it been possible in the din. Our American gunner, Mitchell, is wounded. All the morning we have heard the thundering of the foreign troops, and while it seems too good to be true, our hearts rejoice that deliverance is near. The Chinese exhausted themselves last night, and have doubtless spent the day in fleeing. Between three and four o'clock this afternoon the British Sikhs came through the water-gate, and the rest of the foreign troops came pouring in from various directions. We are released and saved after eight horrible weeks.

1. What is the connection between the politics of imperialism and the fates of ordinary citizens in China?
2. What is Mrs. Lowry's attitude towards the Chinese?

20-7   Theodore Roosevelt, Third Annual Message to Congress (1903)

In the late nineteenth century, advocates of American expansion claimed that the future of the United States depended on a strong navy. Theodore Roosevelt was a major leader in the navy movement and as president strongly supported the naval construction.

I heartily congratulate the Congress upon the steady progress in building up the American Navy. We can not afford a let-up in this great work. To stand still means to go back. There should be no cessation in adding to the effective units of the fighting strength of the fleet. Meanwhile the Navy Department and the officers of the Navy are doing well their part by providing constant service at sea under conditions akin to those of actual warfare. Our officers and enlisted men are learning to handle the battleships, cruisers, and torpedo boats with high efficiency in fleet and squadron formations, and the standard of marksmanship is being steadily raised. The best work ashore is indispensable, but the highest duty of a naval officer is to exercise command at sea.

The establishment of a naval base in the Philippines ought not to be longer postponed. Such a base is desirable in time of peace; in time of war it would be indispensable, and its lack would be ruinous. Without it our fleet would be helpless. Our naval experts are agreed that Subig [Subic] Bay is the proper place for the purpose. The national interests require that the work of fortification and development of a naval station at Subig Bay be begun at an early date; for under the best conditions it is a work which will consume much time. . . .

By the act of June 28, 1902, the Congress authorized the President to enter into treaty with Colombia for the building of the canal across the Isthmus of Panama; it being provided that in the event of failure to secure such treaty after the lapse of a reasonable time, recourse should be had to building a canal through Nicaragua. It has not been necessary to consider this alternative, as I am enabled to lay before the Senate a treaty providing for the building of the canal across the Isthmus of Panama. This was the route which commended itself to the deliberate judgment of the Congress, and we can now acquire by treaty the right to construct the canal over this route. The question now, therefore, is not by which route the isthmian canal shall be built, for that question has been definitely and irrevocably decided. The question is simply whether or not we shall have an isthmian canal. . . .

A new Republic, that of Panama, which was at one time a sovereign state, and at another time a mere department of the successive confederations known as New Granada and Columbia, has now succeeded to the rights which first one and then the other formerly exercised over the Isthmus. But as long as the Isthmus endures, the mere geographical fact of its existence, and the peculiar interest therein which is required by our position, perpetuate the solemn contract which binds the holders of the territory to respect our right to freedom of transit across it, and binds us in return to safeguard for the Isthmus and the world the exercise of that inestimable privilege. . . .

The above recital of facts [not included here] establishes beyond question: First, that the United States has for over half a century patiently and in good faith carried out its obligations under the treaty of 1846; second, that when for the first time it became possible for Colombia to do anything in requital of the services thus repeatedly rendered to it for fifty-seven years by the United States, the Colombian Government preemptorily and offensively refused thus to do its part, even though to do so would have been to its advantage and immeasurably to the advantage of the State of Panama, at that time under its jurisdiction; third, that throughout this period revolutions, riots, and factional disturbances of every kind have occurred one after the other in almost uninterrupted succession, some of them lasting for months and even for years, while the central government was unable to put them down or to make peace with the rebels; fourth, that these disturbances instead of showing any sign of abating have tended to grow more numerous and more serious in the immediate past; fifth, that the control of Colombia over the Isthmus of Panama could not be maintained without the armed intervention and assistance of the United States. In other words, the Government of Colombia, though wholly unable to maintain order on the Isthmus, has nevertheless declined to ratify a treaty the conclusion of which opened the only chance to secure its own stability and to guarantee permanent peace on, and the construction of a canal across, the Isthmus.

Under such circumstances the Government of the United States would have been guilty of folly and weakness, amounting in their sum to a crime against the Nation, had it acted otherwise than it did when the revolution of November 3 last took place in Panama. This great enterprise of building the interoceanic canal can not be held up to gratify the whims, or out of respect to the governmental impotence, or to the even more sinister and evil political peculiarities, of people who, though they dwell afar off, yet, against the wish of the actual dwellers on the Isthmus, assert an unreal supremacy over the territory. The possession of a territory fraught with such peculiar capacities as the Isthmus in question carries with it obligations to mankind. The course of events has shown that this canal can not be built by private enterprise, or by any other nation than our own; therefore it must be built by the United States.

Every effort has been made by the Government of the United States to persuade Colombia to follow a course which was essentially not only to our interests and to the interests of the world, but to the interests of Colombia itself. These efforts have failed; and Colombia, by her persistence in repulsing the advances that have been made, has forced us, for the sake of our own honor, and of the interest and well-being, not merely of our own people, but of the people of the Isthmus of Panama and the people of the civilized countries of the world, to take decisive steps to bring to an end a condition of affairs which had become intolerable. The new Republic of Panama immediately offered to negotiate a treaty with us. This treaty I herewith submit. By it our interests are better safeguarded than in the treaty with Colombia which was ratified by the Senate at its last session. It is better in its terms than the treaties offered to us by the Republics of Nicaragua and Costa Rica. At last the right to begin this great undertaking is made available. Panama has done her part. All that remains is for the American Congress to do its part, and forthwith this Republic will enter upon the execution of a project colossal in its size and of well-nigh incalculable possibilities for the good of this country and the nations of mankind.

By the provisions of the treaty the United States guarantees and will maintain the independence of the Republic of Panama. There is granted to the United States in perpetuity the use, occupation, and control of a strip ten miles wide and extending three nautical miles into the sea at either terminal, with all lands lying outside of the zone necessary for the construction of the canal or for its auxiliary works, and with the islands in the Bay of Panama. The cities of Panama and Colon are not embraced in the canal zone, but the United States assumes their sanitation and, in case of need, the maintenance of order therein; the United States enjoys within the granted limits all the rights, power, and authority which it would possess were it the sovereign of the territory to the exclusion of the exercise of sovereign rights by the Republic. All railway and canal property rights belonging to Panama and needed for the canal pass to the United States, including any property of the respective companies in the cities of Panama and Colon; the works, property, and personnel of the canal and railways are exempted from taxation as well in the cities of Panama and Colon as in the canal zone and its dependencies. Free immigration of the personnel and importation of supplies for the construction and operation of the canal are granted. Provision is made for the use of mili-tary force and the building of fortifications by the United States for the protection of the transit.

1. What interest does the United States have in establishing a canal in Panama?
2. Summarize the efforts and political maneuvering associated with the United States' endeavor to secure the territory that is the site of the proposed canal.

20-8 Mark Twain, "Incident in the Philippines" (1924)

Famous writer Mark Twain had opposed the United States taking possession of the Philippines. His satirical commentary on the battle between U. S. forces and the Moros made fun of the purported Christian mission of U. S. occupation.

. . . This incident burst upon the world last Friday in an official cablegram from the commander of our forces in the Philippines to our government at Washington. The substance of it was as follows:

A tribe of Moros, dark-skinned savages, had fortified themselves in the bowl of an extinct crater not many miles from Jolo; and as they were hostiles, and bitter against us because we have been trying for eight years to take their liberties away from them, their presence in that position was a menace. Our commander, General Leonard Wood, ordered a reconnaissance [*sic*]. It was found that the Moros numbered six hundred, counting women and children; that their crater bowl was in the summit of a peak or mountain twenty-two hundred feet above sea level, and very difficult of access for Christian troops and artillery. . . . Our troops climbed the heights by devious and difficult trails, and even took some artillery with them. . . . [When they] arrived at the rim of the crater, the battle began. Our soldiers numbered five hundred and forty. They were assisted by auxiliaries consisting of a detachment of native constabulary in our pay-their numbers not given-and by a naval detachment, whose numbers are not stated. But apparently the contending parties were about equal as to number-six hundred men on our side, on the edge of the bowl; six hundred men, women, and children in the bottom of the bowl. Depth of the bowl, 50 feet.

General Wood's order was, "Kill or capture the six hundred."

The battle began-it is officially called by that name-our forces firing down into the crater with their artillery and their deadly small arms of precision; the savages furiously returning the fire, probably with brickbats-though this is merely a surmise of mine, as the weapons used by the savages are not nominated in the cablegram. Heretofore the Moros have used knives and clubs mainly; also ineffectual trade-muskets when they had any.

The official report stated that the battle was fought with prodigious energy on both sides during a day and a half, and that it ended with a complete victory for the American arms. The completeness of the victory is established by this fact: that of the six hundred Moros not one was left alive. The brilliancy of the victory is established by this other fact, to wit: that of our six hundred heroes only fifteen lost their lives.

General Wood was present and looking on. His order had been, "Kill or capture those savages." Apparently our little army considered that the "or" left them authorized to kill or capture according to taste, and that their taste had remained what it has been for eight years, in our army out there-the taste of Christian butchers. . . .

Let us now consider two or three details of our military history. In one of the great battles of the Civil War ten per cent of the forces engaged on the two sides were killed and wounded. At Waterloo, where four hundred thousand men were present on the two sides, fifty thousand fell, killed and wounded, in five hours, leaving three hundred and fifty sound and all right for further adventures. Eight years ago, when the pathetic comedy called the Cuban War was played, we summoned two hundred and fifty thousand men. We fought a number of showy battles, and when the war was over we had lost two hundred sixty-eight men out of our two hundred and fifty thousand, in killed and wounded in the field, and just fourteen times as many by the gallantry of the army doctors in the hospitals and camps. We did not exterminate the Spaniards-far from it. In each engagement we left an average of two per cent of the enemy killed or crippled on the field.

Contrast these things with the great statistics which have arrived from that Moro crater! There, with six hundred engaged on each side, we lost fifteen men killed outright, and we had thirty-two wounded. . . . The enemy numbered six hundred-including women and children-and we abolished them utterly, leaving not even a baby alive to cry for its dead mother. This is incomparably the greatest victory that was ever achieved by the Christian soldiers of the United States.

1. What is the author's attitude toward America's actions in the "Incident in the Philippines"?
2. What evidence is there in this text that Twain's tone is bitterly satiric?

PART TWENTY-ONE
THE PROGRESSIVE ERA

21-1 Frederick Winslow Taylor, "A Piece-Rate System" (1896)

As industrialization matured, attention focused on improving efficiency. Scientific management emerged as a means of ordering the industrial and business world. In a sense, scientific management was related to the Progressive idea of ordering the world. Frederick Winslow Taylor was perhaps the most famous advocate of applying science to industry.

The ordinary piece-work system involves a permanent antagonism between employers and men, and a certainty of punishment for each workman who reaches a high rate of efficiency. The demoralizing effect of this system is most serious. Under it, even the best workmen are forced continually to act the part of hypocrites, to hold their own in the struggle against the encroachments of their employers.

The system introduced by the writer, however, is directly the opposite, both in theory and in its results. It takes each workman's interests the same as that of his employer, pays a premium for high efficiency, and soon convinces each man that it is for his permanent advantage to turn out each day the best quality and maximum quantity of work. . . .

Elementary rate-fixing differs from other methods of making piece-work prices in that a careful study is made of the time required to do each of the many elementary operations into which the manufacturing of an establishment may be analyzed or divided. These elementary operations are then classified, recorded, and indexed and when a piece-work price is wanted for work the job is first divided into its elementary operations, the time required to do each elementary operation is found from the records, and the total time for the job is summed up from these data. While this method seems complicated at the first glance, it is, in fact, far simpler and more effective than the old method of recording the time required to do whole jobs of work, and then, after looking over the records of similar jobs, guessing at the time required for any new piece of work.

The differential rate system of piece-work consists briefly, in offering two different rates for the same job, a high price per piece in case the work is finished in the shortest possible time and in perfect condition, and a low price if it takes a longer time to do the job, of if there are any imperfections in the work. (The high rate should be such that the workman can earn more per day than is usually paid in similar establishments.) This is directly the opposite of the ordinary plan of piece-work in which the wages of the workmen are reduced when they increase their productivity.

The system by which the writer proposes managing the men who are on day-work consists in paying men and not *positions*. Each man's wages, as far as possible, are fixed according to the skill and energy with which he performs his work, and not according to the position which he fills. Every endeavor is made to stimulate each man's personal ambition. This involves keeping systematic and careful records of the performance of each man, as to his punctuality, attendance, integrity, rapidity, skill, and accuracy, and a readjustment from time to time of the wages paid him, in accordance with this record.

The advantages of this system of management are:

First. That the manufactures are produced cheaper under it, while at the same time the workmen earn higher wages than are usually paid.

Second. Since the rate-fixing is done from accurate knowledge instead of more or less by guess-work, the motive for holding back on work, or "soldiering," and endeavoring to deceive the employers as to the time required to do work, is entirely removed, and with it the greatest cause for hard feelings and war between the management and the men.

Third. Since the basis from which piece-work as well as day rates are fixed is that of exact observation, instead of being founded upon accident or deception, as is too frequently the case under ordinary systems, the men are treated with greater uniformity and justice, and respond by doing more and better work.

Fourth. It is for the common interest of both the management and the men to conperate in every way, so as to turn out each day the maximum quantity and best quality of work.

Fifth. The system is rapid, while other systems are slow, in attaining the maximum productivity of each machine and man; and when this maximum is once reached, it is automatically maintained by the differential rate.

Sixth. It automatically selects and attracts the best men for each class of work, and it develops many first class men who would otherwise remain slow or inaccurate, while at the same time it discourages and sifts out men who are incurably lazy or inferior.

Finally. One of the chief advantages derived from the above effects of the system is, that it promotes a most friendly feeling between the men and their employers and so renders labor unions and strikes unnecessary. . . .

It is not unusual for the manager of a manufacturing business to go most minutely into every detail of the buying and selling and financiering, and arrange every element of these branches in the most systematic manner and according to principles that have been carefully planned to insure the business against almost any contingency which may arise, while the manufacturing is turned over to a superintendent or foreman, with little or no restrictions as to the principles and methods which he is to pursue, either in the management of his men or the care of the company's plant. . . .

Such managers belong distinctly to the old school of manufacturers; and among them are to be found, in spite of their lack of system, many of the best and most successful men of the country. They believe in men, not in methods, in the management of their shops; and what they would call system in the office and sales departments, would be called red tape by them in the factory. Through their keen insight and knowledge of character they are able to select and train good superintendents, who in turn secure good workmen; and frequently the business prospers under this system (or rather, lack of system) for a term of years.

The modern manufacturer, however, seeks not only to secure the best superintendents and workmen, but to surround each department of his manufacture with the most carefully woven net-work of system and method, which should render the business, for a considerable period at least, independent of the loss of any one man, and frequently of any combination of men.

It is the lack of this system and method which, in the judgment of the writer, constitutes the greatest risk to manufacturing; placing, as it frequently does, the success of the business at the hazard of the health of whims of a few employees.

1. What were the benefits of Taylor's system over the ordinary piece rate system?
2. What distinguished a modern manager from his old-school counterpart?

21-2 William Graham Sumner, What the Social Classes Owe to Each Other (1883)

Advocates of American imperialism tied expansion overseas to the mission of civilizing other peoples. William Graham Sumner was a major supporter of expansion and the right of the United States to spread democracy to other peoples.

There is not a civilized nation that does not talk about its civilizing mission just as grandly as we do. The English, who really have more to boast of it in this respect than anybody else, talk least about it, but the Phariseeism with which they correct and instruct other people has made them hated all over the globe. The French believe themselves the guardians of the highest and purest culture, and that the eyes of all mankind are fixed on Paris, whence they expect oracles of thought and taste. The Germans regard themselves as charged with a mission, especially to us Americans, to save us from egoism and materialism. The Russians, in their books and newspapers, talk about the civilizing mission of Russian in language that might be translated from some of the finest paragraphs of our imperialistic newspapers.

The first principle of Mohammedanism is that we Christians are dogs and infidels, fit only to be enslaved or butchered by Moslems. It is a corollary that wherever Mohammedanism extends it carries, in the belief of its votaries, the highest blessings, and that the whole human race would be enormously elevated if Mohammedanism should supplant Christianity everywhere.

To come, last, to Spain, the Spaniards have, for centuries, considered themselves the most zealous and self-sacrificing Christians, especially charged by the Almighty, on this account, to spread the true religion and civilization over the globe. They think themselves free and noble, leaders in refinement and the sentiments of personal honor, and they despise us as sordid money-grabbers and heretics. I could bring you passages from peninsular authors of the first rank about the grand role of Spain and Portugal in spreading freedom and truth.

Now each nation laughs at all the others when it observes these manifestations of national vanity. You may rely upon it that they are all ridiculous by virtue of these pretensions, including ourselves. The point is that each of them repudiates the standards of the others, and the outlying nations, which are to be civilized, hate all the standards of civilized men.

We assume that what we like and practice, and what we think better, must come as a welcome blessing to Spanish-Americans and Filipinos. This is grossly and obviously untrue. They hate our ways. They are hostile to our ideas. Our religion, language, institutions, and manners offend them. They like their own ways, and if we appear amongst them as rulers, there will be social discord in all the great departments of social interest. The most important thing which we shall inherit from the Spaniards will be the task of suppressing rebellions.

If the United States takes out of the hands of Spain her mission, on the ground that Spain is not executing it well, and if this nation in its turn attempts to be schoolmistress to others, it will shrivel up into the same vanity and self-conceit of which Spain now presents an example. To read our current literature one would think that we were already well on the way to it.

Now, the great reason why all these enterprises which begin by saying to somebody else, "We know what is good for you better than you know yourself and we are going to make you do it," are false and wrong is that they violate liberty; or, to turn the same statement into other words, the reason why liberty, of which we Americans talk so much, is a good thing is that it means leaving people to live out their own lives in their own way, while we do the same.

If we believe in liberty, as an American principle, why do we not stand by it? Why are we going to throw it away to enter upon a Spanish policy of dominion and regulation?

1. *What was Sumner's position on annexing the Philippines and what arguments did heuse to he support that position?*

21-3 Eugene V. Debs, "The Outlook for Socialism in the United States" (1900)

Eugene Debs was the leader of the socialist movement in the United States in the late nineteenth and early twentieth centuries. He ran for president three times. Debs and other socialists saw conditions in the United States and American foreign policy as proving the bankruptcy of capitalism and the ushering in of socialism.

The sun of the passing century is setting upon scenes of extraordinary activity in almost every part of our capitalistic old planet. Wars and rumors of wars are of universal prevalence. In the Philippines our soldiers are civilizing and Christianizing the natives in the latest and most approved styles of the art, and at prices ($13 per month) which commend the blessing to the prayerful consideration of the lowly and oppressed everywhere. . . .

The picture, lurid as a chamber of horrors, becomes complete in its gruesome ghastliness when robed ministers of Christ solemnly declare that it is all for the glory of God and the advancement of Christian civilization. . . .

The campaign this year will be unusually spectacular. The Republican Party "points with pride" to the "prosperity" of the country, the beneficent results of the "gold standard" and the "war record" of the administration. The Democratic Party declares that "imperialism" is the "paramount" issue, and that the country is certain to go to the "demnition bow-wows" if Democratic officeholders are not elected instead of the Republicans. The Democratic slogan is "The Republic vs. the Empire," accompanied in a very minor key by 16 to 1 and "direct legislation where practical."

Both these capitalist parties are fiercely opposed to trusts, though what they propose to do with them is not of sufficient importance to require even a hint in their platforms.

Needless is it for me to say to the thinking workingman that he has no choice between these two capitalist parties, that they are both pledged to the same system and that whether the one or the other succeeds, he will still remain the wage-working slave he is today.

What but meaningless phrases are "imperialism," "expansion," "free silver," "gold standard," etc., to the wage worker? The large capitalists represented by Mr. McKinley and the small capitalists represented by Mr. Bryan are interested in these "issues," but they do not concern the working class.

What the workingmen of the country are profoundly interested in is the private ownership of the means of production and distribution, the enslaving and degrading wage system in which they toil for a pittance at the pleasure of their masters and are bludgeoned, jailed or shot when they protest-this is the central, controlling, vital issue of the hour, and neither of the old party platforms has a word or even a hint about it.

As a rule, large capitalists are Republicans and small capitalists are Democrats, but workingmen must remember that they are all capitalists, and that the many small ones, like the fewer large ones, are all politically supporting their class interests, and this is always and everywhere the capitalist class.

Whether the means of production-that is to say, the land, mines, factories, machinery, etc.-are owned by a few large Republican capitalists, who organize a trust, or whether they be owned by a lot of small Democratic capitalists, who are opposed to the trust, is all the same to the working class. Let the capitalists, large and small, fight this out among themselves.

The working class must get rid of the whole brood of masters and exploiters, and put themselves in possession and control of the means of production, that they may have steady employment without consulting a capitalist employer, large or small, and that they may get the wealth their labor produces, all of it, and enjoy with their families the fruits of their industry in comfortable and happy homes, abundant and wholesome food, proper clothing and all other things necessary to "life, liberty and the pursuit of happiness." It is therefore a question not of "reform," the mask of fraud, but of revolution. The capitalist system must be overthrown, class rule abolished and wage slavery supplanted by cooperative industry.

We hear it frequently urged that the Democratic Party is the "poor man's party," "the friend of labor." There is but one way to relieve poverty and to free labor, and that is by making common property of the tools of labor. . . .

What has the Democratic Party to say about the "property and educational qualifications" in North Carolina and Louisiana, and the proposed general disfranchisement of the Negro race in the Southern states?

The differences between the Republican and Democratic parties involve no issue, no principle in which the working class has any interest. . . .

Between these parties socialists have no choice, no preference. They are one in their opposition to socialism, that is to say, the emancipation of the working class from wage slavery, and every workingman who has intelligence enough to understand the interest of his class and the nature of the struggle in which it is involved will once and for all time sever his relations with them both; and recognizing the class struggle which is being waged between producing workers and non-producing capitalists, cast his lot with the class-conscious, revolutionary Socialist Party, which is pledged to abolish the capitalist system, class rule and wage slavery-a party which does not compromise or fuse, but, preserving inviolate the principles which quickened it into life and now give it vitality and force, moves forward with dauntless determination to the goal of economic freedom.

The political trend is steadily toward socialism. The old parties are held together only by the cohesive power of spoils, and in spite of this they are steadily disintegrating. Again and again they have been tried with the same results, and thousands upon thousands, awake to their duplicity, are deserting them and turning toward socialism as the only refuge and security. Republicans, Democrats, Populists, Prohibitionists, Single Taxers are having their eyes opened to the true nature of the struggle and they are beginning to

Come as the winds come, when
Forests are rended;
Come as the waves come, when
Navies are stranded.

For a time the Populist Party had a mission, but it is practically ended. The Democratic Party has "fused" it out of existence. The "middle-of-the-road" element will be sorely disappointed when the votes are counted, and they will probably never figure in another national campaign. Not many of them will go back to the old parties. Many of them have already come to socialism, and the rest are sure to follow.

There is no longer any room for a Populist Party, and progressive Populists realize it, and hence the "strong-holds" of Populism are becoming the "hotbeds" of Socialism.

It is simply a question of capitalism or socialism, of despotism or democracy, and they who are not wholly with us are wholly against us.

1. According to Debs, what were the differences between the Republican and Democratic parties?
2. For working people, why was the socialism the only true alternative?

21-4   Platform Adopted by the National Negro Committee (1909)

After racial segregation gained constitutional sanction, African Americans founded organizations to protest against prevailing conditions and improvement of their situation.

We denounce the ever-growing oppression of our 10,000,000 colored fellow citizens as the greatest menace that threatens the country. Often plundered of their just share of the public funds, robbed of nearly all part in the government, segregated by common carriers, some murdered with impunity, and all treated with open contempt by officials, they are held in some States in practical slavery to the white community. The systematic persecution of law-abiding citizens and their disfranchisement on account of their race alone is a crime that will ultimately drag down to an infamous end any nation that allows it to be practiced, and it bears most heavily on those poor white farmers and laborers whose economic position is most similar to that of the persecuted race.

The nearest hope lies in the immediate and patiently continued enlightenment of the people who have been inveigled into a campaign of oppression. The spoils of persecution should not go to enrich any class or classes of the population. Indeed persecution of organized workers, peonage, enslavement of prisoners, and even disfranchisement already threaten large bodies of whites in many Southern States.

We agree fully with the prevailing opinion that the transformation of the unskilled colored laborers in industry and agriculture into skilled workers is of vital importance to that race and to the nation, but we demand for the Negroes, as for all others, a free and complete education, whether by city, State or nation, a grammar school and industrial training for all and technical, professional, and academic education for the most gifted.

But the public schools assigned to the Negro of whatever kind or grade will never receive a fair and equal treatment until he is given equal treatment in the Legislature and before the law. Nor will the practically educated Negro, no matter how valuable to the community he may prove, be given a fair return for his labor or encouraged to put forth his best efforts or given the chance to develop that efficiency that comes only outside the school until he is respected in his legal rights as a man and a citizen.

We regard with grave concern the attempt manifest South and North to deny black men the right to work and to enforce this demand by violence and bloodshed. Such a question is too fundamental and clear even to be submitted to arbitration. The late strike in Georgia is not simply a demand that Negroes be displaced, but that proven and efficient men be made to surrender their long-followed means of livelihood to white competitors.

As first and immediate steps toward remedying these national wrongs, so full of peril for the whites as well as the blacks of all sections, we demand of Congress and the Executive:

(1) That the Constitution be strictly enforced and the civil rights guaranteed under the Fourteenth Amendment be secured impartially to all.
(2) That there be equal educational opportunities for all and in all the States, and that public school expenditure be the same for the Negro and white child.
(3) That in accordance with the Fifteenth Amendment the right of the Negro to the ballot on the same terms as other citizens be recognized in every part of the country.

1. Under what conditions did African Americans live?
2. What solutions did the National Negro Committee propose?

21-5 James H. Patten, Chairman of the National Legislative Committee of the American Purity Federation, Testimony Before Congress (1910)

The massive influx of primarily Catholic and Jewish European immigrants from southern and Eastern Europe to the United States created a backlash among native-born Americans who were largely Protestant and had a Western European heritage. Nativist organizations arose and sought to curb foreign immigration seeing them as the cause of crime and illiteracy that threatened the American democratic tradition.

MR. PATTEN: I am positive that the census figures of 1890 show that over one-fifth of our foreign-born criminals are illiterate. As I said a moment ago, the illiteracy test is not proposed as a means of excluding criminals, it is not offered as a substitute for existing laws debarring criminals, but as an additional selective and restrictive measure, and on the ground that, for an enlightened democracy such as we have, on the average, the man who can read and write is more likely to be better fitted for American citizenship than the one who can not. If the steamships can not bring illiterates they will bring literates. Of course an elementary-even a high school-education is no absolute guaranty against rascality. The test is proposed merely as another means of sifting out the more unassimilative aliens. It would seem, as Commissioner-General Sargent argued, that the man who can read, write, and figure must necessarily be better equipped for the struggle for existence-better prepared for American citizenship, and more likely to take up with our standards and ideals, else our whole public-school system is wrong. There are of course individual cases of illiterate persons making excellent citizens, but statistics show, as one would expect, that it is the illiterate who generally has criminal propensities, is averse to country life, settles down in the crowded quarters, takes no permanent interest in the country, lacks a knowledge of a trade, has lower standards of life, a less ambition to seek a better—

MR. K†STERMANN. He may not have had any chance to learn.

MR. PATTEN. That is true, but the public-school system, forms of government, and other institutions are reflections of capacities, characteristics, etc., of people—

MR. K†STERMANN. A good many countries do not offer the opportunities that we offer.

MR. SABATH. How many of those that are employed, we will say, in building the railroads and in the mines can read and write? It is not absolutely necessary that a man should be a scholar, is it, to develop our country, to develop our farms, and to build our railroads? . . .

MR. K†STERMANN. You, as the paid agent of the Immigration Restriction League, seem to be very anxious to have immigrants have proper accommodations and quarters, while the purpose of your league is to exclude them as much as possible and to make it unnecessary to have any immigrant stations?

MR. PATTEN. I beg pardon, but the object of the Immigration Restriction League and of the American Purity Federation is not exclusion, except as to undesirables. Each stands for certain exclusions and restrictions, but neither is opposed to immigration per se. I do not believe an increase in the "head tax," or rather steamship per capita tax, to $10 would increase the steerage rates, and consequently as I do not believe there is a bit of restriction even in it. I think as Mr. Gardner, of this committee, has ably argued in the House, that it would have to be put up to $25 or $50 in order to compel the steamship companies to charge as much or more to this country than they charge to other countries to which they are running and thus materially affect the number coming here. The present rates are from $5 to $65 less than to South America and South Australia. I have considerable data from the steamship companies on that point, and feel quite certain of my conclusions. Now, in order to restrict you would have to make the steamship tax $40 or $50, in my opinion, before the transportation companies which are now charging "all the traffic will bear," would raise their rates sufficiently to deter any number of immigrants from coming.

MR. K†STERMANN. You want to go step by step and eventually reach that point?

MR. PATTEN. That is not the controlling idea or motive with me or the public-spirited organizations I represent, I am sure; and if I could show you the minutes of the meetings of the executive committees, you would find that they have never advocated this increased tax for that purpose whatever the members may think individually or the organizations may do after the illiteracy test becomes a law. The most selective and restrictive measure which the Immigration Restriction League of Boston and the Purity Federation have advocated has been the illiteracy test. I do not believe you can find in their private records or public utterances or in their pamphlets anything to the contrary—
-

MR. K†STERMANN. I should like to refer to one of the pamphlets issued by the League wherein it is stated that the reason so few children were found in American families was simply because they did not want those poor children, if born, exposed to the children of the immigrants, that they do not want them to come together. That is the spirit of your League?

MR. PATTEN. I beg pardon, Mr. KŸstermann, I think if you will look at that pamphlet you will find that that is an article or quotation from an author of international reputation, the late Gen. Francis A. Walker, president of the Massachusetts Institute of Technology and the chief of two United States censuses, who made a very close and thorough statistical study of the question.

MR. K†STERMANN. They were very anxious to quote it. I do not care who said it, they had it in their own pamphlet.

MR. PATTEN. You will remember that the investigations of the industrial commission bore out General Walker's conclusions; for it concluded: "It is a hasty assumption which holds that immigration during the nineteenth century has increased the total population" of the United States. The point being that recent foreign immigration has been a substitution for rather than an addition to our population, in the manner in which your statement indicated. Census statistics show that the population of the South has increased faster out of its own loins alone than has the population of the North out of its loins and from foreign immigration, both together.

MR. SABATH. You are referring to the colored population of the South?

MR. PATTEN. I am referring to the population of the South, either or both, colored and uncolored.

MR. SABATH. Just put in the word "colored."

MR. PATTEN. You can take it either white or black, or both. I think the census will show that the average increase in the native birth rate in the South has been about 30 per cent per decade, whereas in the North it has fallen off to almost nothing, as Walker and the industrial commission point out exclusively in the very States, counties, and localities where recent foreign immigration has competed. There is, for instance, no place in this country where you will find so many old maids, bachelors, late marriages, small families, and so much "race suicide" as you will find in the very towns and communities of the Northeast to which is destined fully 90 per cent of the present influx. I am speaking of the masses, and not of the so-called "flower of society" which is small and dies off everywhere.

There are a number of factors, but the cause of causes, for many reasons, is the enormous inflow and efflux of aliens with lower standards and different ideals. It is the character of the present immigration, the fact that about three-fourths are unmarried male adults, that the bulk comes without any visible means of support, ignorant of our conditions, lacking a knowledge of our language, illiterate, and unused to self-government and self-care; for instance, last year one-fourth of those coming did not have money enough to prepay their passage to this country, and almost one-third of the adults could not read and write. They were unable to speak our language. Less than 10 per cent of them had ever been here before. They were unacquainted with our conditions, and had to find some kind of work at almost any wage, and thus in certain northeast labor centers subjected workers to a cutthroat, ruinous competition, which seems to need protection. They come as birds of passage, about half of those who came have gone back during the last ten years, and have gone back with large savings-"Grasshopper immigrants," Editor John Temple Graves calls them.

1. What immigration policy did Patten claim the American Purity Federation proposes?
2. What impact did Patten claim the current immigration policy has had on the American population?

21-6   Jane Addams, Twenty Years at Hull House (1910)

Based on a similar movement in England, settlement houses arose in American cities in the late nine-teenth century to address various social problems connected to immigration and urbanization. Among others, the settlement houses attracted middle-class, college educated women who had no other employment outlet. Jane Addams founded the most famous settlement house, Hull House in Chicago, where she and others tried to help European immigrants adapt to their new situations.

This paper is an attempt to analyze the motives which underlie a movement based, not only upon conviction, but upon gen-uine emotion, wherever educated young people are seeking an outlet for that sentiment of universal brotherhood, which the best spirit of our times is forcing from an emotion into a motive. These young people accomplish little toward the solution of this social problem, and bear the brunt of being cultivated into unnourished, oversensitive lives. They have been shut off from the common labor by which they live which is a great source of moral and physical health. They feel a fatal want of harmony between their theory and their lives, a lack of coordination between thought and action. I think it is hard for us to realize how seriously many of them are taking to the notion of human brotherhood, how eagerly they long to give tan-gible expression to the democratic ideal. These young men and women, longing to socialize their democracy, are animated by certain hopes which may be thus loosely formulated: that if in a democratic country nothing can be permanently achieved save through the masses of people, it will be impossible to establish a higher political life than the people them-selves crave; that it is difficult to see how the notion of a higher civic life can be fostered save through common intercourse; that the blessings which we associate with a life of refinement and cultivation can be made universal and must be made uni-versal if they are to be permanent; that the good we secure for ourselves is precarious and uncertain, is floating in mid-air, until it is secured for all of us and incorporated into our common life. It is easier to state these hopes than to formulate the line of motives, which I believe to constitute the trend of the subjective pressure toward the Settlement. There is something primordial about these motives, but I am perhaps overbold in designating them as a great desire to share the race life. . . .

We have in America a fast-growing number of cultivated young people who have no recognized outlet for their active faculties. They hear constantly of the great social maladjustment, but no way is provided for them to change it, and their uselessness hangs about them heavily. . . . These young people have had advantages of college, of European travel, and of economic study, but they are sustaining this shock of inaction. They have pet phrases, and they tell you that the things that make us all alike are stronger than the things that make us different. They say that all men are united by needs and sympathies far more permanent and radical than anything that temporarily divides them and sets them in oppo-sition to each other. If they affect art, they say that the decay in artistic expression is due to the decay in ethics, that art when shut away from the human interests and from the great mass of humanity is self-destructive. They tell their elders with all the bitterness of youth that if they expect success from them in business or politics or in whatever lines their ambi-tion for them has run, they must let them consult all of humanity; that they must let them find out what the people want and how they want it. It is only the stronger young people, however, who formulate this. Many of them dissipate their energies in so-called enjoyment. Others not content with that, go on studying and go back to college for their second degrees; not that they are especially fond of study, but because they want something definite to do, and their powers have been trained in the direction of mental accumulation. Many are buried beneath this mental accumulation with low-ered vitality and discontent. . . .

The Settlement . . . is an experimental effort to aid the solution of the social and industrial problems which are engendered by the modern conditions of life in a great city. It insists that these problems are not confined to any one por-tion of a city. It is an attempt to relieve, at the same time, the overaccumulation at one end of society and the destitution at the other, but it assumes that this overaccumulation and destitution is most sorely felt in the things that pertain to social and educational advantages. From its very nature it can stand for no political or social propaganda. It must, in a sense, give the warm welcome of an inn to all such propaganda, if perchance one of them be found an angel. The one thing to be dreaded in the Settlement is that it lose its flexibility, its power of quick adaptation, its readiness to change its methods as its environment may demand. It must be open to conviction and must have a deep and abiding sense of tolerance. It must be hospitable and ready for experiment. It should demand from its residents a scientific patience in the accumulation of facts and the steady holding of their sympathies as one of the best instruments for that accumulation. It must be grounded in a philosophy whose foundation is on the solidarity of the human race, a philosophy which will not waver when the race hap-pens to be represented by a drunken woman or an idiot boy. Its residents must be emptied of all conceit of opinion and all self-assertion, and ready to arouse and interpret the public opinion of their neighborhood. They must be content to live qui-etly side by side with their neighbors, until they grow into a sense of relationship and mutual interests. Their neighbors are held apart by differences of race and language which the residents can more easily overcome. They are bound to see the needs of their neighborhood as a whole, to furnish data for legislation, and to use their influence to secure it. In short, res-idents are pledged to devote themselves to the duties of good citizenship and to the arousing of the social energies which too largely lie dormant in every neighborhood given over to industrialism. They are bound to regard the entire life of their city as organic, to make an effort to unify it, and to protest against its over-differentiation.

It is always easy to make all philosophy point one particular moral and all history adorn one particular tale, but I may be forgiven the reminder that the best speculative philosophy sets forth the solidarity of the human race; that the highest moralists have taught that without the advance and improvement of the whole, no man can hope for any lasting improvement in his own moral or material individual condition; and that the subjective necessity for Social Settlements is therefore identical with that necessity, which urges us on toward social and individual salvation.

1. What situation does Addams claim many young men and women face?
2. What are the characteristics of these young men and women?
3. How did the settlement movement offer a solution?

21-7   Theodore Roosevelt, from *The New Nationalism* (1910)

Municipal reform was a major issue of the Progressive movement. New types of city government were implemented to increase efficiency and eliminate corruption, including the commission form of government.

Practical equality of opportunity for all citizens, when we achieve it, will have two great results. First, every man will have a fair chance to make of himself all that in him lies; to reach the highest point to which his capacities, unassisted by special privilege of his own and unhampered by the special privilege of others, can carry him, and to get for himself and his family substantially what he has earned. Second, equality of opportunity means that the commonwealth will get from every citizen the highest service of which he is capable. No man who carries the burden of the special privileges of another can give to the commonwealth that service to which it is fairly entitled. . . .

Now, this means that our government, national and state, must be freed from the sinister influence or control of special interests. Exactly as the special interests of cotton and slavery threatened our political integrity before the Civil War, so now the great special business interests too often control and corrupt the men and methods of government for their own profit. We must drive the special interests out of politics. That is one of our tasks today. . . .

The true friend of property, the true conservative, is he who insists that property shall be the servant and not the master of the commonwealth; who insists that the creature of man's making shall be the servant and not the master of the man who made it. The citizens of the United States must effectively control the mighty commercial forces which they have themselves called into being. . . .

It has become entirely clear that we must have government supervision of the capitalization, not only of the public service corporations, including, particularly, railways, but of all corporations doing an interstate business. I do not wish to see the nation forced into the ownership of the railways if it can possibly be avoided, and the only alternative is thoroughgoing and effective regulation, which shall be based on a full knowledge of all the facts, including a physical valuation of property. . . .

Combinations in industry are the result of an imperative economic law which cannot be repealed by political legislation. The effort at prohibiting all combination has substantially failed. The way out lies, not in attempting to prevent such combinations, but in completely controlling them in the interest of the public welfare.

1. What benefits did Roosevelt claim practical equality of opportunity would bring to the individual and the nation?
2. What hampered realizing this equality and how could government provide a solution?

21-8   Walker Percy, "Birmingham under the Commission Plan" (1911)

Municipal reform was a major issue of the Progressive movement. New types of city government were implemented to increase efficiency and eliminate corruption, including the commission form of government.

Commission government for the city of Birmingham became effective April 10, 1911. Prior to that time the city government was vested in the mayor and thirty-two aldermen. These aldermen were chosen from different wards in the city and served without legal compensation. For several years prior to the adoption of commission government, the thoughtful, patriotic citizens of Birmingham had regarded, with growing distrust and apprehension the operations of the unpaid ward aldermanic system. Birmingham has always been fortunate in having some honest, intelligent, public-spirited men upon its board of aldermen, but the system, inherently bad, bore in Birmingham its usual fruit of incapacity, unwieldiness, clique, domination, individual greed and graft and the taint of corruption. The leaders in city politics, and the bosses, in and out of office, feeling sure of their position, daily became bolder, more brazen and more contemptuous of decent public opinion.

Believing that with the increasing wealth and importance of the community and the resulting increase in the importance of public contracts handled by the board of aldermen corruption would increase and efficiency diminish; realizing that with the increase in the duties and responsibilities resting upon the board of aldermen it would become more and more difficult to secure good men to fill the positions; and believing that no permanent improvement could be had except by a change in the system of government, I appeared before the state legislature with the avowed intention of procuring the enactment of commission government for the City of Birmingham. In a city primary, shortly preceding the convening of the legislature, the democratic voters of Birmingham declared in favor of commission government by a vote of about ten to one.

Popular sentiment in Birmingham had crystallized so strongly and had been manifested so plainly for commission government, and the interest in this new form of city government had so developed over the state, that there was no open, organized opposition to the passage of legislation on this subject, and the commission bill applying to cities of the size of Birmingham was approved by the governor on the thirty-first of March, 1911.

In drafting the Birmingham bill, I derived more benefit from the Des Moines charter than from any other legislation; and yet, in a few important respects, our commission plan differs from any other. Manifestly, commission government has its fundamentals in the concentration of power and responsibility, coupled with the payment of reasonably adequate compensation. Birmingham has three commissioners. I believe the small number preferable, because of the increased honor and responsibility, and because the smaller number permits, with due regard to economy, the payment of better salaries. Our commissioners, receiving seven thousand dollars each, are the best paid commissioners I know of. . . .

In the election of commissioners, every safeguard that I could devise is thrown around the election to prevent the use of money or, what might be more dangerous, the building up of a machine by the large power of patronage. All city employees are prohibited by law from endeavoring to influence any voter in favor of or against any candidate for commissioner. The Birmingham bill does not permit voters to initiate legislation. I doubt the wisdom or practicability of the initiative in either city or state government. Our law authorizes a referendum to the voters on nothing but the granting of franchises to public utility corporations. Activities in procuring such franchises have been one of the frequent causes of municipal corruption. No referendum is provided on the refusal of such franchises, because the possibilities of corruption and evil on this account are manifestly insignificant. The law contains a provision for elections for the recall of commissioners on petitions signed by three thousand voters. The great power concentrated in the hands of a few men made the recall seem to me most valuable as a check. I want to say frankly, and with regret, that there has always been serious doubt in my mind as to the constitutionality of the recall provision under our state constitution. . . .

Commission government in Birmingham has been an unqualified business success. With the appointment of our commissioners there dawned a new day in our civic progress. We are realizing the fruition of long cherished hopes. The same sort of fidelity, honesty, energy, loyalty and intelligence is being displayed by these public employees that we have been accustomed to expect from private employees. A dollar of city money in Birmingham can buy as much in labor, service, and material as a dollar of individual money. When the commissioners entered upon their duties, Birmingham's floating debt under aldermanic government had been piling up with alarming rapidity. A favored bank had selfishly dominated the city's finances, and the other banking institutions of the city had felt that it was useless for them to consider, or endeavor to aid in, the city's financial problems. Practically all of the Birmingham bankers were enthusiastic believers in commission government, and have rallied in loyal support of the new administration. . . .

The Birmingham commissioners issue monthly a compact summary of their proceedings for the previous month, showing in the simplest and plainest terms all receipts and disbursements of the city and all transactions of the least importance. The first aim of the commissioners was to reduce the current expenses of the city to fit its income. All sinecures were abolished. Operating expenses were cut to the bone, and the regular operating expenses of the city, in the first twenty days the commission was in existence, were reduced in the annual sum of ninety-four thousand five hundred and thirty-four dollars, without decreasing the efficiency of the city government. While the Birmingham commission has resorted to every intelligent economy, it has not hesitated to spend money so as to secure better results and increased efficiency.

The commission has abandoned the use of horses in its fire department and purchased at one time sixteen motor-driven engines for its fire department at a cost of sixty-nine thousand three hundred and twenty-eight dollars. With its large industrial population, one of the most pressing needs of Birmingham is adequate parks and playgrounds; and at the request of the commissioners, some of the most capable and public-spirited men in the community have agreed to serve without compensation as park commissioners for the purpose of devising plans for a park system for the city. There is no "red tape" in the conduct of Birmingham's city affairs. The commissioners devote all of their time to the public business, and a crippled negro mendicant can secure an audience with the commission as easily as a street car magnate.

The work of city government is divided by the commissioners into departments headed by the respective commissioners. Under the law the division into departments can be made and rearranged by the commissioners to suit themselves. But all important questions are passed upon by the entire commission and the recommendations of a commissioner as to his department are in no sense binding upon the board.

The continued success of the Birmingham commission will, of course, depend upon the character of its commissioners, but I confidently predict that in place of the scornful apathy and indifference which formerly characterized the selection of our aldermen, intelligent, public-spirited, enthusiastic and organized interest will be displayed by the best people of Birmingham in maintaining the personnel of the Birmingham commission at its present high standard.

1. Why did Birmingham institute a commission form of city government?
2. How had the commission form of government benefited Birmingham?

21-9   Helen M. Todd, "Getting Out the Vote" (1911)

The movement for woman suffrage began in the mid-nineteenth century. By the early 1900s, several western states had granted women the right to vote, but no success was achieved on the national level. Woman's suffrage groups maintained efforts to pass a constitutional amendment giving women the right to vote.

On a June day last year, six or eight insurgent women met in the library of the Chicago Women's Club and decided to add the Sixteenth Amendment to the Constitution of the United States. . . .

It would be untrue to leave the impression that we found this fraternal feeling toward woman suffrage ready made. It was only achieved in many instances by effort and experience.

The men were sometimes obviously thankful their women folks were incapable of going gallivanting through the country making speeches. Often, as our automobile, covered with banners, stopped in front of the blacksmith shop or on the street corner where we were scheduled to speak, we realized that the temper of the audience was not one of unmixed approval; but they were interested, and above all they were there. The rest was for us to do. Every type of man was represented in these down-State audiences, and every kind of vehicle. The stores were left in charge of whoever was unfortunate enough to have to stay, generally the errand boy, and the rest of the village turned out to "hear the women talk."

We opened our plea for women by showing our audience that the mother and wife could not long protect herself and her children unless she had a vote. That the milk the city mother gave her baby; the school her children were educated in; the purity of the water they drank; the prices she paid for meat and clothes; the very wages her husband received; the sanitary and moral condition of the streets her children passed through were all matters of politics. When once we had clearly established the fact that women wanted to vote to protect their homes we had won a large part of our audience. . .

When we reached Warren the place was decorated with flags and yellow banners. The big street meeting had already gathered. "Let me take up all the time," Mrs. McCulloch said, "because we have only a thirty minutes' stop here." "With all your banners and welcome," she said, getting energetically upon the seat of the automobile, "the man that you have sent to represent you in the Legislature has knifed our Suffrage bill every time it came up. I am just going to tell you your Representative's history and ask you to keep him at home," and she did.

Mixed with the arraignment of Representative Gray was the pathos and wit of the story of the struggles of the women of Illinois in the Legislature to protect its children. When she had finally finished the story of Mr. Gray's part in this struggle you could feel the audience with her. They came crowding about the machine. "All right, we will get somebody else; we never knew about all this. We cannot do much for you ladies because he has got another year to serve," was suggested. This seemed final, and just as the automobile was beginning to move, a crowd of men and women pushing forward a central figure that was half laughing and half resisting bore down upon us and called for the chauffeur to stop. "Here he is!" they shouted. "We went to his house and got him. You just ask him whether he is going to stand for that Suffrage bill this fall and we'll stand back and see what he says. This is Representative Gray." Mrs. McCulloch who had become acquainted with him in the Legislature looked coldly at him. The Rev. Kate Hughes, who had also had the pleasure of meeting him in the same place, sniffed, I might almost say snorted, audibly and looked absently over his head. Dr. Blount greeted him with friendly interest as one would a sinner in whom there were possibilities of repentance. And I, being nearest on the outside, hastily assumed my most ingratiating and feminine air and held out my hand. "Well, Mr. Gray," I said, "will you promise us to stand for our Woman's Suffrage bill this time?" "It looks as if I would have to," he said, disengaging himself with difficulty from the press of the crowd in order to take off his hat. "I have always thought women were about the best things there were in the world, but I never thought you were so in earnest about this voting. If you have really set your hearts on it why there is nothing for me to do but give in. I can't fight against a woman's campaign. I'm for you," he shouted as we drove off amid the laughter and cheers of the crowd.

On the Fourth of July we spoke in the city square. Truths, familiar to city men through a prevalence of speakers, are sometimes new to a down-State audience. We told them that in a country that boasted of its representative government half the population of women were not represented at all, that they were classed with the criminal and insane even though they had given their sons to make a Fourth of July possible. When we had finished, an old man pushed his way to the automobile and gave us some money. He had an old, weather-beaten face and instead of week-day overalls wore a stiff suit of "store" clothes in honor of the Fourth; his trousers guiltless of any crease looked like two sections of stovepipe. So serious and almost forbidding was the expression that we waited for him to speak before making any overtures of friendship. Accustomed as we were to the more mobile city face, we often could not tell from the faces of our audience what they were feeling. This old man might have been going to say, "I hate what you are saying; I wish you would go away," but he handed us a two-dollar bill and leaning over the machine squeezed each of our hands with a grip that brought tears to our eyes. "I would just give anything in the hull world if my wife had been well enough to come along, but she's been poorly all this winter and couldn't stand the long drive. I'm giving you this two dollars for her. The idea," he continued, gazing angrily at us, "of a woman like my wife bein' put along with imbeciles and criminals. Why, she came out with me from New York in the pioneer days when Illinois was nothing but woods and bears and swamps and we drove the hull way in a mover's wagon and took our three children too." . . .

Power and confidence are as valuable assets to a woman as a man; and as one of our party remarked, it is not only the people we have reached on this trip that matters, but we have learned how to do it.

After all, with women, isn't it largely a question of learning how?

There is a comradeship which only comes from working together for a common cause. Although most men know the pleasure of this, comparatively few women have experienced it, and although we were as tired as any pioneer women who had crossed the country in a mover's wagon after this last meeting and our week's campaign, yet our party was loath to break up.

It had been inspiring to depend upon the honesty, personal kindness, the spirit of fair play and neighborliness, the quick response to anyone in sorrow or need, which were characteristics of our country audiences. And we lingered taking to each other and to members of the crowd who were seeing us home until it was very late when I entered the farm-house where I was to spend my last night down State.

Late as it was, the old bed-ridden mother was awake and called softly for me to come in and tell her about the meetin'. "I knew it would be a fine meetin'," she said. "I had my bed turned 'round to the window. I seen the wagons coming in from out of town since morning. I knew you'd be leaving for Chicago early, and I just thought I would wait up for you so's I could hear all about it and tell Lucy. You see," she explained, "Daughter Lucy and the hired girl couldn't both go and leave me alone, since I have had my stroke. Lucy, she was born and brought up to woman's rights, bein' my daughter; but our hired girl's new in our family and she's real ignorant about it. So Lucy she felt it was her duty to send our girl to get converted, and stay to home herself. I'm a believer," she said, "and Maggie ain't. But Lucy she felt terrible put out about it though she didn't let on to me of course, and I made up my mind I'd ask you to just say over what you said so's I could tell it to her. I had hoped," she added, "that I'd last to see the day when women would vote in Illinois, but if Susan B. Anthony can die without seein' it, I guess I can. It's a comfort to see you young women back keepin' up the same fight that we started back East when we was young and spry. It makes us feel as if we hadn't educated you for nothing, for we did educate you. 'What, educate shes!' the men said when we wanted the girls to go to school. 'What's the use spendin' money on educatin' shes?' Well I guess we've showed them what the use was. I've seen that done anyhow." . . .

No words can better express the soul of the woman's movement, lying back of the practical cry of "Votes for Women," better than this sentence which had captured the attention of both Mother Jones and the hired girl, "Bread for all, and Roses too." Not at once; but woman is the mothering element in the world and her vote will go toward helping forward the time when life's Bread, which is home, shelter and security, and the Roses of life, music, education, nature and books, shall be the heritage of every child that is born in the country, in the government of which she has a voice.

There will be no prisons, no scaffolds, no children in factories, no girls driven on the street to earn their bread, in the day when there shall be "Bread for all, and Roses too."

To help to make such a civilization possible is the meaning of "Votes for Women." It was the power of this idea which sent the women of Illinois "down State" on their automobile campaign.

1. *What arguments did the supporters of woman suffrage use to promote a constitutional amendment giving women the right to vote?*
2. *What tactics did the supporters of the amendment use and how successful were they? Why were they successful?*

21-10   Louis Brandeis, Other People's Money and How the Bankers Use It (1913)

The movement for woman suffrage began in the mid-nineteenth century. By the early 1900s, several western states had granted women the right to vote, but no success was achieved on the national level. Woman's suffrage groups maintained efforts to pass a constitutional amendment giving women the right to vote.

The dominant element in our financial oligarchy is the investment banker. Associated banks, trust companies and life insurance companies are his tools. Controlled railroads, public service and industrial corporations are his subjects. Though properly but middlemen, these bankers bestride as masters of America's business world, so that practically no large enterprise can be undertaken successfully without their participation or approval. These bankers are, of course, able men possessed of large fortunes; but the most potent factor in their control of business is not the possession of extraordinary ability or huge wealth. The key to their power is Combination-concentration intensive and comprehensive-advancing on three distinct lines:

First: There is the obvious consolidation of banks and trust companies; the less obvious affiliations-through stock-holdings, voting trusts and interlocking directorates-of banking institutions which are not legally connected; and the joint transactions, gentlemen's agreements, and "banking ethics" which eliminate competition among the investment bankers.

Second: There is the consolidation of railroads into huge systems, the large combinations of public service corporations and the formation of industrial trusts, which, by making businesses so "big" that local, independent banking concerns cannot alone supply the necessary funds, has created dependence upon the associated New York bankers.

But combination, however intensive, along these lines only, could not have produced the Money Trust-another and more potent factor of combination was added.

Third: Investment bankers, like J. P. Morgan & Co., dealers in bonds, stocks and notes, encroached upon the functions of the three other classes of corporations with which their business brought them into contact. They became the directing power in railroads, public service and industrial companies through which our great business operations are conducted-the makers of bonds and stocks. They became the directing power in the life insurance companies, and other corporate reservoirs of the people's savings-the buyers of bonds and stocks. They became the directing power also in banks and trust companies-the depositaries of the quick capital of the country-the life blood of business, with which they and others carried on their operations. Thus four distinct functions, each essential to business, and each exercised, originally, by a distinct set of men, became united in the investment banker. It is to this union of business functions that the existence of the Money Trust is mainly due.

The development of our financial oligarchy followed, in this respect, lines with which the history of political despotism has familiarized us: -usurpation, proceeding by gradual encroachment rather than by violent acts; subtle and often long-concealed concentration of distinct functions, which are beneficent when separately administered, and dangerous only when combined in the same persons. It was by processes such as these that Caesar Augustus became master of Rome. The makers of our own Constitution had in mind like dangers to our political liberty when they provided so carefully for the separation of governmental powers. . . .

The goose that lays golden eggs has been considered a most valuable possession. But even more profitable is the privilege of taking the golden eggs laid by somebody else's goose. The investment bankers and their associates now enjoy that privilege. They control the people through the people's own money. If the bankers' power were commensurate only with their wealth, they would have relatively little influence on American business. Vast fortunes like those of the Astors are no doubt regrettable. They are inconsistent with democracy. They are unsocial. And they seem peculiarly unjust when they represent largely unearned increment. But the wealth of the Astors does not endanger political or industrial liberty. It is insignificant in amount as compared with the aggregate wealth of America, or even of New York City. It lacks significance largely because its owners have only the income from their own wealth. The Astor wealth is static. The wealth of the Morgan associates is dynamic. The power and the growth of power of our financial oligarchs comes from wielding the savings and quick capital of others. In two of the three great life insurance companies the influence of J. P. Morgan & Co. and their associates is exerted without any individual investment by them whatsoever. Even in the Equitable, where Mr. Morgan bought an actual majority of all the outstanding stock, his investment amounts to little more than one-half of one per cent of the assets of the company. The fetters which bind the people are forged from the people's own gold. . . .

The fact that industrial monopolies arrest development is more serious even than the direct burden imposed through extortionate prices. But the most harm-bearing incident of the trusts is their promotion of financial concentration. Industrial trusts feed the money trust. Practically every trust created has destroyed the financial independence of some communities and of many properties; for it has centered the financing of a large part of whole lines of business in New York, and this usually with one of a few banking houses. This is well illustrated by the Steel Trust, which is a trust of trusts;

that is, the Steel Trust combines in one huge holding com-pany the trusts previously formed in the different branches of the steel business. Thus the Tube Trust combined 17 tube mills, located in 16 different cities, scattered over 5 states and owned by 13 different companies. The wire trust combined 19 mills; the sheet steel trust 26; the bridge and structural trust 27; and the tin plate trust 36; all scattered similarly over many states. Finally these and other companies were formed into the United States Steel Corporation, combining 228 companies in all, located in 127 cities and towns, scattered over 18 states. Before the combinations were effected, nearly every one of these companies was owned largely by those who managed it, and had been financed, to a large extent, in the place, or in the state, in which it was located.

1. *What role did Brandeis claim the investment banking industry played in American society?*
2. *Through what means did the investment banking industry pursue its development and how did this pursuit affected American society?*

21-11   Woodrow Wilson, from *The New Freedom* (1913)

This excerpt is from Woodrow Wilson's book published after the campaign, The New Freedom: A Call for the Emancipation of the Generous Energies of a People. Wilson believed federal power should be controlled and limited.

The doctrine that monopoly is inevitable and that the only course open to the people of the United States is to submit to and regulate it found a champion during the campaign of 1912 in the new party or branch of the Republican Party, founded under the leadership of Mr. Roosevelt, with the conspicuous aid,-I mention him with no satirical intention, but merely to set the facts down accurately,-of Mr. George W. Perkins, organizer of the Steel Trust and the Harvester Trust, and with the support of patriotic, conscientious and high-minded men and women of the land. The fact that its acceptance of monopoly was a feature of the new party platform from which the attention of the generous and just was diverted by the charm of a social program of great attractiveness to all concerned for the amelioration of the lot of those who suffer wrong and privation, and the further fact that, even so, the platform was repudiated by the majority of the nation, render it no less necessary to reflect on the party in the country's history. It may be useful, in order to relieve of the minds of many from an error of no small magnitude, to consider now, the heat of a presidential contest being past, exactly what it was that Mr. Roosevelt proposed.

Mr. Roosevelt attached to his platform some very splendid suggestions as to noble enterprises which we ought to undertake for the uplift of the human race; . . . If you have read the trust plank in that platform as often as I have read it, you have found it very long, but very tolerant. It did not anywhere condemn monopoly, except in words; its essential meaning was that the trusts have been bad and must be made to be good. You know that Mr. Roosevelt long ago classified trusts for us as good and bad, and he said that he was afraid only of the bad ones. Now he does not desire that there should be any more of the bad ones, but proposes that they should all be made good by discipline, directly applied by a commission of executive appointment. All he explicitly complains of is lack of publicity and lack of fairness; not the exercise of power, for throughout that plank the power of the great corporations is accepted as the inevitable consequence of the modern organization of industry. All that it is proposed to do is to take them under control and deregulation.

The fundamental part of such a program is that the trusts shall be recognized as a permanent part of our economic order, and that the government shall try to make trusts the ministers, the instruments, through which the life of this country shall be justly and happily developed on its industrial side. . . .

Shall we try to get the grip of monopoly away from our lives, or shall we not? Shall we withhold our hand and say monopoly is inevitable, that all we can do is to regulate it? Shall we say that all we can do is to put government in competition with monopoly and try its strength against it? Shall we admit that the creature of our own hands is stronger than we are? We have been dreading all along the time when the combined power of high finance would be greater than the power of the government.

1. *What political party suggested that monopolies were inevitable?*
2. *How did that party propose to deal with this inevitability?*

21-12 Herbert Croly, Progressive Democracy (1914)

The Progressive movement emerged in the early twentieth century as a broad-based reform movement founded primarily by urban, middle-class reformers. They believed that government could be mobilized to solve the ills of society, Herbert Croly was an early leader of the Progressive movement. In the document, he indicates a deep-rooted change was occurring in American democracy.

While fully admitting that the transition may not be as abrupt as it seems, we have apparently been witnessing during the past year or two the end of one epoch and the beginning of another. A movement of public opinion, which believes itself to be and calls itself essentially progressive, has become the dominant formative influence in American political life.

The best evidence of the power of progressivism is the effect which its advent has had upon the prestige and the fortunes of political leaders of both parties. For the first time attractions and repulsions born of the progressive idea, are determining lines of political association. Until recently a man who wished actively and effectively to participate in political life had to be either a Democrat or a Republican; but now, although Republicanism and Democracy are still powerful political forces, the standing of a politician is determined quite as much by his relation to the progressive movement. The line of cleavage between progressives and non-progressives is fully as important as that between Democrats and Republicans. Political leaders, who have deserved well of their own party but who have offended the progressives, are retiring or are being retired from public life. Precisely what the outcome will be, no one can predict with any confidence; but one result seems tolerably certain. If the classification of the great majority of American voters into Democrats and Republicans is to endure, the significance of both Democracy and Republicanism is bound to be profoundly modified by the new loyalties and the new enmities created by the aggressive progressive intruder. . . .

The complexion, and to a certain extent even the features, of the American political countenance have profoundly altered. Political leaders still pride themselves upon their conservatism, but candid conservatives, in case they come from any other part of the country but the South, often pay for their candor by their early retirement. Conservatism has come to imply reaction. Its substantial utility is almost as much undervalued as that of radicalism formerly was. The whole group of prevailing political values has changed. Proposals for the regulation of public utility companies, which would then have been condemned as examples of administrative autocracy, are now accepted without serious public controversy. Plans of social legislation, which formerly would have been considered culpably "paternal," and, if passed at the solicitation of the labor unions, would have been declared unconstitutional by the courts, are now considered to be a normal and necessary exercise of the police power. Proposed alterations in our political mechanism, which would then have been appraised as utterly extravagant and extremely dangerous, are now being placed on the headlines of political programs and are being incorporated in state constitutions. In certain important respects the radicals of 1904 do not differ in their practical proposals from the conservatives of 1914. . . .

Thus by almost imperceptible degrees reform became insurgent and insurgency progressive. For the first time in four generations American conservatism was confronted by a pervasive progressivism, which began by being dangerously indignant and ended by being far more dangerously inquisitive. Just resentment is useful and indispensable while it lasts; but it cannot last long. If it is to persist, it must be transformed into a thoroughgoing curiosity which will not rest until it has discovered what the abuses mean, how they best can be remedied, and how intimately they are associated with temples and doctrines of the traditional political creed. The conservatives themselves have provoked this curiosity, and they must abide by its results.

Just here lies the difference between modern progressivism and the old reform. The former is coming to be remorselessly inquisitive and unscrupulously thorough. The latter never knew any need of being either inquisitive or thorough. The early political reformers confined their attention to local or to special abuses. Civil service reform furnishes a good example of their methods and their purposes. The spoils system was a very grave evil, which was a fair object of assault; but it could not be successfully attacked and really uprooted merely by placing subordinate public officials under the protection of civil service laws and boards. Such laws and boards might do something to prevent politicians from appropriating the minor offices; but as long as the major offices were the gifts of the political machines, and as long as no attempt was made to perfect expert administrative organization as a necessary instrument of democracy, the agitation for civil service reform remained fundamentally sterile. It was sterile, because it was negative and timid, and because its supporters were content with their early successes and did not grow with the growing needs of their own agitation. In an analogous way the movement towards municipal reform attained a sufficient following in certain places to be embarrassing to local political bosses; but as long as it was a non-partisan movement for "good government" its successes were fugitive and sterile. It did not become really effective until it became frankly partisan, and associated good municipal government with all sorts of changes in economic and political organization which might well be obnoxious to many excellent citizens. In these and other cases the early political reformers were not sufficiently thorough. They failed to carry their analysis of the prevailing evils far or deep enough, and in their choice of remedies they never got beyond the illusions that moral exhortation, legal prohibitions and independent voting constituted a sufficient cure for American political abuses. . . .

All this disconnected political and economic agitation had, however, a value of which the agitators themselves were not wholly conscious. Not only was the attitude of national self-satisfaction being broken down in spots, but the ineffectiveness of these local, spasmodic and restricted agitations had its effect on public opinion and prepared the way for a synthesis of the various phases of reform. When the wave of political "muck-raking" broke over the country, it provided a common bond, which tied reformers together. This bond consisted at first of the indignation which was aroused by the process of exposure; but it did not remain for long merely a feeling. As soon as public opinion began to realize that business exploitation had been allied with political corruption, and that the reformers were confronted, not by disconnected abuses, but by a perverted system, the inevitable and salutary inference began to be drawn. Just as business exploitation was allied with political corruption, so business reorganization must be allied with political reorganization. The old system must be confronted and superseded by a new system-the result of an alert social intelligence as well as an aroused individual conscience.

1. *According to Croly, what are the main differences between "modern progressivism" and "old reform"?*
2. *What connection does Croly make between business and politics?*

PART TWENTY-TWO
WORLD WAR ONE

22-1 The Great War

When war erupted in Europe in the summer of 1914, Americans and the American government immediately proclaimed their neutrality. Woodrow Wilson announced the United States would remain neutral in thought as well as in deed. As the war progressed, Americans wished to stay out of the conflict, even if they were uneasy about the events of the war as played out on foreign battlefields.

> **Source:** Francis Whiting Halsey, *The Literary Digest History of the World War* vol. IV (New York 1920), pp. 26–32.

Thus in the first two months of Germany's unrestricted and intensified submarine warfare—the period ending on March 31—several "overt acts" against the United States had been committed by her—in February, when the Cunarder *Laconia* was sunk and two Americans lost; in March when four American ships—the *Vigilancia,* the *City of Memphis, Illinois, and Healdton*—went down, involving the loss of several more American lives. Since the war began some twenty-five American ships had been sunk by the Teutonic powers, fifteen of them by submarines. On these and on belligerent passenger-ships, including the *Lusitania,* more than 230 Americans had perished—many of them women and children. When Congress assembled in special session on April 2, in response to the President's summons, the whole country was stirred to the depths by these acts of war and looked eagerly for a formal declaration by Congress that war existed with Germany. Congress had scarcely begun its session—indeed, President Wilson was on his way to the Capitol to read his address—when news was printed that another American ship, the freighter *Aztec,* had been torpedoed at the entrance to the English Channel, and that 28 of her crew were missing. Nothing at that time could have prevented a prompt declaration except a decision by Germany to discontinue her unrestricted submarine warfare, and that she failed to make. The Senate on April 4, by a vote of 82 to 6, the House on April 6, by a vote of 373 to 50 , passed the declaration.

Impressive scenes marked the assembling of Congress on April 2. Streets and public places in Washington were thronged with visitors, thousands of them clamorous for war; others, in considerable number pacifists, to whom no patient hearing was granted anywhere. One of the latter came from Massachusetts, and, in a corridor of the Senate wing of the Capitol, assaulted with ill-timed words Senator Lodge of that State, who speedily knocked him down. Outside the Capitol probably 50,000 citizens witnessed the arrival and departure of the President, and, during the delivery of his address, echoed with cheers the sounds of applause that came through the open windows of the Capitol. A squadron of cavalry had escorted the President along Pennsylvania Avenue, now brilliantly lighted, the hour being 8 P.M., while from every window fronting the avenue fluttered the national flag. The President entered the Capitol through troops of cavalry crowded within the shadow of the great white dome, the building elsewhere bathed in a flood of moonlight that brought out every feature of its architecture and from the top of which the figure of Liberty flourished the flag and a torch of gold.

No more thrilling scene was ever witnessed in Congress than the one now seen. The only persons who did not join in storms of applause that broke out at frequent intervals were the Entente and neutral diplomats who were restrained by official etiquette from cheering, and Senators La Follette of Wisconsin, Stone of Missouri, and Lane of Oregon, three of the "wilful men" who, by filibustering on March 4 in the previous Congress, had helped to defeat the Armed Neutrality Bill. Visitors in the galleries, who are ordinarily prohibited from participating in any demonstration made on the floor of the House, chorused in with ringing patriotic cheers, waved their hand flags vigorously and provided every other form of indorsement that was possible. During the tense thirty-eight minutes occupied by the President in reading his address, there occurred scenes the like of which probably had never been seen in any modern legislative chamber. No one could have fully realized that the nation still had two political parties. Observers felt that the President, while reading his address, did not know how thoroughly the whole country not only sympathized with him in the great crisis, but voiced its sincere determination to support him, until he had heard the cheers that greeted a later passage as he delivered it slowly, almost haltingly at times, but with deep emphasis, as follows:

"With a profound sense of the solemn and even tragical character of the step I am taking, and of the grave responsibilities which it involves, but in unhesitating obedience to what I deem my constitutional duty, I advise that the Congress declare the recent course of the Imperial German Government to be in fact nothing less than war against the Government and People of the United States; that it formally accept the status of belligerent which has thus been thrust upon it; and that it take immediate steps not only to put the country in a more thorough state of defense, but also to exert all its power and employ all its resources to bring the Government of the German Empire to terms and end the war."

After the President had completed his address, Senator Lodge went forward and shook his hand warmly, saying: "Mr. President, you have exprest in the loftiest manner possible the sentiments of the American people." Every one of the Supreme Court Judges rose to his feet. Chief Justice White smiled and vigorously clapped his hands, as did Justices Pitney and Clarke. As Lincoln said that this Republic could not exist half slave and half free, so in this issue had man perceived that the world could not exist half German and half free. We, as well as the Entente, had now for our task to put an end to the barbarous doctrine of a superior race and to the assertion that German necessity was above all law. For thirty-two months German armies had been going up and down Europe destroying the beautiful, abusing the weak, murdering the helpless, transforming some of the most beautiful places and regions in the world into deserts. Germans had harnessed science to barbarism and called it "Kultur." They had joined organization to ruthlessness and called it "civilization." The United States could not now pause until Poland had been restored, Serbia liberated, Roumania freed, Belgium returned to her own people, Alsace-Lorraine reunited to France, conspicuous symbols of German tyranny now to be obliterated. All these tyrannies were the handiwork of Germany written on the face of Europe. This country had enlisted, not in a war against the German people, but against a doctrine which the German people held to, and with the German people there could be no peace so long as they held to that doctrine. Our action was regarded as the natural sequence of Lexington.

Berlin, on receipt of the President's address, still declared that there would be no change in the German submarine policy, not even if Congress should adopt the President's views. Germany, moreover, would not declare war, nor would she take any step to wage war against the United States. The submarine war would be continued, as it had been conducted since February 1, but this, officials asserted, was not directed more against the United States than against any other neutral. Nor would there be any change in the treatment of American citizens in Germany, who still had the same freedom as all other neutrals.

A great storm of applause was evoked in the British House of Commons when first mention was made of the address. From the Prime Minister down, all ranks were stirred to the depths. They believed the President had given to Democracy an impetus which would carry it far toward shortening a war which was threatening to drag practically the whole world down to the point of ruin. No other subject was discust in the lobby of Parliament. The United States had gained immensely in prestige, had won a lasting friend and would now have a seat at the peace table. Her voice would be heard in all the Allied councils over post-war trade relations. All agreed that the war had been greatly shortened—not so much by the material assistance America would give, important as that was, as by the blow she had given to the morale of the German people. To Frenchmen, America's intervention appeared as the third big Allied event of the war. The battle of the Marne was the first; the Russian revolution was the second, and America's action the third. It was even greater than the stand made by France at Verdun.

German papers commented on the message bitterly. The *Hamburger Fremdenblatt*, in a leading article, described it as "opening in untruth, continuing in hypocrisy, and ending in blasphemy." The Berlin *Morgen Post* remarked that "just as the whole policy of this professor was insincere, insidious, and malicious from the beginning, so also was this speech with which he tried to plunge and had plunged his people into war." Perhaps no part of the message caused greater annoyance to the German press than the careful differentiation made between America's hostility to the German Government as distinct from its hostility to the German people. The semi-official Berlin *Lokal-Anzeiger* thought it "impossible that the ruler of a nation who has at his disposal the reports of his Ambassador and numerous other sources of information regarding the events of the early part of August, 1914, in Berlin, should really believe that this war was not begun with the assent of the German people."

The *Hannoverische Courier* was inclined to doubt the President's veracity, and even went so far as to suggest a similar thought to its readers by heading its editorial "Wilson Lies." It remarked that the President "concealed his wolf nature in a sheep's clothing of peace." His acts and notes "always breathed so much hypocrisy and love of misrepresentation that it was not difficult to recognize his spiritual kinship to Great Britain." His declaration of war was "alike dishonorable, impudent, and stupid." The *Kolnische Zeitung* thought us "less dangerous as an open enemy than as a neutral." It expected no results because "the American army is not sufficient even to defeat Mexico." The American declaration was "nothing but a gigantic bluff designed to save the sinking British friend, and the billions with which the Entente horse has been backed." The organ of the Krupp firm, the Essen *Rheinisch-Westfalische Zeitung,* thought the war would be over before our troops could appear on the scene, altho if we should arrive in time a cordial welcome was assured us. Fresh ship-loads of ammunition could not go from America to England "because submarines bar the way." New American gold would be thrown into the scales, "but we counter with a war-loan." The American fleet could not perform what the so-called ocean-dominating British fleet had been unable to achieve. Submarines would continue to hold England by the throat." A common remark among Germans was that America had only "a wooden sword."

1. According to this history, what was America's purpose in entering the war?

2. This history of the war was written and published within a year of the war's conclusion. How does it portray American sentiment towards Germany? Does this portrayal correspond to what you know about American neutrality and subsequent involvement in the war?

22-2 Boy Scouts of America from, "Boy Scouts Support the War Effort" (1917)

This is a selection from a pamphlet published by the Boy Scouts of America. The pamphlet encourages vigilantism and loyalty checks, among other patriotic measures. Many Americans became formal or informal loyalty enforcers during the World War I and many individuals were sent to prison for published or unpublished criticisms of the war efforts or Wilsons policies. The Boy Scouts played an important role on the home front, which included planting vegetable gardens and recycling.

To the Members of the Boy Scouts of America!

Attention, Scouts! We are again called upon to do active service for our country! Every one of the 285,661 Scouts and 76,957 Scout Officials has been summoned by President Woodrow Wilson, Commander-in-Chief of the Army and Navy, to serve as a dispatch bearer from the Government at Washington to the American people all over the country. The prompt, enthusiastic, and hearty response of every one of us has been pledged by our [Scout] President, Mr. Livingstone. Our splendid record of accomplishments in war activities promises full success in this new job.

This patriotic service will be rendered under the slogan: "EVERY SCOUT TO BOOST AMERICA" AS A GOVERNMENT DISPATCH BEARER. The World War is for liberty and democracy.

America has long been recognized as the leader among nations standing for liberty and democracy. American entered the war as a sacred duty to uphold the principles of liberty and democracy.

As a democracy, our country faces great danger-not so much from submarines, battleships and armies, because, thanks to our allies, our enemies have apparently little chance of reaching our shores.

Our danger is from within. Our enemies have representatives everywhere; they tell lies; they mispresent the truth; they deceive our own people; they are a real menace to our country.

Already we have seen how poor Russia has been made to suffer because her people do not know the truth. Representatives of the enemy have been very effective in their deceitful efforts to make trouble for the Government.

Fortunately here in America our people are better educated-they want the truth. Our President recognized the justice and wisdom of this demand when in the early stages of the war he created the Committee on Public Information. He knew that the Government would need the confidence, enthusiasm and willing service of every man and woman, every boy and girl in the nation. He knew that the only possible way to create a genuine feeling of partnership between the people and its representatives in Washington was to take the people into his confidence by full, frank statements concerning the reasons for our entering the war, the various steps taken during the war and the ultimate aims of the war.

Neither the President as Commander-in-Chief, nor our army and navy by land and sea, can alone win the war. At this moment the best defense that America has is an enlightened and loyal citizenship. Therefore, we as scouts are going to have the opportunity of rendering real patriotic service under our slogan.

"EVERY SCOUT TO BOOST AMERICA" AS A GOVERNMENT DISPATCH BEARER.

Here is where our service begins. We are to help spread the facts about America and America's part in the World War. We are to fight lies with truth.

We are to help create public opinion "just as effective in helping to bring victory as ships and guns," to stir patriotism, the great force behind the ships and guns. Isn't that a challenge for every loyal Scout?

"EVERY SCOUT TO BOOST AMERICA" AS A GOVERNMENT DISPATCH BEARER: HOW?

As Mr. George Creel, the Chairman of the Committee on Public Information, says in his letter, scouts are to serve as direct special representatives of the Committee on Public Information to keep the people informed about the War and its causes and progress. The Committee has already prepared a number of special pamphlets and other will be prepared. It places upon the members of the Boy Scouts of America the responsibility of putting the information in these pamphlets in homes of the American people. Every Scout will be furnished a credential card by his Scoutmaster. Under the direction of our leaders, the Boy Scouts of America are to serve as an intelligence division of the citizens' army, always prepared and alert to respond to any call which may come from the President of the United States and the Committee on Public Information at Washington.

. . . Each Scoutmaster is to be furnished with a complete set of all of the government publications, in order that all of the members of his troop may be completely informed. Each scout and scout official is expected to seize every opportunity to serve the Committee on Public Information by making available authoritative information. It is up to the Boy Scouts to see that as many people as possible have an intelligent understanding of any and all facts incident to our present national crisis and the World War. . . .

PAMPHLETS NOW READY FOR CIRCULATION

Note:-A set will be sent to every Scoutmaster. You will need to know what is in these pamphlets so as to act as a serviceable bureau of information and be able to give each person the particular intelligence he seeks.

1. *Summarize the role in the war effort prescribed for the Boy Scouts in this pamphlet.*
2. *How does this document represent an attempt to persuade and encourage support for American military involvement and discourage dissent?*

22-3 Letters from the Great Migration (1917)

World War I halted European immigration. As American industry geared up to supply allied war needs, businesses recruited southern African Americans for jobs. Pushed by poverty and racism, pulled by the promise of economic opportunity, approximately 400,000 African Americans migrated to northern cities. The Chicago Defender newspaper played a major role by strongly promoting migration north.

Houston, Texas, 4-29-17.

Dear Sir:

I am a constant reader of the "Chicago Defender" and in your last issue I saw a want ad that appealed to me. I am a Negro, age 37, and am an all round foundry man. I am a cone maker by trade having had about 10 years experience at the business, and hold good references from several shops, in which I have been employed. I have worked at various shops and I have always been able to make good. It is hard for a black man to hold a job here, as prejudice is very strong. I have never been discharged on account of dissatisfaction with my work, but I have been "let out" on account of my color. I am a good brassmelter but i prefer core making as it is my trade. I have a family and am anxious to leave here, but have not the means, and as wages are not much here, it is very hard to save enough to get away with. If you know of any firms that are in need of a core maker and whom you think would send me transportation, I would be pleased to be put in touch with them and I assure you that effort would be appreciated. I am a core maker but I am willing to do any honest work. All I want is to get away from here. I am writing you and I believe you can and will help me. If any one will send transportation, I will arrange or agree to have it taken out of my salary untill full amount of fare is paid. I also know of several good fdry. men here who would leave in a minute, if there only was a way arranged for them to leave, and they are men whom I know personally to be experienced men. I hope that you will give this your immediate attention as I am anxious to get busy and be on my way. I am ready to start at any time, and would be pleased to hear something favorable.

New Orleans, La., June 10, 1917.

Kind Sir:

I read and hear daly of the great chance that a colored parson has in Chicago of making a living with all the priveleg that the whites have and it mak me the most ankious to want to go where I may be able to make a liveing for my self. When you read this you will think it bery strange that being only my self to support that it is so hard, but it is so. everything is gone up but the poor colerd peple wages. I have made sevle afford to leave and come to Chicago where I hear that times is good for us but owing to femail wekness has made it a perfect failure. I am a widow for 9 years. I have very pore learning altho it would not make much diffrent if I would be throughly edacated for I could not get any better work to do, such as house work, washing and ironing and all such work that are injering to a woman with femail wekness and they pay so little for so hard work that it is just enough to pay room rent and a little some thing to eat. I have found a very good remady that I really feeling to belive would cure me if I only could make enough money to keep up my madison and I dont think that I will ever be able to do that down hear for the time is getting worse evry day. I am going to ask if you peple hear could aid me in geting over her in Chicago and seeking out a position of some kind. I can also do plain sewing. Please good peple dont refuse to help me out in my trouble for I am in gret need of help God will bless you. I am going to do my very best after I get over here if God spair me to get work I will pay the expance back. Do try to do the best you can for me, with many thanks for so doing I will remain as ever,

Yours truly.

Philadelphia, Pa., Oct. 7, 1917.

Dear Sir:

I take this method of thanking you for yours early responding and the glorious effect of the treatment. Oh. I do feel so fine. Dr. the treatment reach me almost ready to move I am now housekeeping again I like it so much better than rooming. Well Dr. with the aid of God I am making very good I make $75 per month. I am carrying enough insurance to pay me $20 per week if I am not able to be on duty. I don't have to work hard. dont have to mister every little white boy comes along I havent heard a white man call a colored a nigger you no now-since I been in the state of Pa. I can ride in the electric street and steam cars any where I get a seat. I dont care to mix with white what I mean I am not crazy about being with white folks, but if I have to pay the same fare I have learn to want the same acomidation. and if you are first in a place here shoping you dont have to wait until the white folks get thro tradeing yet amid all this I shall ever love the good old South and I am praying that God may give every well wisher a chance to be a man regardless of his color, and if my going to the front would bring about such conditions I am ready any day-well Dr. I dont want to worry you but read between lines; and maybe you can see a little sense in my weak statement the kids are in school every day I have only two and I guess that all. Dr. when you find time I would be delighted to have a word from the good old home state. Wife join me in sending love you and yours.

I am your friend and patient.

1. Describe the conditions mentioned in these letters that caused the authors to desire to migrate North.
2. How is life in the North considered to be better than what they have experienced elsewhere?

22-4   American Troops in the Trenches (1918)

Since America entered the war in 1917, American troops saw limited action. Even so, American soldiers, known popularly as Doughboys, were exposed to the fullest extent of the horrors of war. The Second Battle of the Marne was a turning point in the war. American and French forces at Chateau-Thierry held off a substantial German attack and were able to repel them in a matter of weeks.

> **Source:** Edwin L. James, "The Americans in the Second Battle of the Marne," *New York Times Current History,* (September 1918), pp. 399–402, reprinted in Alfred B. Hart, *American History Told by Contemporaries* vol. V (New York: MacMillan, 1929), pp. 785–789.

July 18, 1918.—

On a front of forty kilometers, from Fontenoy to Château-Thierry, the Americans and French this morning launched an offensive drive against the German positions. It was the first allied offensive of moment for more than a year. The Americans are playing a large rôle. They are fighting in the Soissons region, the Château-Thierry region, and other points along the big front.

When the German high command started its drive Monday morning [July 15] it started more than the Kaiser planned for. The French and Americans were entirely successful in guarding their secret and the attack at 4:45 o'clock this morning, without one gun of artillery preparation, took the Germans completely by surprise.

The Americans and French had an early breakfast and started out. Then with rolling barrages ahead of them they went on. A big piece of military work, very recent in conception, but of Foch planning, was shown when, at the precise minute, 4:45 o'clock, the French and Americans along nearly thirty miles of front went over the top and against the invaders. As in halting the German drive, the Americans were at two vital points of the allied drive—Soissons and Château-Thierry—and elsewhere as well. On what was done to the ends of the line depended the success of the whole movement.

I was present at the fighting this morning in the Château-Thierry region, where our boys had done so much to aid the allied cause already. Just as the whistle was blown for the doughboys to start, our gunners started barrages with their seventy-fives. Our troops swept down the hill north of the Bois de Belleau toward Torcy. Shooting as they went, the American soldiers advanced on Torcy, and at precisely 5:30 the commander reported that they had captured the town.

A little to the south other Americans swept around Belleau and closed up. Belleau was captured at 8:20 o'clock, and by that time German prisoners began coming back. Captured officers admitted that the coming of the Americans had been a complete surprise. Sweeping north the Americans charged into the Bois de Givry, and after a short fight with Germans, went on down Hill 193 and into the village of Govry. Two hours later these troops had taken the town of Montairs.

In the meanwhile other American detachments with the French had charged the German positions in front of Courchamps and, while held up temporarily, brought up reinforcements, chased the Germans out of the woods, captured eighteen guns, and took possession of Courchamps. . . .

A general review of this operation shows that one reason why the Germans suffered such heavy losses in the woods forming the triangle from Fossoy, to Mézy, to Crezancy, was that the Americans were overwhelmed by such large numbers that the line could not hold, but nevertheless refused to retreat where it could possibly hold a place in the woods. This sent the German advance sweeping over large numbers of nests which sheltered ten, five, or two Americans, and sometimes one, who stuck while the boches passed by and then opened up on them.

Last night tales of heroism of these men were being told. I believe that of all of them the story of Sergeant J. F. Brown was most notable. Brown commanded a detachment of eleven men when the German onslaught came. They had shelter, which saved them under the heavy German bombardment, and when the advancing boche came along they let him pass, and then got ready to turn their machine gun loose. But just then a hundred or more Germans came along. Brown ordered his men to scatter quickly. He ducked into the woods, and saw the Huns put his beloved machine gun out of the war. The Germans passed on. Brown looked around and seemed to be alone. He started toward the Marne, away from his own lines, and met his Captain, also alone.

These two Americans, out there in the woods in the dark, the Captain with an automatic pistol and Brown with an automatic rifle, saw that the boche barrage kept them from getting to their own lines, and so decided to kill all the Germans they could before they themselves were killed. They lay in the thicket while the Germans passed by in large numbers. According to Brown's report, they heard two machine guns going back of them, and decided to go and get them. The two crept close and charged one of the machine guns, which killed the American Captain. Brown got the lone German gunner with his rifle. Then up came an American Corporal, also left alone in the woods, and Brown and the Corporal started after the second German machine gun, behind a clump of bushes.

They got close, and Brown with his automatic rifle killed three Germans, the crew of the gun. Then attracted by the shooting close at hand, up came the eleven men Brown had commanded, each looking for Germans. Brown resumed command, and led the party to where they could see more Germans in a sector of trench taken from the Americans.

These thirteen Americans performed a feat never to be forgotten. The Germans evidently were left in the trenches with machine guns to meet a counter-attack should the Americans make one. Brown posted his twelve men about the Hun position in twelve directions. He took a position where he could rake the trench with his automatic rifle. At a signal the twelve Americans opened up with their rifles from twelve points, and Brown started working his automatic rifle. Brown said he didn't know how many Germans he killed, but fired his rifle until it got so hot he couldn't hold it, and had to rest it across a stump. The Germans then, thinking they were attacked by a large party, decided to surrender. A German Major stepped out of the trench with his hands high, yelling "Kamerad!" Brown laid down his heated rifle, and while three of the hidden Americans guarded him, advanced toward the Major. Then all thirteen Americans moved in and disarmed the Germans. Brown said he didn't know how many there were, but it was more than 100.

Then, with Brown and the Corporal at the head, and the other eleven Americans in the rear, the procession started through the woods, guided by a doughboy's compass, toward the American lines. It wasn't plain sailing. They were behind the German advance, and had to pass it and a space between the fighting Germans and the Americans. On the way through the woods several parties of Germans saw the advancing column, with Brown and the Corporal at its head, and hurriedly surrendered.

Beating through the thicket, Brown led his party to a place where the German advance line was broken. Just as he started over the American lines the Germans laid down a barrage. This got four of the Germans, but didn't touch an American. Brown and his twelve comrades got back with 155 prisoners. The four killed made a total for the thirteen Americans of 159.

American officers were almost dumfounded at the strange tale Brown brought back, but doubt vanished when, soon after he reached regimental headquarters, a military policeman showed up with a large Bundle of maps and plans Brown had taken from dead German officers, killed by his automatic rifle, and, handing them to Brown, said, "Gimme my receipt."

Brown, who is 23 years old, and last year was a shipping clerk, had met this man on the way back, and, turning over the maps, which made a heavy bundle, had stopped while he scribbled out the receipt he demanded. Meanwhile barrage shells were falling all around. This receipt is part of the records of the American army. . . .

July 21.—What a week this has been in the world's history! A week ago, while the French were celebrating Bastille Day, the Germans, strong in hope because of two preceding drives, were making ready for another great effort. On the 15th they launched an attack from Château-Thierry to north of Châlons on a 100-kilometer front. They crossed the Marne and moved a short distance toward their objectives. Then, out of a clear sky, July 18, came Foch's blow from Soissons to Château-Thierry. On Thursday and Friday French and Americans fought ahead, and then today they hit Ludendorff a body blow south of the Marne. The week started with a formidable German offensive. The week ends with a great allied offensive.

Americans, French, English—all the Allies—now face the fury of the German high command, with its great military machine. That machine is big and powerful, but it is not the machine it used to be. The morale of the German Army is weakening from day to day. The size of the German Army is growing surely less day by day.

The morale of the allied armies is getting better every day, and because of America the size of the allied armies is growing day by day. The defeat of Germany is but a matter of time. How much time no one can say. America should rejoice, but America should not be overconfident. But for what France has to be thankful for America has a just right to be thankful for, too.

South of Soissons, where the bitterest fighting of the week took place, it was the Americans who had the good fortune to push the line furthest ahead. Northwest of Château-Thierry, the closest point to Paris, it fell to the Americans to push the Germans back. East of Château-Thierry the Americans drove the enemy back the same day he crossed the Marne. South of Dormans the Americans held the German advance and helped drive the foe back. North of Châlons, the grand objective of the Crown Prince, the Americans stood on the plains and the boche could not pass.

It was the lot of American soldiers to be at vital points, and they made good. It is not to be supposed that Americans were at those points through accident. Perhaps Foch felt that the ultimate, complete victory depended on what the American fighting man could do, and perhaps he thought it best to know now. It seems but fair for America to know and believe that after all the greatest allied gain of this glorious week is the assurance that the American fighting man has no superior. What tens of thousands of them have done in the last week hundreds of thousands will do. The week has changed the nature of the war from an allied defensive to an allied offensive. For the first time in more than a year the Germans are on the defensive.

1. *Is it notable that a graphic description of war at the front is absent from this report?*
2. *How is the American soldier portrayed? How, according to this account, did the participation of American troops affect the course of the war in 1918?*

22-5 Eugene Kennedy, A "Doughboy" Describes the Fighting Front (1918)

The United States entered World War I three years after it started. In 1918, the first American soldiers came to Europe and soon were at the front experiencing combat. This document describes the everyday life of the American soldier at the front.

Thursday, September 12, 1918

Hiked through dark woods. No light allowed, guided by holding on the pack of the man ahead. Stumbled through underbrush for about half mile into an open field where we waited in soaking rain until about 10:00 P.M. We then started on our hike to the St. Mihiel front, arriving on the crest of a hill at 1:00 A.M. I saw a sight which I shall never forget. It was the zero hour and in one instant the entire front as far as the eye could reach in either direction was a sheet of flame while the heavy artillery made the earth quake. The barrage was so intense that for a time we could not make out whether the Americans or Germans were putting it over. After timing the interval between flash and report we knew that the heaviest artillery was less than a mile away and consequently it was ours. We waded through pools and mud across open lots into a woods on a hill and had to pitch tents in mud. Blankets all wet and we are soaked to the skin. Have carried full pack from 10:00 P.M. to 2:00 A.M., without a rest. . . . Despite the cannonading I slept until 8:00 A.M. and awoke to find every discharge of 14-inch artillery shaking our tent like a leaf. Remarkable how we could sleep. No breakfast. . . . The doughboys had gone over the top at 5:00 A.M. and the French were shelling the back areas toward Metz. . . . Firing is incessant, so is rain. See an air battle just before turning in.

Friday, September 13, 1918

Called at 3:00 A.M. Struck tents and started to hike at 5:00 A.M. with full packs and a pick. Put on gas mask at alert position and hiked about five miles to St. Jean, where we unslung full packs and went on about four miles further with short packs and picks. Passed several batteries and saw many dead horses who gave out at start of push. Our doughboys are still shoving and "Jerry" is dropping so many shells on road into no man's land that we stayed back in field and made no effort to repair shell-torn road. Plenty of German prisoners being brought back. . . . Guns booming all the time. . . .

Thursday, October 17, 1918

Struck tents at 8:00 A.M. and moved about four miles to Chatel. Pitched tents on a side hill so steep that we had to cut steps to ascend. Worked like hell to shovel out a spot to pitch tent on. Just across the valley in front of us about two hundred yards distant, there had occurred an explosion due to a mine planted by the "Bosche" [Germans] and set with a time fuse. It had blown two men (French), two horses, and the wagon into fragments. . . . Arriving on the scene we found Quinn ransacking the wagon. It was full of grub. We each loaded a burlap bag with cans of condensed milk, peas, lobster, salmon, and bread. I started back . . . when suddenly another mine exploded, the biggest I ever saw. Rocks and dirt flew sky high. Quinn was hit in the knee and had to go to hospital. . . . At 6:00 P.M. each of our four platoons left camp in units to go up front and throw three foot and one artillery bridge across the Aire River. On way to river we were heavily shelled and gassed. . . . We put a bridge across 75-foot span. . . . Third platoon men had to get into water and swim or stand in water to their necks. The toughest job we had so far. . . .

Monday, October 21, 1918

Fragment from shell struck mess-kit on my back. . . . Equipment, both American and German, thrown everywhere, especially Hun helmets and belts of machine gunners. . . . Went scouting . . . for narrow-gauge rails to replace the ones "Jerry" spoiled before evacuating. Negro engineers working on railroad same as at St. Mihiel, that's all they are good for. . . .

Friday, November 1, 1918

Started out at 4:00 A.M. The drive is on. Fritz is coming back at us. Machine guns cracking, flares and Verry lights, artillery from both sides. A real war and we are walking right into the zone, ducking shells all the way. The artillery is nerve racking and we don't know from which angle "Jerry" will fire next. Halted behind shelter of railroad track just outside of Grand Pre after being forced back off main road by shell fire. Trees splintered like toothpicks. Machine gunners on top of railroad bank. . . . "Jerry" drove Ewell and me into a two-by-four shell hole, snipers' bullets close.

Sunday, November 3, 1918

Many dead Germans along the road. One heap on a manure pile. . . . Devastation everywhere. Our barrage has rooted up the entire territory like a ploughed field. Dead horses galore, many of them have a hind quarter cut off-the Huns need food. Dead men here and there. The sight I enjoy better than a dead German is to see heaps of them. Rain again. Couldn't keep rain out of our faces and it was pouring hard. Got up at midnight and drove stakes to secure shelter-half over us, pulled our wet blankets out of mud and made the bed all over again. Slept like a log with all my equipment in the open. One hundred forty-two planes sighted in evening.

Sunday, November 10, 1918

First day off in over two months. . . . Took a bath and we were issued new underwear but the cooties [lice] got there first. . . . The papers show a picture of the Kaiser entitled "William the Lost," and stating that he had abdicated. Had a good dinner. Rumor at night that armistice was signed. Some fellows discharged their arms in the courtyard, but most of us were too well pleased with dry bunk to get up.

1. *Characterize the author's impressions of and experiences in the war. Overall, what fighting and living conditions are described?*
2. *What attitudes are prevalent toward the enemy? Give examples of latent or overt prejudice as they occur in this account.*

22-6 Newton D. Baker, "The Treatment of German-Americans" (1918)

The spirit of the country seems unusually good, but there is a growing frenzy of suspicion and hostility toward disloyalty. I am afraid we are going to have a good many instances of people roughly treated on very slight evidence of disloyalty. Already a number of men and some women have been "tarred and feathered," and a portion of the press is urging with great vehemence more strenuous efforts at detection and punishment. This usually takes the form of advocating "drum-head courts-martial" and "being stood up against a wall and shot," which are perhaps none too bad for real traitors, but are very suggestive of summary discipline to arouse mob spirit, which unhappily does not take time to weigh evidence.

In Cleveland a few days ago a foreign-looking man got into a street car and, taking a seat, noticed pasted in the window next to him a Liberty Loan poster, which he immediately tore down, tore into small bits, and stamped under his feet. The people in the car surged around him with the demand that he be lynched, when a Secret Service man showed his badge and placed him under arrest, taking him in a car to the police station, where he was searched and found to have two Liberty Bonds in his pocket and to be a non-English Pole. When an interpreter was procured, it was discovered that the circular which he had destroyed had had on it a picture of the German Emperor, which had so infuriated the fellow that he destroyed the circular to show his vehement hatred of the common enemy. As he was unable to speak a single word of English, he would undoubtedly have been hanged but for the intervention and entirely accidental presence of the Secret Service agent.

I am afraid the grave danger in this sort of thing, apart from its injustice, is that the German Government will adopt retaliatory measures. While the Government of the United States is not only responsible for these things, but very zealously trying to prevent them, the German Government draws no fine distinctions.

1. *What does this account represent in terms of the dangers of increased suspicion and vigilante activity encouraged by such measures as the Espionage and Sedition Acts?*
2. *What does the treatment of the Polish man in this account suggest about the particularly precarious position of foreign immigrants in America during the war?*

22-7 An Official Report

A serious and ongoing problem for all armies was a high death rate from contagious diseases. (Penicillin was not developed until the Second World War.) Military officials from all nations knew they faced tremendous waste from a high rate of attrition from diseases they could not control. During the First World War, the American military reported for the first time that battle deaths exceeded deaths from disease. This success was attributed to the use of better-trained medical personnel, compulsory vaccinations for typhoid fever, improved camp sanitation, clean drinking water, better hospital facilities, and the management of highly contagious diseases such as pneumonia, spinal meningitis, and measles through quarantine. Venereal disease was effectively controlled through improved education and medical prophylaxis.

Source: *Official Record of the United State's Part in the Great War*, pp. 145–146.

SUMMARY

1. Of every 100 American soldiers and sailors, who served in the war with Germany, two were killed or died of disease during the period of hostilities.

2. The total battle deaths of all nations in this war were greater than all the deaths in all wars in the previous 100 years.

3. Russian battle deaths were 34 times as heavy as those of the United States, those of Germany 32 times as great, the French 28 times, and the British 18 times as large.

4. The number of American lives lost was 125,500, of which about 10,000 were in the Navy, and the rest in the Army and the marines attached to it.

5. In the American Army the casualty rate in the Infantry was higher than in any other service, and that for officers was higher than for men.

6. For every man killed in battle, six were wounded.

7. Five out of every six men sent to hospitals on account of wounds were cured and returned to duty.

8. In the expeditionary forces battle losses were twice as large as deaths from disease.

9. In this war the death rate from disease was lower, and the death rate from battle was higher, than in any other

previous American war.

    10. Inoculation, clean camps, and safe drinking water practically eliminated typhoid fever among our troops in this war.

    11. Pneumonia killed more soldiers than were killed in battle. Meningitis was the next most serious disease.

    12. Of each 100 cases of venereal disease recorded in the United States, 96 were contracted before entering the Army, and only 4 afterwards.

    13. During the entire war available hospital facilities in the American Expeditionary Forces have been in excess of the needs.

1. What was the significance of the expenditure on public health in this environment?
2. How could stricter health measures apply to the military than in civilian life?

22-8 Woodrow Wilson, The Fourteen Points (1918)

As the end of World War I approached, President Woodrow Wilson issued his plans for future permanent peace in his Fourteen Points. At the Treaty of Versailles, Wilson's idealistic program fell victim to the more realistic plans of the French and English.

It will be our wish and purpose that the processes of peace, when they are begun, shall be absolutely open and that they shall involve and permit henceforth no secret understandings of any kind. The day of conquest and aggrandizement is gone by; so is also the day of secret covenants entered into in the interest of particular governments and likely at some unlooked-for moment to upset the peace of the world. . . .

    We entered this war because violations of right had occurred which touched us to the quick and made the life of our own people impossible unless they were corrected and the world secure once for all against their recurrence.

    What we demand in this war, therefore, is nothing peculiar to ourselves. It is that the world be made fit and safe to live in; and particularly that it be made safe for every peace-loving nation which, like our own, wishes to live its own life, determine its own institutions, be assured of justice and fair dealing by the other peoples of the world as against force and selfish aggressions.

    All the peoples of the world are in effect partners in this interest, and for our own part we see very clearly that unless justice be done to others it will not be done to us. The program of the world's peace, therefore, is our program; and that program, the only possible program, as we see it, is this:

1. Open covenants of peace, openly arrived at, after which there shall be no private international understandings of any kind but diplomacy shall proceed always frankly and in the public view.
2. Absolute freedom of navigation upon the seas, outside territorial waters, alike in peace and in war, except as the seas may be closed in whole or in part by international action for the enforcement of international covenants.
3. The removal, so far as possible, of all economic barriers and the establishment of an equality of trade conditions among all the nations consenting to the peace and associating themselves for its maintenance.
4. Adequate guarantees given and taken that national armaments will be reduced to the lowest points consistent with domestic safety.
5. A free, open-minded, and absolutely impartial adjustment of all colonial claims, based upon a strict observance of the principle that in determining all such questions of sovereignty the interests of the populations concerned must have equal weight with the equitable claims of the government whose title is to be determined.
6. The evacuation of all Russian territory and such a settlement of all questions affecting Russia as will secure the best and freest cooperation of the other nations of the world in obtaining for her an unhampered and unembarrassed opportunity for the independent determination of her own political development and national policy and assure her of a sincere welcome into the society of free nations under institutions of her own choosing; and, more than a welcome, assistance also of every kind that she may need and may herself desire. The treatment accorded Russian by her sister nations in the months to come will be the acid test of their good will, of their comprehension of her needs as distinguished from their own interests, and of their intelligent and unselfish sympathy.
7. Belgium, the whole world will agree, must be evacuated and restored, without any attempt to limit the sovereignty which she enjoys in common with all other free nations. No other single act will serve as this will serve to restore confidence among the nations in the laws which they have themselves set and determined for the government of their relations with one another. Without this healing act the whole structure and validity of international law is forever impaired.

8. All French territory should be freed and the invaded portions restored, and the wrong done to France by Prussia in 1871 in the matter of Alsace-Lorraine, which has unsettled the peace of the world for nearly fifty years, should be righted, in order that peace may once more be made secure in the interest of all.

9. A readjustment of the frontiers of Italy should be affected along clearly recognizable lines of nationality.

10. The peoples of Austria-Hungary, whose place among the nations we wish to see safeguarded and assured, should be accorded the freest opportunity of autonomous development.

11. Rumania, Serbia, and Montenegro should be evacuated; occupied territories restored; Serbia accorded free and secure access to the sea; and the relations of the several Balkan states to one another determined by friendly counsel along historically established lines of allegiance and nationality; and international guarantees of the political and economic independence and territorial integrity of the several Balkan states should be entered into.

12. The Turkish portions of the present Ottoman Empire should be assured a secure sovereignty, but the other nationalities which are now under Turkish rule should be assured an undoubted security of life and an absolutely unmolested opportunity of autonomous development, and the Dardanelles should be permanently opened as a free passage to the ships and commerce of all nations under international guarantees.

13. An independent Polish state should be erected which should include the territories inhabited by indisputably Polish populations, which should be assured a free and secure access to the sea, and whose political and economic independence and territorial integrity should be guaranteed by international covenant.

14. A general association of nations must be formed under specific covenants for the purpose of affording mutual guarantees of political independence and territorial integrity to great and small states alike.

In regard to these essential rectifications of wrong and assertions of right we feel ourselves to be intimate partners of all the governments and peoples associated together against the imperialists. We cannot be separated in interest or divided in purpose. We stand together until the end. . . .

An evident principle runs through the whole program I have outlined. It is the principle of justice to all peoples and nationalities, and their right to live on equal terms of liberty and safety with one another, whether they be strong or weak.

Unless this principle be made its foundation no part of the structure of international justice can stand. The people of the United States could act upon no other principle; and to the vindication of this principle they are ready to devote their lives, their honor, and everything that they possess. The moral climax of this the culminating and final war for human liberty has come, and they are ready to put their own strength, their own highest purpose, their own integrity and devotion to the test.

1. *Upon what basis did America enter into World War I according to this document? How does this rationale for involvement determine the provisions of this document?*
2. *Identify the "evident principle" guides the program outlined in this document. How do the provisions of this document represent this principle? Give specific examples of this "evident principle" as it impacts the resolutions of this document.*

22-9   Warren G. Harding, Campaign Speech at Boston (1920)

The end of World War One ushered in a new mood among Americans. After the harsh experience of World War One and twenty years of reform, Americans looked forward to a more tranquil era. In his 1920 presidential campaign, Warren G. Harding focused on this theme in calling for a return to normalcy.

There isn't anything the matter with world civilization, except that humanity is viewing it through a vision impaired in a cataclysmal war. Poise has been disturbed and nerves have been racked, and fever has rendered men irrational; sometimes there have been draughts upon the dangerous cup of barbarity and men have wandered far from safe paths, but the human procession still marches in the right direction.

Here in the United States, we feel the reflex, rather than the hurting wound, but we still think straight, and we mean to act straight, and mean to hold firmly to all that was ours when war involved us, and seek the higher attainments which are the only compensations that so supreme a tragedy may give mankind.

America's present need is not heroics, but healing; not nostrums but normalcy; not revolution, but restoration; not agitation, but adjustment; not surgery but serenity; not the dramatic, but the dispassionate; not experiment but equipoise, not submergence in internationality, but sustainment in triumphant nationality.

It is one thing to battle successfully against world domination by a military autocracy, because the infinite God never intended such a program, but it is quite another thing to revise human nature and suspend the fundamental laws of life and all of life's acquirements.

The world called for peace, and has its precarious variety. America demands peace, formal as well as actual, and means to have it, regardless of political exigencies and campaign issues. If it must be a campaign issue, we shall have peace and discuss it afterwards, because the actuality is imperative, and the theory is only illusive. Then we may set our own house in order. We challenged the proposal that an armed autocrat should dominate the world, it ill becomes us to assume that a rhetorical autocrat shall direct all humanity.

This republic has its ample tasks. If we put an end to false economics which lure humanity to utter chaos, ours will be the commanding example of world leadership today. If we can prove a representative popular government under which a citizenship seeks what it may do for the government rather than what the government may do for individuals, we shall do more to make democracy safe for the world than all armed conflict ever recorded. The world needs to be reminded that all human ills are not curable by legislation, and that quantity of statutory enactment and excess of government offer no substitute for quality of citizenship. . . .

My best judgment of America's needs is to steady down, to get squarely on our feet, to make sure of the right path. Let's get out of the fevered delirium of war, with the hallucination that all the money in the world is to be made in the madness of war and the wildness of its aftermath. Let us stop to consider that tranquility at home is more precious than peace abroad, and that both our good fortune and our eminence are dependent on the normal forward stride of all the American people.

1. *Summarize Harding's view of American foreign and domestic policy after World War I.*
2. *According to Harding's speech, how are peace time politics and governing different from war time politics and governing?*
3. *Identify and explain the general thrust of Harding's speech.*

22-10   Edward Earle Purinton, "Big Ideas from Big Business" (1921)

The end of World War I ushered in a new era that stressed business and materialism. Business figures were prominent government leaders. Business leaders promoted the belief that business ideas and practices could solve the problems of the nation and the world. During this period, the trend was toward larger corporations.

Among the nations of the earth today America stands for one idea: *Business*. National opprobrium? National opportunity. For in this fact is, potentially, the salvation of the world.

Thru business, properly conceived, managed and conducted, the human race is finally to be redeemed. How and why a man works foretells what he will do, think, have, love and be. And real salvation is in doing, thinking, having, giving and being-not in sermonizing and theorizing. I shall base the facts of this article on the personal tours and minute examinations I have recently made of twelve of the world's largest business plants: U.S. Steel Corporation, International Harvester Company, Swift & Company, E. I. du Pont de Nemours & Company, National County Bank, National Cash Register Company, Western Electric Company, Sears, Roebuck & Company, H. J. Heinz Company, Peabody Coal Company, Statler Hotels, Wanamaker Stores.

These organizations are typical, foremost representatives of the commercial group of interests loosely termed "Big Business." A close view of these corporations would reveal to any trained, unprejudiced observer a new conception of modern business activities. Let me draw a few general conclusions regarding the best type of business house and business man.

What is the finest game? Business. The soundest science? Business. The truest art? Business. The fullest education? Business. The fairest opportunity? Business. The cleanest philanthropy? Business. The sanest religion? Business.

You may not agree. That is because you judge business by the crude, mean, stupid, false imitation of business that happens to be located near you.

The finest game is business. The rewards are for everybody, and all can win. There are no favorites-Providence always crowns the career of the man who is worthy. And in this game there is no "luck"-you have the fun of taking chances but the sobriety of guaranteeing certainties. The speed and size of your winnings are for you alone to determine; you needn't wait for the other fellow in the game-it is always your move. And your slogan is not "Down the Other Fellow!" but rather "Beat Your Own Record!" or "Do It Better Today!" or "Make Every Job a Masterpiece!" The great sportsmen of the world are the great business men.

The soundest science is business. All investigation is reduced to action, and by action proved or disproved. The idealistic motive animates the materialistic method. Hearts as well as minds are open to the truth. Capital is furnished for the researches of "pure science"; yet pure science is not regarded pure until practical. Competent scientists are suitably rewarded-as they are not in the scientific schools.

The truest art is business. The art is so fine, so exquisite, that you do not think of it as art. Language, color, form, line, music, drama, discovery, adventure-all the components of art must be used in business to make it of superior character.

The fullest education is business. A proper blend of study, work and life is essential to advancement. The whole man is educated. Human nature itself is the open book that all business men study; and the mastery of a page of this educates you more than the memorizing of a dusty tome from a library shelf. In the school of business, moreover, you teach yourself and learn most from your own mistakes. What you learn here you live out, the only real test.

The fairest opportunity is business. You can find more, better, quicker chances to get ahead in a large business house than anywhere else on earth. The biographies of champion business men show how they climbed, and how you can climb. Recognition of better work, of keener and quicker thought, of deeper and finer feeling, is gladly offered by the men higher up, with early promotion the rule for the man who justifies it. There is, and can be, no such thing as buried talent in a modern business organization.

The cleanest philanthropy is business. By "clean" philanthropy I mean that devoid of graft, inefficiency and professionalism, also of condolence, hysterics and paternalism. Nearly everything that goes by the name of Charity was born a triplet, the other two members of the trio being Frailty and Cruelty. Not so in the welfare departments of leading corporations. Savings and loan funds; pension and insurance provisions; health precautions, instructions and safeguards; medical attention and hospital care; libraries, lectures and classes; musical, athletic and social features of all kinds; recreational facilities and financial opportunities-these types of "charitable institutions" for employees add to the worker's self-respect, self-knowledge and self-improvement, by making him an active partner in the welfare program, a producer of benefits for his employer and associates quite as much as a recipient of bounty from the company. I wish every "charity" organization would send its officials to school to the heads of the welfare departments of the big corporations; the charity would mostly be transformed into capability, and the minimum of irreducible charity left would not be called by that name.

The sanest religion is business. Any relationship that forces a man to follow the Golden Rule rightfully belongs amid the ceremonials of the church. A great business enterprise includes and presupposes this relationship. I have seen more Christianity to the square inch as a regular part of the office equipment of famous corporation presidents than may ordinarily be found on Sunday in a verbalized but not vitalized church congregation. A man is not wholly religious until he is better on week-days than he is on Sunday. The only ripened fruits of creeds are deeds. You can fool your preacher with a sickly sprout or a wormy semblance of character, but you can't fool your employer. I would make every business house a consultation bureau for the guidance of the church whose members were employees of the house.

I am aware that some of the preceding statements will be challenged by many readers. I should not myself have made them, or believed them, twenty years ago, when I was a pitiful specimen of a callow youth and cocksure professional man combined. A thoro knowledge of business has implanted a deep respect for business and real business men.

The future work of the business man is to teach the teacher, preach to the preacher, admonish the parent, advise the doctor, justify the lawyer, superintend the statesman, fructify the farmer, stabilize the banker, harness the dreamer, and reform the reformer. Do all these needy persons wish to have these many kind things done to them by the business man? Alas, no. They rather look down upon him, or askance at him, regarding him as a mental and social inferior-unless he has money or fame enough to tilt their glance upward.

A large variety of everyday lessons of popular interest may be gleaned from a tour of the world's greatest business plants and a study of the lives of their founders. We suggest a few. . . .

Only common experiences will unite the laborer and the capitalist. Each must get the viewpoint of the other by sharing the work, duties and responsibilities of the other. The sons of the families of Swift, McCormick, Wanamaker, Heinz, du Pont, have learned the business from the ground up; they know the trials, difficulties and needs of workers because they *are* workers; and they don't have to settle agitations and strikes because there aren't any.

Further, by councils and committees of employees, management courses for department heads and foremen, plans of referendum and appeal, offers of stock and voting power to workers, employee representation on the board of directors, and other means of sharing authority and responsibility, owners of a business now give the manual workers a chance to think and feel in unison with themselves. All enmity is between strangers. Those who really know each other cannot fight.

1. According to Purinton, what roles did business play in American society?
2. Why did it play that role?

PART TWENTY-THREE

THE 1920S AND MODERN AMERICA

23-1   F. J. Grimke, "Address of Welcome to the Men Who Have Returned from the Battlefront" (1919)

African Americans serving in Europe during World War One discovered that the racism that confronted in the United States was not present in European nations. They came back to America having fought for democracy and were counseled by some African American leaders to continue the fight for freedom and equality that had tasted in Europe.

Young gentlemen, I am glad to welcome you home again after months of absence in a foreign land in obedience to the call of your country-glad that you have returned to us without any serious casualties.

I am sure you have acquitted yourself well; that in the record that you have made for yourselves, during your absence from home, there is nothing to be ashamed of, nothing that will reflect any discredit upon the race with which you are identified. . . .

While you were away you had the opportunity of coming in contact with another than the American type of white man; and through that contact you have learned what it is to be treated as a man, regardless of the color of your skin or race identity. Unfortunately you had to go away from home to receive a man's treatment, to breathe the pure, bracing air of liberty, equality, fraternity. And, while it was with no intention of bringing to you that knowledge, of putting you where you could get that kind of experience, but simply because they couldn't very well get along without you, I am glad nevertheless, that you were sent. You know now that the mean, contemptible spirit of race prejudice that curses this land is not the spirit of other lands; you know now what it is to be treated as a man. And, one of the things that I am particularly hoping for, now that you have had this experience, is that you have come back determined, as never before, to keep up the struggle for our rights until, here in these United States, in this boasted land of the free and home of the brave, every man, regardless of the color of his skin, shall be accorded a man's treatment.

Your trip will be of very little value to the race in this country unless you have come back with the love of liberty, equality, fraternity burning in your souls. . . . In the struggle that is before us, you can do a great deal in helping to better conditions. You, who gave up everything-home, friends, relatives-you who took your lives in your hands and went forth to lay them, a willing sacrifice upon the altar of your country and in the interest of democracy throughout the world, have a right to speak-to speak with authority; and that right you must exercise.

We, who remained at home, followed you while you were away, with the deepest interest; and, our hearts burned with indignation when tidings came to us, as it did from time to time, of the manner in which you were treated by those over you, from whom you had every reason, in view of the circumstances that took you abroad and what it was costing you, to expect decent, humane treatment, instead of the treatment that was accorded you. The physical hardships, incident to a soldier's life in times of war, are trying enough, are hard enough to bear-and, during this world war, on the other side of the water, I understand they were unusually hard. To add to these the insults, the studied insults that were heaped upon you, and for no reason except that you were colored, is so shocking that were it not for positive evidence, it would be almost unbelievable. . . .

I know of nothing that sets forth this cursed American race prejudice in a more odious, execrable light than the treatment of our colored soldiers in this great world struggle that has been going on, by the very government that ought to have shielded them from the brutes that were over them. . . .

If it was worth going abroad to make the world safe for democracy, it is equally worth laboring no less earnestly to make it safe at home. We shall be greatly disappointed if you do not do this-if you fail to do your part.

1. According to Grimke, what should be the attitude and mission of the black soldier returning from World War I?
2. How has the World War I experience shaped and changed the black soldier?
3. How is America's treatment of the black soldier described and compared to how the black soldier may have been treated by "another than the American type of white man"?

23-2   The Sahara of the Bozart (1920)

H. L. Mencken, editor of The American Mercury, wrote from the vanguard of cultural dissent. Mencken was a conservative observer who did not stray from the mainstream, but who also managed to find the flaws in America's institutions and culture. He was ecumenical in his criticisms—few escaped his acid pen and his sharp wit. The Sahara of the Bozart is his classic commentary on the status of the New South.

Source: H.L. Mencken, *Prejudices* 2nd Series, (New York: A. A. Knopf, 1920), pp. 136–154.

> Alas, for the South! Her books have grown fewer—
> She never was much given to literature.

In the lamented J. Gordon Coogler, author of these elegaic lines, there was the insight of a true poet. He was the last bard of Dixie, at least in the legitimate line. Down there a poet is now almost as rare as an oboe-player, a dry-point etcher or a metaphysician. It is, indeed, amazing to contemplate so vast a vacuity. One thinks of the interstellar spaces, of the colossal reaches of the now mythical ether. Nearly the whole of Europe could be lost in that stupendous region of fat farms, shoddy cities and paralyzed cerebrums: one could throw in France, Germany and Italy, and still have room for the British Isles. And yet, for all its size and all its wealth and all the "progress" it babbles of, it is almost as sterile, artistically, intellectually, culturally, as the Sahara Desert. There are single acres in Europe that house more first-rate men than all the states south of the Potomac; there are probably single square miles in America. If the whole of the late Confederacy were to be engulfed by a tidal wave tomorrow, the effect upon the civilized minority of men in the world would be but little greater than that of a flood on the Yang-tse-kiang. It would be impossible in all history to match so complete a drying-up of a civilization.

I say a civilization because that is what, in the old days, the South had, despite the Baptist and Methodist barbarism that reigns down there now. More, it was a civilization of manifold excellences—perhaps the best that the Western Hemisphere has ever seen—undoubtedly the best that These States have ever seen. Down to the middle of the last century, and even beyond, the main hatchery of ideas on this side of the water was across the Potomac bridges. The New England shopkeepers and theologians never really developed a civilization; all they ever developed was a government. They were, at their best, tawdry and tacky fellows, oafish in manner and devoid of imagination; one searches the books in vain for mention of a salient Yankee gentleman; as well look for a Welsh gentleman. But in the south there were men of delicate fancy, urbane instinct and aristocratic manner—in brief, superior men—in brief, gentry. To politics, their chief diversion, they brought active and original minds. It was there that nearly all the political theories we still cherish and suffer under came to birth. It was there that the crude dogmatism of New England was refined and humanized. It was there, above all, that some attention was given to the art of living—that life got beyond and above the state of a mere infliction and became an exhilarating experience. A certain noble spaciousness was in the ancient southern scheme of things. The *Ur*-Confederate had leisure. He liked to toy with ideas. He was hospitable and tolerant. He had the vague thing that we call culture.

But consider the condition of his late empire today. The picture gives one the creeps. It is as if the Civil War stamped out every last bearer of the torch, and left only a mob of peasants on the field. One thinks of Asia Minor, resigned to Armenians, Greeks and wild swine, of Poland abandoned to the Poles. In all that gargantuan paradise of the fourth-rate there is not a single picture gallery worth going into, or a single orchestra capable of playing the nine symphonies of Beethoven, or a single opera-house, or a single theater devoted to decent plays, or a single public monument (built since the war) that is worth looking at, or a single workshop devoted to the making of beautiful things. Once you have counted Robert Loveman (an Ohioan by birth) and John McClure (an Oklahoman) you will not find a single southern poet above the rank of a neighborhood rhymester. Once you have counted James Branch Cabell (a lingering survivor of the *ancien régime*: a scarlet dragonfly imbedded in opaque amber) you will not find a single southern prose writer who can actually write. And once you have—but when you come to critics, musical composers, painters, sculptors, architects and the like, you will have to give it up, for there is not even a bad one between the Potomac mud-flats and the Gulf. Nor an historian, Nor a sociologist. Nor a philosopher. Nor a theologian. Nor a scientist. In all these fields the south is an awe-inspiring blank—a brother to Portugal, Serbia and Esthonia.

Consider, for example, the present estate and dignity of Virginia—in the great days indubitably the premier American state, the mother of Presidents and statesmen, the home of the first American university worthy of the name, the *arbiter elegantiarum* of the western world. Well, observe Virginia to-day. It is years since a first-rate man, save only Cabell, has come out of it; it is years since an idea has come out of it. The old aristocracy went down the red gullet of war; the poor white trash are now in the saddle. Politics in Virginia are cheap, ignorant, parochial, idiotic; there is scarcely a man in office above the rank of a professional job-seeker; the political doctrine that prevails is made up of hand-me-downs from the bumpkinry of the Middle West—Bryanism, Prohibition, vice crusading, all that sort of filthy claptrap; the administration of the law is turned over to professors of Puritanism and espionage; a Washington or a Jefferson, dumped there by some act of God, would be denounced as a scoundrel and jailed overnight. Elegance, *esprit,* culture? Virginia has no art, no literature, no philosophy, no mind or aspiration of her own. Her education has sunk to the Baptist seminary level; not a single contribution to human knowledge has come out of her colleges in twenty-five years; she spends less than half upon her common schools, *per capita,* than any northern state spends. In brief, an intellectual Gobi or Lapland. Urbanity, *politesse,* chivalry? Go to! It was in Virginia that they invented the device of searching for contraband whisky in women's underwear. . . . There remains, at the top, a ghost of the old aristocracy, a bit wistful and infinitely charming. But it has lost all its old leadership to fabulous monsters from the lower depths; it is submerged in an industrial plutocracy that is ignorant and ignominious. The mind of the state, as it is revealed to the nation, is pathetically naïve and inconsequential. It no longer reacts with energy and elasticity to great problems. It has fallen to the bombastic trivialities of the camp-meeting and the chautauqua. Its foremost exponent—if so flabby a thing may be said to have an exponent— is a statesman whose name is synonymous with empty words, broken pledges and false pretenses. One could no more imagine a Lee or a Washington in the Virginia of to-day than one could imagine a Huxley in Nicaragua.

I choose the Old Dominion, not because I disdain it, but precisely because I esteem it. It is, by long odds, the most civilized of the southern states, now as always. It has sent a host of creditable sons northward; the stream kept running into our own time. Virginians, even the worst of them, show the effects of a great tradition. They hold themselves above other southerners, and with sound pretension. If one turns to such a commonwealth as Georgia the picture becomes far darker. There the liberated lower orders of whites have borrowed the worst commercial bounderism of the Yankee and superimposed it upon a culture that, at bottom, is but little removed from savagery. Georgia is at once the home of the cotton-mill sweater and of the most noisy and vapid sort of chamber of commerce, of the Methodist parson turned Savonarola and of the lynching bee. A self-respecting European, going there to live, would not only find intellectual stimulation utterly lacking; he would actually feel a certain insecurity, as if the scene were the Balkans or the China Coast. The Leo Frank affair was no isolated phenomenon. It fitted into its frame very snugly. It was a natural expression of Georgian notions of truth and justice. There is a state with more than half the area of Italy and more population than either Denmark or Norway, and yet in thirty years it has not produced a single idea. Once upon a time a Georgian printed a couple of books that attracted notice, but immediately it turned out that he was little more than an amanuensis for the local blacks—that his works were really the products, not of white Georgia, but of black Georgia. Writing afterward *as* a white man, he swiftly subsided into the fifth rank. And he is not only the glory of the literature of Georgia; he is, almost literally, the whole of the literature of Georgia—nay, of the entire art of Georgia.

Virginia is the best of the south to-day, and Georgia is perhaps the worst. The one is simply senile; the other is crass, gross, vulgar and obnoxious. Between lies a vast plain of mediocrity, stupidity, lethargy, almost of dead silence. In the north, of course, there is also grossness, crassness, vulgarity. The north, in its way, is also stupid and obnoxious. But nowhere in the north is there such complete sterility, so depressing a lack of all civilized gesture and aspiration. One would find it difficult to unearth a second-rate city between the Ohio and the Pacific that isn't struggling to establish an orchestra, or setting up a little theater, or going in for an art gallery, or making some other effort to get into touch with civilization. These efforts often fail, and sometimes they succeed rather absurdly, but under them there is at least an impulse that deserves respect, and that is the impulse to seek beauty and to experiment with ideas, and so to give the life of every day a certain dignity and purpose. You will find no such impulse in the south. There are no committees down there cadging subscriptions for orchestras; if a string quartet is ever heard there the news of it has never come out; an opera troupe, when it roves the land, is a nine days' wonder. The little theater movement has swept the whole country, enormously augmenting the public interest in sound plays, giving new dramatists their chance, forcing reforms upon the commercial theater. Everywhere else the wave rolls high-but along the line of the Potomac it breaks upon a rock-bound shore. There is no little theater beyond. There is no gallery of pictures. No artist ever gives exhibitions. No one talks of such things. No one seems to be interested in such things.

As for the cause of this unanimous torpor and doltishness, this curious and almost pathological estrangement from everything that makes for a civilized culture, I have hinted at it already, and now state it again. The south has simply been drained of all its best blood. The vast blood-letting of the Civil War half exterminated and wholly paralyzed the old aristocracy, and so left the land to the harsh mercies of the poor white trash, now its masters. The war, of course, was not a complete massacre. It spared a decent number of first-rate southerners—perhaps even some of the very best. Moreover, other countries, notably France and Germany, have survived far more staggering butcheries, and even showed marked progress thereafter. But the war not only cost a great many valuable lives; it also brought bankruptcy, demoralization and despair in its train—and so the majority of the first-rate southerners that were left, broken in spirit and unable to live under the new dispensation, cleared out. A few went to South America, to Egypt, to the Far East. Most came north. They were fecund; their progeny is widely dispersed, to the great benefit of the north. A southerner of good blood almost always does well in the north. He finds, even in the big cities, surroundings fit for a man of condition. His peculiar qualities have a high social value, and are esteemed. He is welcomed by the codfish aristocracy as one palpably superior. But in the south he throws up his hands. It is impossible for him to stoop to the common level. He cannot brawl in politics with the grandsons of his grandfather's tenants. He is unable to share their fierce jealousy of the emerging black—the cornerstone of all their public thinking. He is anaesthetic to their theological and political enthusiasms. He finds himself an alien at their feasts of soul. And so he withdraws into his tower, and is heard of no more. Cabell is almost a perfect example. His eyes,

462

for years, were turned toward the past; he became a professor of the grotesque genealogizing that decaying aristocracies affect; it was only by a sort of accident that he discovered himself to be an artist. The south is unaware of the fact to this day; it regards Woodrow Wilson and Col. John Temple Graves as much finer stylists, and Frank L. Stanton as an infinitely greater poet. If it has heard, which I doubt, that Cabell has been hoofed by the Comstocks, it unquestionably views that assault as a deserved rebuke to a fellow who indulges a lewd passion for fancy writing, and is a covert enemy to the Only True Christianity.

Obviously, it is impossible for intelligence to flourish in such an atmosphere. Free inquiry is blocked by the idiotic certainties of ignorant men. The arts, save in the lower reaches of the gospel hymn, the phonograph and the chautauqua harangue, are all held in suspicion. The tone of public opinion is set by an upstart class but lately emerged from industrial slavery into commercial enterprise—the class of "hustling" business men, of "live wires," of commercial club luminaries, of "drive" managers, of forward-lookers and right-thinkers—in brief, of third-rate southerners inoculated with all the worst traits of the Yankee sharper. One observes the curious effects of an old tradition of truculence upon a population now merely pushful and impudent, of an old tradition of chivalry upon a population now quite without imagination. The old repose is gone. The old romanticism is gone. The philistinism of the new type of town-boomer southerner is not only indifferent to the ideals of the old south; it is positively antagonistic to them. That philistinism regards human life, not as an agreeable adventure, but as a mere trial of rectitude and efficiency. It is overwhelmingly utilitarian and moral. It is inconceivably hollow and obnoxious. What remains of the ancient tradition is simply a certain charming civility in private intercourse—often broken down, alas, by the hot rages of Puritanism, but still generally visible. The southerner, at his worst, is never quite the surly cad that the Yankee is. His sensitiveness may betray him into occasional bad manners, but in the main he is a pleasant fellow—hospitable, polite, good-humored, even jovial. . . . But a bit absurd. . . . A bit pathetic.

1. Why does Mencken argue that the Old South was better?
2. What does the title of the essay mean? What was the cultural status of the rest of the country in 1920?
3. How would Henry Grady have reacted to this critique?

23-3 National Origins Quota Act, 1924

Bowing to pressure from nativists and restrictionist groups, Congress passed several measures intended to stem the flow of immigrants into the United States in the post war period. Anti-immigrant sentiment was directed largely at those arriving from eastern and southern European countries, people who native-born white Americans believed to be inassimilable. The National Origins Quota Act of 1924, superceded similar but weaker legislation of 1917 and 1921, and proved to be a most effective instrument in curtailing the entry of "undesirables" into the United States.

Source: Henry Steele Commanger, *Documents of American History,* pp. 192–194; U.S. Bureau of Immigration, *Annual Report of the Commissioner General of Immigration,* (1924), p. 24 ff.

. . . The "Immigration act of 1924" . . . which supplants the so-called quota limit act of May 19, 1921, the latter having expired by limitation at the close of the fiscal year just ended, makes several very important changes not only in our immigration policy but also in the administrative machinery of the Immigration Service. Some of the more important changes in these respects will be briefly referred to.

It will be remembered that the quota limit act of May, 1921, provided that the number of aliens of any nationality admissible to the United States in any fiscal year should be limited to 3 per cent of the number of persons of such nationality who were resident in the United States according to the census of 1910, it being also provided that not more than 20 per cent of any annual quota could be admitted in any one month. Under the act of 1924 the number of each nationality who may be admitted annually is limited to 2 per cent of the population of such nationality resident in the United States according to the census of 1890, and not more than 10 per cent of any annual quota may be admitted in any month except in cases where such quota is less than 300 for the entire year.

Under the act of May, 1921, the quota area was limited to Europe, the Near East, Africa, and Australasia. The countries of North and South America, with adjacent islands, and countries immigration from which was otherwise regulated, such as China, Japan, and countries within the Asiatic barred zone, were not within the scope of the quota law. Under the new act, however, immigration from the entire world, with the exception of the Dominion of Canada, Newfoundland, the Republic of Mexico, the Republic of Cuba, the Republic of Haiti, the Dominican Republic, the Canal Zone, and independent countries of Central and South America, is subject to quota limitations. The various quotas established under the new law are shown in the following proclamation of the President, issued on the last day of the present fiscal year:

BY THE PRESIDENT OF THE UNITED STATES OF AMERICA

A PROCLAMATION

Whereas it is provided in the act of Congress approved May 26, 1924, entitled "An act to limit the immigration of aliens into the United States, and for other purposes" that—

"The annual quota of any nationality shall be two per centum of the number of foreign-born individuals of such nationality resident in continental United States as determined by the United States census of 1890, but the minimum quota of any nationality shall be 100 (Sec. 11 (a)). . . .

"The Secretary of State, the Secretary of Commerce, and the Secretary of Labor, jointly, shall, as soon as feasible after the enactment of this act, prepare a statement showing the number of individuals of the various nationalities resident in continental United States as determined by the United States census of 1890, which statement shall be the population basis for the purposes of subdivision (a) of section 11 (sec. 12 (b)).

"Such officials shall, jointly, report annually to the President the quota of each nationality under subdivision (a) of section 11, together with the statements, estimates, and revisions provided for in this section. The President shall proclaim and make known the quotas so reported." (Sec. 12 (e)).

Now, therefore, I, Calvin Coolidge, President of the United States of America acting under and by virtue of the power in me vested by the aforesaid act of Congress, do hereby proclaim and make known that on and after July 1, 1924, and throughout the fiscal year 1924-1925, the quota of each nationality provided in said Act shall be as follows:

Country or area of birth	Quota 1924–1925
Afghanistan	100
Albania	100
Andorra	100
Arabian peninsula (1, 2)	100
Armenia	124
Australia, including Papua, Tasmania, and all islands appertaining to Australia (3, 4)	121
Austria	785
Belgium (5)	512
Bhutan	100
Bulgaria	100
Cameroon (proposed British mandate)	100
Cameroon (French mandate)	100
China	100
Czechoslovakia	3,073
Danzig, Free City of	228
Denmark (5, 6)	2,789
Egypt	100
Esthonia	124
Ethiopia (Abyssinia)	100
Finland	170
France (1, 5, 6)	3,954
Germany	51,227
Great Britain and Northern Ireland (1, 3, 5, 6)	34,007
Greece	100
Hungary	473
Iceland	100
India (3)	100
Iraq (Mesopotamia)	100

Irish Free State (3)	28,567
Italy, including Rhodes. Dodekanesia, and Castellorizzo (5)	3,845
Japan	100
Latvia	142
Liberia	100
Liechtenstein	100
Lithuania	344
Luxemburg	100
Monaco	100
Morocco (French and Spanish Zones and Tangier)	100
Muscat (Oman)	100
Nauru (proposed British mandate) (4)	100
Nepal	100
Netherlands (1, 5, 6)	1,648
New Zealand (including appertaining islands (3, 4)	100
Norway (5)	6,453
New Guinea, and other Pacific Islands under proposed Australian mandate (4)	100
Palestine (with Trans-Jordan, proposed British mandate)	100
Persia (1)	100
Poland	5,982
Portugal (1, 5)	503
Ruanda and Urundi (Belgium mandate)	100
Rumania	603
Russia, European and Asiatic (1)	2,248
Samoa, Western (4) (proposed mandate of New Zealand)	100
San Marino	100
Siam	100
South Africa, Union of (3)	100
South West Africa (proposed mandate of Union of South Africa)	100
Spain (5)	131
Sweden	9,561
Switzerland	2,081
Syria and the Lebanon (French mandate)	100
Tanganyika (proposed British mandate)	100
Togoland (proposed British mandate)	100
Togoland (French mandate)	100
Turkey	100
Yap and other Pacific islands (under Japanese mandate) (4)	100
Yugoslavia	671

1. (a) Persons born in the portions of Persia, Russia, or the Arabian peninsula situated within the barred zone, and who are admissible under the immigration laws of the United States as quota immigrants, will be charged to the quotas of these countries; and (b) persons born in the colonies, dependencies, or protectorates, or portions thereof, within the barred zone, of France, Great Britain, the Netherlands, or Portugal, who are admissible under the immigration laws of the United States as quota immigrants, will be charged to the quota of the country to which such colony or dependency belongs or by which it is administered as a protectorate.

2. The quota-area denominated "Arabian peninsula" consists of all territory except Muscat and Aden, situated in the portion of that peninsula and adjacent islands, to the southeast of Iraq, or Palestine with Trans-Jordan, and of Egypt.

3. Quota immigrants born in the British self-governing dominions or in the Empire of India, will be charged to the appropriate quota rather than to that of Great Britain and Northern Ireland. There are no quota restrictions for Canada and Newfoundland. . . .

4. Quota immigrants eligible to citizenship in the United States, born in a colony, dependency, or protectorate of any country to which a quota applies will be charged to the quota of that country.

5. In contrast with the law of 1921, the immigration act of 1924 provides that persons born in the colonies or dependencies of European countries situated in Central America, South America, or the islands adjacent to the American continents (except Newfoundland and islands pertaining to Newfoundland, Labrador and Canada), will be charged to the quota of the country to which such colony or dependency belongs.

GENERAL NOTE.—The immigration quotas assigned to the various countries and quota-areas should not be regarded as having any political significance whatever, or as involving recognition of new governments, or of new boundaries, or of transfers of territory except as the United States Government has already made such recognition in a formal and official manner. . . .

CALVIN COOLIDGE.

1. Why was the quota law of 1921 ineffective?

2. How were quotas determined for 1924? Why might Nepal and Syria have the same quota? Which quota was more likely to get filled?

23-4 Advertisements (1925, 1927)

The advertising industry achieved much prominence in the 1920s as the American economy began focusing more strongly on consumption. In newspapers and magazines and on the radio, advertising messages used sophisticated techniques to attract consumers to various products.

Advertisement for Berkey & Gay Furniture Company (1925)

Do they know Your son at MALUCIO's?

There's a hole in the door at Malucio's. Ring the bell and a pair of eyes will look coldly out at you. If you are known you will get in. Malucio has to be careful.

There have been riotous nights at Malucio's. Tragic nights, too. But somehow the fat little man has managed to avoid the law.

Almost every town has its Malucio's. Some, brightly disguised as cabarets-others, mere back street filling stations for pocket flasks.

But every Malucio will tell you the same thing. His best customers are not the ne'er-do-wells of other years. They are the young people-frequently, the best young people of the town.

Malucio has put one over on the American home. Ultimately he will be driven out. Until then THE HOME MUST BID MORE INTELLIGENTLY FOR MALUCIO'S BUSINESS.

There are many reasons why it is profitable and wise to furnish the home attractively, but one of these, and not the least, is-Malucio's.

The younger generation is sensitive to beauty, princely proud, and will not entertain in homes of which it is secretly ashamed.

But make your rooms attractive, appeal to the vaulting pride of youth, and you may worry that much less about Malucio's-and the other modern frivolities that his name symbolizes.

A guest room smartly and tastefully furnished-a refined and attractive dining room-will more than hold their own against the tinsel cheapness of Malucio's.

Nor is good furniture any longer a luxury for the favored few. THE PRESCOTT suite shown above, for instance, is a moderately priced pattern, conforming in every detail to the finest Berkey & Gay standards.

In style, in the selection of rare and beautiful woods, and in the rich texture of the finish and hand decorating, it reveals the skill of craftsmen long expert in the art of quality furniture making.

The PRESCOTT is typical of values now on display at the store of your local Berkey & Gay dealer. Depend on his showing you furniture in which you may take deep pride-beautiful, well built, luxuriously finished, and moderately priced.

There is a Berkey & Gay pattern suited to every home-an infinite variety of styles at prices ranging all the way from $350 to $6,000.

Advertisement for Eveready Flashlight and Battery (1927)

The Song that STOPPED!

A child of five skipped down the garden path and laughed because the sky was blue. "Jane," called her mother from the kitchen window, "come here and help me bake your birthday cake." Little feet sped. "Don't fall," her mother warned.

Jane stood in the kitchen door and wrinkled her nose in joy. Her gingham dress was luminous against the sun. What a child! Dr. and Mrs. Wentworth cherished Jane.

"Go down to the cellar and get mother some preserves . . . the kind you like."

"The preserves are in the cellar," she chanted, making a progress twice around the kitchen. "Heigh-ho a-derry-o, the preserves are . . ." her voice grew fainter as she danced off. " . . . in the . . ."

The thread of song snapped. A soft *thud-thud*. Fear fluttered Mrs. Wentworth's heart. She rushed to the cellar door.

"Mother!" . . . a child screaming in pain. Mrs. Wentworth saw a little morsel of girlhood lying in a heap of gingham and yellow hair at the bottom of the dark stairs.

The sky is still blue. But there will be no birthday party tomorrow. An ambulance clanged up to Dr. Wentworth's house today. Jane's leg is broken.

If a flashlight had been hanging on a hook at the head of the cellar stairs, this little tragedy would have been averted. If Jane had been taught to use a flashlight as carefully as her father, Dr. Wentworth, had taught her to use a toothbrush, a life need not have been endangered.

An Eveready Flashlight is always a convenience and often a life-saver. Keep one about the house, in the car; and take one with you wherever you go. Keep it supplied with fresh Eveready Batteries-the longest-lasting flashlight batteries made. Eveready Flashlights, $1.00 up.

NATIONAL CARBON CO., INC. EVEREADY FLASHLIGHTS & BATTERIES
A THOUSAND THINGS MAY HAPPEN IN THE DARK

1. *What anxieties and prejudices does the Berkey and Gay Furniture advertisement play upon? What method is employed in gaining th attention and loyalty of the prospective buyer?*
2. *How does the Berkey and Gay advertisement appeal the consumer's self-image and desire for social acceptance?*
3. *How does the Eveready advertisement create a need for its product? What methods are used to appeal to the average American consumer?*

23-5 Family Planning (1926)

Margaret Sanger was a controversial figure in her day. She introduced the term birth control to American couples, she encouraged people to explore the pleasures of passionate and sexual love, and she wrote frankly about the topic. She advocated the use of contraceptives for working class people, to control family growth at an economically manageable level, and also to the middle class, to postpone the arrival of children so the couple could build their relationship on the pleasure of intimate knowledge of each other.

Source: Margaret Sanger, *Happiness in Marriage* (1926) pp. 191–203.

PREMATURE PARENTHOOD AND WHY TO AVOID IT

Coming together with widely differing likes and dislikes, varying inheritances and often with widely divergent training and ideals, the two young people who marry will not be long in discovering that they may have much less in common than they had ever dreamed possible.

When Society has tossed them a marriage certificate and the Church has concluded the ceremony which has legally united them, they are then forced back upon their own resources. Society, so to speak, has washed its hands of the young couple, or cast this man and this woman into the deep waters of matrimony, where they are left to sink or swim as best they may.

The certificate of marriage solves nothing. Rather it accentuates the greater and more complex problems of life. To find a solution to this great problem of living together and growing together requires all the combined intelligence and foresight both man and woman can command. Drifting into this relation will offer no solution, for very often those who drift into marriage, drift out of it in the same aimless fashion.

Others, who have not realized that the marriage of a man and woman is not merely a legal sanction for parenthood, but that it is an important relation in itself—the most important one in human life—often find themselves defeated and forced into an accidental and premature parenthood for which they are not financially or spiritually prepared.

Two years at least are necessary to cement the bonds of love and to establish the marriage relation. Parenthood should therefore be postponed by every young married couple until at least the third year of marriage.

Why is this advisable?

When the young wife is forced into maternity too soon, both are cheated out of marital adjustment and harmony that require time to mature and develop. The plunge into parenthood prematurely with all its problems and disturbances, is like the blighting of a bud before it has been given time to blossom.

Even in the fully matured healthy wife pregnancy has a disturbing physiological and nervous reaction. Temporarily the whole character and temperament of the woman undergoes profound changes. Usually nausea, headaches, irritability, loss of appetite, ensue. At the beginning of this period there develop temporary eccentricities that do not belong to the woman in her normal condition.

If the bride is enforced into an unwilling or accidental pregnancy during the honeymoon or the early stages of their marital love, the young husband is deprived of the possible opportunity of knowing his wife during one of the most interesting stages of her development. He has known her in the exciting days of courtship and during the heightened though brief period of the honeymoon, and now, alas, she enters all too soon the ominous days of early pregnancy. Never under such conditions can he know her in the growing beauty and ripening of mature womanhood. He has known her as a romantic girl before marriage—and now as a mother-to-be, frightened, timorous, and physically and nervously upset by the great ordeal she must go through.

Here often begins a spiritual separation between husband and wife. Conscious of his own helplessness, likewise of his own responsibility, the young husband feels it his duty to leave her alone. This enforced separation is spiritual rather than physical. Outwardly the relation may seem the same. It may be a separation only in the sense that no real unity or welding has been attained. Engrossed by this new problem, the young wife may resign herself to the inevitable and enters a state of passive resignation that is deadening to her love-life. She is in no condition to enjoy companionship. Beneath the superficial and conventional expression of happiness at the approaching parenthood, there may rankle a suppressed resentment at the young husband's careless pride in becoming a father. The young bride knows that she is paying too great a price for the brief and happy days of her honeymoon. She has been swept too rapidly from girlhood to motherhood. Love and romance, as many young wives have confessed to me, were but traps leading her to endless travail and enslavement. And this hidden rankling is often directed toward the husband, whom the wife holds responsible for her accidental pregnancy.

This unhappy condition would not have occurred if they had time to become one, if there were a period of two years during which the bonds of love might be firmly cemented, for time alone can produce this unity. It is a process of growth. Married love does not spring fullgrown into life. It is a delicate plant and it grows from the seed. It must be deeply and firmly rooted, nourished by the sunlight of tenderness, courtship and mutual consideration, before it can produce fine flowers and fruits. This period is as essential for human development as the period of body-building and adolescence.

It is a period of mutual adjustment. It is a period of spiritual discovery and exploration, of finding one's self and one's beloved. It is a period for the full and untroubled expression of passionate love. It is a period for cultural development. It thrusts forward its own complex problems-problems, let it be understood, intricately complex in themselves.

Husband and wife must solve many problems only by *living through them,* not by any cut and dried rules and regulations. For marriage brings with it problems that are individual and unique for each couple.

If instead of solving these problems of early parenthood, in which the life of a third person is immediately involved, a child thrusts itself into the lives of young husband and wife, these fundamental problems of marriage are never given the attention they deserve. A new situation arises, and in innumerable cases, love, as the old adage has it, flies out of the window.

We must recognize that the whole position of womanhood has changed today. Not so many years ago it was assumed to be a just and natural state of affairs that marriage was considered as nothing but a preliminary to motherhood. A girl passed from the guardianship of her father or nearest male relative to that of her husband. She had no will, no wishes of her own. Hers not to question why, but merely to fulfill duties imposed upon her by the man into whose care she was given.

Today women are on the whole much more individual. They possess as strong likes and dislikes as men. They live more and more on the plane of social equality with men. They are better companions. We should be glad that there is more enjoyable companionship and real friendship between men and women.

This very fact, it is true, complicates the marriage relation, and at the same time enables it. Marriage no longer means the slavish subservence of the woman to the will of the man. It means, instead, the union of two strong and highly individualized natures. Their first problem is to find out just what the terms of this partnership are to be. Understanding full and complete cannot come all at once, in one revealing flash. It takes time to arrive at a full and sympathetic understanding of each other, and mutually to arrange lives to increase this understanding. Out of the mutual adjustments, harmony must grow and discords gradually disappear.

These results cannot be obtained if the problem of parenthood is thrust upon the young husband and wife before they are spiritually and economically prepared to meet it. For naturally the coming of the first baby means that all other problems must be thrust aside. That baby is a great fact, a reality that must be met. Preparations must be made for its coming. The layette must be prepared. The doctor must be consulted. The health of the wife may need consideration. The young mother will probably prefer to go to the hospital. All of these preparations are small compared to the régime after the coming of the infant.

In the wife who has lived through a happy marriage, for whom the bonds of passionate love have been fully cemented, maternal desire is intensified and matured. Motherhood becomes for such a woman not a penalty or a punishment, but the road by which she travels onward toward completely rounded self-development. Motherhood thus helps her toward the unfolding and realization of her higher nature.

Her children are not mere accidents, the outcome of chance. When motherhood is a mere accident, as so often it is in the early years of careless or reckless marriages, a constant fear of pregnancy may poison the days and nights of the young mother. Her marriage is thus converted into a tragedy. Motherhood becomes for her a horror instead of a joyfully fulfilled function.

Millions of marriages have been blighted, not because of any lack of love between the young husband and wife, but because children have come too soon. Often these brides become mothers before they have reached even physical maturity, before they have completed the period of adolescence. This period in our race is as a rule complete around the age of twenty-three. Motherhood is possible after the first menstruation. But what is physically possible is very often from every other point of view inadvisable. A young woman should be fully matured from every point of view—physically, mentally and psychically before maternity is thrust upon her.

Those who advise early maternity neglect the spiritual foundation upon which marriage must inevitably be built. This takes time. They also ignore the financial responsibility a family brings.

The young couple begin to build a home. They may have just enough to get along together. The young wife, as in so many cases of early marriage these days, decides to continue her work. They are partners in every way—a commendable thing. The young man is just beginning his career—his salary is probably small. Nevertheless, they manage to get along, their hardships are amusing, and are looked upon as fun. Then suddenly one day, the young wife announces her pregnancy. The situation changes immediately. There are added expenses. The wife must give up her work. The husband must go into debt to pay the expenses of the new and joyfully received arrival. The novelty lasts for some time. The young wife assumes the household duties and the ever growing care of the infant. For a time the child seems to bring the couple closer together. But more often there ensues a concealed resentment on the part of the immature mother at the constant drudgery and slavery to the unfortunate child who has arrived too early upon the scene, which has interfered with her love life.

For the unthinking husband, the "proud papa," the blushing bride is converted at once into the "mother of my children." It is not an unusual occurrence to find that three months after the birth of the baby, the parents are thinking and speaking to each other as "mumsy" and "daddy." The lover and sweetheart relation has disappeared forever and the "mamma-papa" relation has taken its place.

Instead of being a self-determined and self-directing love, everything is henceforward determined by the sweet tyranny of the child. I know of several young mothers, despite a great love for the child, to rebel against this intolerable situation. Vaguely feeling that this new maternity has rendered them unattractive to their husbands, slaves to deadly routine of bottles, baths and washing, they have revolted. I know of innumerable marriages which have been wrecked by premature parenthood.

Love has ever been blighted by the coming of children before the real foundations of marriage have been established. Quite aside from the injustice done to the child who has been brought accidentally into the world, this lamentable fact sinks into insignificance when compared to the injustice inflicted by chance upon the young couple, and the irreparable blow to their love occasioned by premature or involuntary parenthood.

For these reasons, in order that harmonious and happy marriage may be established as the foundation for happy homes and the advent of healthy and desired children, premature parenthood must be avoided. Birth Control is the instrument by which this universal problem may be solved.

1. How does Sanger view women and how does she rank their importance in society?
2. How would John Kellogg react to Sanger's advice?
3. How might Sanger's advice conflict with the contemporary views of the dutiful nobility of motherhood and the status children were alleged to convey on a woman?

23-6   Bartolomeo Vanzetti, Court Statement (1927)

In 1920, Nicola Sacco and Bartolomeo Vanzetti were arrested for killing a guard during the robbery of a shoe factory in South Braintree, Massachusetts. With their conviction, based on what some considered flimsy evidence, the two Italian anarchists became symbols and causes célèbres for liberals across the globe. Nevertheless, after several appeals Sacco and Vanzetti were condemned to death and were executed in the electric chair

Now, I should say that I am not only innocent of all these things, not only have I never committed a real crime in my life-though some sins but not crimes-not only have I struggled all my life to eliminate crimes, the crimes that the officials and the official moral condemns, but also the crime that the official moral and the official law sanctions and sanctifies-the exploitation and the oppression of the man by the man, and if there is a reason why I am here as a guilty man, if there is a reason why you in a few minutes can doom me, it is this reason and none else. . . .

We were tried during a time that has now passed into history. I mean by that, a time when there was a hysteria of resentment and hate against the people of our principles, against the foreigner, against slackers. . . .

Well, I have already said that I not only am not guilty . . . but I never commit a crime in my life-I have never stole and I have never killed and I have never spilt blood, and I have fought against crime and I have fought and have sacrificed myself even to eliminate the crimes the law and the church legitimate and sanctify.

This is what I say: I would not wish to a dog or to a snake, to the most low and misfortunate creature of the earth-I would not wish to any of them what I have had to suffer for things that I am not guilty of. But my conviction is that I have suffered for things I am guilty of. I am suffering because I am a radical and indeed I am a radical; I have suffered because I was an Italian, and indeed I am an Italian; I have suffered more for my family and for my beloved than for myself; but I am so convinced to be right that if you could execute me two times, and if I could be reborn two other times, I would live again to do what I have done already.

I have finished. Thank you.

1. What crimes are sanctioned by the church and the law according to Vanzetti? How has he become a victim of this crime?
2. To what "crimes" does Vanzetti admit his guilt? What is his attitude toward the treatment he has received by American justice? To what extent, does it seem, has anti-immigrant sentiment caused the conviction of Sacco and Vanzetti?

PART TWENTY-FOUR
DEPRESSION AND NEW DEAL

24-1 Herbert Hoover, Speech at New York City (1932)

In the presidential election of 1932, Americans faced a clear choice. Republican incumbent Herbert Hoover espoused a philosophy based on rugged individualism and voluntary cooperation. He claimed that the Democratic program proposed by Franklin D. Roosevelt would profoundly change the character of the United States for the worse.

I may say at once that the changes proposed from all these Democratic principals and allies are of the most profound and penetrating character. If they are brought about this will not be the America which we have known in the past.

Let us pause for a moment and examine the American system of government, of social and economic life, which it is now proposed that we should alter. Our system is the product of our race and of our experience in building a nation to heights unparalleled in the whole history of the world. It is a system peculiar to the American people. It differs essentially from all others in the world. It is an American system.

It is founded on the conception that only through ordered liberty, through freedom to the individual, and equal opportunity to the individual will his initiative and enterprise be summoned to spur the march of national progress.

It is by the maintenance of equality of opportunity and therefore of a society absolutely fluid in the movement of its human particles that our individualism departs from the individualism of Europe. We resent class distinction because there can be no rise for the individual through the frozen strata of classes, and no stratification of classes can take place in a mass livened by the free rise of its particles. Thus in our ideals the able and ambitious are able to rise constantly from the bottom to leadership in the community. And we denounce any intent to stir class feeling and class antagonisms in the United States.

This freedom of the individual creates of itself the necessity and the cheerful willingness of men to act cooperatively in a thousand ways and for every purpose as the occasion requires; and it permits such voluntary cooperations to be dissolved as soon as they have served their purpose, and to be replaced by new voluntary associations for new purposes.

There has thus grown within us, to gigantic importance, a new conception. And that is, this voluntary cooperation within the community. Cooperation to perfect the social organization; cooperation for the care of those in distress; cooperation for the advancement of knowledge, of scientific research, of education; cooperative action in a thousand directions for the advancement of economic life. This is self-government by the people outside of government; it is the most powerful development of individual freedom and equal opportunity that has taken place in the century and a half since our fundamental institutions were founded. . . .

We have heard a great deal in this campaign about reactionaries, conservatives, progressives, liberals and radicals. I think I belong to every group. I have not yet heard an attempt by any one of the orators who mouth these phrases to define the principles upon which they base these classifications. There is one thing I can say without any question of doubt-that is, that the spirit of liberalism is to create free men; it is not the regimentation of men under government. It is not the extension of bureaucracy. I have said in this city before now that you cannot extend the mastery of government over the daily life of a people without somewhere making it master of people's souls and thoughts. Expansion of government in business means that the government in order to protect itself from the political consequences of its errors or even its successes is driven irresistibly without peace to greater and greater control of the nation's press and platform. Free speech does not live many hours after free industry and free commerce die. It is a false liberalism that interprets itself into government operation of business. Every step in that direction poisons the very roots of liberalism. It poisons political equality, free speech, free press and equality of opportunity. It is the road not to liberty, but to less liberty. True liberalism is found not in striving to spread bureaucracy, but in striving to set bounds to it. It is found in an endeavor to extend cooperation between free men. True liberalism seeks all legitimate freedom first in the confident belief that without such freedom the pursuit of other blessings is in vain. Liberalism is a force truly of the spirit proceeding from the deep realization that economic freedom cannot be sacrificed if political freedom is to be preserved.

Even if the government conduct of business could give us the maximum of efficiency instead of least efficiency, it would be purchased at the cost of freedom. It would increase rather than decrease abuse and corruption, stifle initiative and invention, undermine development of leadership, cripple mental and spiritual energies of our people, extinguish equality of opportunity, and dry up the spirit of liberty and progress. Men who are going about this country announcing that they are liberals because of their promises to extend the government in business are not liberals; they are reactionaries of the United States.

1. Explain Hoover's opinion of the relationship that exists among government, business, and the individual.

471

*2. What methods does Hoover encourage to ensure the economic and social welfare of all the people?
What does methods does he warn against?*

24-2 FDR's First Inauguration Speech (1932)

*A tense and hopeful nation listened to Franklin Delano Roosevelt deliver his first official address.
Throughout his campaign he promised a New Deal for Americans, but he was very vague as to what
the New Deal would actually be. His overwhelming election to the presidency suggested great faith in
his ultimate ability to lead the country out of the Great Depression. Roosevelt knew that he had to have
the confidence of Americans and the co-operation of Congress to have any chance at success.*

> **Source:** Henry Steele Commanger, *Documents of American History* (New York: Appleton-Century-Crofts,
> 1949), pp. 240–242; F. D. Roosevelt's First Inaugural Address.

President Hoover, Mr. Chief Justice, my friends:

This is a day of national consecration, and I am certain that my fellow-Americans expect that on my induction into
the Presidency I will address them with a candor and a decision which the present situation of our nation impels.

This is pre-eminently the time to speak the truth, the whole truth, frankly and boldly. Nor need we shrink from
honestly facing conditions in our country today. This great nation will endure as it has endured, will revive and will
prosper.

So first of all let me assert my firm belief that the only thing we have to fear is fear itself—nameless, unreasoning,
unjustified terror which paralyzes needed efforts to convert retreat into advance.

In every dark hour of our national life a leadership of frankness and vigor has met with that understanding and
support of the people themselves which is essential to victory. I am convinced that you will again give that support to leadership in these critical days.

In such a spirit on my part and on yours we face our common difficulties. They concern, thank God, only material things. Values have shrunken to fantastic levels; taxes have risen; our ability to pay has fallen, government of all kinds
is faced by serious curtailment of income; the means of exchange are frozen in the currents of trade; the withered leaves
of industrial enterprise lie on every side; farmers find no markets for their produce; the savings of many years in thousands
of families are gone.

More important, a host of unemployed citizens face the grim problem of existence, and an equally great number
toil with little return. Only a foolish optimist can deny the dark realities of the moment.

Yet our distress comes from no failure of substance. We are stricken by no plague of locusts. Compared with the
perils which our forefathers conquered because they believed and were not afraid, we have still much to be thankful for.
Nature still offers her bounty and human efforts have multiplied it. Plenty is at our doorstep, but a generous use of it languishes in the very sight of the supply.

Primarily, this is because the rulers of the exchange of mankind's goods have failed through their own stubbornness and their own incompetence, have admitted their failure and abdicated. Practices of the unscrupulous money changers
stand indicted in the court of public opinion, rejected by the hearts and minds of men.

True, they have tried, but their efforts have been cast in the pattern of an outworn tradition. Faced by failure of
credit, they have proposed only the lending of more money.

Stripped of the lure of profit by which to induce our people to follow their false leadership, they have resorted to
exhortations, pleading tearfully for restored confidence. They know only the rules of a generation of self-seekers.

They have no vision, and when there is no vision the people perish.

The money changers have fled from their high seats in the temple of our civilization. We may now restore that
temple to the ancient truths.

The measure of the restoration lies in the extent to which we apply social values more noble than mere monetary
profit.

Happiness lies not in the mere possession of money; it lies in the joy of achievement, in the thrill of creative effort.

The joy and moral stimulation of work no longer must be forgotten in the mad chase of evanescent profits. These
dark days will be worth all they cost us if they teach us that our true destiny is not to be ministered unto but to minister
to ourselves and to our fellow-men.

Recognition of the falsity of material wealth as the standard of success goes hand in hand with the abandonment of the false belief that public office and high political position are to be valued only by the standards of pride of
place and personal profit; and there must be an end to a conduct in banking and in business which too often has given

to a sacred trust the likeness of callous and selfish wrongdoing.

Small wonder that confidence languishes, for it thrives only on honesty, on honor, on the sacredness of obligations, on faithful protection, on unselfish performance. Without them it cannot live.

Restoration calls, however, not for changes in ethics alone. This nation asks for action, and action now.

Our greatest primary task is to put people to work. This is no unsolvable problem if we face it wisely and courageously.

It can be accomplished in part by direct recruiting by the government itself, treating the task as we would treat the emergency of a war, but at the same time, through this employment, accomplishing greatly needed projects to stimulate and reorganize the use of our natural resources.

Hand in hand with this, we must frankly recognize the overbalance of population in our industrial centers and, by engaging on a national scale in the redistribution, endeavor to provide a better use of the land for those best fitted for the land.

The task can be helped by definite efforts to raise the values of agricultural products and with this the power to purchase the output of our cities.

It can be helped by preventing realistically the tragedy of the growing loss, through foreclosure, of our small homes and our farms.

It can be helped by insistence that the Federal, State and local governments act forthwith on the demand that their cost be drastically reduced.

It can be helped by the unifying of relief activities which today are often scattered, uneconomical and unequal. It can be helped by national planning for and supervision of all forms of transportation and of communications and other utilities which have a definitely public character.

There are many ways in which it can be helped, but it can never be helped merely by talking about it. We must act, and act quickly.

Finally, in our progress toward a resumption of work we require two safeguards against a return of the evils of the old order; there must be a strict supervision of all banking and credits and investments; there must be an end to speculation with other people's money, and there must be provision for an adequate but sound currency.

These are the lines of attack. I shall presently urge upon a new congress in special session detailed measures for their fulfillment, and I shall seek the immediate assistance of the several States.

Through this program of action we address ourselves to putting our own national house in order and making income balance outgo.

Our international trade relations, though vastly important, are, in point of time and necessity, secondary to the establishment of a sound national economy.

I favor as a practical policy the putting of first things first. I shall spare no effort to restore world trade by international economic readjustment, but the emergency at home cannot wait on that accomplishment.

The basic thought that guides these specific means of national recovery is not narrowly nationalistic.

It is the insistence, as a first consideration, upon the interdependence of the various elements in, and parts of, the United States—a recognition of the old and permanently important manifestation of the American spirit of the pioneer.

It is the way to recovery. It is the immediate way. It is the strongest assurance that the recovery will endure.

In the field of world policy I would dedicate this nation to the policy of the good neighbor—the neighbor who resolutely respects himself and, because he does so, respects the rights of others—the neighbor who respects his obligations and respects the sanctity of his agreements in and with a world of neighbors.

If I read the temper of our people correctly, we now realize as we have never before, our interdependence on each other; that we cannot merely take, but we must give as well; that if we are to go forward we must move as a trained and loyal army willing to sacrifice for the good of a common discipline, because, without such discipline, no progress is made, no leadership becomes effective.

We are, I know, ready and willing to submit our lives and property to such discipline because it makes possible a leadership which aims at a larger good.

This I propose to offer, pledging that the larger purposes will bind upon us all as a sacred obligation with a unity of duty hitherto evoked only in time of armed strife.

With this pledge taken, I assume unhesitatingly the leadership of this great army of our people, dedicated to a disciplined attack upon our common problems.

Action in this image and to this end is feasible under the form of government which we have inherited from our ancestors.

Our Constitution is so simple and practical that it is possible always to meet extraordinary needs by changes in emphasis and arrangement without loss of essential form.

That is why our constitutional system has proved itself the most superbly enduring political mechanism the modern world has produced. It has met every stress of vast expansion of territory, of foreign wars, of bitter internal strife, of world relations.

It is to be hoped that the normal balance of executive and legislative authority may be wholly adequate to meet the unprecedented task before us. But it may be that an unprecedented demand and need for undelayed action may call for temporary departure from that normal balance of public procedure.

I am prepared under my constitutional duty to recommend the measures that a stricken nation in the midst of a stricken world may require.

These measures, or such other measures as the Congress may build out of its experience and wisdom, I shall seek, within my constitutional authority, to bring to speedy adoption.

But in the event that the Congress shall fail to take one of these two courses, and in the event that the national emergency is still critical, I shall not evade the clear course of duty that will then confront me.

I shall ask the Congress for the one remaining instrument to meet the crisis—broad executive power to wage a war against the emergency as great as the power that would be given me if we were in fact invaded by a foreign foe.

For the trust reposed in me I will return the courage and the devotion that befit the time, I can do no less.

We face the arduous days that lie before us in the warm courage of national unity; with the clear consciousness of seeking old and precious moral values; with the clean satisfaction that comes from the stern performance of duty by old and young alike.

We aim at the assurance of a rounded and permanent national life.

We do not distrust the future of essential democracy. The people of the United States have not failed. In their need they have registered a mandate that they want direct, vigorous action.

They have asked for discipline and direction under leadership. They have made me the present instrument of their wishes. In the spirit of the gift I take it.

In this dedication of a nation we humbly ask the blessing of God. May He protect each and every one of us! May He guide me in the days to come!

1. *How did Roosevelt convey to his audience that he comprehended the gravity of the problems they faced day to day? Is this political pandering or was it essential for him to communicate empathy?*
2. *What indications are in this speech that suggest Roosevelt is a man of action and that changes are imminent?*
3. *How would a member of Congress hear this speech differently than the ordinary listener?*

24-3 Franklin Delano Roosevelt, Speech at San Francisco (1932)

Campaigning in California in September of 1932, Roosevelt gave this speech to the Commonwealth Club of California, a public affairs speaking forum. In this speech, Roosevelt hoped to explain differences in political ideology between he and Republican President Herbert Hoover. Roosevelt argued that the United States had entered a new era in which only through a strong and active government could provide economic opportunities for the individual while protecting them from the abuses rampant in industry at the time.

As I see it, the task of Government in its relation to business is to assist the development of an economic declaration of rights, an economic constitutional order. This is the common task of statesman and business man. It is the minimum requirement of a more permanently safe order of things. . . .

The Declaration of Independence discusses the problem of Government in terms of a contract. Government is a relation of give and take, a contract, perforce, if we would follow the thinking out of which it grew. Under such a contract rulers were accorded power, and the people consented to that power on consideration that they be accorded certain rights. The task of statesmanship has always been the re-definition of these rights in terms of a changing and growing social order. New conditions impose new requirements upon Government and those who conduct Government. . . .

I feel that we are coming to a view through the drift of our legislation and our public thinking in the past quarter century that private economic power is, to enlarge an old phrase, a public trust as well. I hold that continued enjoyment of that power by any individual or group must depend upon the fulfillment of that trust. The men who have reached the summit of American business life know this best; happily, many of these urge the binding quality of this greater social contract.

The terms of that contract are as old as the Republic, and as new as the new economic order.

Every man has a right to life; and this means that he has also a right to make a comfortable living. He may by sloth or crime decline to exercise that right; but it may not be denied him. We have no actual famine or dearth; our industrial and agricultural mechanism can produce enough and to spare. Our Government formal and informal, political and economic, owes to everyone an avenue to possess himself of a portion of that plenty sufficient for his needs, through his own work.

Every man has a right to his own property; which means a right to be assured, to the fullest extent attainable, in the safety of his savings. By no other means can men carry the burdens of those parts of life which, in the nature of things, afford no chance of labor; childhood, sickness, old age. In all thought of property, this right is paramount; all other property rights must yield to it. If, in accord with this principle, we must restrict the operations of the speculator, the manipulator, even the financier, I believe we must accept the restriction as needful, not to hamper individualism but to protect it.

These two requirements must be satisfied, in the main, by the individuals who claim and hold control of the great industrial and financial combinations which dominate so large a part of our industrial life. They have undertaken to be, not business men, but princes of property. I am not prepared to say that the system which produces them is wrong. I am very clear that they must fearlessly and competently assume the responsibility which goes with the power. So many enlightened business men know this that the statement would be little more than a platitude, were it not for an added implication.

This implication is, briefly, that the responsible heads of finance and industry instead of acting each for himself, must work together to achieve the common end. They must, where necessary, sacrifice this or that private advantage; and in reciprocal self-denial must seek a general advantage. It is here that formal Government-political Government, if you chose-comes in. Whenever in the pursuit of this objective the lone wolf, the unethical competitor, the reckless promoter, the Ishmael or Insull whose hand is against every man's, declines to join in achieving an end recognized as being for the public welfare, and threatens to drag the industry back to a state of anarchy, the Government may properly be asked to apply restraint. Likewise, should the group ever use its collective power contrary to the public welfare, the Government must be swift to enter and protect the public interest.

The Government should assume the function of economic regulation only as a last resort, to be tried only when private initiative, inspired by high responsibility, with such assistance and balance as Government can give, has finally failed. As yet there has been no final failure, because there has been no attempt; and I decline to assume that this Nation is unable to meet the situation.

The final term of the high contract was for liberty and the pursuit of happiness. We have learned a great deal of both in the past century. We know that individual liberty and individual happiness mean nothing unless both are ordered in the sense that one man's meat is not another man's poison. We know that the old "rights of personal competency," the right to read, to think, to speak, to choose and live a mode of life, must be respected at all hazards. We know that liberty to do anything which deprives others of those elemental rights is outside the protection of any compact; and that Government in this regard is the maintenance of a balance, within which every individual may have a place if he will take it; in which every individual may find safety if he wishes it; in which every individual may attain such power as his ability permits, consistent with his assuming the accompanying responsibility.

All this is a long, slow talk. Nothing is more striking than the simple innocence of the men who insist, whenever an objective is present, on the prompt production of a patent scheme guaranteed to produce a result. Human endeavor is not so simple as that. Government includes the art of formulating a policy, and using the political technique to attain so much of that policy as will receive general support; persuading, leading, sacrificing, teaching always, because the greatest duty of a statesman is to educate. But in the matters of which I have spoken, we are learning rapidly, in a severe school. The lessons so learned must not be forgotten, even in the mental lethargy of a speculative upturn. We must build toward the time when a major depression cannot occur again; and if this means sacrificing the easy profits of inflationist booms, then let them go; and good riddance.

1. *What does this document define as the role of government as it relates to business and the welfare of the people?*
2. *What responsibilities, according to Roosevelt, must the heads of finance and industry bear?*

24-4 Share the Wealth

Senator Huey Long of Louisiana became a staunch critic of the New Deal by the end of Roosevelt's first term. Long argued that the New Deal did not go far enough to stop the depression and to restore the nation's economic good health. Long planned to oppose Roosevelt in the 1936 election and he planned to use his Share Our Wealth program as his springboard to the nomination and election. He was convinced that he could portray Roosevelt as a puppet of the wealthy class in America, and that as such, the best interests of those who suffered the most during the depression were ignored.

Source: Huey Long, *Every Man A King* (New Orleans, National Book Co., 1933), pp. 290–298.

475

I had come to the United States Senate with only one project in mind, which was that by every means of action and persuasion I might do something to spread the wealth of the land among all of the people.

I foresaw the depression in 1929. In letters reproduced in this volume, I had predicted all of the consequences many years before they occurred.

The wealth of the land was being tied up in the hands of a very few men. The people were not buying because they had nothing with which to buy. The big business interests were not selling, because there was nobody they could sell to.

One per cent of the people could not eat any more than any other one per cent; they could not wear much more than any other one per cent; they could not live in any more houses than any other one per cent. So, in 1929, when the fortune-holders of America grew powerful enough that one per cent of the people owned nearly everything, ninety-nine per cent of the people owned practically nothing, not even enough to pay their debts, a collapse was at hand.

God Almighty had warned against this condition. Thomas Jefferson, Andrew Jackson, Daniel Webster, Theodore Roosevelt, William Jennings Bryan and every religious teacher known to this earth had declaimed against it. So it was no new matter, as it was termed, when I propounded the line of thought with the first crash of 1929, that the eventful day had arrived when accumulation at the top by the few had produced a stagnation by which the vast multitude of the people were impoverished at the bottom.

There is no rule so sure as that one that the same mill that grinds out fortunes above a certain size at the top, grinds out paupers at the bottom. The same machine makes them both; and how are they made? There is so much in the world, just so much land, so many houses, so much to eat and so much to wear. There is enough—yea, there is more—than the entire human race can consume, if all are reasonable.

All the people in America cannot eat up the food that is produced in America; all the people in America cannot wear out the clothes that can be made in America; nor can all of the people in America occupy the houses that stand in this country, if all are allowed to share in homes afforded by the nation. But when one man must have more houses to live in than ninety-nine other people; when one man decides he must own more foodstuff than any other ninety-nine people own; when one man decides he must have more goods to wear for himself and family than any other ninety-nine people, then the condition results that instead of one hundred people sharing the things that are on earth for one hundred people, that one man, through his gluttonous greed, takes over ninety-nine parts for himself and leaves one part for the ninety-nine.

Now what can this one man do with what is intended for ninety-nine? He cannot eat the food that is intended for ninety-nine people; he cannot wear the clothes that are intended for ninety-nine people; he cannot live in ninety-nine houses at the same time; but like the dog in the manger, he can put himself on the load of hay and he can say:

"This food and these clothes and these houses are mine, and while I cannot use them, my greed can only be satisfied by keeping anybody else from having them."

Wherefore and whence developed the strife in the land of too much, beginning in the year 1929.

I was standing in the lobby of the Roosevelt Hotel in New Orleans on the 23rd day of October, 1929, at lunch time. Mr. R. S. Hecht, President of the powerful Hibernia Bank & Trust Company, walked to the middle of the lobby, approached me and said:

"Governor, hell's broke loose; the biggest crash of everything that you have ever seen. It is going to be sixty days before this country will get back to normal."

"I have expected this crash for three years," I replied. "It is here for many, many years. It cannot end until there is a redistribution of wealth. Make your plans on that basis."

We argued and wrangled for some moments. A few days later I was informed by a member present that at a meeting of the board of directors of his bank he had repeated, without approval, what I had prophesied. I made known my opinion of the then prevailing cause of the national collapse to the people generally. Time is bearing out all I then said.

My philosophy for sharing the work and sharing the wealth by shortening hours and limiting fortunes was first delivered in the United States Senate on April 4, 1932:

Machines are created making it possible to manufacture more in an hour than used to be manufactured in a month; more is produced by the labor of one man than was formerly produced by the labor of a thousand men; fertilizers are available whereby an acre of land can be made to produce from two to three or even four times what it formerly produced; various other inventions and scientific achievements which God has seen fit to disclose to man from time to time make their appearance; but instead of bringing prosperity, ease and comfort, they have meant unemployment; they have meant idleness; they have meant starvation; they have meant pestilence; whereas they should have meant that hours of labor were shortened, that toil was decreased, that more people would be able to consume, that they would have time for pleasure, time for recreation—in fact, everything that could have been done by science and invention and wealth and progress in this country should have been shared among the people. . . .

But, oh, Mr. President, if we could simply let the people enjoy the wealth and the accumulations and the contrivances that we have. If, with the invention of every machine, we could secure the education of every man; if with increased production of every kind there could be less toil, more hours of pleasure and recreation; if there could be a happy and contented people enjoying what the Almighty has made it possible to provide; if there could be people clothed with the materials that we have to clothe them with today, and no place to put them; if the people could be fed with the food that we have to feed them with, and no place to put it; if the people could be sheltered in the homes we have today, that the Federal Land Bank has taken away from them because they cannot pay the interest on the mortgages—if that could be done, if we could distribute this surplus wealth, while leaving these rich people all the luxuries they can possibly use, what a different world this would be.

We can do this. If we do not, we will leave these masters of finance and fame and fortune like the man in the book of old, who said to himself, so the Bible tells us:

"I will pull down my barns, and build greater; and there will I bestow all my fruits and my goods.

"And I will say to my soul: Soul, thou hast much goods laid up for many years; take thine ease, eat, drink and be merry.

"But God said unto him: Thou fool, this night thy soul shalt be required of thee."

While the tax bills were pending before the United States Senate in 1932, I proposed a resolution which provided that the tax bills should be so revamped that no one man should be allowed to have an income of more than one million dollars a year; that no one person should inherit in a lifetime more than five million dollars without working for it.

The effect of that resolution was that when a man made one million dollars in a year, the government of the United States would receive the balance; and when a rich man died, he could not leave one child more than five million dollars, and the balance would go to the government of the United States.

This would have meant that much of the taxes would have been paid by the so-called upper classes, and that instead of the funds of the government being sucked from the bottom and exploited by the classes at the top, the classes at the top would have paid the taxes to be filtered out to the masses at the bottom, through the various general works and compensations supported by the government.

My resolution, however, received only a few votes.

A COMPARISON

Consider the horrible way of the gangster, and then compare his practices with the greed of our mighty fortune-holders in America:

The gangsters have killed hundreds, maybe thousands, to carry out their nefarious rackets to extort money.

The hoarders of wealth have destroyed humanity by millions in their quest for greater accumulation.

From the newborn babe to the man bowed with age, some have been denied the sustenance for life: they have been thrown from the shelter above their heads; to keep children warm they have been placed in the ground, to start a life not in the cradle, but in the grave; half naked bodies have been thrown against the winter's wind; some have become beggars, some thieves, and some have been murderers; others have been driven insane and still others to suicide—all in the wake of the drive that the masters of fortunes may own and control so much that, even in the land of too much to eat and too much to wear, people perish in their shadow.

Jefferson, Jackson, Webster, Lincoln, Theodore Roosevelt and Bryan have clamored to spread our work and our wealth among all the people.

It is the law of God that a nation must free and re-free its people of debt, and spread and re-spread the wealth of the land among all the people.

"Wherefore ye shall do my statutes, and keep my judgments, and do them; and the land shall yield her fruit and ye shall eat your fill, and dwell therein in safety." Leviticus, Chapter 25, verses 18 and 19.

What cycle of events brings the crime wave of robbery and extortion, murder and destruction?

"Who gave Jacob for a spoil and Israel to the robbers? Did not the Lord, for they would not walk in his ways, neither were they obedient unto his law." Isaiah, Chapter 42, verse 24.

In my never changing course for relief and compensation for the Veterans of our wars, livable wages for public employees, a recognition of all hirelings to unite and bargain for the sinews they have to offer,—all to be supported from top heavy accumulations,—I have merely carried through a philosophy to insure diffusing our wealth into the hands of all who must consume our products.

But I saw to it that my views were known to Mr. Roosevelt, then Governor of New York and now President of the United States. Early in his candidacy in a speech delivered in Atlanta, Mr. Roosevelt said:

The millions who are in want will not stand by silently forever while the things to satisfy their needs are within easy reach.

Many of those whose primary solicitude is confined to the welfare of what they call capital have failed to read the lessons of the last few years and have been moved less by calm analysis of the needs of the Nation as a whole than by a blind determination to preserve their own special stakes in the economic disorder.

We may build more factories, but the fact remains that we have enough now to supply all our domestic needs and more, if they are used. No; our basic trouble was not an insufficiency of capital; it was an insufficient distribution of buying power coupled with an oversufficient speculation in production.

Soon thereafter on the basis of such declarations, I became convinced that the best chance for a solution of America's difficulties was through the election of Franklin D. Roosevelt as President.

1. What was Long's rationale for the Share the Wealth program?
2. Why does Long invoke the names of Jefferson, Jackson, Webster, Lincoln and Theodore Roosevelt?
3. Was Long a socialist?

24-5 The Victims of the Ku Klux Klan (1935)

The Ku Klux Klan had experienced substantial growth in the 1920s but quickly declined. But the Klan survived and committed brutal violence against African Americans.

Pierce Harper

After de colored people was considered free an' turned loose de Klu Klux broke out. Some of de colored people commenced to farming like I tol' you an' all de ol' stock dey could pick up after de Yankees left dey took an' took care of. If you got so you made good money an' had a good farm de Klu Klux'd come an' murder you. De gov'ment built de colored people school houses an' de Klu Klux went to work an' burn 'em down. Dey'd go to de jails an' take de colored men out an' knock der brains out an' break der necks an' throw 'em in de river.

Der was a man dat dey taken, his name was Jim Freeman. Dey taken him an' destroyed his stuff an' him 'cause he was making some money. Hung him on a tree in his front yard, right in front of his cabin. Der was some young men who went to de schools de gov'ment opened for de colored folks. Some white widder woman said someone had stole something she own', so dey put these young fellers in jail 'cause dey suspicioned 'em. De Klu Kluxes went to de jail an' took 'em out an' kill 'em. Dat happened de second year after de War.

After de Klu Kluxes got so strong de colored men got together an' made a complaint before de law. De Gov'nor told de law to give 'em de ol' guns in de commissary what de Southern soldiers had use, so dey issued de col'red men old muskets an' told 'em to protect theirselves.

De colored men got together an' organized the 'Malicy [Militia]. Dey had leaders like regular soldiers, men dat led 'em right on. Dey didn't meet 'cept when dey heard de Klu Kluxes was coming to get some of de colored folks. Den de one who knowed dat tol' de leader an' he went 'round an' told de others when an' where dey's meet. Den dey was ready for 'em. Dey's hide in de cabins an' when de Klu Kluxes come dere dey was. Den's when dey found out who a lot of de Klu Kluxes was, 'cause a lot of 'em was killed. Dey wore dem long sheets an' you couldn't tell who dey was. Dey even covered der horses up so you couldn't tell who dey belong to. Men you thought was your friend was Klu Kluxes. You deal wit' em in de stores in de day time an' at night dey come out to your house an' kill you.

Sue Craft

My teacher's name Dunlap-a white teacher teachin' de cullud. De Ku Klux whupped him fo' teachin' us. I saw de Ku Klux ridin' a heap dem days. Dey had hoods pulled ovah der faces. One time dey come to our house twict. Fus' time dey come quiet. It was right 'fore de 'lection o' Grant jus' after slavery. It was fus' time cullud people 'lowed t' vote. Dey ast my father was he goint to vote for Grant. He tell 'em he don' know he goin' vote. After 'lection day come back, whoopin' an' hollerin'. Dey shoot out de winder lights. It was 'cause my father voted for Grant. Dey broke de do' open. My father was a settin' on de bed. I 'member he had a shot gun in his han'. Well, de broke de do' down, an' then father he shoot, an' dey scattered all ovah de fence.

Morgan Ray

. . . I heard a lot about the Klu Klux, but it warn't till long afterwards dat I evah see 'em. It was one night after de work of de day was done and I was takin' a walk near where I worked. Suddenly I heard the hoof beats of horses and I natcherly wuz curious and waited beside the road to see what was coming'. I saw a company of men hooded and wearin' what looked like sheets. Dey had a young cullud man as der prisoner. I wuz too skairt to say anything or ask any questions. I just went on my sweet way. Later I found out dey acclaimed de prisoner had assulted a white woman. Dey strung him up when he wouldn't confess, and shot him full of holes and threw his body in de pond.

1. *According to Pierce Harper's account, in what ways was the Ku Klux Klan responsible for prohibiting the success of African American's after the war?*
2. *What examples are provided of the Klan's ability to terrorize black families and influence their behavior without fear of punishment or retribution?*
3. *In what ways does the Klan seem to be attempting to restore a pre-civil war society in regard to African Americans?*

24-6 Father Charles E. Coughlin, "A Third Party" (1936)

The New Deal drew much criticism from various people calling for a variety of new ideas and programs. Using radio to good effect, Father Charles E. Coughlin, an early New Deal supporter turned critic, suggested a solution to the depression was the printing of more money.

By 1932 a new era of production had come into full bloom. It was represented by the motor car, the tractor and power lathe, which enables the laborer to produce wealth ten times more rapidly than was possible for his ancestors. Within the short expanse of 150 years the problem of production had been solved, due to the ingenuity of men like Arkwright and his loom, Fulton and his steam engine, and Edison and his dynamo. These and a thousand other benefactors of mankind made it possible for the teeming millions of people throughout the world to transfer speedily the raw materials into the thousand necessities and conveniences which fall under the common name of wealth.

Thus, with the advent of our scientific era, with its far-flung fields, its spacious factories, its humming motors, its thundering locomotives, its highly trained mechanics, it is inconceivable how such a thing as a so-called depression should blight the lives of an entire nation when there was a plenitude of everything surrounding us, only to be withheld from us because the so-called leaders of high finance persisted in clinging to an outworn theory of privately issued money, the medium through which wealth is distributed.

I challenged this private control and creation of money because it was alien to our Constitution, which says "Congress shall have the right to coin and regulate the value of money." I challenged this system of permitting a small group of private citizens to create money and credit out of nothing, to issue it into circulation through loans and to demand that borrowers repay them with money which represented real goods, real labor and real service. I advocated that it be replaced by the American system-namely, that the creation and control of money and credit are the rights of the people through their democratic government. . . .

No man in modern times received such plaudits from the poor as did Franklin Roosevelt when he promised to drive the money changers from the temple-the money changers who had clipped the coins of wages, who had manufactured spurious money and who had brought proud America to her knees.

March 4, 1933! I shall never forget the inaugural address, which seemed to re-echo the very words of Christ Himself as He actually drove the money changers from the temple.

The thrill that was mine was yours. Through dim clouds of the depression this man Roosevelt was, as it were, a new savior of his people! . . .

Such were our hopes in the springtime of 1933.

My friends, what have we witnessed as the finger of time turned the pages of the calendar? Nineteen hundred and thirty-three and the National Recovery Act which multiplied profits for the monopolists; 1934 and the AAA which raised the price of foodstuffs by throwing back God's best gifts into His face; 1935 and the Banking Act which rewarded the exploiters of the poor, the Federal Reserve bankers and their associates, by handing over to them the temple from which they were to have been cast! . . .

Alas! The temple still remains the private property of the money changers. The golden key has been handed over to them for safekeeping-the key which now is fashioned in the shape of a double cross.

1. *What factors, according to Coughlin, are responsible for the depression of the U.S. economy? What solutions does he offer?*
2. *How does Coughlin use the biblical image of Jesus driving moneychangers from the temple to characterize Roosevelt's promises and subsequent failure to deliver on that promise?*

24-7 Mrs. Henry Weddington, Letter to President Roosevelt (1938)

Through his folksy manner and Fireside Chats on the radio, President Franklin D. Roosevelt connected with the American people. He received many letters from Americans, such as the one from Mrs. Henry Weddington, on various subjects. Many told of their situation and asked for help.

Dear President Roosevelt:

I really don't know exactly how to begin this letter to you. Perhaps I should first tell you who I am. I am a young married woman. I am a Negro. . . . I believe that you are familiar with the labor situation among the Negroes, but I want you to know how I and many of us feel about it and what we expect of you.

My husband is working for the W.P.A. doing skilled labor. Before he started on this we were on relief for three months. We were three months trying to get relief. While trying to obtain relief I lost my unborn child. I believe if I had sufficient food this would not have happened. My husband was perfectly willing to work but could not find it. Now I am pregnant again. He is working at Tilden Tech. School where there are more white than colored. Every month more than one hundred persons are given private employment and not one of them are colored. It isn't that the colored men are not as skilled as the white, it is the fact that they are black and therefore must not get ahead.

We are citizens just as much or more than the majority of this country. . . . We are just as intelligent as they. This is supposed to be a free country regardless of color, creed or race but still we are slaves. . . . Won't you help us? I'm sure you can. I admire you and have very much confidence in you. I believe you are a real Christian and non-prejudiced. I have never doubted that you would be elected again. I believe you can and must do something about the labor conditions of the Negro.

Why must our men fight and die for their country when it won't even given them a job that they are fitted for? They would much rather fight and die for their families or race. Before it is over many of them might. We did not ask to be brought here as slaves, nor did we ask to be born black. We are real citizens of this land and must and will be recognized as such! . . . If you are a real Christian you can not stand by and let these conditions exist.

My husband is young, intelligent and very depressed over this situation. We want to live, not merely exist from day to day, but to live as you or any human being desires to do. We want our unborn children to have an equal chance as the white. We don't want them to suffer as we are doing now because of race prejudice. My husband is 22 and I am 18 years of age. We want to own just a comfortable home by the time he reaches his early thirties. Is that asking too much? But how can we do that when the $26 he makes every two weeks don't hardly last the two weeks it should. I can manage money rather well but still we don't have the sufficient amount of food or clothes to keep us warm. . . . I would appreciate it very much if you would give this letter some consideration and give me an answer. I realize that you are a very busy person and have many problems but please give this problem a little thought also.

I will close thanking you in advance.
Sincerely and hopefully yours
Mrs. Henry Weddington

1. *Describe the conditions under which Mrs. Henry Weddington and her husband live and work. What disadvantages or prejudices are experienced by the Weddington's as a result of their race?*
2. *Summarize the method and attitude of this appeal? In what way is this appeal, perhaps, representative of the complaints of countless Americans during this time period?*

PART TWENTY-FIVE
WORLD WAR TWO

25-1 Albert Einstein, Letter to President Roosevelt (1939)

This letter from Albert Einstein warned Franklin Roosevelt that German researchers were close to making an atomic bomb. Inspired by Einstein (and his fellow scientists), Roosevelt organized a secret project (known later as the Manhattan project), to ensure that the United States had a bomb before Germany. In later life, Albert Einstein, committed to peace, regretted sending this letter.

Albert Einstein
Old Grove Rd.
Nassau Point
Peconic, Long Island
August 2nd, 1939
F. D. Roosevelt,
President of the United States,
White House
Washington, D. C.

Sir:

Some recent work by E. Fermi and L. Szilard, which has been communicated to me in manuscript, leads me to expect that the element uranium may be turned into a new and important source of energy in the immediate future. Certain aspects of the situation which has arisen seem to call for watchfulness and, if necessary, quick action on the part of the Administration. I believe therefore that it is my duty to bring to your attention the following facts and recommendations:

In the course of the last four months it has been made probable-through the work of Joliot in France as well as Fermi and Szilard in America-that it may become possible to set up a nuclear chain reaction in a large mass of uranium, by which vast amount of power and large quantities of new radium-like elements would be generated. Now it appears almost certain that this could be achieved in the immediate future.

This new phenomenon would also lead to the construction of bombs, and it is conceivable-though much less certain-that extremely powerful bombs of a new type may thus be constructed. A single bomb of this type, carried by boat and exploded in a port, might very well destroy the whole port together with some of the surrounding territory. However, such bombs might very well prove to be too heavy for transportation by air.

The United States has only very poor ores of uranium in moderate quantities. There is some good ore in Canada and the former Czechoslovakia, while the most important source of uranium is the Belgian Congo.

In view of this situation you may think it desirable to have some permanent contact maintained between the Administration and the group of physicists working on chain reactions in America. One possible way of achieving this might be for you to entrust with this task a person who has your confidence and who could perhaps serve in an inofficial capacity. His task might comprise the following:

a)   to approach Government Departments, keep them informed of the further development, and put forward recommendations for Government action, giving particular attention to the problem of securing a supply of uranium ore for the United States:

b)   to speed up the experimental work, which is at present being carried on within the limits of the budgets of University laboratories, by providing funds, if such funds be required, through his contacts with private persons who are willing to make contributions for this cause, and perhaps also by obtaining the co-operation of industrial laboratories which have the necessary equipment.

I understand that Germany has actually stopped the sale of uranium from the Czechoslovakian mines which she has taken over. That she should have taken such early action might perhaps be understood on the ground that the son of the German Under-Secretary of State, von Weizsacker, is attached to the Kaiser-Wilhelm-Institut in Berlin where some of the American work on uranium is now being repeated.

Yours very truly,
[signed] Albert Einstein

1. *Identify Einstein's description of the potential energy and destructive power of the new bomb. Based on what we know of the atomic bomb today, discuss the accuracy of Einstein's predictions.*
2. *Summarize Einstein's recommendations to the president regarding further research and development of the bomb.*

25-2 Charles Lindbergh, Radio Address (1941)

The American First Committee was formed by famed aviator Charles Lindbergh and others to keep the United States out of World War Two. After war broke out in Europe, the Committee waged a campaign against American entry.

There are many viewpoints from which the issues of this war can be argued. Some are primarily idealistic. Some are primarily practical. One should, I believe, strive for a balance of both. But, since the subjects that can be covered in a single address are limited, tonight I shall discuss the war from a viewpoint which is primarily practical. It is not that I believe ideals are unimportant, even among the realities of war; but if a nation is to survive in a hostile world, its ideals must be backed by the hard logic of military practicability. If the outcome of war depended upon ideals alone, this would be a different world than it is today.

I know I will be severely criticized by the interventionists in America when I say we should not enter a war unless we have a reasonable chance of winning. That, they will claim, is far too materialistic a viewpoint. They will advance again the same arguments that were used to persuade France to declare war against Germany in 1939. But I do not believe that our American ideals, and our way of life, will gain through an unsuccessful war. And I know that the United States is not prepared to wage war in Europe successfully at this time. We are no better prepared today than France was when the interventionists in Europe persuaded her to attack the Siegfried line.

I have said before, and I will say again, that I believe it will be a tragedy to the entire world if the British Empire collapses. That is one of the main reasons why I opposed this war before it was declared and why I have constantly advocated a negotiated peace. I did not feel that England and France had a reasonable chance of winning. France has now been defeated; and, despite the propaganda and confusion of recent months, it is now obvious that England is losing the war. I believe this is realized even by the British Government. But they have one last desperate plan remaining. They hope that they may be able to persuade us to send another American Expeditionary Force to Europe, and to share with England militarily, as well as financially, the fiasco of this war.

I do not blame England for this hope, or for asking for our assistance. But we now know that she declared a war under circumstances which led to the defeat of every nation that sided with her from Poland to Greece. We know that in the desperation of war England promised to all those nations armed assistance that she could not send. We know that she misinformed them, as she has misinformed us, concerning her state of preparation, her military strength, and the progress of the war.

In time of war, truth is always replaced by propaganda. I do not believe we should be too quick to criticize the actions of a belligerent nation. There is always the question whether we, ourselves, would do better under similar circumstances. But we in this country have a right to think of the welfare of America first, just as the people in England thought first of their own country when they encouraged the smaller nations of Europe to fight against hopeless odds. When England asks us to enter this war, she is considering her own future and that of her Empire. In making our reply, I believe we should consider the future of the United States and that of the Western Hemisphere.

It is not only our right, but it is our obligation as American citizens, to look at this war objectively and to weigh our chances for success if we should enter it. I have attempted to do this, especially from the standpoint of aviation; and I have been forced to the conclusion that we cannot win this war for England, regardless of how much assistance we extend.

I ask you to look at the map of Europe today and see if you can suggest any way in which we could win this war if we entered it. Suppose we had a large army in America, trained and equipped. Where would we send it to fight? The campaigns of the war show only too clearly how difficult it is to force a landing, or to maintain an army, on a hostile coast.

Suppose we took our Navy from the Pacific and used it to convoy British shipping. That would not win the war for England. It would, at best, permit her to exist under the constant bombing of the German air fleet. Suppose we had an air force that we could send to Europe. Where could it operate? Some of our squadrons might be based in the British Isles, but it is physically impossible to base enough aircraft in the British Isles alone to equal in strength the aircraft that can be based on the continent of Europe.

I have asked these questions on the supposition that we had in existence an Army and an air force large enough and well enough equipped to send to Europe; and that we would dare to remove our Navy from the Pacific. Even on this basis, I do not see how we could invade the continent of Europe successfully as long as all of that continent and most of

Asia is under Axis domination. But the fact is that none of these suppositions are correct. We have only a one-ocean Navy. Our Army is still untrained and inadequately equipped for foreign war. Our air force is deplorably lacking in modern fighting planes.

When these facts are cited, the interventionists shout that we are defeatists, that we are undermining the principles of democracy, and that we are giving comfort to Germany by talking about our military weakness. But everything I mention here has been published in our newspapers and in the reports of congressional hearings in Washington. Our military position is well known to the governments of Europe and Asia. Why, then, should it not be brought to the attention of our own people?

I say it is the interventionists in America as it was in England and in France, who give comfort to the enemy. I say it is they who are undermining the principles of democracy when they demand that we take a course to which more than 80 percent of our citizens are opposed. I charge them with being the real defeatists, for their policy has led to the defeat of every country that followed their advice since this war began. There is no better way to give comfort to an enemy than to divide the people of a nation over the issue of foreign war. There is no shorter road to defeat than by entering a war with inadequate preparation. Every nation that has adopted the interventionist policy of depending on someone else for its own defense has met with nothing but defeat and failure. . . .

There is a policy open to this Nation that will lead to success-a policy that leaves us free to follow our own way of life and to develop our own civilization. It is not a new and untried idea. It was advocated by Washington. It was incorporated in the Monroe Doctrine. Under its guidance the United States became the greatest Nation in the world.

It is based upon the belief that the security of a nation lies in the strength and character of its own people. It recommends the maintenance of armed forces sufficient to defend this hemisphere from attack by any combination of foreign powers. It demands faith in an independent American destiny. This is the policy of the America First Committee today. It is a policy not of isolation, but of independence; not of defeat, but of courage. It is a policy that led this Nation to success during the most trying years of our history, and it is a policy that will lead us to success again. . . .

The United States is better situated from a military standpoint than any other nation in the world. Even in our present condition of unpreparedness no foreign power is in a position to invade us today. If we concentrate on our own defenses and build the strength that this Nation should maintain, no foreign army will ever attempt to land on American shores.

War is not inevitable for this country. Such a claim is defeatism in the true sense. No one can make us fight abroad unless we ourselves are willing to do so. No one will attempt to fight us here if we arm ourselves as a great nation should be armed. Over a hundred million people in this Nation are opposed to entering the war. If the principles of democracy mean anything at all, that is reason enough for us to stay out. If we are forced into a war against the wishes of an overwhelming majority of our people, we will have proved democracy such a failure at home that there will be little use fighting for it abroad.

The time has come when those of us who believe in an independent American destiny must band together and organize for strength. We have been led toward war by a minority of our people. This minority has power. It has influence. It has a loud voice. But it does not represent the American people. During the last several years I have traveled over this country from one end to the other. I have talked to many hundreds of men and women, and I have letters from tens of thousands more, who feel the same way as you and I.

Most of these people have no influence or power. Most of them have no means of expressing their convictions, except by their vote which has always been against this war. They are the citizens who have had to work too hard at their daily jobs to organize political meetings. Hitherto, they have relied upon their vote to express their feelings; but now they find that it is hardly remembered except in the oratory of a political campaign. These people, the majority of hard-working American citizens, are with us. They are the true strength of our country. And they are beginning to realize, as you and I, that there are times when we must sacrifice our normal interests in life in order to insure the safety and the welfare of our Nation.

Such a time has come. Such a crisis is here. That is why the America First Committee has been formed-to give voice to the people who have no newspaper, or newsreel, or radio station at their command; to the people who must do the paying, and the fighting, and the dying if this country enters the war.

1. *Summarize Lindbergh's opinion of the war in general, and specifically of America's role in it. What is Lindbergh's justification for this opinion?*
2. *Analyze and describe Lindbergh's articulation of the policy of the "America First Comittee." In what way does this committee exist to assist the majority of Americans?*

25-3　Franklin D. Roosevelt, The Four Freedoms (1941)

This selection from Roosevelt's annual address to Congress is his argument for American involvement in the war, tied to his Lend-Lease act which provided military supplies for England. Many Americans, including the famous aviator Charles Lindbergh, were isolationist and pacifist and believed intervention would be futile and that the United States should remain uninvolved in European wars.

Armed defense of democratic existence is now being gallantly waged in four continents. If that defense fails, all the population and all the resources of Europe, Asia, Africa and Australasia will be dominated by the conquerors. The total of those populations and their resources . . . greatly exceeds the sum total of the population and the resources of the whole of the Western Hemisphere-many times over.

In times like these it is immature-and incidentally untrue-for anybody to brag that an unprepared America, single-handed, and with one hand tied behind its back, can hold off the whole world.

No realistic American can expect from a dictator's peace international generosity, or return of true independence, or world disarmament, or freedom of expression, or freedom of religion-or even good business. . . .

The need of the moment is that our actions and our policy should be devoted primarily-almost exclusively-to meeting this foreign peril. For all our domestic problems are now a part of the great emergency.

Just as our national policy in internal affairs has been based upon a decent respect for the rights and the dignity of all our fellow men within our gates, so our national policy in foreign affairs has been based on a decent respect for the rights and dignity of all nations, large and small. And the justice of morality must and will win in the end.

Our national policy is this:

First, by an impressive expression of the public will and without regard to partisanship, we are committed to all-inclusive national defense.

Second, by an impressive expression of the public will and without regard to partisanship, we are committed to full support of all those resolute peoples, everywhere, who are resisting aggression and are thereby keeping war away from our hemisphere. By this support, we express our determination that the democratic cause shall prevail, and we strengthen the defense and security of our own nation.

Third, by an impressive expression of the public will and without regard to partisanship, we are committed to the proposition that principles of morality and considerations for our own security will never permit us to acquiesce in a peace dictated by aggressors and sponsored by appeasers. We know that enduring peace cannot be bought at the cost of other people's freedom. . . .

I also ask this Congress for authority and for funds sufficient to manufacture additional munitions and war supplies of many kinds, to be turned over to those nations which are now in actual war with aggressor nations.

Our most useful and immediate role is to act as an arsenal for them as well as for ourselves. They do not need man power. They do need billions of dollars' worth of the weapons of defense. . . .

Let us say to the democracies, "We Americans are vitally concerned in your defense of freedom. We are putting forth our energies, our resources, and our organizing powers to give you the strength to regain and maintain a free world. We shall send you, in ever-increasing numbers, ships, planes, tanks, guns. This is our purpose and our pledge." . . .

There is nothing mysterious about the foundations of a healthy and strong democracy. The basic things expected by our people of their political and economic systems are simple.

They are:

Equality of opportunity for youth and for others.

Jobs for those who can work.

Security for those who need it.

The ending of special privilege for the few.

The preservation of civil liberties for all.

The enjoyment of the fruits of scientific progress in a wider and constantly rising standard of living.

These are the simple and basic things that must never be lost sight of in the turmoil and unbelievable complexity of our modern world. The inner and abiding strength of our economic and political systems is dependent upon the degree to which they fulfill these expectations. . . .

In the future days, which we seek to make secure, we look forward to a world founded upon four essential human freedoms.

The first is freedom of speech and expression everywhere in the world.

The second is freedom of every person to worship God in his own way everywhere in the world.

The third is freedom from want, which, translated into world terms, means economic understandings which will secure to every nation a healthy peacetime life for its inhabitants everywhere in the world.

The fourth is freedom from fear-which, translated into world terms, means a world-wide reduction of armaments to such a point and in such a thorough fashion that no nation will be in a position to commit an act of physical aggression against any neighbor-anywhere in the world.

That is no vision of a distant millennium. It is a definite basis for a kind of world attainable in our own time and generation. That kind of world is the very antithesis of the so-called new order of tyranny which the dictators seek to create with the crash of a bomb.

To that new order we oppose the greater conception-the moral order. A good society is able to face schemes of world domination and foreign revolutions alike without fear.

Since the beginning of our American history we have been engaged in change-in a perpetual peaceful revolution-a revolution which goes on steadily, quietly adjusting itself to changing conditions-without the concentration camp or the quicklime in the ditch. The world order which we seek is the cooperation of free countries, working together in a friendly, civilized society.

1. *Summarize Roosevelt's description of America's national policy as it is identified in this document.*
2. *Identify the "four freedoms" outlined in this speech, and explain what bearing these freedoms have upon American policy entering WWII.*

25-4 Franklin Delano Roosevelt, Annual Message to Congress (1941)

Recognizing the need to gain public support for American involvement in World War Two, President Roosevelt outlined the danger that existed and the promise of the future that he felt was based on four freedoms.

I address you, the Members of the Seventy-seventh Congress, at a moment unprecedented in the history of the Union. I use the word "unprecedented," because at no previous time has American security been as seriously threatened from without as it is today. . . .

Every realist knows that the democratic way of life is at this moment being directly assailed in every part of the world-assailed either by arms or by secret spreading of poisonous propaganda by those who seek to destroy unity and promote discord in nations still at peace.

During 16 months this assault has blotted out the whole pattern of democratic life in an appalling number of independent nations, great and small. The assailants are still on the march, threatening other nations, great and small.

Therefore, as your President, performing my constitutional duty to "give to the Congress information of the state of the Union," I find it necessary to report that the future and the safety of our country and of our democracy are overwhelmingly involved in events far beyond our borders.

Armed defense of democratic existence is now being gallantly waged in four continents. If that defense fails, all the population and all the resources of Europe, Asia, Africa, and Australasia will be dominated by the conquerors. The total of those populations and their resources greatly exceeds the sum total of the population and resources of the whole of the Western Hemisphere-many times over.

In times like these it is immature-and incidentally untrue-for anybody to brag that an unprepared America, single-handed, and with one hand tied behind its back, can hold off the whole world.

No realistic American can expect from a dictator's peace international generosity, or return of true independence, or world disarmament, or freedom of expression, or freedom of religion-or even good business.

Such a peace would bring no security for us or for our neighbors. "Those who would give up essential liberty to purchase a little temporary safety deserve neither liberty nor safety." . . .

The need of the moment is that our actions and our policy should be devoted primarily-almost exclusively-to meeting this foreign peril. For all our domestic problems are now a part of the great emergency. . . .

Our national policy is this:

First, by an impressive expression of the public will and without regard to partisanship, we are committed to all-inclusive national defense.

Second, by an impressive expression of the public will and without regard to partisanship, we are committed to full support of all those resolute peoples, everywhere, who are resisting aggression and are thereby keeping war away from our hemisphere. By this support, we express our determination that the democratic cause shall prevail, and we strengthen the defense and security of our own Nation.

Third, by an impressive expression of the public will and without regard to partisanship, we are committed to the proposition that principles of morality and considerations for our own security will never permit us to acquiesce in a peace dictated by aggressors and sponsored by appeasers. We know that enduring peace cannot be bought at the cost of other people's freedom. . . .

I . . . ask this Congress for authority and for funds sufficient to manufacture additional munitions and war supplies of many kinds, to be turned over to those nations which are now in actual war with aggressor nations.

Our most useful and immediate role is to act as an arsenal for them as well as for ourselves. They do not need manpower. They do need billions of dollars' worth of the weapons of defense.

The time is near when they will not be able to pay for them in ready cash. We cannot, and will not, tell them they must surrender merely because of present inability to pay for the weapons which we know they must have. . . .

Let us say to the democracies, "We Americans are vitally concerned in your defense of freedom. We are putting forth our energies, our resources, and our organizing powers to give you the strength to regain and maintain a free world. We shall send you, in ever-increasing numbers, ships, planes, tanks, guns. This is our purpose and our pledge."

In fulfillment of this purpose we will not be intimidated by the threats of dictators that they will regard as a breach of international law and as an act of war our aid to the democracies which dare to resist their aggression. Such aid is not an act of war, even if a dictator should unilaterally proclaim it so to be.

When the dictators are ready to make war upon us, they will not wait for an act of war on our part. . . .

As men do not live by bread alone, they do not fight by armaments alone. Those who man our defenses, and those behind them who build our defenses, must have the stamina and courage which come from an unshakable belief in the manner of life which they are defending. The mighty action which we are calling for cannot be based on a disregard of all things worth fighting for.

The Nation takes great satisfaction and much strength from the things which have been done to make its people conscious of their individual stake in the preservation of democratic life in America. Those things have toughened the fiber of our people, have renewed their faith and strengthened their devotion to the institutions we make ready to protect.

Certainly this is no time to stop thinking about the social and economic problems which are the root cause of the social revolution which is today a supreme factor in the world.

There is nothing mysterious about the foundations of a healthy and strong democracy. The basic things expected by our people of their political and economic systems are simple. They are:

Equality of opportunity for youth and for others.

Jobs for those who can work.

Security for those who need it.

The ending of special privilege for the few.

The preservation of civil liberties for all.

The enjoyment of the fruits of scientific progress in a wider and constantly rising standard of living.

These are the simple and basic things that must never be lost sight of in the turmoil and unbelievable complexity of our modern world. The inner and abiding strength of our economic and political systems is dependent upon the degree to which they fulfill these expectations. . . .

In the future days, which we seek to make secure, we look forward to a world founded upon four essential human freedoms.

The first is freedom of speech and expression everywhere in the world.

The second is freedom of every person to worship God in his own way everywhere in the world.

The third is freedom from want, which, translated into world terms, means economic understandings which will secure to every nation a healthy peacetime life for its inhabitants everywhere in the world.

The fourth is freedom from fear-which, translated into world terms, means a world-wide reduction of armaments to such a point and in such a thorough fashion that no nation will be in a position to commit an act of physical aggression against any neighbor-anywhere in the world.

That is no vision of a distant millennium. It is a definite basis for a kind of world attainable in our own time and generation. . . .

To that high concept there can be no end save victory.

---

1. What is Roosevelt's opinion of the safety of American democracy in the face of a threat to freedom abroad? What, according to this document, does Roosevelt propose is the best way for the United States assist its allies in the war effort?

2. What freedoms is America dedicated to help to secure for its allies? How does the naming of these freedoms place America squarely in opposition to the Axis powers?

3. Summarize the significance of this speech as it defines American foreign policy regarding involvement in the war.

25-5   A. Philip Randolph, "Why Should We March?" (1942)

Stressing that African Americans supported the war effort, black leaders observed that they also wanted to win the war for democracy at home and abroad. Their intent was to eliminate racism and imperialism. In support of the so-called "Double V," victory at war and at home, African American and others participated in mass protest meetings.

Though I have found no Negroes who want to see the United Nations lose this war, I have found many who, before the war ends, want to see the stuffing knocked out of white supremacy and of empire over subject peoples. American Negroes, involved as we are in the general issues of the conflict, are confronted not with a choice but with the challenge both to win democracy for ourselves at home and to help win the war for democracy the world over.

There is no escape from the horns of this dilemma. There ought not to be escape. For if the war for democracy is not won abroad, the fight for democracy cannot be won at home. If this war cannot be won for the white peoples, it will not be won for the darker races.

Conversely, if freedom and equality are not vouchsafed the peoples of color, the war for democracy will not be won. Unless this double-barreled thesis is accepted and applied, the darker races will never wholeheartedly fight for the victory of the United Nations. That is why those familiar with the thinking of the American Negro have sensed his lack of enthusiasm, whether among the educated or uneducated, rich or poor, professional or nonprofessional, religious or secular, rural or urban, north, south, east or west.

That is why questions are being raised by Negroes in church, labor union and fraternal society; in poolroom, barbershop, schoolroom, hospital, hair-dressing parlor; on college campus, railroad, and bus. One can hear such questions asked as these: What have Negroes to fight for? What's the difference between Hitler and that "cracker" Talmadge of Georgia? Why has a man got to be Jim Crowed to die for democracy? If you haven't got democracy yourself, how can you carry it to somebody else?

What are the reasons for this state of mind? The answer is: discrimination, segregation, Jim Crow. Witness the navy, the army, the air corps; and also government services at Washington. In many parts of the South, Negroes in Uncle Sam's uniform are being put upon, mobbed, sometimes even shot down by civilian and military police, and on occasion lynched. Vested political interests in race prejudice are so deeply entrenched that to them winning the war against Hitler is secondary to preventing Negroes from winning democracy for themselves. This is worth many divisions to Hitler and Hirohito. While labor, business, and farm are subjected to ceilings and doors and not allowed to carry on as usual, these interests trade in the dangerous business of race hate as usual.

When the defense program began and billions of the taxpayers' money were appropriated for guns, ships, tanks and bombs, Negroes presented themselves for work only to be given the cold shoulder. North as well as South, and despite their qualifications, Negroes were denied skilled employment. Not until their wrath and indignation took the form of a proposed protest march on Washington, scheduled for July 1, 1941, did things begin to move in the form of defense jobs for Negroes. The march was postponed by the timely issuance (June 25, 1941) of the famous Executive Order No. 8802 by President Roosevelt. But this order and the President's Committee on Fair Employment Practice, established thereunder, have as yet only scratched the surface by way of eliminating discriminations on account of race or color in war industry. Both management and labor unions in too many places and in too many ways are still drawing the color line.

It is to meet this situation squarely with direct action that the March on Washington Movement launched its present program of protest mass meetings. Twenty thousand were in attendance at Madison Square Garden, June 16; sixteen thousand in the Coliseum in Chicago, June 26; nine thousand in the City Auditorium of St. Louis, August 14. Meetings of such magnitude were unprecedented among Negroes. The vast throngs were drawn from all walks and levels of Negro life—businessmen, teachers, laundry workers, Pullman porters, waiters, and red caps; preachers, crapshooters, and social workers; jitterbugs and Ph.D.'s. They came and sat in silence, thinking, applauding only when they considered the truth was told, when they felt strongly that something was going to be done about it.

The March on Washington Movement is essentially a movement of the people. It is all Negro and pro-Negro, but not for that reason anti-white or anti-Semitic, or anti-Catholic, or anti-foreign, or anti-labor. Its major weapon is the nonviolent demonstration of Negro mass power. Negro leadership has united back of its drive for jobs and justice. "Whether Negroes should march on Washington, and if so, when?" will be the focus of a forthcoming national conference. For the plan of a protest march has not been abandoned. Its purpose would be to demonstrate that American Negroes are in deadly earnest, and all out for their full rights. No power on earth can cause them today to abandon their fight to wipe out every vestige of second class citizenship and the dual standards that plague them.

A community is democratic only when the humblest and weakest person can enjoy the highest civil, economic, and social rights that the biggest and most powerful possess. To trample on these rights of both Negroes and poor whites is such a commonplace in the South that it takes readily to anti-social, anti-labor, anti-Semitic and anti-Catholic propaganda. It was because of laxness in enforcing the Weimar constitution in republican Germany that Nazism made headway. Oppression of the Negroes in the United States, like suppression of the Jews in Germany, may open the way for a fascist dictatorship.

By fighting for their rights now, American Negroes are helping to make America a moral and spiritual arsenal of democracy. Their fight against the poll tax, against lynch law, segregation, and Jim Crow, their fight for economic, political, and social equality, thus becomes part of the global war for freedom.

1. *What steps have been taken to right the social and racial injustices at home during wartime? What has been the response of the government to these steps?*

25-6   Japanese Relocation Order February 19, 1942

The Japanese attack on Pearl Harbor concerned the government that a Japanese invasion of the west coast was imminent. The War Department urged Roosevelt to order the evacuation of all Japanese and Japanese-Americans on the west coast to relocation centers. This action was debated openly in government and in California before it was implemented with the full knowledge of the American people.

Source: Henry Steele Commanger, *Documents of American History* (New York: Appleton-Century-Crofts, 1949), pp. 464–465; Japanese Relocation Order; Federal *Register*, vol. VII, No. 38.

EXECUTIVE ORDER

Authorizing the Secretary of War to Prescribe Military Areas

Whereas the successful prosecution of the war requires every possible protection against espionage and against sabotage to national-defense materials, national-defense premises, and national-defense utilities. . . .

Now, therefore, by virtue of the authority vested in me as President of the United States, and Commander in Chief of the Army and Navy, I hereby authorize and direct the Secretary of War, and the Military Commanders whom he may from time to time designate, whenever he or any designated Commander deems such action necessary or desirable, to prescribe military areas in such places and of such extent as he or the appropriate Military Commander may determine, from which any or all persons may be excluded, and with respect to which, the right of any person to enter, remain in, or leave shall be subject to whatever restrictions the Secretary of War or the appropriate Military Commander may impose in his discretion. The Secretary of War is hereby authorized to provide for residents of any such area who are excluded therefrom, such transportation, food, shelter, and other accommodations as may be necessary, in the judgment of the Secretary of War or the said Military Commander, and until other arrangements are made, to accomplish the purpose of this order. The designation of military areas in any region or locality shall supersede designations of prohibited and restricted areas by the Attorney General under the Proclamations of December 7 and 8, 1941, and shall supersede the responsibility and authority of the Attorney General under the said Proclamations in respect of such prohibited and restricted areas.

I hereby further authorize and direct the Secretary of War and the said Military Commanders to take such other steps as he or the appropriate Military Commander may deem advisable to enforce compliance with the restrictions applicable to each Military area hereinabove authorized to be designated, including the use of Federal troops and other Federal Agencies, with authority to accept assistance of state and local agencies.

I hereby further authorize and direct all Executive Departments, independent establishments and other Federal Agencies, to assist the Secretary of War or the said Military Commanders in carrying out this Executive Order, including the furnishing of medical aid, hospitalization, food, clothing, transportation, use of land, shelter, and other supplies, equipment, utilities, facilities, and services. . . .

FRANKLIN D. ROOSEVELT

1. Why is this order vaguely worded?
2. Why would American citizens permit this to happen?

25-7 Sterling A. Brown, "Out of Their Mouths" (1942)

As these excerpts show, African American folklore provided a vital outlet for wryly protesting against white supremacy and discrimination in the South.

Deep South-a *Soliloquy*:

"Why do you reckon white folks act like they do? I sit home studying them. A cracker is like this. He will cut his own throat just to see a Negro die along with him. Further and more, they're fussing and squabbling among theirselves so much that a man can creep up behind them unbeknownst to 'em and hit 'em on the head.

"Take Talmadge, that narrow-minded rascal. All this trouble, war, soldiers being killed by the thousands, hostages being killed, bombs falling on women and little children-and all he can do is woof about 'coeducation of the races' or 'segregation.' Somebody ought to dump him on his head in some sea or other.

"This war now. It looks like they don't want you in the navy, army, or marines. Just like before the war they didn't want you anywhere you could make a dime out of it. When those Japs first started out in the Pacific, I thought Negroes ought to thank their lucky stars that they weren't on those ships going down with the white folks. Then I got to studying and knew I was wrong. Onliest way we can get anything out of this war is to put all we can in it. That's my best judgment.

"The diffunce between the northern and the southern Negro is that the northern is a freeborn-minded Negro, but the southern is trained to say Yes-sir and No-sir all the time. That don't mean the southern Negro won't fight, but he's just more kinderhearted. The gurvenmrent is exchanging them, sending one to the north and one to the south.

"These crackers will chase a Negro like he was a jackrabbit. There ain't no right in their heart or soul.

"Do you think they will elect President Roosevelt for a fourth term? They'd better, if they know what's good for the country. I don't wish him no hard luck, but I hope he will wear out in his job. But I hope that won't be for many a long year. Yessir, I hope he dies in the White House. But I hope he lives forever. He's the best friend the Negro ever had. Bar none, Lincoln, Washington, Teddy Roosevelt. And Mrs. Roosevelt, she's the greatest woman living today.

"The party-I don't give two cents for party. My question is who's gonna do most for me, my people, all the poor people. I'm a New Dealite.

"It's remarkable how the Negro continues to keep coming on. Right out of slavery, the Negro jumped into teaching college. Course he ain't perfect. Cutting, fighting, laziness. A lot of Negroes have gone to hell and destruction fooling around with numbers and that mess. But you can't fault the Negro for that. Not much diffunce between a man robbing you in the nighttime with a gun, and robbing you in the daytime with knowledge.

"The Negroe's obstacles made a man out of him. Depression, lynching, all like that, the Negro kept coming, smiling and singing. They come on like the Japs before Singapore. You bend back the middle, the niggers (I mean Negroes) flow around the edges.

"I'm patriotic. I've got a boy in camp. Yessir, some of my blood is in the army. I love my country but I don't like the way they doing us down here in the South. . . .

Southern White Editor: "These fellows come down here and instead of doing the job with common sense, they go at it in a crusading way. They just blow open prejudices. So the died-in-the-wool traditionalist backs up, god-damning this and that to hell. The way these crusaders go about they hurt some real friends of the Negro."

Negro journalist: "Some of these southern liberals used to want to accelerate Negro progress. Now it seems that all they want to do is put on the brakes.

"A lot of white women are up in arms because they have to bring up their own children."

Dr. P. talking: . . . "The road-cop pulled up and told me I'd been exceeding the speed limit, that he'd been pacing me on the whole trip. I told him the car wouldn't go much over 40. It was a red Chrysler with wire wheels, sorta fancy. I knew he didn't like the looks of it with me behind the wheel. Both of us argued back and forth. Finally he said,'I don't know whether to shoot you or take you to jail.' "

"I said, 'Well, it won't make any difference to me. One's about as bad as the other.'

"He said, 'You don't act like you're scared at all.'

"I spoke right up. 'Why you're the last man in the world I'd be scared of. You're the law. You're supposed to be my protection.' "

"Man, that threw him off balance. He finally said, 'Well, Doc, you'd better watch yourself. There's a couple fellows in a pepped-up Ford (that's a Ford with a Frontenac head) on the road that are kinda mean. They'd like to pick you up in a car like this. So you take it easy now.' "

"Then he growled at me, 'But you know damn well you were doing more than 40 miles an hour.' "

White liberal: "This Negro soldier was sitting on a seat opposite to a white man. The bus was not crowded, and he wasn't sitting in front of any white. But the driver came back and told him to move. He refused. The driver shouted, 'I'm gonna move you.' The Negro took his coat off and said, 'Well I'm fixing to go off and fight for democracy. I might as well start right now.' And I want to tell you that bus driver backed down. It did me good to see it."

Harlemite (shortly after Pearl Harbor): "All these radio announcers talking about yellow this, yellow that. Don't hear them calling the Nazis white this, pink that. What in hell color do they think the Chinese are anyway! And those Filipinos on Bataan? And the British Imperial Army, I suppose they think they're all blondes?"

Folk Tales: "They're telling the story that a cracker running a lunchroom at a railroad junction got a wire ordering lunches for 500 soldiers. He got together all the bread and eggs and chickens and coffee and stuff he could. When the troop train pulled in he saw they were Negroes. He ran to the officer in charge: 'You said 500 *soldiers*. Those are just Nigra boys.' The officer told him they were soldiers in the uniform of their country. Man kept on: 'You said *soldiers*. I can't serve those boys in my place.' The captain wouldn't budge. Finally the man said to the white officers, 'Well, y'all can come in and eat but I'll have to put their food in boxes. I reckon I can stir up that many boxes.'

" 'No; these men must eat hot food.'

"But that cracker wouldn't give in. So the boys went unfed. The story goes that all the townspeople went together and put in so much money apiece to save white supremacy and the lunchroom man's money."

1. Summarize the speaker's attitude toward the war and the black man's involvement in it.
2. Compare and Contrast the various perspectives upon everyday life offered in this document. How do these perspectives represent a cross section of American attitudes and experiences regarding race?
3. Cite and analyze the various experiences with prejudice, in word and deed, that are depicted in the piece.

PART TWENTY-SIX
COLD WAR

26-1 George F. Kennan, "Long Telegram" (1946)

In 1946, the wartime alliance between the United States and the Soviet Union was falling apart. In his "Long Telegram," Foreign Service officer George F. Kennan suggested that the systems of the United States and the Soviet Union were incompatible and that Soviet security depended on destroying the American way of life. His ideas were foundations of Cold War foriegn policy.

We have here a political force committed fanatically to the belief that with US there can be no permanent *modus vivendi*, that it is desirable and necessary that the internal harmony of our society be disrupted, our traditional way of life be destroyed, the international authority of our state be broken, if Soviet power is to be secure. This political force has complete power of disposition over energies of one of world's greatest peoples and resources of world's richest national territory, and is borne along by deep and powerful currents of Russian nationalism. In addition, it has an elaborate and far flung apparatus for exertion of its influence in other countries, and apparatus of amazing flexibility and versatility, managed by people whose experience and skill in underground methods are presumably without parallel in history. Finally, it is seemingly inaccessible to considerations of reality in its basic reactions. For it, the vast fund of objective fact about human society is not, as with us, the measure against which outlook is constantly being tested and re-formed, but a grab bag from which individual items are selected arbitrarily and tendentiously to bolster an outlook already preconceived. This is admittedly not a pleasant picture. Problem of how to cope with this force in [*is*] undoubtedly greatest task our diplomacy has ever faced and probably greatest it will ever have to face. It should be point of departure from which our political general staff work at present juncture should proceed. It should be approached with same thoroughness and care as solution of major strategic problem in war, and if necessary, with no smaller outlay in planning effort. I cannot attempt to suggest all answers here. But I would like to record my conviction that problem is within our power to solve-and that without recourse to any general military conflict. And in support of this conviction there are certain observations of a more encouraging nature I should like to make:

(1) Soviet power, unlike that of Hitlerite Germany, is neither schematic nor adventuristic. It does not work by fixed plans. It does not take unnecessary risks. Impervious to logic of reason, and it is highly sensitive to logic of force. For this reason it can easily withdraw-and usually does-when strong resistance is encountered at any point. Thus, if the adversary has sufficient force and makes clear his readiness to use it, he rarely has to do so. If situations are properly handled there need be no prestige-engaging showdowns.

(2) Gauged against Western World as a whole, Soviets are still by far the weaker force. Thus, their success will really depend on degree of cohesion, firmness and vigor which Western World can muster. And this is factor which it is within our power to influence.

(3) Success of Soviet system, as form of internal power, is not yet finally proven. It has yet to be demonstrated that it can survive supreme test of successive transfer of power from one individual or group to another. Lenin's death was first such transfer, and its effects wracked Soviet state for 15 years. After Stalin's death or retirement will be second. But even this will not be final test. Soviet internal system will now be subjected, by virtue of recent territorial expansions, to series of additional strains which once proved severe tax on Tsardom. We here are convinced that never since termination of civil war have mass of Russian people been emotionally farther removed from doctrines of Communist Party than they are today. In Russia, party has now become a great and-for the moment-highly successful apparatus of dictatorial administration, but it has ceased to be a source of emotional inspiration. Thus, internal soundness and permanence of movement need not yet be regarded as assured.

(4) All Soviet propaganda beyond Soviet security sphere is basically negative and destructive. It should therefore be relatively easy to combat it by any intelligent and really constructive program.

For these reasons I think we may approach calmly and with good heart problem of how to deal with Russia. As to how this approach should be made, I only wish to advance, by way of conclusion, following comments:

(1) Our first step must be to apprehend, and recognize for what it is, the nature of the movement with which we are dealing. We must study it with same courage, detachment, objectivity, and same determination not to be emotionally provoked or unseated by it, with which doctor studies unruly and unreasonable individual.

(2) We must see that our public is educated to realities of Russian situation. I cannot over-emphasize importance of this. Press cannot do this alone. It must be done mainly by Government, which is necessarily more experienced and better informed on practical problems involved. In this we need not be deterred by [ugliness?] of picture. I am convinced

that there would be far less hysterical anti-Sovietism in our country today if realities of this situation were better understood by our people. There is nothing as dangerous or as terrifying as the unknown. It may also be argued that to reveal more information on our difficulties with Russia would reflect unfavorably on Russian-American relations. I feel that if there is any real risk here involved, it is one which we should have courage to face, and sooner the better. But I cannot see what we would be risking. Our stake in this country, even coming on heels of tremendous demonstrations of our friendship for Russian people, is remarkably small. We have here no investments to guard, no actual trade to lose, virtually no citizens to protect, few cultural contacts to preserve. Our only stake lies in what we hope rather than what we have; and I am convinced we have better chance of realizing those hopes if our public is enlightened and if our dealings with Russians are placed entirely on realistic and matter-of-fact basis.

(3) Much depends on health and vigor of our own society. World communism is like malignant parasite which feeds only on diseased tissue. This is point at which domestic and foreign policies meet. Every courageous and incisive measure to solve internal problems of our own society, to improve self-confidence, discipline, morale and community spirit of our own people, is a diplomatic victory over Moscow worth a thousand diplomatic notes and joint communiq≥s. If we cannot abandon fatalism and indifference in face of deficiencies of our own society, Moscow will profit-Moscow cannot help profiting by them in its foreign policies.

(4) We must formulate and put forward for other nations a much more positive and constructive picture of sort of world we would like to see than we have put forward in past. It is not enough to urge people to develop political processes similar to our own. Many foreign peoples, in Europe at least, are tired and frightened by experiences of past, and are less interested in abstract freedom than in security. They are seeking guidance rather than responsibilities. We should be better able than Russians to give them this. And unless we do, Russians certainly will.

(5) Finally we must have courage and self-confidence to cling to our own methods and conceptions of human society. After all, the greatest danger that can befall us in coping with this problem of Soviet communism, is that we shall allow ourselves to become like those with whom we are coping.

1. *What are Kennan's beliefs regarding the state of Russian power and the threat Russia poses to America?*
2. *Summarize the steps Kennan suggests to combat the threat and spread of Russian power.*

26-2   Kenneth MacFarland, "The Unfinished Work" (1946)

The end of World War Two was greeted with celebration and uncertainty. After 15 years of economic depression and war, American worried about the future. They also wanted the wartime conditions to end.

One who traveled about over the country a year ago this month, talking with taxi drivers, bell hops, policemen, business employees, and others who reflect the thinking of the man-on-the-street, found the conversation all to be along the same lines. The war was over, the boys would be coming home now, rationing would end. Truman was doing better than expected, we must resolutely work together to build one world in which war would be outlawed and the principles of the Atlantic Charter would hold sway. The keynote a year ago was one of joyous relief that the bloodiest conflict in all history had ended in complete victory over the enemy, and a feeling of faith that we had at last learned our lesson sufficiently well to outlaw war. There was confidence that an effective United Nations organization would be developed.

But today, one year after, that buoyant faith has turned to cynicism. Hope in the United Nations is largely gone. The average American has already resigned himself to a future in which there will be at least two worlds instead of one. Having given up his hope for a better world, the average man has ceased to realize how terribly important it is that we keep striving, and he has settled down to bickering over a myriad of minor issues here on the domestic scene. . . .

There is a strange fear and insecurity in America today. The people fear that in winning the war we introduced a new power into the world which may in turn engulf us. As James Reston says in a recent article,

"Among the reflective people of the country, among the leaders of the communities and those who aspire to political office, fear for the security of America and doubt about the ability of America to solve its own problems seem stronger today than ever in memory.

"It is an astonishing fact, but after an unprecedented war in which the enemies on the field of battle were entirely defeated, the people seem to feel less secure than they did before they were attacked, or even when the tide of war was running strongest against them."

In this year that has passed since the ending of the war we have found we cannot immediately shut off the hates that were generated during the struggle. Racial tensions have burst into open flame. Minority groups are being terrorized by hoodlums who seek only personal gain from such persecution. There is unprecedented confusion in our political life.

Special interest groups raise slush funds to purge congressmen who failed to support their particular legislative programs. Many politicians totally forget the sacred obligation of public office holding and appeal to the basest motives to win re-election. Yes, America has retrogressed to a dangerous degree in the 387 days since General MacArthur proclaimed to the world that Japan had surrendered unconditionally. We have lost the faith that won the fight just when we needed it most to win the peace. *We have demobilized our patriotism far too soon. . . .*

Today there is a powerfully organized force that is working unceasingly to prolong the confusion. This is the first post-war period in which we have had to contend with a highly organized effort to prevent recovery. *We are fools unless we awaken to the fact that a great campaign is being carried on in America today to perpetuate chaos, and that campaign is being directed from abroad by a force that wants democracy to fail.* This highly organized and well financed power reaches into key positions in numerous organizations and publications, institutions of learning, and into the government itself. There is the new, the unprecedented, and by far the most dangerous element in the clashing cross currents which torment our times.

The identical force which is spreading the gospel of despair and dissension in America today is almost solely responsible for the black cloud that obscures the sunshine of peace on the international horizon. Out in Salt Lake City on the twelfth day of last month, America's only living Ex-President, Herbert Clark Hoover, said,

"The dominant note in the world today is not one of hope and confidence, but rather one of fear and frustration. . . . Far from freedom having been expanded in this war, it has been shrunk to far fewer nations than a quarter of a century ago . . . and it is Russia that blocks the almost universal desire for peace."

It is Russia, Hoover said, that is deliberately stalling the peace conference while it communizes Eastern Europe and exploits its economic resources. Whether we agree with Mr. Hoover or not, it can scarcely be gainsaid that behind the iron curtain which Russia has drawn across Europe lie eleven nations that were formerly independent-and that represents more countries than Hitler ever conquered. Yes, we cannot deny that the beautiful blue Danube, which turned brown when Hitler's legions marched in, has now turned to red.

No doubt the vast population of Russia yearns for peace as ardently as we do. Yet between that great people and ourselves stands the Russian government. That government consists of a group of revolutionaries who are determined that no other Russian government shall come to power the same way they did. Skilled in the school of sabotage and intrigue, that government stands today as an absolute dictatorship, wielding the power of Russia in world councils, and withholding the knowledge of the world from its own people.

So ominous is the threat of this new and unpredictable world power that the average man has all but abandoned his high hopes for permanent peace. . . .

It is in such a world and such a time that September comes again, and the miracle of the great American school system once more unfolds before eyes that have grown tired of searching for light. As millions of bright eyed youngsters put their books under their arms and trudge to school each September the world never fails to take on renewed hope. There is a dawn of a better day in the faces of the children and it simply will not be denied. Let us use this occasion and this inspiration to arouse ourselves from aimless lethargy and "to rededicate ourselves to the unfinished work." These children *must* have a future. We cannot deny them. We must build a better world. We cannot fail.

To what specific ends shall these high resolves be directed? Briefly, the goals are these:

First, *let us make democracy work.* As John Fischer so well states in his "Scared Men in the Kremlin," it is not the Red army but the communistic *idea* that we must overcome. This can be done only by demonstrating conclusively to the world that it is democracy, and not the regimented society of Russia, that can best eliminate unemployment, avoid depressions, and develop a world in which war cannot survive. We must unite behind this goal and demonstrate by actual practice the limitless power and possibilities of the democratic way of life.

Secondly, *our leadership must constantly call forth our best instead of so frequently appealing to our worst.* Our political leaders must have faith in an aroused and properly led America. Not once in our history have our people betrayed or forsaken a great leader who held out a great ideal and based his plea upon moral grounds. Our leaders must return to that great premise and be done with appeals to greed, selfishness, group interest, and class hatred.

Third, *we must rededicate ourselves to the determination that we shall not be pushed around by any dictatorship, that we shall not compromise with the immortal democratic principle of the dignity and freedom of the individual citizen everywhere.*

And finally, *we must not grow faint in our efforts to outlaw war.* The alternative is death. As the Baruch Report declares, "The choice is between the quick and the dead." Harold Fey put it well when he said that after every war the nations have put their trust in weapons which have but compounded their jeopardy. Now God has grown weary of the age old cycle. Lifting the lid on the atom, God has at last said to the world, "Choose life, or choose death, but *choose!*"

We, the living, *must* rededicate ourselves to the unfinished work.

1. How is the state of American security and stability one year after the end of World War I described in this document?

2. What, according to MacFarland, has been the influence of Russia upon world peace and stability?
3. What steps must be followed in order to "build a better world" in the post-war era?

26-3   George Marshall, The Marshall Plan (1947)

In this speech, delivered at the Harvard University commencement in 1947, Secretary of State Marshall articulated a plan for American aid to Europe. The plan was designed to fill the power vacuum in Europe and to help Europe reconstruct itself after the devastation of war. Marshall even extended the promise of aid to the Soviet-dominated countries of Eastern Europe. The program was remarkably successful and by the early 1950s the Western European economy was much recovered.

The truth of the matter is that Europe's requirements for the next three or four years of foreign food and other essential products-principally from America-are so much greater than her present ability to pay that she must have substantial additional help or face economic, social, and political deterioration of a very grave character. . . .

Aside from the demoralizing effect on the world at large and the possibilities of disturbances arising as a result of the desperation of the people concerned, the consequences of the economy of the United States should be apparent to all. It is logical that the United States should do whatever it is able to do to assist in the return of normal economic health in the world, without which there can be no political stability and no assured peace. Our policy is directed not against any country or doctrine but against hunger, poverty, desperation, and chaos. Its purpose should be the revival of a working economy in the world so as to permit the emergence of political and social conditions in which free institutions can exist.

Such assistance, I am convinced, must not be on a piecemeal basis as various crises develop. Any assistance that this Government may render in the future should provide a cure rather than a mere palliative. Any government that is willing to assist in the task of recovery will find full cooperation, I am sure, on the part of the United States Government. Any government which maneuvers to block the recovery of other countries cannot expect help from us. Furthermore, governments, political parties, or groups which seek to perpetuate human misery in order to profit there from politically or otherwise will encounter the opposition of the United States.

It is already evident that, before the United States Government can proceed much further in its efforts to alleviate the situation and help start the European world on its way to recovery, there must be some agreement among the countries of Europe as to the requirements of the situation and the part those countries themselves will take in order to give proper effect to whatever action might be undertaken by this Government.

It would be neither fitting nor efficacious for this Government to undertake to draw up unilaterally a program designed to place Europe on its feet economically. This is the business of the Europeans. The initiative, I think, must come from Europe. The role of this country should consist of friendly aid in the drafting of a European program and of later support of such a program so far as it may be practical for us to do so. The program should be a joint one, agreed to by a number, if not all, European nations.

1. According to the Marshall plan, what is the relationship between the welfare of Europe and the welfare of America? How must America act to ensure the economic health of European Nations?
2. What does this plan stipulate regarding how assistance should be rendered to nations in need? What is Europe's responsibility? What will be the role of the United States? What is expected in return for U.S. assistance?

26-4   Containment (1947)

Diplomat George Kennan, writing as "X" in Foreign Affairs magazine, articulated the concept of containment, which became the basis for U.S. policy with the Soviet Union for the duration of the Cold War. Kennan's conception of this policy was based on the history and development of the Communist regime in the Soviet Union in consideration of the goals of that government. Containment required that in response to all impulses of Soviet expansion and aggression, the United States must be prepared to commit itself to a long-term policy of stopping or obstructing Soviet ambitions in what ever form they might take. Containment also required huge capital investment by the United States.

Source: "X", "The Sources of Soviet Conduct," *Foreign Affairs* vol. 25 no. 4 (July 1947), pp. 566–582.

THE SOURCES OF SOVIET CONDUCT

The political personality of Soviet power as we know it today is the product of ideology and circumstances: ideology inherited by the present Soviet leaders from the movement in which they had their political origin, and circumstances of the power which they now have exercised for nearly three decades in Russia. There can be few tasks of psychological analysis more difficult than to try to trace the interaction of these two forces and the relative role of each in the determination of official Soviet conduct. Yet the attempt must be made if that conduct is to be understood and effectively countered.

* * *

The outstanding circumstance concerning the Soviet regime is that down to the present day this process of political consolidation has never been completed and the men in the Kremlin have continued to be predominantly absorbed with the struggle to secure and make absolute the power which they seized in November 1917. They have endeavored to secure it primarily against forces at home, within Soviet society itself. But they have also endeavored to secure it against the outside world. For ideology, as we have seen, taught them that the outside world was hostile and that it was their duty eventually to overthrow the political forces beyond their borders. The powerful hands of Russian history and tradition reached up to sustain them in this feeling. Finally, their own aggressive intransigence with respect to the outside world began to find its own reaction; and they were soon forced, to use another Gibbonesque phrase, "to chastise the contumacy" which they themselves had provoked. It is an undeniable privilege of every man to prove himself right in the thesis that the world is his enemy; for if he reiterates it frequently enough and makes it the background of his conduct he is bound eventually to be right.

* * *

Now it lies in the nature of the mental world of the Soviet leaders, as well as in the character of their ideology, that no opposition to them can be officially recognized as having any merit or justification whatsoever. Such opposition can flow, in theory, only from the hostile and incorrigible forces of dying capitalism. As long as remnants of capitalism were officially recognized as existing in Russia, it was possible to place on them, as an internal element, part of the blame for the maintenance of a dictatorial form of society. But as these remnants were liquidated, little by little, this justification fell away; and when it was indicated officially that they had been finally destroyed, it disappeared altogether. And this fact created one of the most basic of the compulsions which came to act upon the Soviet régime: since capitalism no longer existed in Russia and since it could not be admitted that there could be serious or widespread opposition to the Kremlin springing spontaneously from the liberated masses under its authority, it became necessary to justify the retention of the dictatorship by stressing the menace of capitalism abroad.

. . . In 1924 Stalin specifically defended the retention of the "organs of suppression" meaning, among others, the army and the secret police, on the ground that "as long as there is a capitalist encirclement there will be danger of intervention with all the consequences that flow from that danger." In accordance with that theory, and from that time on, all internal opposition forces in Russia have consistently been portrayed as the agents of foreign forces of reaction antagonistic to Soviet power.

By the same token, tremendous emphasis has been placed on the original Communist thesis of a basic antagonism between the capitalist and Socialist worlds. It is clear, from many indications, that this emphasis is not founded in reality. The real facts concerning it have been confused by the existence abroad of genuine resentment provoked by Soviet philosophy and tactics and occasionally by the existence of great centers of military power, notably the Nazi régime in Germany and the Japanese Government of the late 1930's, which did indeed have aggressive designs against the Soviet Union. But there is ample evidence that the stress laid in Moscow on the menace confronting Soviet society from the world outside its borders is founded not in the realities of foreign antagonism but in the necessity of explaining away the maintenance of dictatorial authority at home.

Now the maintenance of this pattern of Soviet power, namely, the pursuit of unlimited authority domestically, accompanied by the cultivation of the semi-myth of implacable foreign hostility, has gone far to shape the actual machinery of Soviet power as we know it today. Internal organs of administration which did not serve this purpose became vastly swollen. The security of Soviet power came to rest on the iron discipline of the Party, on the severity and ubiquity of the secret police, and on the uncompromising economic monopolism of the state. The "organs of suppression," in which the Soviet leaders had sought security from rival forces, became in large measure the masters of those whom they were designed to serve. Today the major part of the structure of Soviet power is committed to the perfection of the dictatorship and to the maintenance of the concept of Russia as in a state of siege, with the enemy lowering beyond the walls. And the millions of human beings who form that part of the structure of power must defend at all costs this concept of Russia's position, for without it they are themselves superfluous.

As things stand today, the rulers can no longer dream of parting with these organs of suppression. The quest for absolute power, pursued now for nearly three decades with a ruthlessness unparalleled (in scope at least) in modern times, has again produced internally, as it did externally, its own reaction. The excesses of the police apparatus have fanned the potential opposition to the régime into something far greater and more dangerous than it could have been before those excesses began.

But least of all can the rulers dispense with the fiction by which the maintenance of dictatorial power has been defended. For this fiction has been canonized in Soviet philosophy by the excesses already committed in its name; and it is now anchored in the Soviet structure of thought by bonds far greater than those of mere ideology.

Of the original ideology, nothing has been officially junked. Belief is maintained in the basic badness of capitalism, in the inevitability of its destruction, in the obligation of the proletariat to assist in that destruction and to take power into its own hands. But stress has come to be laid primarily on those concepts which relate most specifically to the Soviet régime itself: to its position as the sole truly Socialist régime in a dark and misguided world, and to the relationships of power within it.

The first of these concepts is that of the innate antagonism between capitalism and Socialism. We have seen how deeply that concept has become imbedded in foundations of Soviet power. It has profound implications for Russia's conduct as a member of international society. It means that there can never be on Moscow's side any sincere assumption of a community of aims between the Soviet Union and powers which are regarded as capitalist. It must invariably be assumed in Moscow that the aims of the capitalist world are antagonistic to the Soviet régime, and therefore to the interests of the peoples it controls. If the Soviet government occasionally sets its signature to documents which would indicate the contrary, this is to be regarded as a tactical manoeuvre permissible in dealing with the enemy (who is without honor) and should be taken in the spirit of *caveat emptor*. Basically, the antagonism remains. It is postulated. And from it flow many of the phenomena which we find disturbing in the Kremlin's conduct of foreign policy: the secretiveness, the lack of frankness, the duplicity, the wary suspiciousness, and the basic unfriendliness of purpose. These phenomena are there to stay, for the foreseeable future. There can be variations of degree and of emphasis. When there is something the Russians want from us, one or the other of these features of their policy may be thrust temporarily into the background; and when that happens there will always be Americans who will leap forward with gleeful announcements that "the Russians have changed," and some who will even try to take credit for having brought about such "changes." But we should not be misled by tactical manoeuvres. These characteristics of Soviet policy, like the postulate from which they flow, are basic to the internal nature of Soviet power, and will be with us, whether in the foreground or the background, until the internal nature of Soviet power is changed.

This means that we are going to continue for a long time to find the Russians difficult to deal with. It does not mean that they should be considered as embarked upon a do-or-die program to overthrow our society by a given date. The theory of the inevitability of the eventual fall of capitalism has the fortunate connotation that there is no hurry about it. The forces of progress can take their time in preparing the final *coup de grâce*. Meanwhile, what is vital is that the "Socialist fatherland"—that oasis of power which has been already won for Socialism in the person of the Soviet Union—should be cherished and defended by all good Communists at home and abroad, its fortunes promoted, its enemies badgered and confounded. The promotion of premature, "adventuristic" revolutionary projects abroad which might embarrass Soviet power in any way would be an inexcusable, even a counter-revolutionary act. The cause of Socialism is the support and promotion of Soviet power, as defined in Moscow.

This brings us to the second of the concepts important to contemporary Soviet outlook. That is the infallibility of the Kremlin. The Soviet concept of power, which permits no focal points of organization outside the Party itself, requires that the Party leadership remain in theory the sole repository of truth. For if truth were to be found elsewhere, there would be justification for its expression in organized activity. But it is precisely that which the Kremlin cannot and will not permit.

The leadership of the Communist Party is therefore always right, and has been always right ever since in 1929 Stalin formalized his personal power by announcing that decisions of the Politburo were being taken unanimously.

On the principle of infallibility there rests the iron discipline of the Communist Party. In fact, the two concepts are mutually self-supporting. Perfect discipline requires recognition of infallibility. Infallibility requires the observance of discipline. And the two together go far to determine the behaviorism of the entire Soviet apparatus of power. But their effect cannot be understood unless a third factor be taken into account: namely, the fact that the leadership is at liberty to put forward for tactical purposes any particular thesis which it finds useful to the cause at any particular moment and to require the faithful and unquestioning acceptance of that thesis by the members of the movement as a whole. This means that truth is not a constant but is actually created, for all intents and purposes, by the Soviet leaders themselves. It may vary from week to week, from month to month. It is nothing absolute and immutable—nothing which flows from objective reality. It is only the most recent manifestation of the wisdom of those in whom the ultimate wisdom is supposed to reside, because they represent the logic of history.

The accumulative effect of these factors is to give to the whole subordinate apparatus of Soviet power an unshakeable stubbornness and steadfastness in its orientation. This orientation can be changed at will by the Kremlin but by no other power. Once a given party line has been laid down on a given issue of current policy, the whole Soviet governmental machine, including the mechanism of diplomacy, moves inexorably along the prescribed path, like a persistent toy automobile wound up and headed in a given direction, stopping only when it meets with some unanswerable force. The individuals who are the components of this machine are unamenable to argument or reason which comes to them from outside sources. Their whole training has taught them to mistrust and discount the glib persuasiveness of the outside world. Like the white dog before the phonograph, they hear only the "master's voice." And if they are to be called off from the purposes last dictated to them, it is the master who must call them off. Thus the foreign representative cannot hope that his words will make any impression on them. The most that he can hope is that they will be transmitted to those at the top, who are capable of changing the party line. But even those are not likely to be swayed by any normal logic in the words of the bourgeois representative. Since there can be no appeal to common purposes, there can be no appeal to common mental approaches. For this reason, facts speak louder than words to the ears of the Kremlin; and words carry the greatest weight when they have the ring of reflecting, or being backed up by, facts of unchallengeable validity.

But we have seen that the Kremlin is under no ideological compulsion to accomplish its purposes in a hurry. Like the Church, it is dealing in ideological concepts which are of long-term validity, and it can afford to be patient. It has no right to risk the existing achievements of the revolution for the sake of vain baubles of the future. The very teachings of Lenin himself require great caution and flexibility in the pursuit of Communist purposes. Again, these precepts are fortified by the lessons of Russian history: of centuries of obscure battles between nomadic forces over the stretches of a vast unfortified plain. Here caution, circumspection, flexibility and deception are the valuable qualities; and their value finds natural appreciation in the Russian or the oriental mind. Thus the Kremlin has no compunction about retreating in the face of superior force. And being under the compulsion of no timetable, it does not get panicky under the necessity for such retreat. Its political action is a fluid stream which moves constantly, wherever it is permitted to move, toward a given goal. Its main concern is to make sure that it has filled every nook and cranny available to it in the basin of world power. But if it finds unassailable barriers in its path, it accepts these philosophically and accommodates itself to them. The main thing is that there should always be pressure, unceasing constant pressure, toward the desired goal. There is no trace of any feeling in Soviet psychology that that goal must be reached at any given time.

These considerations make Soviet diplomacy at once easier and more difficult to deal with than the diplomacy of individual aggressive leaders like Napoleon and Hitler. On the one hand it is more sensitive to contrary force, more ready to yield on individual sectors of the diplomatic front when that force is felt to be too strong, and thus more rational in the logic and rhetoric of power. On the other hand it cannot be easily defeated or discouraged by a single victory on the part of its opponents. And the patient persistence by which it is animated means that it can be effectively countered not by sporadic acts which represent the momentary whims of democratic opinion but only by intelligent long-range policies on the part of Russia's adversaries—policies no less steady in their purpose, and no less variegated and resourceful in their applications, than those of the Soviet Union itself.

In these circumstances it is clear that the main element of any United States policy toward the Soviet Union must be that of a long-term, patient but firm and vigilant containment of Russian expansive tendencies. It is important to note, however, that such a policy has nothing to do with outward histrionics: with threats or blustering or superfluous gestures of outward "toughness." While the Kremlin is basically flexible in its reaction to political realities, it is by no means unamenable to considerations of prestige. Like almost any other government, it can be placed by tactless and threatening gestures in a position where it cannot afford to yield even though this might be dictated by its sense of realism. The Russian leaders are keen judges of human psychology, and as such they are highly conscious that loss of temper and of self-control is never a source of strength in political affairs. They are quick to exploit such evidences of weakness. For these reasons, it is a *sine qua non* of successful dealing with Russia that the foreign government in question should remain at all times cool and collected and that its demands on Russian policy should be put forward in such a manner as to leave the way open for a compliance not too detrimental to Russian prestige.

1. What was the basic contention of containment?
2. Did it work?
3. How did Kennan describe the character of the ambitions of the Soviet Union?

26-5 Harry S Truman, The Truman Doctrine (1947)

World War II left Europe economically devastated and politically unstable. Early in 1947, it appeared that Turkey and Greece would fall under Soviet influence. In this famous speech, Truman outlines his support for a policy of aggressive containment of the Soviet Union not only in Turkey and Greece, but all over the world. In the words of his secretary of state, Dean Acheson, the Truman administration worried that like apples in a barrel infected by one rotten one, the corruption of Greece would infect Iran and all of the east.

At the present moment in world history nearly every nation must choose between alternative ways of life. The choice is too often not a free one.

One way of life is based upon the will of the majority, and is distinguished by free institutions, representative government, free elections, guaranties of individual liberty, freedom of speech and religion, and freedom from political oppression.

The second way of life is based upon the will of a minority forcibly imposed upon the majority. It relies upon terror and oppression, a controlled press and radio, fixed elections, and the suppression of personal freedoms.

I believe that it must be the policy of the United States to support free peoples who are resisting attempted subjugation by armed minorities or by outside pressures.

I believe that we must assist free peoples to work out their own destinies in their own way.

I believe that our help should be primarily through economic and financial aid, which is essential to economic stability and orderly political processes.

The world is not static, and the status quo is not sacred. But we cannot allow changes in the status quo in violation of the Charter of the United Nations by such methods as coercion, or by such subterfuges as political infiltration. In helping free and independent nations to maintain their freedom, the United States will be giving effect to the principles of the Charter of the United Nations. . . .

The seeds of totalitarian regimes are nurtured by misery and want. They spread and grow in the evil soil of poverty and strife. They reach their full growth when the hope of a people for a better life has died.

We must keep that hope alive.

The free peoples of the world look to us for support in maintaining their freedoms.

If we falter in our leadership, we may endanger the peace of the world-and we shall surely endanger the welfare of our own Nation.

1. *Identify and summarize the choice that faces every nation according to Truman. What does this choice entail?*
2. *Explain Truman's vision of the United States' foreign policy responsibilities.*

26-6 Ronald Reagan, Testimony Before the House Un-American Activities Committee (1947)

The worsening relations between the Soviet Union and the United States was evidenced by an anti-communist movement led by the House Un-American Activities Committee. Hollywood and the film industry were prime targets of the Committee. In hearing actors such as Ronald Reagan were called to testify on communist influence in Hollywood.

The Committee met at 10:30 A.M. [October 23, 1947], the Honorable J. Parnell Thomas (Chairman) presiding.

THE CHAIRMAN: The record will show that Mr. McDowell, Mr. Vail, Mr. Nixon, and Mr. Thomas are present. A Subcommittee is sitting.

Staff members present:

Mr. Robert E. Stripling, Chief Investigator; Messrs. Louis J. Russell, H. A. Smith, and Robert B. Gatson, Investigators; and Mr. Benjamin Mandel, Director of Research.

MR. STRIPLING: When and where were you born, Mr. Reagan?

MR. REAGAN: Tampico, Illinois, February 6, 1911.

MR. STRIPLING: What is your present occupation?

MR. REAGAN: Motion-picture actor.

MR. STRIPLING: How long have you been engaged in that profession?

MR. REAGAN: Since June 1937, with a brief interlude of three and a half years-that at the time didn't seem very brief.

MR. STRIPLING: What period was that?

MR. REAGAN: That was during the late war.

MR. STRIPLING: What branch of the service were you in?

MR. REAGAN: Well, sir, I had been for several years in the Reserve as an officer in the United States Calvary, but I was assigned to the Air Corp.

MR. STRIPLING: Are you the president of the guild at the present time?

MR. REAGAN: Yes, sir. . . .

MR. STRIPLING: As a member of the board of directors, as president of the Screen Actors Guild, and as an active member, have you at any time observed or noted within the organization a clique of either Communists or Fascists who were attempting to exert influence or pressure on the guild?

MR. REAGAN: Well, sir, my testimony must be very similar to that of Mr. [George] Murphy and Mr. [Robert] Montgomery. There has been a small group within the Screen Actors Guild which has consistently opposed the policy of the guild board and officers of the guild, as evidenced by the vote on various issues. That small clique referred to has been suspected of more or less following the tactics that we associated with the Communist Party.

MR. STRIPLING: Would you refer to them as a disruptive influence within the guild?

MR. REAGAN: I would say that at times they have attempted to be a disruptive influence.

MR. STRIPLING: You have no knowledge yourself as to whether or not any of them are members of the Communist Party?

MR. REAGAN: No, sir, I have no investigative force, or anything, and I do not know.

MR. STRIPLING: Has it ever been reported to you that certain members of the guild were Communists?

MR. REAGAN: Yes, sir, I have heard different discussions and some of them tagged as Communists.

MR. STRIPLING: Would you say that this clique has attempted to dominate the guild?

MR. REAGAN: Well, sir, by attempting to put over their own particular views on various issues. . . .

MR. STRIPLING: Mr. Reagan, there has been testimony to the effect here that numerous Communist-front organizations have been set up in Hollywood. Have you ever been solicited to join any of those organizations or any organization which you consider to be a Communist-front organization?

MR. REAGAN: Well, sir, I have received literature from an organization called the Committee for a Far-Eastern Democratic Policy. I don't know whether it is Communist or not. I only know that I didn't like their views and as a result I didn't want to have anything to do with them. . . .

MR. STRIPLING: Would you say from your observation that this is typical of the tactics or strategy of the Communists, to solicit and use the names of prominent people to either raise money or gain support.

MR. REAGAN: I think it is in keeping with their tactics, yes, sir.

MR. STRIPLING: Do you think there is anything democratic about those tactics?

MR. REAGAN: I do not, sir.

MR. STRIPLING: Mr. Reagan, what is your feeling about what steps should be taken to rid the motion-picture industry of any Communist influences?

MR. REAGAN: Well, sir, ninety-nine percent of us are pretty well aware of what is going on, and I think, within the bounds of our democratic rights and never once stepping over the rights given us by democracy, we have done a pretty good job in our business of keeping those people's activities curtailed. After all, we must recognize them at present as a political party. On that basis we have exposed their lies when we came across them, we have opposed their propaganda, and I can certainly testify that in the case of the Screen Actors Guild we have been eminently successful in preventing them from, with their usual tactics, trying to run a majority of an organization with a well-organized minority. In opposing those people, the best thing to do is make democracy work. . . .

Sir, I detest, I abhor their philosophy, but I detest more than that their tactics, which are those of the fifth column, and are dishonest, but at the same time I never as a citizen want to see our country become urged, by either fear or resentment of this group that we ever compromise with any of our democratic principles through that fear or resentment. I still think that democracy can do it.

1. Summarize Reagan's experience with and attitude toward the influence of the Communist party within the Screen Actor's Guild community.
2. What is Reagan's overall opinion of the communist influence in Hollywood and how best to combat it?

26-7   Joseph R. McCarthy, from Speech Delivered to the Women's Club of Wheeling, West Virginia (1950)

The junior senator from Wisconsin, Joseph McCarthy, launched a virulent anticommunist crusade that affected Americans from all walks of life. In this 1950 speech, McCarthy began his campaign of accusations claiming to have the names of communists in the government. None of McCarthy's suspicions were proven and he eventually lost favor with the American public.

Five years after a world war has been one, men's hearts should anticipate a long peace, and men's minds should be free from the heavy weight that comes from war. But this is not such a period-for this is not a period of peace. This is a time of the "cold war." This is a time when all the world is split into two vast, increasingly hostile armed camps. . . .

The reason why we find ourselves in a position of impotency is not because our only powerful potential enemy has sent men to invade our shores, but rather because of the traitorous actions of those who have been treated so well by this Nation. It has not been the less fortunate or members of minority groups who have been selling this Nation out, but rather those who have had all the benefits that the wealthiest nation on earth has to offer-the finest homes, the finest college education, and the finest jobs in Government.

This is glaringly true in the State Department. There the bright young men who are born with silver spoons in their mouths are the ones who have been the worst. . . . In my opinion, the State Department, which is one of the most important government departments, is thoroughly infested with Communists.

I have in my hand 57 cases of individuals who would appear to be either card carrying members or certainly loyal to the Communist Party, but who nevertheless are still helping to shape our foreign policy. . . .

As you know, very recently the Secretary of State proclaimed his loyalty to a man guilty of what has always been considered as the most abominable of all crimes-of being a traitor to the people who gave him a position of great trust. The Secretary of State in attempting to justify his continued devotion to the man who sold out the Christian world to the atheistic world, referred to Christ's Sermon on the Mount as a justification and reason therefor, and the reaction of the American people to this would have made the heart of Abraham Lincoln happy.

When this pompous diplomat in striped pants, with a phony British accent, proclaimed to the American people that Christ on the Mount endorsed communism, high treason, and a betrayal of a sacred trust, the blasphemy was so great that it awakened the dormant indignation of the American people.

He has lighted the spark which is resulting in a moral uprising and will end only when the whole sorry mess of twisted, warped thinkers are swept from the national scene so that we may have a new birth of national honesty and decency in government.

1. *What is the threat that McCarthy warns against? From where does it originate?*
2. *Summarize the specific charges the McCarthy proclaims in this speech. How does he intend to deal with those he charges?*

26-8   National Security Council Memorandum Number 68 (1950)

The emerging Cold War led some United States officials to view the world as dividing into two hostile spheres. The Soviet-dominated sphere was considered a threat to survival of the American-led free world. A major issue concerned nuclear weapons and the need to maintain the American lead in the arms race.

Within the past thirty-five years the world has experienced two global wars of tremendous violence. It has witnessed two revolutions-the Russian and the Chinese-of extreme scope and intensity. It has also seen the collapse of five empires-the Ottoman, the Austro-Hungarian, German, Italian and Japanese-and the drastic decline of two major imperial systems, the British and the French. During the span of one generation, the international distribution of power has been fundamentally altered. For several centuries it had proved impossible for any one nation to gain such preponderant strength that a coalition of other nations could not in time face it with greater strength. The international scene was marked by recurring periods of violence and war, but a system of sovereign and independent states was maintained, over which no state was able to achieve hegemony.

Two complex sets of factors have now basically altered this historical distribution of power. First, the defeat of Germany and Japan and the decline of the British and French Empires have interacted with the development of the United States and the Soviet Union in such a way that power has increasingly gravitated to these two centers. Second, the Soviet Union, unlike previous aspirants to hegemony, is animated by a new fanatic faith, antithetical to our own, and seeks to impose its absolute authority over the rest of the world. Conflict has, therefore, become endemic and is waged, on the part of the Soviet Union, by violent or non-violent methods in accordance with the dictates of expediency. With the development of increasingly terrifying weapons of mass destruction, every individual faces the ever-present possibility of annihilation should the conflict enter the phase of total war.

On the one hand, the people of the world yearn for relief from the anxiety arising from the risk of atomic war. On the other hand, any substantial further extension of the area under the domination of the Kremlin would raise the possibility that no coalition adequate to confront the Kremlin with greater strength could be assembled. It is in this context that this Republic and its citizens in the ascendancy of their strength stand in their deepest peril. . . .

Military Evaluation of U.S. and U.S.S.R. Atomic Capabilities

1. The United States now has an atomic capability, including both numbers and deliverability, estimated to be adequate, if effectively utilized, to deliver a serious blow against the war-making capacity of the U.S.S.R. It is doubted whether such a blow, even if it resulted in the complete destruction of the contemplated target systems, would cause the U.S.S.R. to sue for terms or present *[prevent]* Soviet forces from occupying Western Europe against such ground resistance as could presently be mobilized. A very serious initial blow could, however, so reduce the capabilities of the U.S.S.R. to supply and equip its military organization and its civilian population as to give the United States the prospect of developing a general military superiority in a war of long duration.

2. As the atomic capability of the U.S.S.R. increases, it will have an increased ability to hit at our atomic bases and installations and thus seriously hamper the ability of the United States to carry out an attack such as that outlined above. It is quite possible that in the near future the U.S.S.R. will have a sufficient number of atomic bombs and a sufficient deliverability to raise a question whether Britain with its present inadequate air defense could be relied upon as an advance base from which a major portion of the U.S. attack could be launched.

It is estimated that, within the next four years, the U.S.S.R. will attain the capability of seriously damaging vital centers of the United States, provided it strikes a surprise blow and provided further that the blow is opposed by no more effective opposition than we now have programmed. Such a blow could so seriously damage the United States as to greatly reduce its superiority in economic potential.

Effective opposition to this Soviet capability will require among other measures greatly increased air warning systems, air defenses, and vigorous development and implementation of a civilian defense program which has been thoroughly integrated with the military defense systems.

In time the atomic capability of the U.S.S.R. can be expected to grow to a point where, given surprise and no more effective opposition than we now have programmed, the possibility of a decisive initial attack cannot be excluded.

3. In the initial phases of an atomic war, the advantages of initiative and surprise would be very great. A police state living behind an iron curtain has an enormous advantage in maintaining the necessary security and centralization of decision required to capitalize on this advantage.

4. For the moment our atomic retaliatory capability is probably adequate to deter the Kremlin from a deliberate direct military attack against ourselves or other free peoples. However, when it calculates that it has a sufficient atomic capability to make a surprise attack on us, nullifying our atomic superiority and creating a military situation decisively in its favor, the Kremlin might be tempted to strike swiftly and with stealth. The existence of two large atomic capabilities in such a relationship might well act, therefore, not as a deterrent, but as an incitement to war.

5. A further increase in the number and power of our atomic weapons is necessary in order to assure the effectiveness of any U.S. retaliatory blow, but would not of itself seem to change the basic logic of the above points. Greatly increased general air, ground and sea strength, and increased air defense and civilian defense programs would also be necessary to provide reasonable assurance that the free world could survive an initial surprise atomic attack of the weight which it is estimated the U.S.S.R. will be capable of delivering by 1954 and still permit the free world to go on to the eventual attainment of its objectives. Furthermore, such a build-up of strength could safeguard and increase our retaliatory power, and thus might put off for some time the date when the Soviet Union could calculate that a surprise blow would be advantageous. This would provide additional time for the effects of our policies to produce a modification of the Soviet system.

6. If the U.S.S.R. develops a thermonuclear weapon ahead of the U.S., the risks of greatly increased Soviet pressure against all the free world, or an attack against the U.S., will be greatly increased.

7. If the U.S. develops a thermonuclear weapon ahead of the U.S.S.R., the U.S. should for the time being be able to bring increased pressure on the U.S.S.R. . . .

In the light of present and prospective Soviet atomic capabilities, the action which can be taken under present programs and plans, however, becomes dangerously inadequate, in both timing and scope, to accomplish the rapid progress toward the attainment of the United States political, economic, and military objectives which is now imperative.

A continuation of present trends would result in a serious decline in the strength of the free world relative to the Soviet Union and its satellites. This unfavorable trend arises from the inadequacy of current programs and plans rather than from any error in our objectives and aims. These trends lead in the direction of isolation, not by deliberate decision but by lack of the necessary basis for a vigorous initiative in the conflict with the Soviet Union.

Our position as the center of power in the free world places a heavy responsibility upon the United States for leadership. We must organize and enlist the energies and resources of the free world in a positive program for peace which will frustrate the Kremlin design for world domination by creating a situation in the free world to which the Kremlin will be compelled to adjust. Without such a cooperative effort, led by the United States, we will have to make gradual withdrawals under pressure until we discover one day that we have sacrificed positions of vital interest.

It is imperative that this trend be reversed by a much more rapid and concerted build-up of the actual strength of both the United States and the other nations of the free world. The analysis shows that this will be costly and will involve significant domestic financial and economic adjustments.

The execution of such a build-up, however, requires that the United States have an affirmative program beyond the solely defensive one of countering the threat posed by the Soviet Union. This program must light the path to peace and order among nations in a system based on freedom and justice, as contemplated in the Charter of the United Nations. Further, it must envisage the political and economic measures with which and the military shield behind which the free world can work to frustrate the Kremlin design by the strategy of the cold war; for every consideration of devotion to our fundamental values and to our national security demands that we achieve our objectives by the strategy of the cold war, building up our military strength in order that it may not have to be used. The only sure victory lies in the frustration of the Kremlin design by the steady development of the moral and material strength of the free world and its projection into the Soviet world in such a way as to bring about an internal change in the Soviet system. Such a positive program-harmonious with our fundamental national purpose and our objectives-is necessary if we are to regain and retain the initiative and to win and hold the necessary popular support and cooperation in the United States and the rest of the free world.

1. *What does NSC-68 reveal regarding the atomic capabilities of the United States? What does it predict regarding the atomic capabilities of the U.S.S.R.?*
2. *What is the assessment of the ability of the United State to achieve and maintain superiority over the Soviet Union?*
3. *Describe the kind of plan this resolution calls for.*

26-9 Senator Joseph McCarthy's telegram to President Truman following the 'Wheeling (W.Va.) Speech,' February 11, 1950

Here is the complete text of Senator Joseph McCarthy's telegram to President Truman regarding communist infiltration into the State Department.

In a Lincoln Day speech at Wheeling Thursday night I stated that the State Department harbors a nest of communists and communist sympathizers who are helping to shape our foreign policy. I further stated that I have in my possession the names of 57 commuists who are in the State Department at present. A State Department spokesman flatly denied this and claimed that there is not a single communist in the department. You can convince yourself of the falsity of the State Department claim very easily. You will recall that you personally appointed a board to screen State Department employees for the purpose of weeding out fellow travelers. Your board did a pains-taking job, and named hundreds which it listed as "dangerous to the security of the nation," because of communistic connections. While the records are not available to me, I know absolutely that of one group of approximately 300 certified to the Secretary for discharge, he actually discharged only approximately 80. I understand that this was done after lengthy consultation with Alger Hiss. I would suggest therefore, Mr. President, that you simply pick up your phone and ask Mr. Acheson how many of those whom your board had labeled as dangers, he failed to discharge. The day the House Un-American Activities Committee exposed Alger Hiss as an important link in an international communist spy ring, you signed an order forbidding the State Department giving to the Congress any information in regard to the disloyalty or the communistic connections of anyone in that Department, despite this State Department blackout, we have been able to compile a list of 57 communists in the State Department. This list is available to you, but you can get a much longer list by ordering the Secretary Acheson to give you a list of these whome your own board listed as being disloyal, and who are still working in the State Department. I believe the following is the minimum which can be expected of you in this case

That you demand that Acheson give you and the proper Congressional committee the names and a complete report on all of those who were placed in the Department by Alger Hiss, and all of those still working in the State Department who were listed by your board as bad security risks because of the communistic connections.

That under no circumstances could a Congressional committee obtain any information or help from the Executive Department in exposing communists.

Failure on your part will label the Democratic Party of being the bed-fellow of international communism. Certainly this label is not deserved by the hundreds of thousands of loyal American Democrats throughout the nation, and by the sizable number of able loyal Democrats in both the Senate and the House.

1. *What was McCarthy's proof that communists had infiltrated the State Department?*
2. *What did he want President Truman to do about communist infiltration?*

PART TWENTY-SEVEN
CONSENSUS AND CONFORMITY

27-1 The Kinsey Report (1948)

Dr. Kinsey's scientific study on sexual behavior in humans arrested public attention. Through Kinsey's findings, humans were described as highly sexual and sexually complex beings. The study also confirmed that humans, far from repressing their urges, sought a variety of outlets for sexual satisfaction. The 12,000 subjects studied for his report revealed that people engaged in a variety of sexual activities and often did so outside of marriage.

> **Source:** Alfred C. Kinsey, et al., *Sexual Behavior in the Human Male* (Philadelphia: W. B. Sanders, 1948), pp. 263–273.

MARITAL STATUS AND SEXUAL OUTLET

Among the social factors affecting sexual activity, marital status is the one that would seem most likely to influence both the frequencies and the sources of the individual's outlet. The data, however, need detailed analyses.

Social and Legal Limitations

In Social and religious philosophies, there have been two antagonistic interpretations of sex. There have been cultures and religions which have inclined to the hedonistic doctrine that sexual activity is justifiable for its immediate and pleasurable return; and there have been cultures and religions which accept sex primarily as the necessary means of procreation, to be enjoyed only in marriage, and then only if reproduction is the goal of the act. The Hebrews were among the Asiatics who held this ascetic approach to sex; and Christian sexual philosophy and English-American sex law is largely built around these Hebraic interpretations, around Greek ascetic philosophies, and around the asceticism of some of the Roman cults (Angus 1925, May 1931).

A third possible interpretation of sex as a normal biologic function, acceptable in whatever form it is manifested, has hardly figured in either general or scientific discussions. By English and American standards, such an attitude is considered primitive, materialistic or animalistic, and beneath the dignity of a civilized and educated people. Freud has contributed more than the biologists toward an adoption of this biologic viewpoint.

Since English-American moral codes and sex laws are the direct outcome of the reproductive interpretation of sex, they accept no form of socio-sexual activity outside of the marital state; and even marital intercourse is more or less limited to particular times and places and to the techniques which are most likely to result in conception. By this system, no socio-sexual outlet is provided for the single male or for the widowed or divorced male, since they cannot legally procreate; and homosexual and solitary sources of outlet, since they are completely without reproductive possibilities, are penalized or frowned upon by public opinion and by the processes of the law.

Specifically, English-American legal codes restrict the sexual activity of the unmarried male by characterizing all pre-marital, extra-marital, and post-marital intercourse as rape, statutory rape, fornication, adultery, prostitution, association with a prostitute, incest, delinquency, a contribution to delinquency, assault and battery, or public indecency—all of which are offenses with penalties attached. However it is labelled, all intercourse outside of marriage (non-marital intercourse) is illicit and subject to penalty by statute law in most of the states of the Union, or by the precedent of the common law on which most courts, in all states, chiefly depend when sex is involved. In addition to their restrictions on hetero-sexual intercourse, statute law and the common law penalize all homosexual activity, and all sexual contacts with animals; and they specifically limit the techniques of marital intercourse. Mouth-genital and anal contacts are punishable as crimes whether they occur in heterosexual or homosexual relations and whether in or outside of marriage. Such manual manipulation as occurs in the petting which is common in the younger generation has been interpreted in some courts as an impairment of the morals of a minor, or even as assault and battery. The public exhibition of any kind of sexual activity, including self masturbation, or the viewing of such activity, is punishable as a contribution to delinquency or as public indecency.

There have been occasional court decisions which have attempted to limit the individual's right to solitary masturbation; and the statutes of at least one state (Indiana Acts 1905, ch. 169, & 473, p. 584) rule that the encouragement of self masturbation is an offense punishable as sodomy. Under a literal interpretation of this law, it is possible that a teacher, biologist, psychologist, physician or other person who published the scientifically determinable fact that masturbation does no physical harm might be prosecuted for encouraging some person to "commit masturbation." There have been penal commitments of adults who have given sex instruction to minors, and there are evidently some courts who are inclined to interpret all sex instruction as a contribution to the delinquency of minors. In state controlled penal and mental institutions, and in homes for dependent children, the administrations are authorized to establish rules of sexual behavior which go beyond the definitions of courtroom law. It is the usual practice in such institutions to impose penalties, including physical punishment, for masturbation, and we have histories from at least two institutions which imposed equally severe penalties for nocturnal emissions. The United States Naval Academy at Annapolis considers evidence of masturbation sufficient grounds for refusing admission to a candidate (U.S. Naval Acad. Regul., June 1940). It is probable that the courts would defend the right of the administrators of institutions to impose such ultimate restrictions upon the sexual outlets of their charges.

Concepts of sexual perversion depend in part on this same reproductive interpretation of sex. Sodomy laws are usually indefinite in their descriptions of acts that are punishable; perversions are defined as unnatural acts, acts contrary to nature, bestial, abominable, and detestable. Such laws are interpretable only in accordance with the ancient tradition of the English common law which, as has already been indicated, is committed to the doctrine that no sexual activity is justifiable unless its objective is procreation.

Official church attitudes toward contraception and abortion similarly stem from the demand that there be no interference with reproduction. They are consistent in denying the use of contraceptives in marriage and in intercourse which is outside of marriage, for intercourse outside of marriage is illegal and not a legitimate source of procreation. Medical and presumably scientific data which are adduced in support of the objections to contraception and abortion, are rationalizations or confusions of the real issue, which is the reproductive value of any kind of sexual behavior.

In addition to establishing restrictions by way of the statutory and common law, society at large, and each element in it, have developed mores that even more profoundly affect the frequency of sexual activity and the general pattern of behavior. Some of the community attitudes fortify certain of the legal interpretations, even though no segment of society accepts the whole of the legal code, as its behavior and expressed attitudes demonstrate (Chapter 10). Often the social proscriptions involve more than is in the law, and the individual who conforms with the traditions of the social level to which he belongs, is restricted in such detail as the written codes never venture to cover. Group attitudes become his "conscience," and he accepts group interpretations, thinking them the product of his own wisdom. Each type of sex act acquires values, becomes right or wrong, socially useful or undesirable. Esthetic values are attached: limitations are set on the times and places where sexual relations may be had; the social niceties (and the law) forbid the presence of witnesses to sexual acts; there are standards of physical cleanliness and supposed requirements of hygiene and sanitation which may become more important than the gratification of sexual drives; the forms of courtesy between men and women may receive especial attention when sexual relations are involved; the effect of the relations upon the sexual partner, the effect upon the subsequent sexual, marital, or business relations with the partner, the effect upon the subject's own self esteem or subsequent mental or physical happiness, or conflict—may all be involved in the decision to have, or not to have, a socio-sexual relation. While the decision seems to rest upon personal desires, ideals, and concepts of esthetics, the individual's standards are very largely set by the mores of the social level to which he belongs. In the end, their effect is strongly to limit his opportunity for intercourse, or for most other types of sexual activity, especially if he is unmarried, widowed, separated, or divorced.

A lower level male has fewer esthetic demands and social forms to satisfy. By the time he becomes an adolescent, he has learned that it is possible to josh any passing girl, ask for a simple social date, and, inside of a few minutes, suggest intercourse. Such financial resources as will provide a drink, tickets for a movie, or an automobile ride, are at that level sufficient for making the necessary approaches. Such things are impossible for most better educated males. Education develops a demand for more elaborate recreation and more extended social contacts. The average college male plans repeated dates, dinners, expensive entertainments, and long-time acquaintances before he feels warranted in asking for a complete sexual relation. There is, in consequence, a definitely greater limitation on the heterosexual activities of the educated portion of the population, and a higher frequency of solitary outlets in that group. Upper level males rationalize their lack of socio-sexual activities in terms of right and wrong, but it is certain that the social formalities have a great deal to do with their chastity.

In any case, at any social level, the human animal is more hampered in its pursuit of sexual contacts than the primitive anthropoid in the wild; and, at any level, the restrictions would appear to be most severe for males who are not married. One should expect, then, that the sexual histories of unmarried males would contrast sharply with the histories of married adults; and that, at the end of two thousand years of social monitoring, at least some unmarried males might be found who follow the custom and the law and live abstinent, celibate, sublimated, and wholly chaste lives. Scientists will, however, want to examine the specific data showing the effect of marital status on the human male's total sexual outlet, and on his choice of particular outlets (if he has any) in his single, married, or post-marital states.

TOTAL SEXUAL OUTLET

The mean frequencies of total sexual outlet for the married males are always, at all age levels, higher than the total outlets for single males; but, as already pointed out (Chapter 6), essentially all single males have regular and usually frequent sexual outlet, whether before marriage, or after being widowed, separated, or divorced. Of the more than five thousand males who have contributed to the present study, only 1 per cent has lived for as much as five years (after the onset of adolescence and outside of old age) without orgasm.

As previously recorded, the mean frequency of the total outlet for the single males between 16 and 20 is (on the basis of the U. S. Corrections) about 3.3 per week (Table 60, Figures 50-52). The mean frequency of total outlet for the married male is about 4.8 per week, which is 47 per cent above the average outlet of the single male. At 30, the frequencies for the married males are about 18 per cent above those of the single males, and approximately this relation holds for some period of years. Beyond 40 years of age, the single males may actually exceed the married males in their sexual frequencies. In adolescent years, the restrictions upon the sexual activity of the unmarried male are greatest. He finds it more difficult to locate sources of outlet and he has not learned the techniques for approaching and utilizing those sources when they are available. Nevertheless, his frequency between adolescence and 16 does average about 3.0 per week and between 16 and 20 it amounts to nearly 3.4 per week. This represents arousal that leads to orgasm on an average of about every other day. By the time he is 30, the single male has become much more efficient in his social approaches and does not lag far behind the married individual in his performance. Considering the physical advantage which the married individual has in securing intercourse without going outside of his own home, it is apparent that the older single male develops skills in making social approaches and finding places for sexual contacts which far exceed the skills of married persons. Beau Brummels and Casanovas are not married males. A few of the married males who are involved in promiscuous extra-marital activity are the only ones whose facilities begin to compare with those found among unmarried groups. It is notable that in the male homosexual, where long-term unions are not often maintained and new partners are being continually sought, there are many persons who preserve this same facility for making social contacts for long periods of years.

The differences that exist between the total activities of the younger married male and the younger unmarried male are, to some degree, a measure of the effectiveness of the social pressures that keep the single male's performance below his native capacity; although the lower rates in the single males may depend, in part, upon the possibility that less responsive males may not marry so young, or may never marry. On the other hand, the fact that the single male, from adolescence to 30 years of age, does have a frequency of nearly 3.0 per week is evidence of the ineffectiveness of social restrictions and of the imperativeness of the biologic demands. For those who like the term, it is clear that there is a sexual drive which cannot be set aside for any large portion of the population, by any sort of social convention. For those who prefer to think in simpler terms of action and reaction, it is a picture of an animal who, however civilized or cultured, continues to respond to the constantly present sexual stimuli, albeit with some social and physical restraints.

In addition to the differences in frequencies of total outlet between married and single males, there are minor differences in incidence and in range of variation in the groups. Between adolescence and 15 years of age, 95 per cent of the unmarried boys have some sort of sexual outlet. From 16 to 35 years of age, 99 per cent or more of these males are engaging in some form of sexual activity (Table 60). Among the married males, a full 100 per cent is sexually active between 16 and 35 years of age. Beyond 35, the incidence figures drop for single males, and at a somewhat faster rate than for married males. The differences are not great.

The range of variation in frequency of outlet in any particular age group is also nearly identical for single and married males. In both populations (Table 49), there are individuals who engage in sexual activity only a few times a year, and there are some who engage in sexual activities regularly 3 or 4 or more times per day (29 or more per week). The lower average rates for single males are not dependent upon the fact that there are no high-rating individuals in that group, but upon the fact that there is a large number of the single males who have lower rates, and a larger number of married males who have higher rates. At least half of the younger married males have outlets which average 3 or more per week, whereas only a third of the single males fall into that category.

Throughout both single and married histories, there is a steady decline in total sexual outlet in successive age groups (Chapter 7). After 30 years of age this decline in any 5-year period (Figures 50-52) is very nearly as great as the differences between married and single males of the same age group. Age is eventually as important as all of the social, moral, and legal factors which differentiate single from married histories.

1. *Contrast Kinsey's report to John Kellogg's thoughts on appropriate sexual comportment.*
2. *Is the behavior Kinsey documents representative of a sudden change in human sexual and social conduct, or a more realistic and scientific presentation of human behavior that the more visible social commentators of the turn of the century would not and could not recognize? What changes occurred in American society to make this research and its publication possible?*

27-2 *Brown v. Board of Education* (1954)

This landmark Supreme Court decision was the outcome of three years of litigation by the father of Linda Brown, an elementary school student from Topeka, Kansas. In this decision, the Court declared segregated schools unconstitutional. In subsequent decisions, it ruled that schools be desegregated with all deliberate speed. Somewhat reluctantly, President Dwight Eisenhower oversaw the process in the South in the 1950s, which culminated in the dramatic desegregation of the Little Rock, Arkansas, high school in 1957 under the protection of the National Guard.

Mr. Chief Justice Warren delivered the opinion of the Court

These cases come to us from the States of Kansas, South Carolina, Virginia, and Delaware. They are premised on different facts and different local conditions, but a common legal question justifies their consideration together in this consolidated opinion.

In each of the cases, minors of the Negro race, through their legal representatives, seek the aid of the courts in obtaining admission to the public schools of their community on a nonsegregated basis. In each instance, they had been denied admission to schools attended by white children under laws requiring or permitting segregation according to race. This segregation was alleged to deprive the plaintiffs of the equal protection of the laws under the Fourteenth Amendment. In each of the cases other than the Delaware case, a three-judge federal district court denied relief to the plaintiffs on the so-called "separate but equal" doctrine announced by this Court in *Plessy v. Ferguson*, 163 U.S. 537. Under that doctrine, equality of treatment is accorded when the races are provided substantially equal facilities, even though these facilities be separate. In the Delaware case, the Supreme Court of Delaware adhered to that doctrine, but ordered that the plaintiffs be admitted to the white schools because of their superiority to the Negro schools.

The plaintiffs contended that segregated public schools are not "equal" and cannot be made "equal," and that hence they are deprived of the equal protection of the laws. . . .

In the first cases in this Court construing the Fourteenth Amendment, decided shortly after its adoption, the Court interpreted it as proscribing all state-imposed discriminations against the Negro race. The doctrine of "separate but equal" did not make its appearance in this Court until 1896 in the case of *Plessy v. Ferguson, supra*, involving not education but transportation. American courts have since labored with the doctrine for over half a century. In this Court, there have been six cases involving the "separate but equal" doctrine in the field of public education. . . . In none of these cases was it necessary to examine the doctrine to grant relief to the Negro plaintiff. And in *Sweatt v. Painter* . . . the Court expressly reserved decision on the question of whether *Plessy v. Ferguson* should be held inapplicable to public education.

In the instant cases, that question is directly presented. Here, unlike *Sweatt v. Painter*, there are findings below that the Negro and white schools involved have been equalized, or are being equalized, with respect to buildings, curricula, qualifications and salaries of teachers, and other "tangible" factors. Our decision, therefore, cannot turn on merely a comparison of these tangible factors in the Negro and white schools involved in each of the cases. We must look instead to the effect of segregation itself on public education.

In approaching this problem, we cannot turn the clock back to 1868 when the Amendment was adopted, or even to 1896 when *Plessy v. Ferguson* was written. We must consider public education in the light of its full development and its present place in American life throughout the Nation. Only in this way can it be determined if segregation in public schools deprives these plaintiffs of the equal protection of the laws.

Today, education is perhaps the most important function of state and local governments. Compulsory school attendance laws and the great expenditures for education both demonstrate our recognition of the importance of education to our democratic society. It is required in the performance of our most basic public responsibilities, even service in the armed forces. It is the very foundation of good citizenship. Today it is a principal instrument in awakening the child to cultural values, in preparing him for later professional training, and in helping him to adjust normally to his environment. In these days, it is doubtful that any child may reasonably be expected to succeed in life if he is denied the opportunity of an education. Such an opportunity, where the state has undertaken to provide it, is a right which must be made available to all on equal terms.

We come then to the question presented: Does segregation of children in public schools solely on the basis of race, even though the physical facilities and other "tangible" factors may be equal, deprive the children of the minority group of equal education opportunities? We believe that it does.

In *Sweatt v. Painter* . . . in finding that a segregated law school for Negroes could not provide them equal education opportunities, the Court relied in large part on "those qualities which are incapable of objective measurement but which make for greatness in a law school." In *McLaurin v. Oklahoma State Regents* . . . the Court, in requiring that a Negro admitted to a white graduate school be treated like all other students, again resorted to intangible considerations: ". . . his ability to study, to engage in discussions and exchange views with other students, and in general, to learn his profession." Such considerations apply with added force to children in grade and high schools. To separate them from others of similar age and qualifications solely because of their race generates a feeling of inferiority as to their status in the community that may affect their hearts and minds in a way unlikely ever to be undone. The effect of this separation on their educational opportunities was well stated by a finding in the Kansas case by a court which nevertheless felt compelled to rule against the Negro plaintiffs:

Segregation of white and colored children in public schools has a detrimental effect upon the colored children. The impact is greater when it has the sanction of the law; for the policy of separating the races is usually interpreted as denoting the inferiority of the Negro group. A sense of inferiority affects the motivation of a child to learn. Segregation with the sanction of law, therefore, has a tendency to retard the education and mental development of negro children and to deprive them of some of the benefits they would receive in a racial[ly] integrated school system.

Whatever may have been the extent of psychological knowledge at the time of *Plessy v. Ferguson*, this finding is amply supported by modern authority. Any language in *Plessy v. Ferguson* contrary to this finding is rejected.

We conclude that in the field of public education the doctrine of "separate but equal" has no place. Separate educational facilities are inherently unequal. Therefore, we hold that the plaintiffs and others similarly situated for whom the actions have been brought are, by reason of the segregation complained of, deprived of the equal protection of the laws guaranteed by the Fourteenth Amendment. This disposition makes unnecessary any discussion whether such segregation also violates the Due Process Clause of the Fourteenth Amendment.

1. *What is the function and significance of education in America according to this decision?*
2. *Identify and explain the opinion of the Court regarding the effects of "separate but equal" education upon African American students.*

27-3 Ladies Home Journal, "Young Mother" (1956)

The post-World War Two years witnessed a tremendous baby boom that led to great interest in family life. The mother was seen as the person responsible for maintaining the house, raising the children, and caring for the husband. In some cases, the mother not only received little or no help, but often was an unequal partner in the family and received little recognition for the work she did.

Mrs. Gould: As editors and parents we are extremely interested in this whole problem. The welfare of our society depends upon the type of children you young mothers and others like you are able to bring up. Anything that affects the welfare of young families is most crucial, and I do feel that the young mother, any young mother in our day, should get far more general recognition and attention than she does-not so much for her own sake as for society as a whole, or just out of sheer common sense.

Miss Hickey: And understanding. I think there is a lack of understanding, too. Since it would take all day to tell what a busy woman does all day . . . how about your high points?

Mrs. Petry: I would say in the morning-breakfast and wash time. I put the breakfast out, leave the children to eat it and run into the bathroom-that is where the washer is-and fill it up. I come back into the kitchen and shove a little in the baby's mouth and try to keep the others eating. Then I go back in the bathroom and put the clothes in the wringer and start the rinse water. That is about the end of the half-hour there. I continue then to finish the wash, and either put them out or let them see one program they like on television, and then I go out and hang the wash up.

Miss Hickey: You put that outside?

Mrs. Petry: Yes. Then I eat.

Mrs. Gould: Can you sit down and eat in peace? Are the children outdoors at that time or watching television?

Mrs. Petry: They are supposed to be outside, but they are usually running in and out. Somebody forgot something he should have eaten, or wants more milk, or a toy or something. Finally I lock the screen door. I always read something while I'm eating-two meals a day I read. When my husband isn't there, and if I am alone, or maybe just one child at the table, I read something quick. But I time it. I take no more than half an hour for eating and reading.

Miss Hickey: You work on schedule quite a bit. Why do you do that?

Mrs. Petry: Because I am very forgetful. I have an orange crayon and I write "defrost" on the refrigerator every now and then, or I forget to defrost it. If I think of something while I am washing, I write it on the mirror with an eyebrow pencil. It must sound silly, but that is the only way I can remember everything I have to do. . . .

Miss Hickey: Mrs. Ehrhardt, your quietest half-hour?

Mrs. Ehrhardt: I would say . . . that when I go out to take the wash in. There is something about getting outdoors-and I don't get out too often, except to hang out the wash and to bring it in. I really enjoy doing it. If it is a nice day, I stand outside and fold it outdoors. I think that is my quietest hour.

Miss Hickey: How often do you and your husband go out together in the evening?

Mrs. Ehrhardt: Not often. An occasional movie, which might be every couple of months or so, on an anniversary. This year is the first year we celebrated on the day we were married. We were married in June. We always celebrated it, but it might be in July or August.

It depends on our babysitter. If you cannot get anyone, you just cannot go out. I am not living near my family and I won't leave the children with teenagers. I would be afraid it might be a little hectic, and a young girl might not know what to do. So we don't get out very often. . . .

Miss Hickey: Let us hear about Mrs. Petry's recreation.

Mrs. Petry: Oh, I went to work in a department store that opened in Levittown. I begged and begged my husband to let me work, and finally he said I could go once or twice a week. I lasted for three weeks, or should I say he lasted for three weeks.

Mrs. Gould: You mean you worked in the daytime?

Mrs. Petry: Three evenings, from six until nine, and on Saturday.

Mrs. Gould: And your husband took care of the children during that time?

Mrs. Petry: Yes, but the third week, he couldn't stand it anymore, Saturday and all. In fact, I think he had to work that Saturday, so I asked if I could just come in to the store during the week. My husband was hoping they would fire me, but they didn't. But I could see that it wasn't really fair to him, because I was going out for my own pleasure.

Mrs. Gould: In other words, your working was your recreation. Mrs. Petry: Yes, and I enjoyed it very much.

Miss Hickey: Why did you feel you wanted to do this?

Mrs. Petry: To see some people and talk to people, just to see what is going on in the world. . . .

Miss Hickey: How about your shopping experiences?

Mrs. McKenzie: Well, I don't go in the evening, because I cannot depend on Ed being home; and when he is there, he likes to have me there too. I don't know. Usually all three of the children go shopping with me. At one time I carried two and dragged the other one along behind me in the cart with the groceries. It is fun to take them all. Once a man stopped me and said, "Lady, did you know your son is eating hamburger?" He had eaten a half- pound of raw hamburger. When corn on the cob was so expensive, my oldest one begged me to buy corn on the cob, so I splurged and bought three ears for thirty-nine cents. When I got to the check-out counter, I discovered he had eaten all three, so he had to pay for the cobs.

Miss Hickey: You go once a week?

Mrs. McKenzie: Once a week or every ten days now, depending on how often I have the use of the car. That day we usually go to the park, too. . . .

Miss Hickey: Tell us about your most recent crisis.

Mrs. McKenzie: I had given a birthday party for fifteen children in my little living room, which is seven by eleven. The next morning my son, whose birthday it had been, broke out with the measles, so I had exposed fifteen children to measles, and I was the most unpopular mother in the neighborhood.

He was quite sick, and it snowed that day. Ed took Lucy sleigh riding. Both of them fell off the sled and she broke both the bones in her arm.

Mrs. Gould: Did she then get the measles?

Mrs. McKenzie: She did, and so did the baby. . . . My main problem was being in quarantine for a month. During this time that all three had measles and Lucy had broken her arm, we got a notice from the school that her tuberculin test was positive-and that meant that one of the adults living in our home had active tuberculosis. It horrified me. I kept thinking, "Here I sit killing my three children with tuberculosis." But we had to wait until they were over their contagion period before we could all go in and get x-rayed.

Miss Hickey: And the test was not correct?

Mrs. McKenzie: She had had childhood tuberculosis, but it was well healed and she was all right. About eight of ten have had childhood tuberculosis and no one knows it.

Mrs. Gould: It is quite common, but it is frightening when it occurs to you. Were your children quite sick with measles?

Mrs. McKenzie: Terribly ill.

Mrs. Gould: They had high temperatures?

Mrs. McKenzie: My children are a great deal like my father. Anything they do, they do to extreme. They are violently ill, or they are as robust as can be. There is no in-between. . . .

508

Dr. Montagu: There is one very large question I would like to ask. What in your lives, as they are at present, would you most like to see changed or modified?

Mrs. Ehrhardt: Well, I would like to be sure my husband's position would not require him to be transferred so often. I would like to stay in place long enough to take a few roots in the community. It would also be nice to have someone help with the housework, but I don't think I would like to have anyone live in. The houses nowadays are too small. I think you would bump into each other. Of course, I have never had any one in, so I cannot honestly give an opinion.

Mrs. Townsend: At the present time, I don't think there is anything that I would like to change in the household. We happen to be very close, and we are all very happy. I will admit that there are times when I am a little overtired, and I might be a little more than annoyed with the children, but actually it doesn't last too long. We do have a problem where we live now. There aren't any younger children for my children to play with. Therefore, they are underneath my heels just constantly, and I am not able to take the older children out the way I would like to, because of the two babies.

Miss Hickey: You have been in how many communities?Mrs. Townsend:I have lived in Louisiana, California, New York, and for a short period in Columbia, South Carolina. . . .

Miss Hickey: Mrs. Petry, what would you change?

Mrs. Petry: I would like more time to enjoy my children. I do take time, but if I do take as much time as I like, the work piles up. When I go back to work I feel crabby, and I don't know whether I'm mad at the children, or mad at the work or just mad at everybody sometimes.

I would also like to have a little more rest and a little more time to spend in relaxation with my husband. We never get to go out together, and the only time we have much of a conversation is just before we go to bed. And I would like to have a girl come and do my ironing.

I am happy there where we live because this is the first time we have stayed anywhere for any length of time. It will be two years in August, and it is the first home we have really had. That is why my husband left the Navy. I nearly had a nervous collapse, because it seemed I couldn't stand another minute not having him home and helping, or not helping, but just being there.

1. What vision of Suburban American life is formed from these accounts?
2. What seems to be the prescribed roles for women in these accounts?

27-4 Student Nonviolent Coordinating Committee, Statement of Purpose (1960)

The Statement of Purpose of the SNCC (pronounced "snick"), was adopted at a conference held at Shaw University in April 1960. The statement was adopted at the insistence of James Lawson, a former theology student at Vanderbilt University and one of the leaders of the Nashville student movement.

We affirm the philosophical or religious ideal of nonviolence as the foundation of our purpose, the presupposition of our faith, and the manner of our action. Nonviolence as it grows from Judaic-Christian tradition seeks a social order of justice permeated by love. Integration of human endeavor represents the crucial first step toward such a society.

Through nonviolence, courage displaces fear; love transforms hate. Acceptance dissipates prejudice; hope ends despair. Peace dominates war; faith reconciles doubt. Mutual regard cancels enmity. Justice for all overthrows injustice. The redemptive community supersedes systems of gross social immorality.

Love is the central motif of nonviolence. Love is the force by which God binds man to Himself and man to man. Such love goes to the extreme; it remains loving and forgiving even in the midst of hostility. It matches the capacity of evil to inflict suffering with an even more enduring capacity to absorb evil, all the while persisting in love.

By appealing to conscience and standing on the moral nature of human existence, nonviolence nurtures the atmosphere in which reconciliation and justice become actual possibilities.

1. Identify and describe the basic premises of the Student Nonviolent Coordinating Committee.

PART TWENTY-EIGHT
THE CHANGING LIBERAL STATE

28-1 Dwight D. Eisenhower, Decision Not to Intervene at Dien Bien Phu (1954)

Initially, Eisenhower considered coming to the aid of the French at Dien Bien Phu. However, he insisted that in order to obtain American assistance, the French had to internationalize the war and to promise freedom for Laos, Cambodia, and Vietnam if and when the communists were defeated. The French would not agree to Eisenhowers terms, so Eisenhower refused to commit American forces. The first document is from a letter Eisenhower wrote on April 26, 1954 to Alfred Gruenther, who was on Eisenhowers staff during World War II, served as Ikes chief of staff at NATO, and later was himself Supreme Allied Commander of NATO forces. The second document is an excerpt from a letter Eisenhower wrote to Swede Hazlett, a boyhood friend, with whom Eisenhower corresponded in long, frank, and revealing letters. This letter was written the day after the letter to Gruenther. The third document comes from the diary kept by James C. Hagerty, Eisenhowers press secretary. The excerpt is from the entry for April 26, 1954.

Dwight D. Eisenhower to Alfred Gruenther, April 26, 1954

As you know, you and I started more than three years ago trying to convince the French that they could not win the Indo-China war and particularly could not get real American support in that region unless they would unequivocally pledge independence to the Associated States upon the achievement of military victory. Along with this-indeed as a corollary to it-this administration has been arguing that no Western power can go to Asia militarily, except as one of a concert of powers, which concert must include local Asiatic peoples.

To contemplate anything else is to lay ourselves open to the charge of imperialism and colonialism or-at the very least-of objectionable paternalism. Even, therefore, if we could by some sudden stroke assure the saving of the Dien Bien Phu garrison, I think that under the conditions proposed by the French, the free world would lose more than it would gain.

Dwight D. Eisenhower to Swede Hazlett, April 27, 1954

In my last letter I remember that I mentioned Dien Bien Phu. It still holds out and while the situation looked particularly desperate during the past week, there now appears to be a slight improvement and the place may hold on for another week or ten days. The general situation in Southeast Asia, which is rather dramatically epitomized by the Dien Bien Phu battle, is a complicated one that has been a long time developing. . . .

For more than three years I have been urging upon successive French governments the advisability of finding some way of "internationalizing" the war; such action would be proof to all the world and particularly to the Viet Namese that France's purpose is not colonial in character but is to defeat Communism in the region and to give the natives their freedom. The reply has always been vague, containing references to national prestige, Constitutional limitations, inevitable effects upon the Moroccan and Tunisian peoples, and dissertations on plain political difficulties and battles within the French Parliament. The result has been that the French have failed entirely to produce any enthusiasm on the part of the Vietnamese for participation in the war. . . .

In any event, any nation that intervenes in a civil war can scarcely expect to win unless the side in whose favor it intervenes possesses a high morale based upon a war purpose or cause in which it believes. The French have used weasel words in promising independence and through this one reason as much as anything else, have suffered reverses that have been really inexcusable.

James C. Hagerty, Diary, Monday, April 26, 1954

Indochina. The President said that the French "are weary as hell." He said that it didn't look as though Dienbienphu could hold out for more than a week and would fall possibly sooner. Reported that the British thought that the French were not putting out as much as they could, but that he did not necessarily agree with their viewpoint. "The French go up and down every day-they are very volatile. They think they are a great power one day and they feel sorry for themselves the next day." The President said that if we were to put one combat soldier into Indochina, then our entire prestige would be at stake, not only in that area but throughout the world. . . . The President said the situation looked very grim this morning, but that he and Dulles were doing everything they could to get the free countries to act in concert. In addition, he said "there are plenty of people in Asia, and we can train them to fight well. I don't see any reason for American ground troops to be committed in Indochina, don't think we need it, but we can train their forces and it may be necessary for us eventually to use some of our planes or aircraft carriers off the coast and some of our fighting craft we have in that area for support."

1. Explain Eisenhower's reasoning for desiring an "internationalized" war effort.
2. Explain Eisenhower's opinion regarding the commitment of American military forces in Viet Nam.

28-2 Charles Sherrod, Student Nonviolent Coordinating Committee Memorandum (1961)

SNCC was a major civil rights group that actively participated in the civil rights movement in the South. Their campaign in Albany, Georgia showed the need to educate the local African American community about their rights and the importance the black churches played in mobilizing community support for mass meetings and the struggle to achieve their rights.

The Albany we found in October when we came down as SNCC field workers was quite different from the Albany we now know. Naturally, though, many things remain the same. The swift flowing, cool waters of the Flint River still cut off the east side of the city from the west. The paved streets remind visitors that civilization may be thought to exist in the area while the many dusty, sandy roadways in residential areas cause one to wonder where tax money goes. Beautiful homes against green backgrounds with lawns rolling up and down hills and around corners held up by the deep roots of palm and pine trees untouched by years of nature's movement, sunny days with moonlit nights-this was the Albany we had been introduced to in October. But this was not the real Albany; the real Albany was seen much later.

Albany is known by its people to be "liberal." Located in the center of such infamous counties as "Terrible Terrell," "Dogging Douglas," "Unmitigated Mitchell," "Lamentable Lee," "Unbearable Baker," and the "Unworthy Worth County." It stands out as the only metropolitan area of any prominence in Southwest Georgia. It is the crossroads of rural people in villages and towns within a radius of ninety miles. It was principally because of its location that Albany was chosen as the beachhead for Democracy in *DEEP Southwest Georgia.*

Initially, we met with every obstacle possible. We had come down with the idea of setting up office in Albany and moving on shortly to Terrell County. This idea was short-lived. We found that it would take more time than we thought to present this city of 23,000 Negroes with the idea that freedom is worth sacrifice. . . .

The first obstacle to remove . . . was the mental block in the minds of those who wanted to move but were unable for fear that we were not who we said we were. But when people began to hear us in churches, social meetings, on the streets, in the poolhalls, lunchrooms, nightclubs, and other places where people gather, they began to open up a bit. We would tell them of how it feels to be in prison, what it means to be behind bars, in jail for the cause. We explained to them that we had stopped school because we felt compelled to do so since so many of us were in chains. We explained further that there were worse chains than jail and prison. We referred to the system that imprisons men's minds and robs them of creativity. We mocked the systems that teaches men to be good Negroes instead of good men. We gave an account of the many resistances of injustice in the courts, in employment, registration, and voting. The people knew that such evils existed but when we pointed them out time and time again and emphasized the need for concerted action against them, the people began to think. At this point, we started to illustrate what had happened in Montgomery, Macon, Nashville, Charlotte, Atlanta, Savannah, Richmond, Petersburg, and many other cities where people came together and protested against an evil system. . . .

From the beginning we had, as Student Nonviolent Coordinating Committee field people, visited the NAACP Youth Chapter, introduced ourselves and outlined our project for Voter-Registration. We pointed out differences between the two organizations and advanced the hope that we could work together.

From this point we initiated meetings in the churches of the city. We had introduced ourselves to the Baptist Ministerial Alliance and the Interdenominational Alliance. We were given their support as groups and many churches opened their doors to us; others were afraid for one reason or another.

To these churches we drew the young people from the College, Trade and General High schools, and on the street. They were searching for a meaning in life. Nine committees were formed-Typists, Clubs, Writing, Telephone, Campus, communication, Sunday School communication, Ministerial communication, Boy and Girl Scouts, and a central committee of eighteen persons. Some of those were members of the NAACP Youth Chapter. They kept coming to the workshops we were holding every night at different churches. . . .

That same morning, five or six of us got together at the home of a local citizen and planned again to go to the bus terminal. At three o'clock, nine students approached the bus station, which is located only one block away from the predominantly "Negro" business area. Upon seeing the neatly dressed students walk toward the station, a large number came from the poolrooms, lunchrooms, liquor stores, and other places. . . .

The stories of faraway cities and their protests turned over in their minds. Was this a dream or was it really happening here in Albany? The students symbolized in the eyes of them who looked on, the expression of years of resentment-for police brutality, for poor housing, for dis[e]nfranchisement, for inferior education, for the whole damnable system. The fruit of years of prayer and sacrifice stood the ageless hatched-men of the South, the policeman, but the children of the new day stood tall, fearless before the legal executioners of the blacks in the DEEP south.

The bus station was full of men in blue but up through the mass of people past the men with guns and billies ready, into the terminal, they marched, quiet and quite clean. They were allowed to buy tickets to Florida but after sitting in the waiting room, they were asked to leave under the threat of arrest. They left as planned and later filed affidavits with the Interstate Commerce Commission. The idea had been delivered. In the hearts of the young and of the old, from that moment on, Segregation was dead-the funeral was to come later.

There was a meeting of minds which came about as a result of this action. It was a momentous occasion! The gathering was scheduled for one Friday evening, at a citizen's home. The proposed number of five had grown to a total of twenty interested persons who had been invited by the initial five. No one imagined the importance of this meeting. Its objective was to organize and thereby discipline a group to negotiate with the city officials. It was generally understood that the entire group would go before the officials but later three men were chosen to represent the group (THE ALBANY MOVEMENT). This committee presented to the Mayor the displeasure of the community with Segregation as connected with the following: Train station, Bus terminal, Library, Parks, Hospitals, City Buses, Juries, Jobs and other public facilities. There was no reasonable consequence of the meeting with the Mayor; it was as if there had never been communication.

But the importance of this meeting of the representatives of the Albany community at the home of a citizen lies in its structure. The real issue immediately took the floor in the form of a question: Would the organizations involved be willing to lose their identity as separate groups and cooperate under the name of "THE ALBANY MOVEMENT"? All of the organizations had to caucus-Baptist Ministerial Alliance, Interdenominational Alliance, Criterion Club, Lincoln Heights Improvement Association, Federated Women Clubs of Albany, National Association for the Advance of Colored People and its coordinate groups-Youth Council-Albany Voters League, and the Student Nonviolent Coordinating Committee. There were other interested persons who were members of such groups as the American Legion, Masons, Elks, etc., but not there as official representatives. These groups later gave their support. After a short period of deliberation the groups were ready to give their opinions. All of the groups were willing to lose their identit[ies] in the local organization except the NAACP, whose delegates requested time to receive directives from the national office.

The Albany Movement soon grew to the statue of "Spokesman" for the "Negro" community; a representative social unit with extraordinary powers of negotiations had been born. . . .

[T]he first mass meeting was called at one of the larger churches in the city-Mount Zion. A week before the meeting, enthusiasm had already been developing. There was a men's day exercise at which the Reverend Ralph Abernathy, Treasurer of the Southern Christian Leadership Conference, was the main speaker. He had been invited by the local church, but his soul-searching message touched the hearts of many, mounting enthusiastic anticipation for the mass meeting.

The night of the first Mass Meeting came! The church was packed before eight o'clock. People were everywhere, in the aisles, sitting and standing in the choir stands, hanging over the railing of the balcony upstairs, sitting in trees outside near windows, and about twenty or thirty ministers sat on the pulpit in chairs and on the floor side by side. There was no bickering. Soon a young doctor of the community took charge of the gathering, leading in the freedom songs which have grown out of the student movement during the last two years. Petitions were laid before Almighty God by one of the ministers and a challenge was directed to the assembly by the young doctor. Then arose a tall, silver-haired, outspoken veteran of the struggle. He spoke [in a] slow and determined [manner]. He referred to attempts last year to unify the community in protest against literary abuse of black men in the local paper and filled in with vivid detail the developments to the date of the Mass Meeting. Appearing also on the program was the indefatigable, only, local Negro lawyer, C. B. King. He stood flatfooted and thundered with his explosive deep voice, striking at both the inaction of the church and its hypocrisy. He also condemned local leadership in other areas for procrastination. At times he sounded like the prophet of doom but before he had finished, in his highly polished speech, he declared that our only hope was unity. This had been the real reason for the Mass Meeting-to weld the community into one bond of reason and emotion. The force to do this was generated by accounts of the released who individually described the physical situation and mental state of each, in jail.

When the last speaker among the students, Bertha Gober, had finished, there was nothing left to say. Tears filled the eyes of hard, grown men who had known personally and seen with their own eyes merciless atrocities committed by small men without conscience. As Bertha, with her small frame and baby voice told of spending Thanksgiving in jail along with other physical inconveniences, there was not a dry eye to be found. And when we rose to sing "We Shall Overcome," nobody could imagine what kept the top of the church on four corners. It was as if everyone had been lifted up on high and had been granted voices to sing with the celestial chorus in another time and in another place.

I threw my head back and closed my eyes as I sang with my whole body. I remembered walking dusty roads for weeks without food. I remembered staying up all night for two and three nights in succession writing and cutting stencils and memeographing and wondering-How Long? I remembered thinking about home, a thousand miles away and fun, games, dancing, movies, boatrides, tennis, chess, swimming,-LIFE; this was history.

But when I momentarily opened my eyes something good happened to me. I saw standing beside a dentist of the city, a man of the streets singing and smiling with joyful tears in his eyes and beside him a mailman with whom I had become acquainted along with people from all walks of life. It was then that I felt deep down within where it really counts, a warm feeling and all I could do was laugh out loud in the swelling of the singing.

1. Summarize and characterize the extent and process of organization as the SNCC began its work in Albany.
2. Describe the events accompanying the beginning of "The Albany Movement" as they are depicted in this account. In what ways is the movement seen as a unifying and empowering force in the struggle for civil rights?

28-3   John F. Kennedy, Cuban Missile Address (1962)

This is an excerpt from the television address President Kennedy gave on October 22, 1962, to the American people, letting them know about the security threat posed by the Soviets in Cuba and his willingness to take strong aggressive action against it. It is interesting to note that while all this transpired the Soviet Union already had missiles stationed in Siberia which were within range of the West Coast and that the United States had missiles in Europe that were certainly within range of the Soviet Union's major population centers.

Good evening, my fellow citizens. This Government, as promised, has maintained the closest surveillance of the Soviet military build-up on the island of Cuba. Within the past week unmistakable evidence has established the fact that a series of offensive missile sites is now in preparation on that imprisoned island. The purposes of these bases can be none other than to provide a nuclear strike capability against the Western Hemisphere.

Upon receiving the first preliminary hard information of this nature last Tuesday morning [October 16] at 9:00 A.M., I directed that our surveillance be stepped up. And now having confirmed and completed our evaluation of the evidence and our decision on a course of action, this Government feels obliged to report this new crisis to you in fullest detail.

The characteristics of these new missile sites indicate two distinct types of installations. Several of them include medium-range ballistic missiles capable of carrying a nuclear warhead for a distance of more than 1,000 nautical miles. Each of these missiles, in short, is capable of striking Washington, D.C., the Panama Canal, Cape Canaveral, Mexico City, or any other city in the southeastern part of the United States, in Central America, or in the Caribbean area.

Additional sites not yet completed appear to be designed for intermediate-range ballistic missiles capable of traveling more than twice as far-and thus capable of striking most of the major cities in the Western Hemisphere, ranging as far north as Hudson Bay, Canada, and as far south as Lima, Peru. In addition, jet bombers, capable of carrying nuclear weapons, are now being uncrated and assembled in Cuba, while the necessary air bases are being prepared.

This urgent transformation of Cuba into an important strategic base-by the presence of these large, long-range, and clearly offensive weapons of sudden mass destruction-constitutes an explicit threat to the peace and security of all the Americas, in flagrant and deliberate defiance of the Rio Pact of 1947, the traditions of this nation and Hemisphere, the Joint Resolution of the Eighty-seventh Congress, the Charter of the United Nations, and my own public warnings to the Soviets on September 4 and 13.

This action also contradicts the repeated assurances of Soviet spokesmen, both publicly and privately delivered, that the arms build-up in Cuba would retain its original defensive character and that the Soviet Union had no need or desire to station strategic missiles on the territory of any other nation. . . .

In that sense missiles in Cuba add to an already clear and present danger-although it should be noted the nations of Latin America have never previously been subjected to a potential nuclear threat.

But this secret, swift, and extraordinary build-up of Communist missiles-in an area well known to have a special and historical relationship to the United States and the nations of the Western Hemisphere, in violation of Soviet assurances, and in defiance of American and hemispheric policy-this sudden, clandestine decision to station strategic weapons for the first time outside of Soviet soil-is a deliberately provocative and unjustifiable change in the status quo which cannot be accepted by this country if our courage and our commitments are ever to be trusted again by either friend or foe.

1. Summarize Kennedy's description of the nuclear capability present in Cuba.
2. Describe Kennedy's beliefs regarding the necessity of an American response to the nuclear build-up in Cuba.

28-4 Students for a Democratic Society, The Port Huron Statement (1962)

Raised in relative safety and prosperity, while middle-class college students in the early 1960s saw the civil rights movement and the Cold War as evidence that the principles of equality and justice they had been taught were not practiced fully in the United States. Seeking to realize these goals, some students formed radical groups to work for social and political change. These groups helped spearhead the youth movement of the 1960s.

We are the people of this generation, bred in at least modest comfort, housed now in the universities, looking uncomfortably to the world we inherit.

When we were kids the United States was the wealthiest and strongest country in the world; the only one with the atom bomb, the least scarred by modern war, an initiator of the United Nations that we thought would distribute Western influence throughout the world. Freedom and equality for each individual, government of, by, and for the people-these American values we found good, principles by which we could live as men. Many of us began maturing in complacency.

As we grew, however, our comfort was penetrated by events too troubling to dismiss. First, the permeating and victimizing fact of human degradation, symbolized by the Southern struggle against racial bigotry, compelled most of us from silence to activism. Second, the enclosing fact of the Cold War, symbolized by the presence of the Bomb, brought awareness that we ourselves, and our friends, and millions of abstract "others" we knew more directly because of our common peril, might die at any time. We might deliberately ignore, or avoid or fail to feel all other human problems, but not these two, for these were too immediate and crushing in their impact, too challenging in the demand that we as individuals take the responsibility for encounter and resolution.

1. What factors identified in this statement have impacted the lives of the younger generation more than any others? What have been the effects of these factors upon this generation?

28-5 John Lewis, Address at the March on Washington (1963)

A high point of the civil rights movement was the March on Washington. A number of civil rights leaders, including Martin Luther King, Jr., spoke in favor a civil rights law. John Lewis was a leader of the Student Nonviolent Coordinating Committee.

We march today for jobs and freedom, but we have nothing to be proud of, for hundreds and thousands of our brothers are not here-they have no money for their transportation, for they are receiving starvation wages . . . or no wages, at all.

In good conscience, we cannot support the Administration's civil rights bill, for it is too little, and too late. There's not one thing in the bill that will protect our people from police brutality.

The voting section of the bill will not help the thousands of citizens who want to vote. . . .

What is in the bill that will protect the homeless and starving people of this nation? What is there in this bill to ensure the equality of a maid who earns $5.00 a week in the home of a family whose income is $100,000 a year?

The bill will not protect young children and old women from police dogs and fire hoses for engaging in peaceful demonstrations. . . .

For the first time in 100 years this nation is being awakened to the fact that segregation is evil and it must be destroyed in all forms. Our presence today proves that we have been aroused to the point of action.

We are now involved in a serious revolution. This nation is still a place of cheap political leaders who build their careers on immoral compromise and ally themselves with open forms of political, economic, and social exploitation. . . . The party of Kennedy is also the party of Eastland. The party of Javits is also the party of Goldwater. Where is our party?

I want to know-which side is the federal government on?

The revolution is at hand, and we must free ourselves of the chains of political and economic slavery. The non-violent revolution is saying, "We will not wait for the courts to act, for we have been waiting hundreds of years. We will not wait for the President, nor the Justice Department, nor Congress, but we will take matters into our own hands, and create a great source of power, outside of any national structure that could and would assure us victory." . . . We cannot be patient, we do not want to be free gradually, we want our freedom, and we want it now. We can not depend on any political party, for both the Democrats and Republicans have betrayed the basic principles of the Declaration of Independence. . . .

The revolution is a serious one. Mr. Kennedy is trying to take the revolution out of the streets and put it in the courts. Listen, Mr. Kennedy, listen. Mr. Congressman, listen, fellow citizens-the black masses are on the march for jobs and freedom, and we must say to the politicians that there won't be a "cooling-off period."

We won't stop now. All of the forces of Eastland, Barnett, and Wallace won't stop this revolution. The next time we march, we won't march on Washington, but will march through the South, through the Heart of Dixie, the way Sherman did-nonviolently. We will make the action of the past few months look petty. And I say to you, WAKE UP AMERICA!

1. What deficiencies in the Civil Rights Bill are identified in this speech?
2. What is Lewis' attitude toward the government's stance and progress on civil rights?
3. Describe the type of revolution that is proposed by Lewis.

28-6 The Civil Rights Act of 1964

Partially in response to the march on Washington, Congress passed a civil rights act that attempted to provide African Americans with the rights they had been granted them ninety years earlier. One of the provisions included ensuring voting rights for African Americans.

TITLE I

Voting Rights

Sec. 101 (2). No person acting under color of law shall-

(A) in determining whether any individual is qualified under State law or laws to vote in any Federal election, apply any standard, practice, or procedure different form the standards, practices, or procedures applied under such law or laws to other individuals within the same county, parish, or similar political subdivision who have been found by State officials to be qualified to vote; . . . .

(C) employ any literacy test as a qualification for voting in any Federal election unless (i) such test is administered to each individual wholly in writing; and (ii) a certified copy of the test and of the answers given by the individual is furnished to him within twenty-five days of the submission of his request made within the period of time during which records and papers are required to be retained and preserved pursuant to Title III of the Civil Rights Act of 1960. . . .

TITLE II

Injunctive Relief Against Discrimination in Places of Public Accommodation

Sec. 201. (a) All persons shall be entitled to the full and equal enjoyment of the goods, services, facilities, privileges, advantages, and accommodations of any place of public accommodation, as defined in this section, without discrimination or segregation on the ground of race, color, religion, or national origin.

(b) Each of the following establishments which serves the public is a place of public accommodation within the meaning of this title if its operations affect commerce, or if discrimination or segregation by it is supported by State action:

(1) any inn, motel, or other establishment which provides lodging to transient guests, other than an establishment located within a building which contains not more than five rooms for rent or hire and which is actually occupied by the proprietor of such establishment as his residence;

(2) any restaurant, cafeteria, lunch room, lunch counter, soda fountain, or other activity principally engaged in selling food for consumption on the premises. . . .

(3) any motion picture house, theater, concert hall, sports arena, stadium, or other place of exhibition or entertainment. . . .

(d) Discrimination or segregation by an establishment is supported by State action within the meaning of this title if such discrimination or segregation (1) is carried on under color of any law, statute, ordinance, or regulation; or (2) is carried on under color of any custom or usage required or enforced by officials of the State or political subdivision thereof. . . .

Sec. 202. All persons shall be entitled to be free, at any establishment or place, from discrimination or segregation of any kind on the ground of race, color, religion, or national origin, if such discrimination or segregation is or purports to be required by any law, statute, ordinance, regulation, rule, or order of a State or any agency or political subdivision thereof. . . .

Sec. 206. (a) Whenever the Attorney General has reasonable cause to believe that any person or group of persons is engaged in a pattern of practice of resistance to the full enjoyment of any of the rights secured by this title, the Attorney General may bring a civil action in the appropriate district court of the United States by filing with it a complaint . . . requesting such preventive relief, including an application for a permanent or temporary injunction, restraining order or other order against the person or persons responsible for such pattern or practice, as he deems necessary to insure the full enjoyment of the rights herein described.

TITLE IV

Nondiscrimination in Federally Assisted Programs

Sec. 601. No person in the United States shall, on the ground of race, color, or national origin, be excluded from participation in, be denied the benefits of, or be subjected to discrimination under any program or activity receiving Federal financial assistance.

1. What provisions are stipulated in this act regarding voting rights?
2. What practical impact does this act have in regard to access to "public accommodation"?

28-7   The Tonkin Gulf Incident (1964)

After several years of having American troops serving in Vietnam, the United States vastly expanded their military involvement in that nation. The incident that triggered the escalation was the purported firing by North Vietnam on American ships in the Gulf of Tonkin. In response, Congress passed a resolution that gave President Johnson vastly increased war powers.

President Johnson's Message to Congress

Last night I announced to the American people that North Vietnamese regime had conducted further deliberate attacks against US. naval vessels operating in international waters, and that I had therefore directed air action against gunboats and supporting facilities used in these hostile operations. This air action has now been carried out with substantial damage to the boats and facilities. Two US. aircraft were lost in the action.

After consultation with the leaders of both parties in the Congress, I further announced a decision to ask the Congress for a resolution expressing the unity and determination of the United States in supporting freedom and in protecting peace in southeast Asia.

These latest actions of the North Vietnamese regime have given a new and grave turn to the already serious situation in southeast Asia. Our commitments in that area are well known to the Congress. They were first made in 1954 by President Eisenhower. They were further defined in the Southeast Asia Collective Defense Treaty approved by the Senate in February 1955.

This treaty with its accompanying protocol obligates the United States and other members to act in accordance with their constitutional processes to meet Communist aggression against any of the parties or protocol states.

Our policy in southeast Asia has been consistent and unchanged since 1954. I summarized it on June 2 in our simple propositions:

1. America keeps her word. Here as elsewhere, we must and shall honor our commitments.
2. The issue is the future of southeast Asia as a whole. A threat to any nation in that region is a threat to all, and a threat to us.
3. Our purpose is peace. We have no military, political, or territorial ambitions in the area.
4. This is not just a jungle war, but a struggle for freedom on every front of human activity. Our military and economic assistance to South Vietnam and Laos in particular has the purpose of helping these countries to repel aggression and strengthen their independence.

The threat to the free nations of southeast Asia has long been clear. The North Vietnamese regime has constantly sought to take over South Vietnam and Laos. This Communist regime has violated the Geneva accords for Vietnam. It has systematically conducted a campaign of subversion, which included the direction, training, and supply of personnel and arms for the conduct of guerrilla warfare in South Vietnamese territory. In Laos, the North Vietnamese regime has maintained military forces, used Laotian territory for infiltration into South Vietnam, and most recently carried out combat operations-all in direct violation of the Geneva agreements of 1962.

In recent months, the actions of the North Vietnamese regime have become steadily more threatening. . . .

As President of the United States I have concluded that I should now ask the Congress, on its part, to join in affirming the national determination that all such attacks will be met, and that the United States will continue in its basic policy of assisting the free nations of the area to defend their freedom.

As I have repeatedly made clear, the United States intends no rashness, and seeks no wider war. We must make it clear to all that the United States is united in its determination to bring about the end of Communist subversion and aggression in the area. We seek the full and effective restoration of the international agreements signed in Geneva in 1954, with respect to South Vietnam, and again in Geneva in 1962, with respect to Laos. . . .

Joint Resolution of Congress

To promote the maintenance of international peace and security in southeast Asia.

Whereas naval units of the Communist regime in Vietnam, in violation of the principles of the Charter of the United Nations and of international law, have deliberately and repeatedly attacked United States naval vessels lawfully present in international waters, and have thereby created a serious threat to international peace; and

Whereas these attacks are part of a deliberate and systematic campaign of aggression that the Communist regime in North Vietnam has been waging against its neighbors and the nations joined with them in the collective defense of their freedom; and

Whereas the United States is assisting the peoples of southeast Asia to protect their freedom and has no territorial, military or political ambitions in that area, but desires only that these peoples should be left in peace to work out their own destinies in their own way; Now, therefore, be it

Resolved by the Senate and House of Representatives of the United States of America in Congress assembled, that the Congress approves and supports the determination of the President, as Commander in Chief, to take all necessary measures to repel any armed attack against the forces of the United States and to prevent further aggression.

SEC. 2. The United States regards as vital to its national interest and to world peace the maintenance of international peace and security in southeast Asia. Consonant with the Constitution of the United States and the Charter of the United Nations and in accordance with its obligations under the Southeast Asia Collective Defense Treaty, the United States is, therefore, prepared, as the President determines, to take all necessary steps, including the use of armed force, to assist any member or protocol state of the Southeast Asia Collective Defense Treaty requesting assistance in defense of its freedom.

SEC. 3. This resolution shall expire when the President shall determine that the peace and security of the area is reasonably assured by international conditions created by action of the United Nations or otherwise, except that it may be terminated earlier by concurrent resolution of the Congress.

1. How does Johnson summarize U.S. policy in Southeast Asia?
2. Identify and explain the reasons given in this resolution for United States involvment in Viet Nam.

28-8 Lyndon B. Johnson, Commencement Address at Howard University (1965)

The passage of the Civil Rights Act in 1964 did not end the struggle for civil rights. In his 1965 speech, President Lyndon Johnson suggested the next step was guaranteeing equal opportunity through government programs on health, antipoverty, and other programs.

Our earth is the home of revolution.

In every corner of every continent men charged with hope contend with ancient ways in pursuit of justice. They reach for the newest of weapons to realize the oldest of dreams: that each may walk in freedom and pride, stretching his talents, enjoying the fruits of the earth.

Our enemies may occasionally seize the day of change. But it is the banner of our revolution they take. And our own future is linked to this process of swift and turbulent change in many lands. But nothing, in any country, touches us more profoundly, nothing is more freighted with meaning for our own destiny, than the revolution of the Negro American.

In far too many ways American Negroes have been another nation: deprived of freedom, crippled by hatred, the doors of opportunity closed to hope.

In our time change has come to this nation too. Heroically, the American Negro-acting with impressive restraint-has peacefully protested and marched, entered the courtrooms and the seats of government, demanding a justice long denied. The voice of the Negro was the call to action. But it is a tribute to America that, once aroused, the courts and the Congress, the President and most of the people, have been the allies of progress.

Thus we have seen the high court of the country declare that discrimination based on race was repugnant to the Constitution, and therefore void. We have seen-in 1957, 1960, and again in 1964-the first civil rights legislation in almost a century. . . .

The voting rights bill will be the latest, and among the most important, in a long series of victories. But this victory-as Winston Churchill said of another triumph for freedom-"is not the end. It is not even the beginning of the end. But it is, perhaps, the end of the beginning."

That beginning is freedom; and the barriers to that freedom are tumbling. Freedom is the right to share, fully and equally, in American society-to vote, to hold a job, to enter a public place, to go to school. It is the right to be treated, in every part of our national life, as a man equal in dignity and promise to all others.

But freedom is not enough. You do not wipe away the scars of centuries by saying: Now, you are free to go where you want, do as you desire, and choose the leaders you please.

You do not take a man who, for years, has been hobbled by chains, liberate him, bring him to the starting line of a race, saying "you are free to compete with all the others," and still justly believe you have been completely fair.

Thus it is not enough to open the gates of opportunity. All our citizens must have the ability to walk through those gates.

This is the next and the more profound stage of the battle for civil rights. We seek not just freedom but opportunity-not just legal equity but human ability-not just equality as a right and a theory, but equality as a fact and a result.

For the task is to give twenty million Negroes the same chance as every other American to learn and grow-to work and share in society-to develop their abilities-physical, mental, and spiritual, and to pursue their individual happiness.

To this end equal opportunity is essential, but not enough. Men and women of all races are born with the same range of abilities. But ability is not just the product of birth. It is stretched or stunted by the family you live with, and the neighborhood you live in-by the school you go to, and the poverty or richness of your surroundings. It is the product of a hundred unseen forces playing upon the infant, the child, and the man.

This graduating class at Howard University is witness to the indomitable determination of the Negro American to win his way in American life.

The number of Negroes in schools of high learning has almost doubled in fifteen years. The number of nonwhite professional workers has more than doubled in ten years. The median income of Negro college women now exceeds that of white college women. And these are the enormous accomplishments of distinguished individual Negroes-many of them graduates of this institution.

These are proud and impressive achievements. But they only tell the story of a growing middle class minority, steadily narrowing the gap between them and their white counterparts.

But for the great majority of Negro Americans-the poor, the unemployed, the uprooted and dispossessed-there is a grimmer story. They still are another nation. Despite the court orders and the laws, the victories and speeches, for them the walls are rising and the gulf is widening. . . .

We are not completely sure why this is. The causes are complex and subtle. But we do know the two broad basic reasons. And we know we have to act.

First, Negroes are trapped-as many whites are trapped-in inherited, gateless poverty. They lack training and skills. They are shut in slums, without decent medical care. Private and public poverty combine to cripple their capacities.

We are attacking these evils through our poverty program, our education program, our health program and a dozen more-aimed at the root causes of poverty.

We will increase, and accelerate, and broaden this attack in years to come, until this most enduring of foes yields to our unyielding will.

But there is a *second* cause-more difficult to explain, more deeply grounded, more desperate in its force. It is the devastating heritage of long years of slavery; and a century of oppression, hatred and injustice.

For Negro poverty is not white poverty. Many of its causes and many of its cures are the same. But there are differences-deep, corrosive, obstinate differences-radiating painful roots into the community, the family, and the nature of the individual.

These differences are not racial differences. They are solely and simply the consequence of ancient brutality, past injustice, and present prejudice. They are anguishing to observe. For the Negro they are a reminder of oppression. For the white they are a reminder of guilt. But they must be faced, and dealt with, and overcome; if we are to reach the time when the only difference between Negroes and whites is the color of their skin.

Nor can we find a complete answer in the experience of other American minorities. They made a valiant, and largely successful effort to emerge from poverty and prejudice. The Negro, like these others, will have to rely mostly on his own efforts. But he cannot do it alone. For they did not have the heritage of centuries to overcome. They did not have a cultural tradition which had been twisted and battered by endless years of hatred and hopelessness. Nor were they excluded because of race or color-a feeling whose dark intensity is matched by no other prejudice in our society.

Nor can these differences be understood as isolated infirmities. They are a seamless web. They cause each other. They result from each other. They reinforce each other. Much of the Negro community is buried under a blanket of history and circumstance. It is not a lasting solution to lift just one corner. We must stand on all sides and raise the entire cover if we are to liberate our fellow citizens.

One of the differences is the increased concentration of Negroes in our cities. More than 73 per cent of all Negroes live in urban areas compared with less than 70 per cent of whites. Most of them live in slums. And most of them live together; a separated people. Men are shaped by their world. When it is a world of decay ringed by an invisible wall-when escape is arduous and uncertain, and the saving pressures of a more hopeful society are unknown-it can cripple the youth and desolate the man.

There is also the burden a dark skin can add to the search for a productive place in society. Unemployment strikes most swiftly and broadly at the Negro. This burden erodes hope. Blighted hope breeds despair. Despair brings indifference to the learning which offers a way out. And despair coupled with indifference is often the source of destructive rebellion against the fabric of society. . . .

Perhaps most important-its influence radiating to every part of life-is the breakdown of the Negro family structure. For this, most of all, white America must accept responsibility. It flows from centuries of oppression and persecution of the Negro man. It flows from the long years of degradation and discrimination which have attacked his dignity and assaulted his ability to provide for his family. . . .

Unless we work to strengthen the family-to create conditions under which most parents will stay together-all the rest: schools and playgrounds, public assistance and private concern-will not be enough to cut completely the circle of despair and deprivation.

There is no single easy answer to all these problems.

Jobs are part of the answer. They bring the income which permits a man to provide for his family.

Decent homes in decent surroundings and a chance to learn are part of the answer.

Welfare and social programs better designed to hold families together are part of the answer.

Care for the sick is part of the answer.

An understanding heart by all Americans is also part of the answer.

To all these fronts-and a dozen more-I will dedicate the expanding efforts of my administration. . . .

It is the glorious opportunity of this generation to end the one huge wrong of the American nation-and in so doing to find America for ourselves, with the same immense thrill of discovery which gripped those who first began to realize that here, at last, was a home for freedom.

All it will take is for all of us to understand what this country is and what it must become.

The Scripture promises: "I shall light a candle of understanding in thine heart, which shall not be put out."

Together, and with millions more, we can light that candle of understanding in the heart of America.

And, once lit, it will never go out.

1. Why, according to Johnson, is it not enough to free African Americans from the bondage of prejudice? What more must be done?
2. Identify and explain the reasons identified in this address why African Americans have not universally been able to take advantage of equal opportunities for success.
3. What are the answers that Johnson proposes for dealing with the disadvantages that confront African Americans in their struggle for equality?

28-9   Stokely Carmichael and Charles Hamilton, from *Black Power* (1967)

By the late 1960s, some civil rights activists had become frustrated with what they considered a lack of progress. A new, activist movement arose around the idea of Black Power that rejected the nonviolent, integrationist rhetoric of the past for a more racially defined, confrontational approach.

The advocates of Black Power reject the old slogans and meaningless rhetoric of previous years in the civil rights struggle. The language of yesterday is indeed irrelevant: progress, non-violence, integration, fear of "white backlash," coalition. . . .

One of the tragedies of the struggle against racism is that up to this point there has been no national organization which could speak to the growing militancy of young black people in the urban ghettos and the black-belt South. There has been only a "civil rights" movement, whose tone of voice was adapted to an audience of middle-class whites. It served as a sort of buffer zone between that audience and angry young blacks. It claimed to speak for the needs of a community, but it did not speak in the tone of that community. None of its so-called leaders could go into a rioting community and be listened to. In a sense, the blame must be shared-along with the mass media-by those leaders for what happened in Watts, Harlem, Chicago, Cleveland, and other places. Each time the black people in those cities saw Dr. Martin Luther King get slapped they became angry. When they saw little black girls bombed to death in a church and civil rights workers ambushed and murdered, they were angrier; and when nothing happened, they were steaming mad. We had nothing to offer that they could see, except to go out and be beaten again. We helped to build their frustration.

We had only the old language of love and suffering. And in most places-that is, from the liberals and middle class-we got back the old language of patience and progress. . . .

Such language, along with admonitions to remain non-violent and fear the white backlash, convinced some that that course was the only course to follow. It misled some into believing that a black minority could bow its head and get whipped into a meaningful position of power. The very notion is absurd. . . .

There are many who still sincerely believe in that approach. From our viewpoint, rampaging white mobs and white night-riders must be made to understand that their days of free head-whipping are over. Black people should and must fight back. Nothing more quickly repels someone bent on destroying you than the unequivocal message: "O.K., fool, make your move, and run the same risk I run-of dying."

Next we deal with the term "integration." According to its advocates, social justice will be accomplished by "integrating the Negro into the mainstream institutions of the society from which he has been traditionally excluded." This concept is based on the assumption that there is nothing of value in the black community and that little of value could be created among black people. The thing to do is to siphon off the "acceptable" black people into the surrounding middle-class white community.

The goals of integrationists are middle-class goals, articulated primarily by a small group of Negroes with middle-class aspirations or status. . . .

Secondly, while color blindness may be a sound goal ultimately, we must realize that race is an overwhelming fact of life in this historical period. There is no black man in the country who can live "simply as a man." His blackness is an ever-present fact of this racist society, whether he recognizes it or not. It is unlikely that this or the next generation will witness the time when race will no longer be relevant in the conduct of public affairs and in public policy decision-making. . . .

"Integration" as a goal today speaks to the problem of blackness not only in an unrealistic way but also in a despicable way. It is based on complete acceptance of the fact that in order to have a decent house or education, black people must move into a white neighborhood or send their children to a white school. This reinforces, among both black and white, the idea that "white" is automatically superior and "black" is by definition inferior. For this reason, "integration" is a subterfuge for the maintenance of white supremacy.

1. What attitudes are expressed in this document regarding the nonviolent civil rights movement?
2. What is the reason for rejection the word "integration"?

28-10   Donald Wheeldin, "The Situation in Watts Today" (1967)

In the mid-1960s, a number of cities experienced violent race riots. The worst occurred in 1965 in the Watts section of Los Angeles. The riot had strong repercussions on political life in California. Two years after the Watts riot, Donald Wheeldin reviewed the African American situation.

To answer the question, "what is the situation in Watts today?" is, perforce, to provide an answer to what the situation holds for every single Negro who lives in the United States.

The great though tragic Watts uprising in August, 1965, in which 36 persons (mostly Negroes) were slaughtered by police, 1,032 injured, 3,436 jailed, and $40 millions in property destroyed, is now held as responsible for the stunning defeat of Governor Edmund G. (Pat) Brown for re-election in California. Following his defeat, Brown charged that Watts and subsequent ghetto explosions brought on "the white backlash" that sent him into total political eclipse.

This is, of course, such an unsophisticated political estimate-omitting so many important factors-that, by itself, it becomes a substantial argument explaining his defeat. However, it has become popular for politicians, preachers, police officials and Negro "spokesmen" to blame everything on Watts-ranging from the Governor's defeat to the arrest of a teenager, anywhere in the state. Actually, the Governor's failure lies not in the star of Watts but, rather, in himself and his own inept coterie of underlings.

The inherent peril of Watts today, ghetto for many of Los Angeles 420,000 Negroes, is that nothing has really changed since that fateful week in August, 1965. If anything, the situation has grown alarmingly worse.

Burned-out buildings, vacant lots, boarded-up businesses still pockmark the main areas there. At the corner of 103rd Street and Compton Avenue, heart of its business section, is to be seen Mayor Sam Yorty's optimum contribution towards "an improved Watts community." It consists of a printed statement proclaiming free pony rides for the kids, over the mayor's signature. Further east on 103rd Street at Lou Dillon Avenue is to be found an old abandoned gas station that now headquarters a new organization called the Sons of Watts Improvement Association.

"Sons of Watts," ages 20-26, claim a membership of nearly 100, drawn from former neighborhood gangs.

Their stated purpose is to rebuild Watts into a prosperous community by seeking a return of job-supplying businesses and industry.

How have they been advised to do this?

They've gotten a few traffic signs posted and been urged to distribute 100 containers bearing a legend "Keep Watts Clean" in which people are asked to drop their empty bottles and trash.

Meanwhile, the Los Angeles business community boasts getting "thousands of jobs" for Watts residents which Negro spokesmen in the area contradict as being only "a few hundred." However, Aerojet General Corporation, a huge West Coast outfit with kingsized military contracts, has taken $4.5 million of government money to set up a Watts Manufacturing Company that now hires Watts Negroes to make tents for the Armed Forces. It estimates keeping "200 people busy for the next two years."

The above-mentioned are the piddling answers to a community where today 42 out of every 100 men are reported unemployed and among whom many are unemployable. Watts is the community where Los Angeles voters recently denied funds for building a hospital despite 1960 health statistics disclosing: a death rate 22.3 percent higher than the rest of Los Angeles; 65 percent of all tuberculin reactors; 46 percent of the venereal diseases; and 42 percent of all food poisoning in the city.

Stark and graphic as they are, the statistics alone do not convey the real situation in Watts. Like other black ghettos throughout the country, it is mired in a racism that threatens to suck the substance from the American Dream and turn it into a nightmare. The bald fact of Watts is that black people there are not quite considered eligible for membership in the human family. . . .

Earlier, last May, all the tree top tall tensions that erupted in the Watts explosion threatened to break out anew after the gunning down of Leonard Deadwyler, young Negro father, rushing his pregnant wife to the hospital. After his car had pulled to the curb and stopped, Jerald Bova, a white policeman, trained his gun through the side-window and fired. He later termed it "an accident." Bova had a prior record of brutality towards Negroes.

At the massed funeral services for Deadwyler, following a fifteen block long march, Rev. W. H. Johnson, speaking on behalf of Watts ministers said: "No man's life in Watts . . . is worth more than the price of a bullet. Any innocent man may be killed in Watts. It is a jungle where inhumanity is the order of the day."

It was within this context that the late Los Angeles Police Chief William Parker poured acid into the wounds of the Negro community-as he had so often on prior occasions-by taking to the television and blistering the Negro community and its leaders as stupid and totally lacking in respect for his brand of law and order. Parker's sentiment was echoed by Mayor Yorty.

This turn of events caused great consternation, frightening some Negro leaders. Others became angered. All were worried and concerned. As a result, a hastily called meeting brought together the widest diversity of Negro groups united for the single purpose of challenging Parker and his "get tough" policy and treatment of Negroes. Sole condition for membership was being a Negro. Black spokesmen ranged from the churches to the Communists; Nationalists to the NAACP; social clubs to society matrons. They formed the Temporary Alliance of Local Organizations (TALO). During the summer, TALO financed and placed in Watts and throughout South Los Angeles a volunteer Community Alert Patrol to observe and report on police malpractices.

The CAP, equipped with 2-way radios, was an impressive step forward as it entered the ghetto areas to the cheers of the people who readily cooperate with the Negro volunteers in keeping the peace. It wasn't long before the Mexican community asked its help in setting up such a patrol in its area. Even the police who had bitterly resented CAP's presence, earlier, was forced to call on it for help in a number of cases. This volunteer action represented a first, halting step toward acquiring some "black power."

Meanwhile, others in TALO sought to press with the Los Angeles Police Commission and Chief Parker for a redress of Watts community grievances. While in the process, Parker died and some of the immediate pressures on the community receded. TALO, no longer with a single unifying object, began to dissolve. . . .

The largest and probably most noble single thrust in an effort to retrieve and make life bearable in Watts has been undertaken by the Presbyterians through Westminster House.

With a paid staff of 100 social workers under the leadership of dedicated Morris Samuel (Father Sam) the Center is spending 66 percent of its $1,148,150 budget on a job training and employment program for Watts Negro youth.

Bluntly, this, too, is doomed to fail. Why? Because the shrinking job market, alone, will be unable to absorb the trainees. And the government doesn't have enough post offices in which to employ the rest. Beyond that what has as yet to be understood is that racism is a prop that undergirds and helps sustain this economic system. Finger-in-the-dike methods won't change it. Only a successful challenge to those who preside over it will usher in a new and different set of race relations. The power and direction of the system's present rulers are best illustrated in California by the McCone Commission Report, official document dealing with the so-called Watts Riots.

The Commission, headed by John McCone, former CIA director, spent 100 days and $250,000 in order to ". . . bring into clear focus . . . the economic and sociological conditions in our city that underlay the gathering anger . . ." It, of course, does neither.

The Report turns out to be a commingling of police public relations and anti-Negro bias. So much so that sole Negro Commission member Rev. James Edward Jones caused to be published a separate comment in which he "violently disagreed" with part of its "unjustified projection." The Report was blasted by the State Civil Rights Commission as "superficial, unoriginal and unimaginative." . . .

The most compelling lesson of Watts today is that it simply is not a matter of geographic location. It kaleidoscopes the situation in which we Negroes find ourselves throughout the country. It is only a matter of degree. We're trapped in a culture pattern that has seen our parents jobless and on relief; members of our families disintegrate through poor health and slum housing; and finally, we find ourselves as inheritors of a cruel and seemingly unending cycle of economic brinkmanship in an affluent society which has brought us to the breaking point. That breaking point is demonstrated in Watts and elsewhere in the country in a thousand clashes between Negroes and police since "That Was The Week That Was" in August, 1965. . . .

Nothing short of maximal government intervention on a scale equal to that now committed to the destruction of Vietnam can avert a major race holocaust in our country in our time. And there is nothing in the Johnson Administration or on the political horizon generally, that indicates any serious thought is being given the matter.

This is the reality now, leading inexorably toward a major national race crisis.

And when these present times are analyzed by future historians to unravel the whys and wherefores their starting point may well be that volatile black ghetto tucked away in South Los Angeles named Watts.

1. Summarize the author's description of African American life in Los Angeles after the Watts riots.
2. What, according to the author, are the causes of the problems in Watts? What are the solutions?
3. What is the significance of Watts, its problems and the steps necessary to deal with those problems, as it relates to the rest of America?

28-11 Vietnamization (1969)

By 1969 Nixon had to recognize that America was in an untenable situation in Vietnam. To stay in the war sapped American resources and prestige, and devastated morale at home. To leave the war would acknowledge that the forces of Communism had prevailed. It appeared that the only honorable way out of the conflict was to force the South Vietnamese to assume responsibility for their own defense.

> **Source:** Henry Steele Commager, "Nixon's Address on Vietnamizing the War, November 3, 1969" *Documents on American History* (New York: Appleton-Century-Crofts, 1965), pp. 738–741.

. . . Tonight I want to talk to you on a subject of deep concern to all Americans and to many people in all parts of the world—the war in Vietnam.

I believe that one of the reasons for the deep division about Vietnam is that many Americans have lost confidence in what their Government has told them about our policy. The American people cannot and should not be asked to support a policy which involves the overriding issues of war and peace unless they know the truth about that policy . . . .

In January I could only conclude that the precipitate withdrawal of American forces from Vietnam would be a disaster not only for South Vietnam but for the United States and for the cause of peace.

For the South Vietnamese, our precipitate withdrawal would inevitably allow the Communists to repeat the massacres which followed their takeover in the North fifteen years before. . . .

For the United States, this first defeat in our nation's history would result in a collapse of confidence in American leadership not only in Asia but throughout the world.

Three American Presidents have recognized the great stakes involved in Vietnam and understood what had to be done. . . .

For the future of peace, precipitate withdrawal would thus be a disaster of immense magnitude.

—A nation cannot remain great if it betrays its allies and lets down its friends.

—Our defeat and humiliation in South Vietnam without question would promote recklessness in the councils of those great powers who have not yet abandoned their goals of world conquest.

—This would spark violence wherever our commitments help maintain the peace—in the Middle East, in Berlin, eventually even in the Western Hemisphere.

Ultimately, this would cost more lives. It would not bring peace; it would bring more war.

For these reasons I rejected the recommendation that I should end the war by immediately withdrawing all our forces. I chose instead to change American policy on both the negotiating front and the battlefront.

In order to end a war fought on many fronts, I initiated a pursuit for peace on many fronts.

In a television speech on May 14, in a speech before the United Nations, and on a number of other occasions, I set forth our peace proposals in great detail.

—We have offered the complete withdrawal of all outside forces within one year.

—We have proposed a cease-fire under international supervision.

—We have offered free elections under international supervision, with the Communists participating in the organization and conduct of the elections as an organized political force. The Saigon Government has pledged to accept the result of the elections.

We have not put forth our proposals on a take-it-or-leave-it basis. We have indicated that we are willing to discuss the proposals that have been put forth by the other side. We have declared that anything is negotiable, except the right of the people of South Vietnam to determine their own future. At the Paris peace conference, Ambassador Lodge has demonstrated our flexibility and good faith in forty public meetings.

Hanoi has refused even to discuss our proposals. They demand our unconditional acceptance of their terms, which are that we withdraw all American forces immediately and unconditionally and that we overthrow the Government of South Vietnam as we leave.

We have not limited our peace initiatives to public forums and public statements. I recognized in January that a long and bitter war like this usually cannot be settled in a public forum. That is why, in addition to the public statements and negotiations, I have explored every possible private avenue that might lead to a settlement. . . .But the effect of all the public, private, and secret negotiations which have been undertaken since the bombing halt a year ago and since this administration came into office on January 20 can be summed up in one sentence: No progress whatever has been made except agreement on the shape of the bargaining table. Now, who is at fault?

It has become clear that the obstacle in negotiating an end to the war is not the President of the United States. It is not the South Vietnamese Government.

The obstacle is the other side's absolute refusal to show the least willingness to join us in seeking a just peace. It will not do so while it is convinced that all it has to do is to wait for our next concession, and our next concession after that one, until it gets everything it wants.

There can now be no longer any question that progress in negotiation depends only on Hanoi's deciding to negotiate, to negotiate seriously. . . .

Now let me turn, however, to a more encouraging report on another front.

At the time we launched our search for peace, I recognized we might not succeed in bringing an end to the war through negotiation.

I therefore put into effect another plan to bring peace—a plan which will bring the war to an end regardless of what happens on the negotiating front. It is in line with a major shift in U. S. foreign policy which I described in my press conference at Guam on July 25.

Let me briefly explain what has been described as the Nixon doctrine—a policy which not only will help end the war in Vietnam but which is an essential element of our program to prevent future Vietnams. . . .

I laid down in Guam three principles as guidelines for future American policy toward Asia:

—First, the United States will keep all of its treaty commitments.

—Second, we shall provide a shield if a nuclear power threatens the freedom of a nation allied with us or of a nation whose survival we consider vital to our security.

—Third, in cases involving other types of aggression, we shall furnish military and economic assistance when requested in accordance with our treaty commitments. But we shall look to the nation directly threatened to assume the primary responsibility of providing the manpower for its defense.

After I announced this policy, I found that the leaders of the Philippines, Thailand, Vietnam, South Korea, and other nations which might be threatened by Communist aggression welcomed this new direction in American foreign policy.

The defense of freedom is everybody's business—not just America's business. And it is particularly the responsibility of the people whose freedom is threatened. In the previous administration we Americanized the war in Vietnam. In this administration we are Vietnamizing the search for peace.

The policy of the previous administration not only resulted in our assuming the primary responsibility for fighting the war but, even more significantly, did not adequately stress the goal of strengthening the South Vietnamese so that they could defend themselves when we left. . . .

Let me now turn to our program for the future.

We have adopted a plan which we have worked out in cooperation with the South Vietnamese for the complete withdrawal of all U. S. combat ground forces and their replacement by South Vietnamese forces on an orderly scheduled timetable. This withdrawal will be made from strength and not from weakness. As South Vietnamese forces become stronger, the rate of American withdrawal can become greater.

I have not and do not intend to announce the timetable for our program. There are obvious reasons for this decision, which I am sure you will understand. As I have indicated on several occasions, the rate of withdrawal will depend on developments on three fronts.

One of these is the progress which can be, or might be, made in the Paris talks. An announcement of a fixed timetable for our withdrawal would completely remove any incentive for the enemy to negotiate an agreement. They would simply wait until our forces had withdrawn and then move in.

The other two factors on which we will base our withdrawal decisions are the level of enemy activity and the progress of the training program of the South Vietnamese forces. I am glad to be able to report tonight progress on both of these fronts has been greater than we anticipated when we started the program in June for withdrawal. As a result, our timetable for withdrawal is more optimistic now than when we made our first estimates in June.

This clearly demonstrates why it is not wise to be frozen in on a fixed timetable. We must retain the flexibility to base each withdrawal decision on the situation as it is at that time rather than on estimates that are no longer valid.

Along with this optimistic estimate, I must in all candor leave one note of caution: If the level of enemy activity significantly increases, we might have to adjust our timetable accordingly.

However, I want the record to be completely clear on one point.

At the time of the bombing halt just a year ago, there was some confusion as to whether there was an understanding on the part of the enemy that if we stopped the bombing of North Vietnam, they would stop the shelling of cities in South Vietnam. I want to be sure that there is no misunderstanding on the part of the enemy with regard to our withdrawal program.

We have noted the reduced level of infiltration, the reduction of our casualties, and are basing our withdrawal decisions partially on those factors.

If the level of infiltration or our casualties increase while we are trying to scale down the fighting, it will be the result of a conscious decision by the enemy.

Hanoi could make no greater mistake than to assume that an increase in violence will be to its advantage. If I conclude that increased enemy action jeopardizes our remaining forces in Vietnam, I shall not hesitate to take strong and effective measures to deal with that situation.

This is not a threat. This is a statement of policy which as Commander in Chief of our Armed Forces I am making in meeting my responsibility for the protection of American fighting men wherever they may be.

My fellow Americans, I am sure you can recognize from what I have said that we really only have two choices open to us if we want to end this war:

—I can order an immediate, precipitate withdrawal of all Americans from Vietnam without regard to the effects of that action.

—Or we can persist in our search for a just peace, through a negotiated settlement if possible or through continued implementation of our plan for Vietnamization if necessary—a plan in which we will withdraw all of our forces from Vietnam on a schedule in accordance with our program, as the South Vietnamese become strong enough to defend their own freedom.

I have chosen this second course. It is not the easy way. It is the right way. It is a plan which will end the war and serve the cause of peace, not just in Vietnam, but in the Pacific and in the world.

In speaking of the consequences of a precipitate withdrawal, I mentioned that our allies would lose confidence in America.

Far more dangerous, we would lose confidence in ourselves. Oh, the immediate reaction would be a sense of relief that our men were coming home. But as we saw the consequences of what we had done, inevitable remorse and divisive recrimination would scar our spirit as a people.

We have faced other crises in our history and have become stronger by rejecting the easy way out and taking the right way in meeting our challenges. Our greatness as a nation has been our capacity to do what had to be done when we knew our course was right.

I recognize that some of my fellow citizens disagree with the plan for peace I have chosen. . . . I would be untrue to my oath of office if I allowed the policy of this nation to be dictated by the minority who hold that point and who try to impose it on the Nation by mounting demonstrations in the street.

For almost two hundred years, the policy of this nation has been made under our Constitution by those leaders in the Congress and in the White House elected by all of the people. If a vocal minority; however fervent its cause, prevails over reason and the will of the majority, this nation has no future as a free society.

And now I would like to address a word, if I may, to the young people of this nation who are particularly concerned—and I understand why they are concerned—about this war.

I respect your idealism.

I share your concern for peace.

I want peace as much as you do. . . .

I have chosen a plan for peace, I believe it will succeed.

If it does succeed, what the critics say now won't matter. If it does not succeed, anything I say then won't matter.

I know it may not be fashionable to speak of patriotism or national destiny these days. But I feel it is appropriate to do so on this occasion.

Two hundred years ago this nation was weak and poor. But even then, America was the hope of millions in the world. Today we have become the strongest and richest nation in the world. The wheel of destiny has turned so that any hope the world has for the survival of peace and freedom will be determined by whether the American people have the moral stamina and the courage to meet the challenge of free-world leadership.

Let historians not record that when America was the most powerful nation in the world we passed on the other side of the road and allowed the last hopes for peace and freedom of millions of people to be suffocated by the forces of totalitarianism. . . .

1. *How did Nixon set up the premise of Vietnamization?*
2. *Since the United States, and therefore the forces of democracy, was losing the war, how was the Communist regime of North Vietnam portrayed as an ignoble and undeserving victor?*
3. *What type of action did Nixon propose?*

PART TWENTY-NINE
THE STRUGGLE FOR SOCIAL CHANGE

29-1   John F. Kennedy, Inaugural Address (1961)

In many ways, John Kennedy, his young wife Jackie, and their two small children personified the New Frontier and the hopes of a new, postwar America. This speech, with its now famous lines, has itself symbolized the Kennedy legacy-which, after his assassination in November of 1963-unified a generation.

My fellow citizens:

We observe today not a victory of party but a celebration of freedom-symbolizing an end as well as a beginning-signifying renewal as well as change. For I have sworn before you and Almighty God the same solemn oath our forebears prescribed nearly a century and three quarters ago.

The world is very different now. For man holds in his mortal hands the power to abolish all form of human poverty and to abolish all form of human life. And, yet, the same revolutionary beliefs for which our forebears fought are still at issue around the globe-the belief that the rights of man come not from the generosity of the state but from the hand of God.

We dare not forget today that we are the heirs of that first revolution. Let the word go forth from this time and place, to friend and foe alike, that the torch has been passed to a new generation of Americans-born in this century, tempered by war, disciplined by a cold and bitter peace, proud of our ancient heritage-and unwilling to witness or permit the slow undoing of those human rights to which this nation has always been committed, and to which we are committed today.

Let every nation know, whether it wish us well or ill, that we shall pay any price, bear any burden, meet any hardship, support any friend or oppose any foe in order to assure the survival and success of liberty.

This much we pledge-and more.

To those old allies whose cultural and spiritual origins we share, we pledge the loyalty of faithful friends. United, there is little we cannot do in a host of new co-operative ventures. Divided, there is little we can do-for we dare not meet a powerful challenge at odds and split asunder.

To those new states whom we now welcome to the ranks of the free, we pledge our world that one form of colonial control shall not have passed merely to be replaced by a far more iron tyranny. We shall not always expect to find them supporting our every view. But we shall always hope to find them strongly supporting their own freedom-and to remember that, in the past, those who foolishly sought to find power by riding on the tiger's back inevitably ended up inside.

To those peoples in the huts and villages of half the globe struggling to break the bonds of mass misery, we pledge our best efforts to help them help themselves, for whatever period is required-not because the Communists are doing it, not because we seek their votes, but because it is right. If the free society cannot help the many who are poor, it can never save the few who are rich.

To our sister republics south of our border, we offer a special pledge-to convert our good words into good deeds-in a new alliance for progress-to assist free men and free Governments in casting off the chains of poverty. But this peaceful revolution of hope cannot become the prey of hostile powers. Let all our neighbors know that we shall join with them to oppose aggression or subversion anywhere in the Americas. And let every other power know that this Hemisphere intends to remain the master of its own house.

To that world assembly of sovereign states, the United Nations, our last best hope in an age where the instruments of war have far outpaced the instruments of peace, we renew our pledge of support-to prevent its becoming merely a forum for invective-to strengthen its shield of the new and the weak-and to enlarge the area to which its writ may run.

Finally, to those nations who would make themselves our adversary, we offer not a pledge but a request: that both sides begin anew the quest for peace, before the dark powers of destruction unleashed by science engulf all humanity in planned or accidental self-destruction.

We dare not tempt them with weakness. For only when our arms are sufficient beyond doubt can we be certain beyond doubt that they will never be employed.

But neither can two great and powerful groups of nations take comfort from their present course-both sides overburdened by the cost of modern weapons, both rightly alarmed by the steady spread of the deadly atom, yet both racing to alter that uncertain balance of terror that stays the hand of mankind's final war.

So let us begin anew-remembering on both sides that civility is not a sign of weakness and sincerity is always subject to proof. Let us never negotiate out of fear. But let us never fear to negotiate.

Let both sides explore what problems unite us instead of belaboring the problems that divide us.

Let both sides for the first time formulate serious and precise proposals for the inspection and control of arms-and bring the absolute power to destroy other nations under the absolute control of all nations.

Let both sides join to invoke the wonders of science instead of its terrors. Together let us explore the stars, conquer the deserts, eradicate disease, tap the ocean depths and encourage the arts and commerce.

Let both sides unite to heed in all corners of the earth the command of Isaiah-to "undo the heavy burdens . . . (and) let the oppressed go free."

And if a beachhead of co-operation can be made in the jungles of suspicion, let both sides join in the next task: creating, not a new balance of power, but a new world of law, where the strong are just and the weak secure and the peace preserved forever.

All this will not be finished in the first 100 days. Nor will it be finished in the first 1,000 days, nor in the life of this Administration, nor even perhaps in our lifetime on this planet. But let us begin.

In your hands, my fellow citizens, more than in mine, will rest the final success or failure of our course. Since this country was founded, each generation has been summoned to give testimony to its national loyalty. The graves of young Americans who answered that call encircle the globe.

Now the trumpet summons us again-not as a call to battle, though embattled we are-but a call to bear the burden of a long twilight struggle, year in and year out, "rejoicing in hope, patient in tribulation"-a struggle against the common enemies of man: tyranny, poverty, disease, and war itself.

Can we forge against these enemies a grand and global alliance, north and south, east and west, that can assure a more fruitful life for all mankind? Will you join in that historic effort?

In the long history of the world, only a few generations have been granted the role of defending freedom in its hour of maximum danger. I do not shrink from this responsibility-I welcome it. I do not believe that any of us would exchange places with any other people or any other generation. The energy, the faith and the devotion which we bring to this endeavor will light our country and all who serve it-and the glow from that fire can truly light the world.

And so, my fellow Americans: Ask not what your country will do for you-ask what you can do for your country.

My fellow citizens of the world: Ask not what America will do for you, but what together we can do for the freedom of man.

Finally, whether you are citizens of America or of the world, ask of us the same high standards of strength and sacrifice that we shall ask of you. With a good conscience our only sure reward, with history the final judge of our deeds, let us go forth to lead the land we love, asking His blessing and His help, but knowing that here on earth God's work must truly be our own.

1. Identify and analyze the foreign policy laid out in this address.
2. In what ways is this speech a call for a new beginning?

29-2 The Feminist Mystique (1963)

Journalist Betty Freidan wrote The Feminine Mystique to expose the social mechanisms used to oppress women. In theory, middle class women were provided with the same opportunities as men, but social expectations regarding men and women were not equal and did not change significantly over time. More than at any other time in recent history, the 1950s were a period during which women were assaulted with articles and images that defined their existence in the domestic sphere and required them to register supine contentment with that status. As Friedan undertook to define "the problem that has no name," she launched a new era in the movement for women's rights.

Source: Betty Friedan, *The Feminine Mystique,* (New York: Norton, 1963), pp. 15–32.

THE PROBLEM THAT HAS NO NAME

The problem lay buried, unspoken, for many years in the minds of American women. It was a strange stirring, a sense of dissatisfaction, a yearning that women suffered in the middle of the twentieth century in the United States. Each suburban wife struggled with it alone. As she made the beds, shopped for groceries, matched slipcover material, ate peanut butter sandwiches with her children, chauffeured Cub Scouts and Brownies, lay beside her husband at night—she was afraid to ask even of herself the silent question—"Is this all?"

For over fifteen years there was no word of this yearning in the millions of words written about women, for women, in all the columns, books and articles by experts telling women their role was to seek fulfillment as wives and mothers. Over and over women heard in voices of tradition and of Freudian sophistication that they could desire no greater destiny than to glory in their own femininity. Experts told them how to catch a man and keep him, how to breastfeed children and handle their toilet training, how to cope with sibling rivalry and adolescent rebellion; how to buy a dishwasher, bake bread, cook gourmet snails, and build a swimming pool with their own hands; how to dress, look, and act more feminine and make marriage more exciting; how to keep their husbands from dying young and their sons from growing into delinquents. They were taught to pity the neurotic, unfeminine, unhappy women who wanted to be poets or physicists or presidents. They learned that truly feminine women do not want careers, higher education, political rights—the independence and the opportunities that the old-fashioned feminists fought for. Some women, in their forties and fifties, still remembered painfully giving up those dreams, but most of the younger women no longer even thought about them. A thousand expert voices applauded their femininity, their adjustment, their new maturity. All they had to do was devote their lives from earliest girlhood to finding a husband and bearing children.

* * *

By the end of the fifties, the United States birthrate was overtaking India's. The birth-control movement, renamed Planned Parenthood, was asked to find a method whereby women who had been advised that a third or fourth baby would be born dead or defective might have it anyhow. Statisticians were especially astounded at the fantastic increase in the number of babies among college women. Where once they had two children, now they had four, five, six. Women who had once wanted careers were now making careers out of having babies. So rejoiced *Life* magazine in a 1956 paean to the movement of American women back to the home.

In a New York hospital, a woman had a nervous breakdown when she found she could not breastfeed her baby. In other hospitals, women dying of cancer refused a drug which research had proved might save their lives: its side effects were said to be unfeminine. "If I have only one life, let me live it as a blonde," a larger-than-life-sized picture of a pretty, vacuous woman proclaimed from newspaper, magazine, and drugstore ads. And across America, three out of every ten women dyed their hair blonde. They ate a chalk called Metrecal, instead of food, to shrink to the size of the thin young models. Department-store buyers reported that American women, since 1939, had become three and four sizes smaller. "Women are out to fit the clothes, instead of vice-versa," one buyer said.

Interior decorators were designing kitchens with mosaic murals and original paintings, for kitchens were once again the center of women's lives. Home sewing became a million-dollar industry. Many women no longer left their homes, except to shop, chauffeur their children, or attend a social engagement with their husbands. Girls were growing up in America without ever having jobs outside the home. In the late fifties, a sociological phenomenon was suddenly remarked: a third of American women now worked, but most were no longer young and very few were pursuing careers. They were married women who held part-time jobs, selling or secretarial, to put their husbands through school, their sons through college, or to help pay the mortgage. Or they were widows supporting families. Fewer and fewer women were entering professional work. The shortages in the nursing, social work, and teaching professions caused crises in almost every American city. Concerned over the Soviet Union's lead in the space race, scientists noted that America's greatest source of unused brainpower was women. But girls would not study physics: it was "unfeminine." A girl refused a science fellowship at Johns Hopkins to take a job in a real-estate office. All she wanted, she said, was what every other American girl wanted—to get married, have four children and live in a nice house in a nice suburb.

The suburban housewife—she was the dream image of the young American women and the envy, it was said, of women all over the world. The American housewife—freed by science and labor-saving appliances from the drudgery, the dangers of childbirth and the illnesses of her grandmother. She was healthy, beautiful, educated, concerned only about her husband, her children, her home. She had found true feminine fulfillment. As a housewife and mother, she was respected as a full and equal partner to man in his world. She was free to choose automobiles, clothes, appliances, supermarkets; she had everything that women ever dreamed of.

In the fifteen years after World War II, this mystique of feminine fulfillment became the cherished and self-perpetuating core of contemporary American culture. Millions of women lived their lives in the image of those pretty pictures of the American suburban housewife, kissing their husbands goodbye in front of the picture window, depositing their stationwagonsful of children at school, and smiling as they ran the new electric waxer over the spotless kitchen floor. They baked their own bread, sewed their own and their children's clothes, kept their new washing machines and dryers running all day. They changed the sheets on the beds twice a week instead of once, took the rug-hooking class in adult education, and pitied their poor frustrated mothers, who had dreamed of having a career. Their only dream was to be perfect wives and mothers; their highest ambition to have five children and a beautiful house, their only fight to get and keep their husbands. They had no thought for the unfeminine problems of the world outside the home; they wanted the men to make the major decisions. They gloried in their role as women, and wrote proudly on the census blank: "Occupation: housewife."

* * *

If a woman had a problem in the 1950's and 1960's, she knew that something must be wrong with her marriage, or with herself. Other women were satisfied with their lives, she thought. What kind of a women was she if she did not feel this mysterious fulfillment waxing the kitchen floor? She was so ashamed to admit her dissatisfaction that she never knew how many other women shared it. If she tried to tell her husband, he didn't understand what she was talking about. She did not really understand it herself. For over fifteen years women in America found it harder to talk about this problem than about sex. Even the psychoanalysts had no name for it. When a women went to a psychiatrist for help, as many women did, she would say, "I'm so ashamed," or "I must be hopelessly neurotic." "I don't know what's wrong with women today," a suburban psychiatrist said uncasily. "I only know something is wrong because most of my patients happen to be women. And their problem isn't sexual." Most women with this problem did not go to see a psychoanalyst, however, "There's nothing wrong really," they kept telling themselves. "There isn't any problem."

But on an April morning in 1959, I heard a mother of four, having coffee with four other mothers in a suburban development fifteen miles from New York, say in a tone of quiet desperation, "the problem." And the others knew, without words, that she was not talking about a problem with her husband, or her children, or her home. Suddenly they realized they all shared the same problem, the problem that has no name. They began, hesitantly, to talk about it. Later, after they had picked up their children at nursery school and taken them home to nap, two of the women cried, in sheer relief, just to know they were not alone.

Gradually I came to realize that the problem that has no name was shared by countless women in America

* * *

Just what was this problem that has no name? What were the words women used when they tried to express it? Sometimes a woman would say "I feel empty somehow . . . incomplete." Or she would say, "I feel as if I don't exist." Sometimes she blotted out the feeling with a tranquilizer. Sometimes she thought the problem was with her husband, or her children, or that what she really needed was to redecorate her house, or move to a better neighborhood, or have an affair, or another baby. Sometimes, she went to a doctor with symptoms she could hardly describe: "A tired feeling . . . I get so angry with the children it scares me . . . I feel like crying without any reason." (A Cleveland doctor called it "the housewife's syndrome.") A number of women told me about great bleeding blisters that break out on their hands and arms. "I call it the housewife's blight," said a family doctor in Pennsylvania. "I see it so often lately in these young women with four, five and six children who bury themselves in their dishpans. But it isn't caused by detergent and it isn't cured by cortisone."

* * *

In 1960, the problem that has no name burst like a boil through the image of the happy American housewife. In the television commercials the pretty housewives still beamed over their foaming dishpans and *Time's* cover story on "The Suburban Wife, an American Phenomenon" protested: "Having too good a time . . . to believe that they should be unhappy." But the actual unhappiness of the American housewife was suddenly being reported—from the *New York Times* and *Newsweek* to *Good Housekeeping* and CBS Television ("The Trapped Housewife"), although almost everybody who talked about it found some superficial reason to dismiss it. It was attributed to incompetent appliance repairmen (*New York Times*), or the distances children must be chauffeured in the suburbs (*Time*), or too much PTA (*Redbook*). Some said it was the old problem—education: more and more women had education, which naturally made them unhappy in their role as housewives. "the road from Freud to Frigidaire, from Sophocles to Spock, has turned out to be a bumpy one," reported the *New York Times* (June 28, 1960). "Many young women—certainly not all—whose education plunged them into a world of ideas feel stifled in their homes. They find their routine lives out of joint with their training. Like shut-ins, they feel left out. In the last year, the problem of the educated housewife has provided the meat of dozens of speeches made by troubled presidents of women's colleges who maintain, in the face of complaints, that sixteen years of academic training is realistic preparation for wifehood and motherhood."

There was much sympathy for the educated housewife. ("Like a two-headed schizophrenic . . . once she wrote a paper on the Graveyard poets; now she writes notes to the milkman. Once she determined the boiling point of sulphuric acid; now she determines her boiling point with the overdue repairman. . . . The housewife often is reduced to screams and tears. . . . No one, it seems, is appreciative, least of all herself, of the kind of person she becomes in the process of turning from poetess into shrew.")

* * *

A bitter laugh was beginning to be heard from American women. They were admired, envied, pitied, theorized over until they were sick of it, offered drastic solutions or silly choices that no one could take seriously. They got all kinds of advice from the growing armies of marriage and child-guidance counselors, psychotherapists, and armchair psychologists, on how to adjust to their role as housewives. No other road to fulfillment was offered to American women in the middle of the twentieth century. Most adjusted to their role and suffered or ignored the problem that has no name. It can be less painful, for a women, not to hear the strange, dissatisfied voice stirring within her.

It is no longer possible to ignore that voice, to dismiss the desperation of so many American women. This is not what being a woman means, no matter what the experts say. For human suffering there is a reason; perhaps the reason has not been found because the right questions have not been asked, or pressed far enough. I do not accept the answer that there is no problem because American women have luxuries that women in other times and lands never dreamed of; part of the strange newness of the problem is that it cannot be understood in terms of the age-old material problems of man: poverty, sickness, hunger, cold. The women who suffer this problem have a hunger that food cannot fill. It persists in women whose husbands are struggling interns and law clerks, or prosperous doctors and lawyers; in wives of workers and executives who make $5,000 a year or $50,000. It is not caused by lack of material advantages; it may not even be felt by women preoccupied with desperate problems of hunger, poverty or illness. And women who think it will be solved by more money, a bigger house, a second car, moving to a better suburb, often discover it gets worse.

It is no longer possible today to blame the problem on loss of femininity: to say that education and independence and equality with men have made American women unfeminine. I have heard so many women try to deny this dissatisfied voice within themselves because it does not fit the pretty picture of femininity the experts have given them. I think, in fact, that this is the first clue to the mystery: the problem cannot be understood in the generally accepted terms by which scientists have studied women, doctors have treated them, counselors have advised them, and writers have written about them. Women who suffer this problem, in whom this voice is stirring, have lived their whole lives in the pursuit of feminine fulfillment. They are not career women (although career women may have other problems); they are women whose greatest ambition has been marriage and children. For the oldest of these women, these daughters of the American middle class, no other dream was possible. The ones in their forties and fifties who once had other dreams gave them up and threw themselves joyously into life as housewives. For the youngest, the new wives and mothers, this was the only dream. They are the ones who quit high school and college to marry, or marked time in some job in which they had no real interest until they married. These women are very "feminine" in the usual sense, and yet they still suffer the problem.

* * *

If the secret of feminine fulfillment is having children, never have so many women, with the freedom to choose, had so many children, in so few years, so willingly. If the answer is love, never have women searched for love with such determination. And yet there is a growing suspicion that the problem may not be sexual, though it must somehow be related to sex. I have heard from many doctors evidence of new sexual problems between man and wife—sexual hunger in wives so great their husbands cannot satisfy it. "We have made women a sex creature," said a psychiatrist at the Margaret Sanger marriage counseling clinic. "She has no identity except as a wife and mother. She does not know who she is herself. She waits all day for her husband to come home at night to make her feel alive. And now it is the husband who is not interested. It is terrible for the women, to lie there, night after night, waiting for her husband to make her feel alive." Why is there such a market for books and articles offering sexual advice? The kind of sexual orgasm which Kinsey found in statistical plentitude in the recent generations of American women does not seem to make this problem go away.

On the contrary, new neuroses are being seen among women—and problems as yet unnamed as neuroses—which Freud and his followers did not predict, with physical symptoms, anxieties, and defense mechanisms equal to those caused by sexual repression. And strange new problems are being reported in the growing generations of children whose mothers were always there, driving them around, helping them with their homework—an inability to endure pain or discipline or pursue any self-sustained goal of any sort, a devastating boredom with life. Educators are increasingly uneasy about the dependence, the lack of self-reliance, of the boys and girls who are entering college today. "We fight a continual battle to make our students assume manhood," said a Columbia dean.

* * *

Can the problem that has no name be somehow related to the domestic routine of the housewife? When a woman tries to put the problem into words, she often merely describes the daily life she leads. What is there in this recital of comfortable domestic detail that could possibly cause such a feeling of desperation? Is she trapped simply by the enormous demands of her role as modern housewife: wife, mistress, mother, nurse, consumer, cook, chauffeur; expert on interior decoration, child care, appliance repair, furniture refinishing, nutrition, and education? Her day is fragmented as she rushes from dishwasher to washing machine to telephone to dryer to station wagon to supermarket, and delivers Johnny to the Little League field, takes Janey to dancing class, gets the lawnmower fixed and meets the 6:45. She can never spend more than 15 minutes on any one thing; she has no time to read books, only magazines; even if she had time, she has lost the power to concentrate. At the end of the day, she is so terribly tired that sometimes her husband has to take over and put the children to bed.

This terrible tiredness took so many women to doctors in the 1950's that one decided to investigate it. He found, surprisingly, that his patients suffering from "housewife's fatigue" slept more than an adult needed to sleep—as much as ten hours a day—and that the actual energy they expended on housework did not tax their capacity. The real problem must be something else, he decided—perhaps boredom. Some doctors told their women patients they must get out of the house for a day, treat themselves to a movie in town. Others prescribed tranquilizers. Many suburban housewives were taking tranquilizers like cough drops. "You wake up in the morning, and you feel as if there's no point in going on another day like this. So you take a tranquilizer because it makes you not care so much that it's pointless."

It is easy to see the concrete details that trap the suburban housewife, the continual demands on her time. But the chains that bind her in her trap are chains in her own mind and spirit. They are chains made up of mistaken ideas and misinterpreted facts, of incomplete truths and unreal choices. They are not easily seen and not easily shaken off.

How can any women see the whole truth within the bounds of her own life? How can she believe that voice inside herself, when it denies the conventional, accepted truths by which she has been living? And yet the women I have talked to, who are finally listening to that inner voice, seem in some incredible way to be groping through to a truth that has defied the experts.

* * *

I began to see in a strange new light the American return to early marriage and the large families that are causing the population explosion; the recent movement to natural childbirth and breastfeeding; suburban conformity, and the new neuroses, character pathologies and sexual problems being reported by the doctors. I began to see new dimensions to old problems that have long been taken for granted among women: menstrual difficulties, sexual frigidity, promiscuity, pregnancy fears, childbirth depression, the high incidence of emotional breakdown and suicide among women in their twenties and thirties, the menopause crises, the so-called passivity and immaturity of American men, the discrepancy between women's tested intellectual abilities in childhood and their adult achievement, the changing incidence of adult sexual orgasm in American women, and persistent problems in psychotherapy and in women's education.

If I am right, the problem that has no name stirring in the minds of so many American women today is not a matter of loss of femininity or too much education, or the demands of domesticity. It is far more important than anyone recognizes. It is the key to these other new and old problems which have been torturing women and their husbands and children, and puzzling their doctors and educators for years. It may well be the key to our future as a nation and a culture. We can no longer ignore that voice within women that says: "I want something more than my husband and children and my home."

1. What is "the problem that has no name"?
2. What similarities are there between the problem that has no name and the advertising goals of those who wrote Workingman's Wife?
3. What were the roots of this problem?

29-3   Lyndon Johnson, The War on Poverty (1964)

Lyndon Johnson had served in Roosevelt's New Deal administrations and believed in the power of government to provide for the poor and to solve social problems. His Great Society package became the most massive reform movement in America's history, and its effects would touch more groups than any other reform movement. It is not an understatement to say that the Great Society changed the very face and to a certain extent structure of American society. The Economic Opportunity Act, proposed in this speech to Congress, was a $947.5 million appropriation to wage war on poverty. It included establishing the Job Corps, VISTA (Volunteers in Service to America), and new education programs including work-study for college students and grants for elementary education in poor districts.

I have called for a national war on poverty. Our objective: total victory.

There are millions of Americans-one fifth of our people-who have not shared in the abundance which has been granted to most of us, and on whom the gates of opportunity have been closed.

What does this poverty mean to those who endure it?

It means a daily struggle to secure the necessities for even a meager existence. It means that the abundance, the comforts, the opportunities they see all around them are beyond their grasp.

Worst of all, it means hopelessness for the young.

The young man or woman who grows up without a decent education, in a broken home, in a hostile and squalid environment, in ill health or in the face of racial injustice-that young man or woman is often trapped in a life of poverty.

He does not have the skills demanded by a complex society. He does not know how to acquire those skills. He faces a mounting sense of despair which drains initiative and ambition and energy. . . .

The war on poverty is not a struggle simply to support people, to make them dependent on the generosity of others.

It is a struggle to give people a chance.

It is an effort to allow them to develop and use their capacities, as we have been allowed to develop and use ours, so that they can share, as others share, in the promise of this nation.

We do this, first of all, because it is right that we should.

For the establishment of public education and land grant colleges through agricultural extension and encouragement to industry, we have pursued the goal of a nation with full and increasing opportunities for all its citizens.

The war on poverty is a further step in that pursuit.

We do it also because helping some will increase the prosperity of all.

Our fight against poverty will be an investment in the most valuable of our resources-the skills and strength of our people.

And in the future, as in the past, this investment will return its cost many fold to our entire economy.

If we can raise the annual earnings of 10 million among the poor by only $1,000 we will have added $14 billion a year to our national output. In addition we can make important reductions in public assistance payments which now cost us $4 billion a year, and in the large costs of fighting crime and delinquency, disease and hunger.

This is only part of the story.

Our history has proved that each time we broaden the base of abundance, giving more people the chance to produce and consume, we create new industry, higher production, increased earnings and better income for all.

Giving new opportunity to those who have little will enrich the lives of all the rest.

Because it is right, because it is wise, and because, for the first time in our history, it is possible to conquer poverty, I submit, for the consideration of the Congress and the country, the Economic Opportunity Act of 1964.

The Act does not merely expand old programs or improve what is already being done.

It charts a new course.

It strikes at the causes, not just the consequences of poverty.

It can be a milestone in our one-hundred-eighty-year search for a better life for our people.

1. What is the war on poverty and why is it necessary according to Johnson?
2. What specific plans or methods are outlined in this address to combat poverty?

29-4   National Organization for Women, Statement of Purpose (1966)

The civil rights movement stimulated other groups to seek improvement of their conditions. In 1966, a group of feminist leaders founded NOW to fight for equal rights with men.

We, men and women who hereby constitute ourselves as the National Organization for Women, believe that the time has come for a new movement toward true equality for all women in America, and toward a fully equal partnership of the sexes, as part of the worldwide revolution of human rights now taking place within and beyond our national borders.

The purpose of **NOW** is to take action to bring women into full participation in the mainstream of American society now, exercising all the privileges an responsibilities thereof in truly equal partnership with men.

WE BELIEVE the time has come to move beyond the abstract argument, discussion, and symposia over the status and special nature of women which have raged in America in recent years; the time has come to confront, with concrete action, the conditions that now prevent women from enjoying the equality of opportunity and freedom of choice which is their right, as individual Americans, and as human beings.

NOW is dedicated to the proposition that women, first and foremost, are human beings, who, like all other people in our society, must have the chance to develop their fullest human potential. We believe that women can achieve such equality only by accepting to the full the challenges and responsibilities they share with all other people in our society, as part of the decision-making mainstream of American political, economic, and social life.

WE ORGANIZE to initiate or support action, nationally, or in any part of this nation, by individuals or organizations, to break through the silken curtain of prejudice and discrimination against women in government, industry, the professions, the churches, the political parties, the judiciary, the labor unions, in education, science, medicine, law, religion, and every other field of importance in American society. . . .

Despite all the talk about the status of American women in recent years, the actual position of women in the United States has declined, and is declining, to an alarming degree throughout the 1950's and 1960's. . . . Working women are becoming increasingly-not less-concentrated on the bottom of the job ladder. As a consequence full-time women workers today earn on the average only 60% of what men earn, and that wage gap has been increasing over the past twenty-five years in every major industry group. . . .

Further, with higher education increasingly essential in today's society, too few women are entering and finishing college or going on to graduate or professional school. . . .

In all the professions considered of importance to society, and in the executive ranks of industry and government, women are losing ground. Where they are present it is only a token handful. . . .

Official pronouncement of the advance in the status of women hide not only the reality of this dangerous decline, but the fact that nothing is being done to stop it. The excellent reports of the President's Commission on the Status of Women and of the State Commissions have not been fully implemented. Such Commissions have power only to advise. They have no power to enforce their recommendations; nor have they the freedom to organize American women and men to press for action on them. The reports of these commissions have, however, created a basis upon which it is now possible to build.

Discrimination in employment on the basis of sex is now prohibited by federal law, in Title VII of the Civil Rights Act of 1964. . . . Until now, too few women's organizations and official spokesmen have been willing to speak out against these dangers facing women. Too many women have been restrained by the fear of being called "feminist."

There is no civil rights movement to speak for women, as there has been for Negroes and other victims of discrimination. The National Organization for Women must therefore begin to speak.

WE BELIEVE that the power of American law, and the protection guaranteed by the U.S. Constitution to the civil rights of all individuals, must be effectively applied and enforced to isolate and remove patterns of sex discrimination, to ensure equality of opportunity in employment and education, and equality of civil and political rights and responsibilities on behalf of women, as well as for Negroes and other deprived groups.

WE REALIZE that women's problems are linked to many broader questions of social justice; their solution will require concerted action by many groups. . . .

WE DO NOT ACCEPT the token appointment of a few women to high-level positions in government and industry as a substitute for a serious continuing effort to recruit and advance women according to their individual abilities. To this end, we urge American government and industry to mobilize the same resources of ingenuity and command with which they have solved problems of far greater difficulty than those now impeding the progress of women.

WE BELIEVE that this nation has a capacity at least as great as other nations, to innovate new social institutions which will enable women to enjoy true equality of opportunity and responsibility in society, without conflict with their responsibilities as mothers and homemakers. . . .

. . . WE REJECT the assumption that these problems are the unique responsibility of each individual woman, rather than a basic social dilemma which society must solve. . . .

WE BELIEVE that it is an essential for every girl to be educated to her full potential of human ability as it is for every boy-with the knowledge that such education is the key to effective participation in today's economy and that, for a girl as for a boy, education can only be serious where there is expectation that it will be used in society. . . .

WE REJECT the current assumptions that a man must carry the sole burden of supporting himself, his wife, and family, and that a woman is automatically entitled to lifelong support by a man upon her marriage, or that marriage, home, and family are primarily woman's world and responsibility-hers to dominate-his to support. We believe that a true partnership between the sexes demands a different concept of marriage, and equitable sharing of the responsibilities of home and children and of the economic burdens of their support. We believe that proper recognition should be given to the economic and social value of homemaking and child care. . . .

WE BELIEVE that women must now exercise their political rights and responsibilities as American citizens. They must refuse to be segregated on the basis of sex into separate-and-not-equal ladies' auxiliaries in the political parties, and they must demand representation according to their numbers in the regularly constituted party committees-at local, state, and national levels-and in the informal power structure, participating fully in the selection of candidates and political decision making, and running for office themselves. . . .

NOW WILL HOLD ITSELF INDEPENDENT OF ANY POLITICAL PARTY in order to mobilize the political power of all women and men intent on our goals. . . .

WE BELIEVE that women will do most to create a new image of women by acting now, and by speaking out in behalf of their own equality, freedom, and human dignity-not in pleas for special privilege, nor in enmity toward men, who are also victims of the current, half-equality between the sexes-but in an active, self-respecting partnership with men. By so doing, women will develop confidence in their own ability to determine actively, in partnership with men, the conditions of their life, their choices, their future, and their society.

1. *What is the status of women in American Society according to this document? How has this status changed in the decades previous to this document?*
2. *What steps must be taken to rectify what is seen as inequality between the sexes in terms of opportunity and self-actualization?*

3. *Assess of the level of political and social awareness of gender inequality and the effectiveness of the actions taken to correct inequalities between the sexes.*

29-5 The Gay Liberation Front, *Come Out* (1970)

The Gay Liberation movement arose to secure rights for people who faced the hostility of society and discrimination because of their sexual preference. One of the goals of the gay movement was to have people publicly declare their sexual preference and not keep it secret.

Pat: The first question I would like to ask you to discuss is what is your concept of the movement?

Kay: People are always asking me what the movement means, I am always asking other people what the movement means, and I don't quite know myself. For 9 or 10 years, the movement has meant to me personally the peace movement.

Bernard: Kay, the movement means something a little bit wider than you have expressed. Movements have developed all over the world, and the movement has meant to me-I've in the movement over 50 years-any attempt to change. Whether it be political change, social change, or economic change. The movement, as I understand it, means that people organize or even work privately and individually to make changes in the country. Historically there are times when you work individually, and there have been times when the movement catches up masses of people as it did in Russia before the revolution. Now the movement includes people who want to make changes whether they be Panthers who are changing the system for black people, or Woman's Liberation who are concerned with changes for women, or socialists who are concerned with changes in the system. Or whether it be an organization like the Gay Liberation Front concerned with fighting against the oppression of homosexuals, but fighting within the framework of the wider movement. These problems are not isolated, but within the context of the oppression of the system against us all.

Bob: The movement today gets me a little up-tight. I find people saying I am the movement. The movement can be 5 people who refuse to pay the subway fare. During the Christmas week vigil there was a little old lady marching with me and she had on her Dove button. She was terribly non-violent and marching for what she believed was right: she wanted political prisoners freed. A cop hassled us and I was very angry. I called him a pig. She said, "Let me do it." She was sort of a hooker type-sort of a tough old broad, and she charmed him. She came back and said, "You have your way, and I have mine." That's true. This woman is as much a part of the movement as I, even though we are working in different ways.

Pat: I would like to ask you specifically-what ways have you found to get involved in the movement?

Bernard: Well, my first activity was when I was 5 years old. My parents had organized the first Student Friends of the Russian Revolution. I had a tray of little red flags and I put them on people and got money from them. When I was about 13 lots of us were arrested for picketing and handing out leaflets and demonstrating. We were helping the workers who were locked out, we were protesting the war budgets, we were protesting growing unemployment. At college, I helped organize the first NSL-The National Student League-which is the granddaddy of all student organizations. Also the John Reed Club. As time went on I got more and more involved but always from a political end because I was convinced that nothing but a change in the system could change the oppressions against blacks, against women, against children who were being unfairly employed at the time. Also against homosexuals. Now I'm working with homosexuals in the movement because I'm convinced that only in getting our rightful place in the movement and demanding an end to our own oppression can we ever really make changes for homosexuals.

Bob: I was instrumental in forming the 7 Arts chapters of CORE [Congress of Racial Equality]. Most of my past work has been with non-whites. In this chapter we demanded rights for Black people in show business. The first thing we did was break down the industrial shows. No non-caucasian had ever been hired. We threw a picket line around 8th Ave. and 57th St. where most of the Auto show rooms are. We also got off to the World's Fair-that was one of the times I was busted.

Kay: It seems that we had been arrested together. I was arrested at the World's Fair too. Politics make strange cell mates. I think I got into the movement first as a Quaker. As a Quaker I looked out my window in the West Village and noticed a lot of children smashing things. I thought in a few years they'll be big enough to push the button and, you know, somebody ought to do something now. I sort of got kidnapped by the children and started a thing called Workshop of Children which I ran for three years. During this time the civil rights thing was building up but since I was working with these children who had a great deal of trouble with the law, I felt I couldn't be arrested. I thought they couldn't distinguish between civil disobedience and crime exactly. However, as soon as that thing folded I was delighted to go to jail at the CORE demonstration you referred to, Bob.

Bob: I wasn't delighted.

Kay: I volunteered to be arrested and the Pinkerton men were so new and so non-violent it was really difficult. I finally had to dance on the bar at the Schaffer Pavillion. Then I worked with the Survivors of Nagasaski Hiroshima who were traveling around the world. I worked with the people at New England Committee for Non-violent Action. We participated in the blockade at the missile base of Lamakaza, in Canada, at the white house, at prisons, and at submarine bases. And I went into the Peace Corps. I can't think of any other exciting things to brag about.

Bob: I went south after the civil rights bill was signed. We went to a public swimming pool in one demonstration. Myself, a very big black girl, and a black boy. We had a big hassle getting in; but finally we demanded in, and we got in. Wc joined hands and jumped into the water. There were about 50 people when we got there and in one or two seconds there were three. . . .

Bernard: In the early days of demonstrations the thing we had to fear the most were the mounted police. Most of us were under the hooves of police horses all the time. Young children, men, women-even old people. What I found was that this kind of reaction to us brought a stronger commitment from us. And also brought more and more people to the movement. I wonder if the powers that be are aware that they build the movement themselves with their actions.

Pat: It seems here as you talk about your own experiences and some of the thoughts and feelings which have come to you from those experiences we're getting a fuller meaning of the word oppression. So we might tie it up here by saying the movement is making changes in the establishment where it oppresses us. Your experiences seem to have been radicalizing. If you are in a situation where you see the extreme degrees of the establishment oppression-you see the actual physical effects on people-you become radicalized. Like you were saying, Bernard-about-

Bernard: -about the system being it's worst enemy.

Pat: I would like to ask you how you see the Gay Liberation Movement.

Bernard: I see the Gay Liberation Movement as a process which will help liberate gay people by making them fully part of the whole liberation movement. The movement for change in the system that will eventually annihilate any form of oppression. Before GLF I was active in these movements, but anonymously-nobody was conscious of the fact that I was homosexual. I think the only way we can gain respect for ourselves and any of the help that we need from everyone else in overcoming our oppression is by showing that we participate even though they don't understand why we participate. I think even among a lot of our own people we have to fight for the right to participate as homosexuals.

Bob: I've always been active as a homosexual. Openly, but never publicly. In the past six or seven months I have suddenly found myself living the life of a public homosexual. I find resentment in many parts of the movement. When I find it, I confront it. This is very healthy for me; and it's very healthy for the movement. We cant hold the movement up as being any better or any worse than the rest of us. Gay Liberation to me is seeing 35 or 40 homosexuals marching as homosexuals in a vigil to free political prisoners. We have been political prisoners, and we will be political prisoners. Homosexuals are beginning to see themselves as an oppressed minority. I don't think homosexuality is a magic tie that binds us all but in a sense there is something. It's being proud of ourselves. And I think that's what liberation will help us find-a pride that we can just stand up and be proud of ourselves as human beings.

Bernard: I want to bring up the past in one way. When I was among young people, we had no way of expressing this. I never felt sick, although the attitude then was that we were a sickness. I could only fight this when I talked to individuals. We had no public way of fighting it. And it's exciting to be able to do it now, and the fight must be a very conscious fight.

Bob: Kay, do you have anything to say. Say something, we'll have Women's Liberation after us if you don't.

Kay: I'm very new in GLF and I don't have a great deal to say to people who want to know what it is. I see half of the gay liberation as a sort of attempt to try to change other people outside of ourselves-to try to make them stop oppressing us. But the half that interests me most now, at the beginning of my gay liberation, is self liberation. I was never open or public. I always felt that I had to be a secret homosexual, and I was terrified. Indeed I am now. This article is the first time I have ever come out in a public way, and I find that a great deal of the oppression is built into myself-is built into us. So I still expect when I come out, people are going to dislike me because I am homosexual. People do dislike homosexuals. On the other hand, I myself have disliked my own homosexuality, so perhaps it's not going to be as bad as I thought.

Bernard: Although I haven't been a public homosexual, among my friends, it was always known. What interests me now is that, although I was completely loved, for me, being a homosexual, I find that now that I'm getting active in GLF thcrc's a rcscntment. People wonder why I have to work as a homosexual in the movement. Why I can't take it up wherever I am in the movement. I don't think you can take it up wherever you are in the movement. It's only possible when we are working as a homosexual to take it up. I think that we should-those of us who can-be public as well as open.

535

1. *What seem to be the common experiences and goals of those involved in "the movement"?*
2. *What role does the Gay Liberation Front play in the larger scene of social protest and in the realm of personal liberation?*

29-6   *Swann v. Charlotte-Mecklenburg Board of Education* (1971)

Desegregation of public schools moved slowly in spite of the Brown decision. Swann v. Charlotte-Mecklenburg Board of Education upheld that busing was an acceptable solution to the de facto segregation that resulted from shifting residential patterns. In 1998, Swann was challenged by the parents of a white student who argued that the thirty-year-old ruling discriminated against both races when they tried to get into magnet schools, which accept students by a lottery system. When a U.S. District Court judge ruled that the Charlotte-Mecklenburg school system had achieved desegregation in September, 1999, a divided school board appealed the decision, which is still pending.

> **Source:** Henry Steele Commager, *Swann v. Charlotte-Mecklenburg Board of Education, Documents in American History* (New York: Appleton-Century-Crofts, 1965), pp. 756–760.

BURGER, C. J. We granted certiorari in this case to review important issues as to the duties of school authorities and the scope of powers of federal courts under this Court's mandates to eliminate racially separate public schools established and maintained by state action. . . .

This case and those argued with it arose in states having a long history of maintaining two sets of schools in a single school system deliberately operated to carry out a governmental policy to separate pupils in schools solely on the basis of race. That was what *Brown v. Board of Education* was all about. These cases present us with the problem of defining in more precise terms than heretofore the scope of the duty of school authorities and district courts in implementing *Brown I* and the mandate to eliminate dual systems and establish unitary systems at once. Meanwhile district courts and courts of appeals have struggled in hundreds of cases with a multitude and variety of problems under this Court's general directive. Understandably, in an area of evolving remedies, those courts had to improvise and experiment without detailed or specific guidelines. This court, in *Brown I*, appropriately dealt with the large constitutional principles; other federal courts had to grapple with the flinty, intractable realities of day-to-day implementation of those constitutional commands. Their efforts, of necessity, embraced a process of "trial and error," and our effort to formulate guidelines must take into account their experience. . . .

The central issue in this case is that of student assignment, and there are essentially four problem areas:

(1) to what extent racial balance or racial quotas may be used as an implement in a remedial order to correct a previously segregated system;

(2) whether every all-Negro and all-white school must be eliminated as an indispensable part of a remedial process of desegregation;

(3) what are the limits, if any, on the rearrangement of school districts and attendance zones, as a remedial measure; and

(4) what are the limits, if any, on the use of transportation facilities to correct state-enforced racial school segregation.

(1) RACIAL BALANCES OR RACIAL QUOTAS

The constant theme and thrust of every holding from *Brown I* to date is that state-enforced separation of races in public schools is discrimination that violates the Equal Protection Clause. The remedy commanded was to dismantle dual school systems.

We are concerned in these cases with the elimination of the discrimination inherent in the dual school systems, not with myriad factors of human existence which can cause discrimination in a multitude of ways on racial, religious, or ethnic grounds. The target of the cases from *Brown I* to the present was the dual school system. The elimination of racial discrimination in public schools is a large task and one that should not be retarded by efforts to achieve broader purposes lying beyond the jurisdiction of school authorities. One vehicle can carry only a limited amount of baggage. It would not serve the important objective of *Brown I* to seek to use school desegregation cases for purposes beyond their scope, although desegregation of schools ultimately will have impact on other forms of discrimination. We do not reach in this case the question whether a showing that school segregation is a consequence of other types of state action, without any discriminatory action by the school authorities, is a constitutional violation requiring remedial action by a school desegregation decree. This case does not present that question and we therefore do not decide it.

Our objective in dealing with the issues presented by these cases is to see that school authorities exclude no pupil of a racial minority from any school, directly or indirectly, on account of race; it does not and cannot embrace all the problems of racial prejudice, even when those problems contribute to disproportionate racial concentrations in some schools.

In this case it is urged that the District Court has imposed a racial balance requirement of 71%-29% on individual schools. The fact that no such objective was actually achieved—and would appear to be impossible—tends to blunt that claim, yet in the opinion and order of the District Court of December 1, 1969, we find that court directing:

"that efforts should be made to reach a 71–29 ratio in the various schools so that there will be no basis for contending that one school is racially different from the others . . . , that no school [should] be operated with an all-black or predominantly black student body, [and] that pupils of all grades [should] be assigned in such a way that as nearly as practicable the various schools at various grade levels have about the same proportion of black and white students."

The District Judge went on to acknowledge that variation "from that norm may be unavoidable." This contains intimations that the "norm" is a fixed mathematical racial balance reflecting the pupil constituency of the system. If we were to read the holding of the District Court to require, as a matter of substantive constitutional right, any particular degree of racial balance or mixing, that approach would be disapproved and we would be obliged to reverse. The constitutional command to desegregate schools does not mean that every school in every community must always reflect the racial composition of the school system as a whole. . . .

We see therefore that the use made of mathematical ratios was no more than a starting point in the process of shaping a remedy, rather than an inflexible requirement. From that starting point the District Court proceeded to frame a decree that was within its discretionary powers, an equitable remedy for the particular circumstances. As we said in *Green*, a school authority's remedial plan or a district court's remedial decree is to be judged by its effectiveness. Awareness of the racial composition of the whole school system is likely to be a useful starting point in shaping a remedy to correct past constitutional violations. In sum, the very limited use made of mathematical ratios was within the equitable remedial discretion of the District Court.

(2) ONE-RACE SCHOOLS

The record in this case reveals the familiar phenomenon that in metropolitan areas minority groups are often found concentrated in one part of the city. In some circumstances certain schools may remain all or largely of one race until new schools can be provided or neighborhood patterns change. Schools all or predominantly of one race in a district of mixed population will require close scrutiny to determine that school assignments are not part of state-enforced segregation.

In light of the above, it should be clear that the existence of some small number of one-race, or virtually one-race, schools within a district is not in and of itself the mark of a system which still practices segregation by law. The district judge or school authorities should make every effort to achieve the greatest possible degree of actual desegregation and will thus necessarily be concerned with the elimination of one-race schools. No *per se* rule can adequately embrace all the difficulties of reconciling the competing interests involved; but in a system with a history of segregation the need for remedial criteria of sufficient specificity to assure a school authority's compliance with its constitutional duty warrants a presumption against schools that are substantially disproportionate in their racial composition. Where the school authority's proposed plan for conversion from a dual to a unitary system contemplates the continued existence of some schools that are all or predominantly of one race, they have the burden of showing that such school assignments are genuinely non-discriminatory. The court should scrutinize such schools, and the burden upon the school authorities will be to satisfy the court that their racial composition is not the result of present or past discriminatory action on their part.

An optional majority-to-minority transfer provision has long been recognized as a useful part of every desegregation plan. Provision for optional transfer of those in the majority racial group of a particular school to other schools where they will be in the minority is an indispensable remedy for those students willing to transfer to other schools in order to lessen the impact on them of the state-imposed stigma of segregation. In order to be effective, such a transfer arrangement must grant the transferring student free transportation and space must be made available in the school to which he desires to move. . . .

(3) REMEDIAL ALTERING OF ATTENDANCE ZONES

The maps submitted in these cases graphically demonstrate that one of the principal tools employed by school planners and by courts to break up the dual school system has been a frank—and sometimes drastic—gerrymandering of school districts and attendance zones. An additional step was pairing, "clustering," or "grouping" of schools with attendance assignments made deliberately to accomplish the transfer of Negro students out of formerly segregated Negro schools and transfer of white students to formerly all-Negro schools. More often than not, these zones are neither compact nor contiguous; indeed they may be on opposite ends of the city. As an interim corrective measure, this cannot be said to be beyond the broad remedial powers of a court.

Absent a constitutional violation there would be no basis for judicially ordering assignment of students on a racial basis. All things being equal, with no history of discrimination, it might well be desirable to assign pupils to schools nearest their homes. But all things are not equal in a system that has been deliberately constructed and maintained to enforce racial segregation. The remedy for such segregation may be administratively awkward, inconvenient and even bizarre in some situations and may impose burdens on some; but all awkwardness and inconvenience cannot be avoided in the interim period when remedial adjustments are being made to eliminate the dual school systems.

No fixed or even substantially fixed guidelines can be established as to how far a court can go, but it must be recognized that there are limits. The objective is to dismantle the dual school system. "Racially neutral" assignment plans proposed by school authorities to a district court may be inadequate; such plans may fail to counteract the continuing effects of past school segregation resulting from discriminatory location of school sites or distortion of school size in order to achieve or maintain an artificial racial separation. When school authorities present a district court with a "loaded game board," affirmative action in the form of remedial altering of attendance zones is proper to achieve truly nondiscriminatory assignments. In short, an assignment plan is not acceptable simply because it appears to be neutral.

In this area, we must of necessity rely to a large extent, as this Court has for more than sixteen years, on the informed judgment of the district courts in the first instance and on courts of appeals.

We hold that the pairing and grouping non-contiguous school zones is a permissable tool and such action is to be considered in light of the objectives sought. Judicial steps in shaping such zones going beyond combinations of contiguous areas should be examined in light of what is said [above] concerning the objectives to be sought. Maps do not tell the whole story since non-contiguous school zones may be more accessible to each other in terms of the critical travel time, because of traffic patterns and good highways, than schools geographically closer together. Conditions in different localities will vary so widely that no rigid rules can be laid down to govern all situations.

(4) TRANSPORTATION OF STUDENTS

The scope of permissable transportation of students as an implement of a remedial decree has never been defined by this Court and by the very nature of the problem it cannot be defined with precision. No rigid guidelines as to student transportation can be given for application to the infinite variety of problems presented in thousands of situations. Bus transportation has been an integral part of the public education system for years, and was perhaps the single most important factor in the transition from the one-room schoolhouse to the consolidated school. Eighteen million of the nation's public school children, approximately 39%, were transported to their schools by bus in 1969-1970 in all parts of the country.

The importance of bus transportation as a normal and accepted tool of educational policy is readily discernible in this and the companion case. The Charlotte school authorities did not purport to assign students on the basis of geographically drawn zones until 1965 and then they allowed almost unlimited transfer privileges. The District Court's conclusion that assignment of children to the school nearest their home serving their grade would not produce an effective dismantling of the dual system is supported by the record.

Thus the remedial techniques used in the District court's order were within that court's power to provide equitable relief; implementation of the decree is well within the capacity of the school authority.

The decree provided that the buses used to implement the plan would operate on direct routes. Students would be picked up at schools near their homes and transported to the schools they were to attend. The trips for elementary school pupils average about seven miles and the District Court found that they would take "not over thirty-five minutes at the most." This system compares favorably with the transportation plan previously operated in Charlotte under which each day 23,600 students on all grade levels were transported an average of fifteen miles one way for an average trip requiring over an hour. In these circumstances, we find no basis for holding that the local school authorities may not be required to employ bus transportation as one tool of school desegregation. Desegregation plans cannot be limited to the walk-in school.

An objection to transportation of students may have validity when the time or distance of travel is so great as to risk either the health of the children or significantly impinge on the educational process. District courts must weigh the soundness of any transportation plan in light of what is said . . . above. It hardly needs stating that the limits on time of travel will vary with many factors, but probably with none more than the age of the students. The reconciliation of competing values in a desegregation case is, of course, a difficult task with many sensitive facets but fundamentally no more so than remedial measures courts of equity have traditionally employed.

The Court of Appeals, searching for a term to define the equitable remedial power of the district courts, used the term "reasonableness." In *Green, supra*, this Court used the term "feasible" and by implication, "workable," "effective," and "realistic" in the mandate to develop "a plan that promises realistically to work, and . . . to work *now*." On the facts of this case, we are unable to conclude that the order of the District Court is not reasonable, feasible and workable. However, in seeking to define the scope of remedial power or the limits on remedial power of courts in an area as sensitive as we deal with here, words are poor instruments to convey the sense of basic fairness inherent in equity. Substance, not semantics, must govern, and we have sought to suggest the nature of limitations without frustrating the appropriate scope of equity.

At some point, these school authorities and others like them should have achieved full compliance with this Court's decision in *Brown I*. The systems will then be "unitary" in the sense required by our decisions in *Green* and *Alexander*.

It does not follow that the communities served by such systems will remain demographically stable, for in a growing, mobile society, few will do so. Neither school authorities nor district courts are constitutionally required to make year-by-year adjustments of the racial composition of student bodies once the affirmative duty to desegregate has been accomplished and racial discrimination through official action is eliminated from the system. This does not mean that federal courts are without power to deal with future problems; but in the absence of a showing that either the school authorities or some other agency of the State has deliberately attempted to fix or alter demographic patterns to affect the racial composition of the schools, further intervention by a district court should not be necessary.

For the reasons herein set forth, the judgment of the Court of Appeals is affirmed as to those parts in which it affirmed the judgment of the District Court. The order of the District Court dated August 7, 1970, is also affirmed. It is so ordered.

1. How is this ruling in the lineage of Brown v. Board of Education of Topeka?
2. How would this ruling improve education?
3. What was the nature of segregation that existed in the United States by 1971?
4. Why was the Nixon administration resistant to this decision?

29-7 *Roe v. Wade* (1973)

Voting 7–2 in 1973, the Supreme Court struck down state laws preventing abortion in the first trimester of pregnancy. The decision also set guidelines for abortion in the second and third trimesters. Roe v. Wade was based on the grounds that extant state laws prohibiting abortion were unconstitutional, as they violated the right to privacy implicitly guaranteed in the 9th and 14th amendments.

Source: Henry Steele Commager, *Roe v. Wade, Documents of American History* (New York: Appleton-Century-Crofts, 1965), pp. 798–800.

BLACKMUN, J. . . . We forthwith acknowledge our awareness of the sensitive and emotional nature of the abortion controversy, of the vigorous opposing views, even among physicians, and of the deep and seemingly absolute convictions that the subject inspires. One's philosophy, one's experiences, one's exposure to the raw edges of human existence, one's religious training, one's attitudes toward life and family and their values, and the moral standards one establishes and seeks to observe, are all likely to influence and to color one's thinking and conclusions about abortion.

In addition, population growth, pollution, poverty, and racial overtones tend to complicate and not to simplify the problem.

Our task, of course, is to resolve the issue by constitutional measurement free of emotion and of predilection. We seek earnestly to do this, and, because we do, we have inquired into, and in this opinion place some emphasis upon, medical and medical-legal history and what that history reveals about man's attitudes toward the abortive procedure over the centuries. . . .

The Texas statutes that concern us here are Arts. 1191-1194 and 1196 of the State Penal Code. These make it a crime to "procure an abortion," as therein defined, or to attempt one, except with respect to "an abortion procured or attempted by medical advice for the purpose of saving the life of the mother." Similar statutes are in existence in a majority of the states. . . .

The principal thrust of appellant's attack on the Texas statutes is that they improperly invade a right, said to be possessed by the pregnant women, to choose to terminate her pregnancy. Appellant would discover this right in the concept of personal "liberty" embodied in the Fourteenth Amendment's Due Process Clause; or in personal, marital, familial, and sexual privacy said to be protected by the Bill of Rights or its penumbras, *see Griswold v. Connecticut*, 381 U. S. 479 (1965); *Eisenstadt v. Baird*, 405 U. S. 438 (1972); *id.*, at 460 (White, J., concurring); or among those rights reserved to the people by the Ninth Amendment, *Griswold v. Connecticut*, 381 U. S., at 486 (Goldberg, J., concurring) . . . .

The Constitution does not explicitly mention any right of privacy. In a line of decisions, however, going back perhaps as far as *Union Pacific R. Co. v. Botsford,* 141 U. S. 250, 251 (1891), the Court has recognized that a right of personal privacy, or a guarantee of certain areas or zones of privacy, does exist under the Constitution. . . .

This right of privacy, whether it be founded in the Fourteenth Amendment's concept of personal liberty and restrictions upon state action, as we feel it is, or, as the District Court determined, in the Ninth Amendment's reservation of rights to the people, is broad enough to encompass a women's decision whether or not to terminate her pregnancy. The detriment that the state would impose upon the pregnant woman by denying this choice altogether is apparent. Specific and direct harm medically diagnosable even in early pregnancy may be involved. Maternity, or additional offspring, may force upon the woman a distressful life and future. Psychological harm may be imminent. Mental and physical health may be taxed by child care. There is also the distress, for all concerned, associated with the unwanted child, and there is the problem of bringing a child into a family already unable, psychologically and otherwise, to care for it. In other cases, as in this one, the additional difficulties and continuing stigma of unwed motherhood may be involved. All these are factors the woman and her responsible physician necessarily will consider in consultation.

On the basis of elements such as these, appellants and some *amici* argue that the woman's right is absolute and that she is entitled to terminate her pregnancy at whatever time, in whatever way, and for whatever reason she alone chooses. With this we do not agree. Appellants' arguments that Texas either has no valid interest at all in regulating the abortion decision, or no interest strong enough to support any limitation upon the woman's sole determination, is unpersuasive. The Court's decisions recognizing a right of privacy also acknowledge that some state regulation in areas protected by that right is appropriate. As noted above, a state may properly assert important interests in safeguarding health, in maintaining medical standards, and in protecting potential life. At some point in pregnancy, these respective interests become sufficiently compelling to sustain regulation of the factors that govern the abortion decision. The privacy right involved, therefore, cannot be said to be absolute. . . .

We therefore conclude that the right of personal privacy includes the abortion decision, but that this right is not unqualified and must be considered against important state interests in regulation.

We note that those federal and state courts that have recently considered abortion law challenges have reached the same conclusion. . .

The appellee and certain *amici* argue that the fetus is a "person" within the language and meaning of the Fourteenth Amendment. In support of this they outline at length and in detail the well-known facts of fetal development. If this suggestion of personhood is established, the appellant's case, of course, collapses, for the fetus' right to life is then guaranteed specifically by the Amendment. The appellant conceded as much as reargument. On the other hand, the appellee conceded on reargument that no case could be cited that holds that a fetus is a person within the meaning of the Fourteenth Amendment.

The Constitution does not define "person" in so many words. Section 1 of the Fourteenth Amendment contains three references to "person." The first, in defining "citizens," speaks of "persons born or naturalized in the United States." The word also appears both in the Due Process Clause and in the Equal Protection Clause. "Person" is used in other places in the Constitution. . . . in nearly all these instances, the use of the word is such that it has application only postnatally. None indicates, with any assurance, that it has any possible pre-natal application.

Texas urges that, apart from the Fourteenth Amendment, life begins at conception and is present throughout pregnancy, and that, therefore, the state has a compelling interest in protecting that life from and after conception. We need not resolve the difficult question of when life begins. When those trained in the respective disciplines of medicine, philosophy, and theology are unable to arrive at any consensus, the judiciary, at this point in the development of man's knowledge, is not in a position to speculate as to the answer. . . .

In areas other than criminal abortion the law has been reluctant to endorse any theory that life, as we recognize it, begins before live birth or to accord legal rights to the unborn except in narrowly defined situations and except when the rights are contingent upon live birth. . . .

In short, the unborn have never been recognized in the law as persons in the whole sense. . . .

In view of all this, we do not agree that, by adopting one theory of life, Texas may override the rights of the pregnant woman that are at stake. We repeat, however, that the state does have an important and legitimate interest in preserving and protecting the health of the pregnant woman, whether she be a resident of the state or a nonresident who seeks medical consultation and treatment there, and that it has still *another* important and legitimate interest in protecting the potentiality of human life. These interests are separate and distinct. Each grows in substantiality as the woman approaches term and, at a point during pregnancy, each becomes "compelling."

With respect to the state's important and legitimate interests in the health of the mother, the "compelling" point, in the light of present medical knowledge, is at approximately the end of the first trimester. This is so because of the now established medical fact, referred to above . . . , that until the end of the first trimester mortality in abortion is less than mortality in normal childbirth. It follows that, from and after this point, a state may regulate the abortion procedure to the extent that the regulation reasonably relates to the preservation and protection of maternal health. . . .

With respect to the state's important and legitimate interest in potential life, the "compelling" point is at viability. This is so because the fetus then presumably has the capability of meaningful life outside the mother's womb. State regulation protective of fetal life after viability thus has both logical and biological justifications. If the state is interested in protecting fetal life after viability, it may go so far as to proscribe abortion during that period except when it is necessary to preserve the life or health of the mother.

Measured against these standards, Art. 1196 of the Texas Penal Code, in restricting legal abortions to those "procured or attempted by medical advice for the purpose of saving the life of the mother," sweeps too broadly. The statute makes no distinction between abortions performed early in pregnancy and those performed later, and it limits to a single reason, "saving" the mother's life, the legal justification for the procedure. The statute, therefore, cannot survive the constitutional attack made upon it here. . . .

To summarize and to repeat:

1. A state criminal abortion statute of the current Texas type, that excepts from criminality only a *life saving* procedure on behalf of the mother, without regard to pregnancy stage and without recognition of the other interests involved, is violative of the Due Process Clause of the Fourteenth Amendment.

(a) For the stage prior to approximately the end of the first trimester, the abortion decision and its effectuation must be left to the medical judgment of the pregnant woman's attending physician.

(b) For the stage subsequent to approximately the end of the first trimester, the state, in promoting its interest in the health of the mother, may, if it chooses, regulate the abortion procedure in ways that are reasonably related to maternal health.

(c) For the stage subsequent to viability the state, in promoting its interest in the potentiality of human life, may, if it chooses, regulate, and even proscribe, abortion except where it is necessary, in appropriate medical judgment, for the preservation of the life or health of the mother. . . .

1. *What ramifications does this law have for women's rights?*
2. *On what elements did the court base its decision?*
3. *What is the role of the state in this matter? At what point does the interest of the state begin? Why?*

29-8 Ione Malloy, Southie Won't Go (1975)

Federally mandated busing for school integration stimulated strong protests among white residents in South Boston. Attempts of integrating schools touched off riots such as the one described by Ione Malloy.

From my homeroom window I watched the school buses empty one by one, while an administrator, Mr. Gizzi, checked each student's class program to see whether the student belonged at the high school. As I watched, a girl's piercing screams rose from the front lobby. Troopers began running toward the building. Trooper squad cars blocked off G Street down the hill so the buses couldn't move. Mr. Gizzi stayed with the buses. Over the intercom the secretary's voice cried, "We need help here on the second floor. Please send help to the office." Isolated on the second floor in the front corner of the building, in a small room attached to two adjoining rooms, I again felt the terror of not knowing what was coming from what direction, feeling unable to protect myself or the students from an unidentified danger.

I have never had a desire to flee, just to protect the students, though I don't like the feeling of being trapped. I closed the door, turned out the lights, and told my homeroom students we would stay there and help each other. We waited-two white girls, Kathryn and Becky; James, a small, long-haired white boy; and Jeffrey, a black. In a few minutes the door opened. The gym teacher, carrying an umbrella, stood there with a trooper, their faces anxious. "Have you seen Jane?" they asked, then hurried away. What had happened? Why was the teacher carrying an umbrella? Who was Jane, and where might she have gone, we wondered, but there was no chance to ask. They had already shut the door behind them.

Then came a call for all teachers not assigned to homerooms to report to the front lobby. The call was repeated several times.

About forty minutes later, I was amazed when, from my window, I saw the last bus empty. Several minutes later the intercom announced that the school day would begin. Students should proceed to their first class. Instead, everyone just sat, afraid to move, paralyzed by the unknown.

There were only twenty minutes left in the first class, senior English. The seniors were upset. There had been fights in the South Cafeteria, in the third floor lavatory, and in room 303 on the third floor down the hall, they told me. Because the fights had broken out simultaneously, the seniors felt they had been planned. Just then the intercom requested custodians to report to the third floor lavatory and to the South Cafeteria. "To clean up the blood," the seniors explained.

Although the seniors wanted to discuss the fights, I said we would first take a quick, objective, one-word test. I was a little angry. It was better to get their minds focused on something else. In the few remaining minutes, I let them take the Luscher color preference test and talk about the correlation of color with personality. Most of them chose yellow, red, or blue in their color preference. They are a good class.

When I passed room 303 a few minutes later, the students were pushing at the door to get out. A trooper was holding them in. I told two boys at the door to go in and help their teacher. They asked, "Help *her?*" It hadn't occurred to them that she might need their help. Jack Kennedy, administrator, passed me in the corridor, his face white and drained. I stopped in the teachers' room to comb my hair. My face in the mirror looked ghastly. It must take the body time to recover its equilibrium, even after the mind has composed itself.

As I walked around the school, and felt the mood of the school, I thought, "This school is DEATH. The mood of the school is black."

The troopers were happy, however, I was surprised to see. One said, "This is more like it. It gets the old adrenalin going."

My sophomores, a mixed class of black and white students, also wanted to talk about the incidents. They explained how the fight before school had started at the front lobby door. A black girl and a white boy were going through the front lobby-the boy first. He let the door slam on her. She screamed; a black male jumped to her defense, and the fight was on. A trooper pushed a white boy back over a desk and dislocated his shoulder. A black student on the stairs started screaming insults at the white students-among them Michael Faith-and Faith lunged for him. Fights broke out everywhere in the lobby. Students rushed down from the classrooms, or out of their homerooms to aid the secretaries when they called for help on the intercom.

Anne was upset because a trooper in the cafeteria had grabbed a black girl and called her "nigger." "Nobody calls me 'nigger.' " Anne said. "My friend got her comb and got a piece of his red meat."

I played dumb and, for the benefit of white students, said, "But I hear black kids call each other 'nigger,' and they don't seem to mind." Anne said, "Nobody's called me 'nigger.' I don't care who he is." Louis, a black student who has come to school regularly in a taxi even when Atkins called for a boycott, sat back confidently in his fine pressed suit and said, "It's all right when another black person calls me a 'nigger,' but not a white person. Then it's an insult. If I don't know a person and he calls me 'nigger,' I don't say anything until I find out how he feels about me."

Anne said, "I hate this school. I don't never want to come back."

I concluded, "We all need more understanding.". . .

There was a faculty meeting after school. Dr. Reid took the toll of casualities and names involved in fights. Unconsciously he wiped his brow with the classic tragic sweep of his hand and said, "I don't know what we can do. We were all at our posts doing our jobs. But if a youngster will insult and another responds with his fists, there's nothing we can do-except encourage them to watch their mouths and language."

Dr. Reid announced he would like to have an honor roll assembly for sophomores. Mrs. Marie Folkart, the oldest, most respected member of the faculty, raised her hand: She hoped he wouldn't have an assembly. Usually very deferential to her, he disagreed, "I don't know about that. I think maybe we should."

The assembly, the first this year, is scheduled for Friday, a day when attendance is the lowest. . . .

The sophomore assembly convened as planned. Classes filed to assigned seats room by room without incident. Troopers lined the auditorium. The mood was ugly.

Dr. Reid entered from the rear of the hall. As he moved down the center aisle to the stage, he urged the students to stand. He stopped at my class. Martin wouldn't stand because Siegfried, behind him, wouldn't. Then James sat down-later, he told me, because the black kids-Martin and Siegfried-wouldn't stand. Dr. Reid insisted, and I insisted, but Martin refused. Dr. Reid proceeded on. Again I thought, "This school is death."

After the pledge of allegience to the flag, Dr. Reid lectured on the courtesy of standing when a guest comes to one's home. A few students snickered. When he alluded to the troopers, the black boys in the row behind me yelled, "Get them out." Then Dr. Reid outlined the sports plan for the winter and told the assembly, "We will be together for the year. After that I don't know. But we're here, and we had better make the best of it. And let's have a little courtesy toward one another. Let's treat each other with respect and watch what we say to one another-treat each other with a little kindness. A smile goes a long way if someone accidentally bumps you, instead of pushing back." The students listened respectfully.

Then, as both black and white students crossed the stage to accept their honor roll cards from Dr. Reid, the assembly applauded.

Students left the auditorium room by room.

During the day, girl students traveled the school in roving gangs of blacks and whites, bursting out of classes at any provocation, spreading consternation among the police. "They're in holiday mood," I told the police, dismayed at the prospect of chasing pretty girls back to classrooms.

At the end of the day in homeroom, I told Martin, "Dr. Reid has put his life on the line about desegregation because it is the law. His house in South Boston is guarded. Then he asks you to stand in the assembly, and you refuse. He is your friend, the friend of all of us, and you should know that." James said to Martin, "That's right, Dr. Reid has guards."

A neighborhood crowd chanted at Dr. Reid outside the school this morning. . . .

A librarian at the Boston Public Library in Copley Square told me there are enough kids in the library all day to have school there. He doesn't know where they come from. . . .

The number of troopers in the building was increased instead of decreased, contrary to what the troopers had anticipated Friday when I talked to them.

The two black boys-Martin and Jeffrey-and one white girl, Kathryn, were present in my homeroom today. Expecting a boycott, I was surprised to see any white students in school until I learned that a walkout of white students was anticipated at 9:45 A.M., when the parents, now gathering on the sidewalk, planned to walk in to protest the presence of steel combs in the school.

Walkers (or white students) were permitted to leave by the side doors, if they preferred, so as not to be identified and, perhaps, intimidated by the now divided community. In South Boston families once friends are now enemies, since half support the antibusing boycott and the other half feel they have to educatc their children.

Television cameras recorded Dr. Reid facing the protesters outside the building in the morning sunshine. He told them, "The black parents have elected no biracial council; the white students have elected none; the white parents have elected none. And frankly, the number of fights last week made me afraid."

In class Anne described the walkout. "The white kids said, 'See you Tuesday, niggers.' If the black kids had a walkout, I'd go, too. The white kids have to go, or they'll get beaten up." Gretchen, a diligent and intelligent white student, who had attended the advanced classes of the New York public schools, listened. I give her extra reading and reports because she is highly motivated. Besides Gretchen, there were five black students in the class.

I left school at the end of the day by the front lobby staircase, passing the Greek frieze laboriously painted by the art teachers in neutral dark brown last September before school began. The frieze had been nightly mutilated with spray paint and daily repaired by the art department, until finally they gave up. The frieze is now hideous: The faces are black blobs, or white blobs, or faceless with black holes for eyes. Looking at them, one teacher shuddered, "The hatred is getting to me."

1. *How is the situation described in this Boston school a microcosm of race tensions and relations in America?*
2. *What social pressures are at work on the attitudes and actions of the students in the school?*
3. *In what ways does this account provide a very personal perspective on a national problem?*

29-9 Jimmy Carter, The "Malaise" Speech (1979)

During Carter's presidency the American economy was beset with inflation and high interest rates while foreign policy was troubled. By midpoint in his term, Carter's popularity was lower than any of the previous five presidents at a similar stage. Part of the problem was the enormous disparity between Carter's promises and his performance. Carter gave this speech after canceling an address on energy policy and retreating with his advisers at Camp David in 1979. Although Carter never used the term in this speech, it became known as his "malaise" speech because he complained publicly of a malaise of the American spirit.

Good evening.

This is a special night for me. Exactly three years ago, on July 15, 1976, I accepted the nomination of my party to run for President of the United States. I promised you a President who is not isolated from the people, who feels your pain, and who shared your dreams and who draws his strength and his wisdom from you. . . .

Ten days ago I had planned to speak to you again about a very important subject-energy. For the fifth time I would have described the urgency of the problem and laid out a series of legislative recommendations to the Congress. But as I was preparing to speak, I began to ask myself the same question that I now know has been troubling many of you. Why have we not been able to get together as a nation to resolve our serious energy problem?

It's clear that the true problems of our Nation are much deeper-deeper than gasoline lines or energy shortages, deeper even than inflation or recession. And I realize more than ever that as President I need your help. So, I decided to reach out and listen to the voices of America.

I invited to Camp David people from almost every segment of our society-business and labor, teachers and preachers, Governors, mayors, and private citizens. And then I left Camp David to listen to other Americans, men and women like you. It has been an extraordinary ten days, and I want to share with you what I've heard. . . .

These ten days confirmed my belief in the decency and the strength and the wisdom of the American people, but it also bore out some of my long-standing concerns about our Nation's underlying problems.

I know, of course, being president, that government actions and legislation can be very important. That's why I've worked hard to put my campaign promises into law-and I have to admit, with just mixed success. But after listening to the American people I have been reminded again that all the legislation in the world can't fix what's wrong with America. So,

I want to speak to you first tonight about a subject even more serious than energy or inflation. I want to talk to you right now about a fundamental threat to American democracy.

I do not mean our political and civil liberties. They will endure. And I do not refer to the outward strength of America, a nation that is at peace tonight everywhere in the world, with unmatched economic power and military might.

The threat is nearly invisible in ordinary ways. It is a crisis of confidence. It is a crisis that strikes at the very heart and soul and spirit of our national will. We can see this crisis in the growing doubt about the meaning of our own lives and in the loss of a unity of purpose for our Nation.

The erosion of our confidence in the future is threatening to destroy the social and the political fabric of America. . . .

The symptoms of this crisis of the American spirit are all around us. For the first time in the history of our country a majority of our people believe that the next five years will be worse than the past five years. Two-thirds of our people do not even vote. The productivity of American workers is actually dropping, and the willingness of Americans to save for the future has fallen below that of all other people in the Western world. . . .

Often you see paralysis and stagnation and drift. You don't like it, and neither do I. What can we do?

First of all, we must face the truth, and then we can change our course. We simply must have faith in each other, faith in our course. We simply must have faith in each other, faith in our ability to govern ourselves, and faith in the future of this Nation. Restoring that faith and that confidence to America is now the most important task we face. It is a true challenge of this generation of Americans. . . .

We are at a turning point in our history. There are two paths to choose. One is a path I've warned about tonight, the path that leads to fragmentation and self-interest. Down that road lies a mistaken idea of freedom, the right to grasp for ourselves some advantage over others. That path would be one of constant conflict between narrow interests ending in chaos and immobility. It is a certain route to failure.

All the traditions of our past, all the lessons of our heritage, all the promises of our future point to another path, the path of common purpose and the restoration of American values. That path leads to true freedom for our Nation and ourselves. We can take the first steps down that path as we begin to solve our energy problems. . . .

1. Explain what is wrong with America as it is described in this speech.
2. Identify and describe the steps outlined by Carter necessary to deal with the crisis of confidence.
3. How is this speech quite different from many other presidential addresses?

30-1 House Judiciary Committee, Conclusion on Impeachment Resolution (1974)

During the 1972 presidential race, several employees of the Committee to Re-Elect the President (CREEP), a branch of Richard Nixons reelection campaign, broke into the Democratic Party headquarters, searched through files, and installed listening devices. They were caught. Nixon initially denied that anyone in the White House was involved. But after one of the burglars admitted during his trial that Republican officials had known about their activities, several White House officials admitted their involvement and resigned. As more disclosures followed, it became clear that Nixon administration officials had wiretapped journalists and politicians as well as the Democratic headquarters, broken into the office of the psychiatrist treating Daniel Ellsberg (who had leaked the Pentagon Papers about Vietnam to the New York Times which helped to further erode public support for the war), and paid off the burglars to ensure their silence. Nixons presidency was already shadowed by scandalhis vice president, Spiro Agnew, had been forced to resign after he was indicted on bribery and tax evasion charges, while Nixon himself had been investigated for tax evasion after he took huge deductions for donating his vice presidential papers to the National Archives. Newspapers, a Senate committee, and a Special Counsel investigated Nixons involvement in the break-in, and John Dean, the former White House counsel under Nixon, testified that the president had known about the cover-up. Nixon, of course, was not forthcoming in the matter, and when it was revealed that he had tape-recorded all his meetings in the White House, the investigators sought those tapes in order to find out what Nixon knew. In the end, it took a Supreme Court ruling to force Nixon to hand over the tapes. The following is a copy of the conclusion of the House of Representatives on their consideration of the Impeachment Resolution for President Nixon, prepared and released before Nixon was ordered by the Court to release the tapes. Nixon resigned less than a month after this report was issued.

After the Committee on the Judiciary had debated whether or not it should recommend Article I to the House of Representatives, 27 of the 38 Members of the Committee found that the evidence before it could only lead to one conclusion: that Richard M. Nixon, using the powers of his high office, engaged, personally and through his subordinates and agents, in a course of conduct or plan designed to delay, impede, and obstruct the investigation of the unlawful entry on June 17, 1972, into the headquarters of the Democratic National Committee; to cover up, conceal and protect those responsible; and to conceal the existence and scope of other unlawful activities.

This finding is the only one that can explain the President's involvement in a pattern on undisputed acts that occurred after the break-in and that cannot otherwise be rationally explained.

1. The President's decision on June 20, 1972, not to meet with his Attorney General, his chief of staff, his counsel, his campaign director, and his assistant, John Ehrlichman, whom he had put in charge of the investigation-when the subject of their meeting was the Watergate matter.
2. The erasure of that portion of the recording of the President's conversation with White House chief of staff H. R. Haldeman on June 20, 1972, which dealt with Watergate-when the President stated that the tapes had been under his "sole and personal control."
3. The President's public denial on June 22, 1972, of the involvement of members of the Committee for the Re-election of the President [CREEP] or of the White House staff in the Watergate burglary, in spite of having discussed Watergate, on or before June 22, 1972, with Haldeman, special counsel Charles Colson, and former attorney general John Mitchell [head of CREEP]-all persons aware of that involvement.
4. The President's directive to Haldeman on June 23, 1972, to have the CIA request the FBI to curtail its Watergate investigation.
5. The President's refusal, on July 6, 1972, to inquire and inform himself what Patrick Gray, Acting Director of the FBI, meant by his warning that some of the President's aides were "trying to mortally wound him."
6. The President's discussion with Erlichman on July 8, 1972, of clemency for the Watergate burglars, more than two months before the return of any indictments.
7. The President's public statement on August 29, 1972, a statement later shown to be untrue, that an investigation by [White House counsel] John Dean "indicates no one in the White House staff, no one in the Administration, presently employed, was involved in this very bizarre incident."

8. The President's statement to Dean on September 14, 1972, the day that the Watergate indictments were returned without naming high CRP [CREEP] and White House officials, that Dean had handled his work skillfully, "putting your fingers in the dike every time that leaks have sprung here and sprung there," and that "you just try to button it up as well as you can and hope for the best." . . .

In addition to this evidence, there was before the Committee the following evidence:

1. Beginning immediately after June 17, 1972, the involvement of each of the President's top aides and political associates, Haldeman, Mitchell, Ehrlichman, Colson, Dena, LaRue, Mardinan, Magruder, in the Watergate coverup. . . .

Finally , there was before the Committee a record of public statement by the President between June 22, 1972 and June 9, 1974, deliberately contrived to deceive the courts, the Department of Justice, the Congress and the American people.

President Nixon's course of conduct following the Watergate break-in, as described in Article I, caused action not only by his subordinates but by the agencies of the United States, including the Department of Justice, the FBI, and the CIA. It required perjury, destruction of evidence, obstruction of justice, all crimes. But, most important, it required deliberate, contrived, and continuing deception of the American people.

President Nixon's actions resulted in manifest injury to the confidence of the nation and great prejudice to the cause of law and justice, and was subversive of constitutional government. His actions were contrary to his trust as President and unmindful of the solemn duties of his high office. It was this serious violation of Richard M. Nixon's constitutional obligations as President, and not the fact that violations of Federal criminal statutes occurred, that lies at the heart of Article I.

The Committee find, based upon clear and convincing evidence, that this conduct, detailed in the foregoing pages of this report, constitutes "high crimes and misdemeanors" as that term is used in Article II, Section 4 of the Constitution. Therefore, the Committee recommends that the House of Representatives exercise its constitutional power to impeach Richard M. Nixon.

1. *Summarize the pattern of behavior engaged in by Nixon that leads the House Judiciary Committee to believe that Nixon was involved in a plan to obstruct the investigation into the Watergate burglary.*
2. *What legal violations is Nixon accused of in this document? What more serious injury is Nixon accused of causing?*

30-2   Ronald Reagan, First Inaugural Address (1981)

The 1980 election witnessed a profound change in government policy. President Ronald Reagan focused on reducing taxes, federal government spending, and the size of the federal government to stimulate economic growth and provide more freedom for business and consumers.

These United States are confronted with an economic affliction of great proportions. We suffer from the longest and one of the worst sustained inflations in our national history. It distorts our economic decisions, penalizes thrift, and crushes the struggling young and the fixed-income elderly alike. It threatens to shatter the lives of millions of our people.

Idle industries have cast workers into unemployment, causing human misery and personal indignity. Those who do work are denied a fair return for their labor by a tax system which penalizes successful achievement and keeps us from maintaining full productivity.

But great as our tax burden is, it has not kept pace with public spending. For decades, we have piled deficit upon deficit, mortgaging our future and our children's future for the temporary convenience of the present. To continue this long trend is to guarantee tremendous social, cultural, political, and economic upheavals.

You and I, as individuals, can, by borrowing, live beyond our means, but for only a limited period of time. Why, then, should we think that collectively, as a nation, we are not bound by that same limitation?

We must act today in order to preserve tomorrow. And let there be no misunderstanding-we are going to begin to act, beginning today.

The economic ills we suffer have come upon us over several decades. They will not go away in days, weeks, or months, but they will go away. They will go away because we, as Americans, have the capacity now, as we have had in the past, to do whatever needs to be done to preserve this last and greatest bastion of freedom.

In this present crisis, government is not the solution to our problem.

From time to time, we have been tempted to believe that society has become too complex to be managed by self-rule, that government by an elite group is superior over government for, by, and of the people. But if no one among us is capable of governing himself, then who among us has the capacity to govern someone else? All of us together, in and out of government, must bear the burden. The solutions we seek must be equitable, with no one group singled out to pay a higher price.

We hear much of special interest groups. Our concern must be for a special interest group that has been too long neglected. It knows no sectional boundaries or ethnic and racial divisions, and it crosses political party lines. It is made up of men and women who raise our food, patrol our streets, man our mines and our factories, teach our children, keep our homes, and heal us when we are sick-professionals, industrialists, shopkeepers, clerks, cabbies, and truckdrivers. They are, in short, "We the people," this breed called Americans.

Well, this administration's objective will be a healthy, vigorous, growing economy that provides equal opportunity for all Americans, with no barriers born of bigotry or discrimination. Putting America back to work means putting all Americans back to work. Ending inflation means freeing all Americans from the terror of runaway living costs. All must share in the productive work of this "new beginning" and all must share in the bounty of a revived economy. With the idealism and fair play which are the core of our system and our strength, we can have a strong and prosperous America at peace with itself and the world.

So, as we begin, let us take inventory. We are a nation that has a government-not the other way around. And this makes us special among the nations of the Earth. Our Government has no power except that granted it by the people. It is time to check and reverse the growth of government which shows signs of having grown beyond the consent of the governed.

It is my intention to curb the size and influence of the Federal establishment and to demand recognition of the distinction between the powers granted to the Federal Government and those reserved to the States or to the people. All of us need to be reminded that the Federal Government did not create the States; the States created the Federal Government.

Now, so there will be no misunderstanding, it is not my intention to do away with government. It is, rather, to make it work-work with us, not over us; to stand by our side, not ride on our back. Government can and must provide opportunity, not smother it; foster productivity, not stifle it.

If we look to the answer as to why, for so many years, we achieved so much, prospered as no other people on Earth, it was because here, in this land, we unleashed the energy and individual genius of man to a greater extent than has ever been done before. Freedom and the dignity of the individual have been more available and assured here than in any other place on Earth. The price for this freedom at times has been high, but we have never been unwilling to pay that price.

It is no coincidence that our present troubles parallel and are proportionate to the intervention and intrusion in our lives that result from unnecessary and excessive growth of government. It is time for us to realize that we are too great a nation to limit ourselves to small dreams. We are not, as some would have us believe, doomed to an inevitable decline. I do not believe in a fate that will fall on us no matter what we do. I do believe in a fate that will fall on us if we do nothing. So, with all the creative energy at our command, let us begin an era of national renewal. Let us renew our determination, our courage, and our strength. And let us renew our faith and our hope

1. *Identify and describe the solutions to America's economic problems proposed by Reagan in this address.*
2. *What is Reagan's opinion of the role of government in America's recovery? What is the role of the individual citizens, the states, and the private corporations?*

30-3   Ronald Reagan, Speech to the House of Commons (1982)

The Solidarity movement in Poland threatened the totalitarian regime of that country and indicated the potential weakness of other such regimes in Eastern Europe. This movement and conditions in the Soviet Union led Ronald Reagan to proclaim the failure of communism. He also military strength as the key to peace in the continuing struggle against the Soviet Union.

We're approaching the end of a bloody century plagued by a terrible political invention-totalitarianism. Optimism comes less easily today, not because democracy is less vigorous, but because democracy's enemies have refined their instruments of repression. Yet optimism is in order because day by day democracy is proving itself to be a not at all fragile flower. From Stettin on the Baltic to Varna on the Black Sea, the regimes planted by totalitarianism have had more than thirty years to establish their legitimacy. But none-not one regime-has yet been able to risk free elections. Regimes planted by bayonets do not take root.

The strength of the Solidarity movement in Poland demonstrates the truth told in an underground joke in the Soviet Union. It is that the Soviet Union would remain a one-party nation even if an opposition party were permitted because everyone would join the opposition party. . . .

If history teaches us anything, it teaches self-delusion in the face of unpleasant facts is folly. We see around us the marks of our terrible dilemma-predictions of doomsday, antinuclear demonstrations, an arms race in which the West must, for its own protection, be an unwilling participant. At the same time we see totalitarian forces in the world who seek subversion and conflict around the globe to further their barbarous assault on the human spirit. What, then, is our course? Must civilization perish in a hail of fiery atoms? Must freedom wither in a quiet, deadening accommodation with totalitarian evil? . . .

It may not be easy to see; but I believe we live now at a turning point.

In an ironic sense Karl Marx was right. We are witnessing today a great revolutionary crisis, a crisis where the demands of the economic order are conflicting directly with those of the political order. But the crisis is happening not in the free, non-Marxist West, but in the home of Marxism-Leninism, the Soviet Union. It is the Soviet Union that runs against the tide of history by denying human freedom and human dignity to its citizens. It is also deep in economic difficulty. The rate of growth in the national product has been steadily declining since the fifties and is less than half of what it was then.

The dimensions of this failure are astounding: a country which employs one-fifth of its population in agriculture is unable to feed its own people. . . . The decay of the Soviet experiment should come as no surprise to us. Wherever the comparisons have been made between free and closed societies-West Germany and East Germany, Austria and Czechoslovakia, Malaysia and Vietnam-it is the democratic countries that are prosperous and responsive to the needs of their people. . . .

Our military strength is a prerequisite to peace, but let it be clear we maintain this strength in the hope it will never be used, for the ultimate determinant in the struggle that's now going on in the world will not be bombs and rockets but a test of wills and ideas, a trial of spiritual resolve, the values we hold, the beliefs we cherish, the ideals to which we are dedicated. . . .

I've often wondered about the shyness of some of us in the West about standing for these ideals that have done so much to ease the plight of man and the hardships of our imperfect world. This reluctance to use those vast resources at our command reminds me of the elderly lady whose home was bombed in the Blitz. As the rescuers moved about, they found a bottle of brandy she'd stored behind the staircase, which was all that was left standing. And since she was barely conscious, one of the workers pulled the cork to give her a taste of it. She came around immediately and said, "Here now-there now, put it back. That's for emergencies."

Well, the emergency is upon us. Let us be shy no longer. Let us go to our strength. Let us offer hope. Let us tell the world that a new age is not only possible but probable.

1. What, according to Reagan, are the causes for optimism in the face of international danger?

2. Why does Reagan identify this period of time as a turning point? What action is called for at this turning point in time?

30-4 Ronald Reagan, Address to the National Association of Evangelicals (1983)

The continuing threat of nuclear war and the escalation of the arms race had prompted the call for a nuclear freeze. Ronal Reagan rejected these calls saying it would put the United States in an inferior position to the Soviet Union, threatening the future of America.

During my first press conference as President, in answer to a direct question, I pointed out that, as good Marxist-Leninists, the Soviet leaders have openly and publicly declared that the only morality they recognize is that which will further their cause, which is world revolution. I think I should point out I was only quoting Lenin, their guiding spirit, who said in 1920 that they repudiate all morality that proceeds from supernatural ideas-that's their name for religion-or ideas that are outside class conceptions. Morality is entirely subordinate to the interests of class war. And everything is moral that is necessary for the annihilation of the old, exploiting social order and for uniting the proletariat.

Well, I think the refusal of many influential people to accept this elementary fact of Soviet doctrine illustrates an historical reluctance to see totalitarian powers for what they are. We saw this phenomenon in the 1930's. We see it too often today.

This doesn't mean we should isolate ourselves and refuse to seek an understanding with them. I intend to do everything I can to persuade them of our peaceful intent, to remind them that it was the West that refused to use its nuclear monopoly in the forties and fifties for territorial gain and which now proposes 50-percent cut in strategic ballistic missiles and the elimination of an entire class of land-based, intermediate-range nuclear missiles.

At the same time, however, they must be made to understand that we will never compromise our principles and standards. We will never give away our freedom. We will never abandon our belief in God. And we will never stop searching for a genuine peace. But we can assure none of these things America stands for through the so-called nuclear freeze solutions proposed by some.

The truth is that a freeze now would be a very dangerous fraud, for that is merely the illusion of peace. The reality is that we must find peace through strength.

I would agree to a freeze if only we could freeze the Soviets' global desires. A freeze at current levels of weapons would remove any incentive for the Soviets to negotiate seriously in Geneva and virtually end our chances to achieve the major arms reductions which we have proposed. Instead, they would achieve their objectives through the freeze.

A freeze would reward the Soviet Union for its enormous and unparalleled military buildup. It would prevent the essential and long overdue modernization of United States and allied defenses and would leave our aging forces increasingly vulnerable. And an honest freeze would require extensive prior negotiations on the systems and numbers to be limited and on the measures to ensure effective verification and compliance. And the kind of freeze that has been suggested would be virtually impossible to verify. Such a major effort would divert us completely from our current negotiations on achieving substantial reductions.

A number of years ago, I heard a young father, a very prominent young man in the entertainment world, addressing a tremendous gathering in California. It was during the time of the cold war, and communism and our own way of life were very much on people's minds. And he was speaking to that subject. And suddenly, though, I heard him saying, "I love my little girls more than anything—-" And I said to myself, "Oh, no, don't. You can't-don't say that." But I had underestimated him. He went on: "I would rather see my little girls die now, still believing in God, than have them grow up under communism and one day die no longer believing in God."

There were thousands of young people in that audience. They came to their feet with shouts of joy. They had instantly recognized the profound truth in what he had said, with regard to the physical and the soul and what was truly important.

Yes, let us pray for the salvation of all of those who live in that totalitarian darkness-pray they will discover the joy of knowing God. But until they do, let us be aware that while they preach the supremacy of the state, declare its omnipotence over individual man, and predict its eventual domination of all peoples on the Earth, they are the focus of evil in the modern world.

It was C. S. Lewis who, in his unforgettable "Screwtape Letters," wrote: "The greatest evil is not done now in those sordid 'dens of crime' that Dickens loved to paint. It is not even done in concentration camps and labor camps. In those we see its final result. But it is conceived and ordered (moved, seconded, carried and minuted) in clear, carpeted, warmed, and well-lighted offices, by quiet men with white collars and cut fingernails and smooth-shaven cheeks who do not need to raise their voice."

Well, because these "quiet men" do not "raise their voices," because they sometimes speak in soothing tones of brotherhood and peace, because, like other dictators before them, they're always making "their final territorial demand," some would have us accept them at their word and accommodate ourselves to their aggressive impulses. But if history teaches anything, it teaches that simple-minded appeasement or wishful thinking about our adversaries is folly. It means the betrayal of our past, the squandering of our freedom.

So, I urge you to speak out against those who would place the United States in a position of military and moral inferiority. You know, I've always believed that old Screwtape reserved his best efforts for those of you in the church. So, in your discussions of the nuclear freeze proposals, I urge you to beware the temptation of pride-the temptation of blithely declaring yourselves above it all and label both sides equally at fault, to ignore the facts of history and the aggressive impulses of an evil empire, to simply call the arms race a giant misunderstanding and thereby remove yourself from the struggle between right and wrong and good and evil.

I ask you to resist the attempts of those who would have you withhold your support for our efforts, this administration's efforts, to keep America strong and free, while we negotiate real and verifiable reductions in the world's nuclear arsenals and one day, with God's help, their total elimination.

While America's military strength is important, let me add here that I've always maintained that the struggle now going on for the world will never be decided by bombs or rockets, by armies or military might. The real crisis we face today is a spiritual one; at root, it is a test of moral will and faith.

Whittaker Chambers, the man whose own religious conversion made him a witness to one of the terrible traumas of our time, the Hiss-Chambers case, wrote that the crisis of the Western World exists to the degree in which the West is indifferent to God, the degree to which it collaborates in communism's attempt to make man stand alone without God. And then he said, for Marxism-Leninism is actually the second oldest faith, first proclaimed in the Garden of Eden with the words of temptation, "Ye shall be as gods."

The Western World can answer this challenge, he wrote, "but only provided that its faith in God and the freedom He enjoins is as great as communism's faith in Man."

I believe we shall rise to the challenge. I believe that communism is another sad, bizarre chapter in human history whose last pages even now are being written. I believe this because the source of our strength in the quest for human freedom is not material, but spiritual. And because it knows no limitation, it must terrify and ultimately triumph over those who would enslave their fellow man. For in the words of Isaiah: "He giveth power to the faint; and to them that have no might He increased strength. . . . But they that wait upon the Lord shall renew their strength; they shall mount up with wings as eagles; they shall run, and not be weary. . . ."

Yes, change your world. One of our Founding Fathers, Thomas Paine, said, "We have it within our power to begin the world over again." We can do it, doing together what no one church could do by itself.

God bless you, and thank you very much.

1. What is the foreign policy, specifically in relation to the Soviet Union, articulated in this speech?
2. How does Reagan weave spiritual concerns into this political address? What is his plea to his audience?

30-5 T. Boone Pickens, "My Case for Reagan" (1984)

The Reagan administration had clear-cut differences with the Democrats over the roles of government and the private sector. Reagan followed a pro-business program that sought to reduce federal spending and power while providing freer rein for business to stimulate the economy. The document shows why leaders of big business supported Reagan.

When businessmen consider why they should support President Reagan's reelection, their analysis should come down to two important questions: What has allowed their companies to grow and prosper? What makes business opportunities in America different from those in any other country?

The answer is free enterprise. Our economic system is what keeps Americans employed, clothed, housed, and nourished. That system makes it possible for every American to attain his or her dream of material or spiritual wealth. It truly makes ours the land of opportunity. This year voters will have a clear choice between a President who believes in retaining the maximum amount possible of the nation's wealth in the private sector and a challenger who supports a greater role for government.

More than any other President in the last 30 years, Ronald Reagan understands the importance of free enterprise. He knows that this country's markets should be allowed to operate freely and competitively. That's the philosophy he brought to the White House in 1981, and we've seen how beneficial the results are. Since President Reagan took office, inflation has dropped from nearly 14% to approximately 4%, and the prime rate has fallen from 20% to 13%.

By reducing government intervention, Reagan has injected a new competitive spirit into the marketplace. There is now an atmosphere that encourages business efficiency. For example, merger and acquisition activity, properly undertaken within the constraints of antitrust laws, has allowed companies and even entire industries to restructure and become more efficient and financially sound. Shareholders have reaped the rewards of their investments, and the government has received additional revenues as taxes are paid on those gains.

In contrast, Walter Mondale does not appear to understand what makes America work. His proposals would more heavily tax individuals and corporations, inhibit capital formation, and use government as the primary means to stimulate employment.

The cheapest, most effective way to create jobs is to encourage business growth, not to devise complicated and costly federal programs. Ronald Reagan has proved that. His policies have invigorated the market and put more Americans to work. Economic recovery is the best jobs programs this country has had. A record 107 million people are currently employed, five million more than when the Carter-Mondale Administration left office.

But Reagan has done even more for the average worker than stimulate employment. Through his tax policies, Americans are now taking home more pay. They have more money for their children's education, a new home, retirement, and investments. Some 42 million Americans have invested in shares of publicly owned companies, either directly or through mutual funds, compared with 30 million in 1980.

We've seen tangible evidence that Ronald Reagan's policies are working for America. That's important for everyone in this country. The health of U.S. business is critical to our nation's survival. We do, indeed, have a responsibility to support candidates who understand that principle-a responsibility not just to ourselves but to all citizens.

I am frequently asked by high school and college students how they can attain success from modest beginnings. My answer is simple. Like many business executives, I owe my success to the free enterprise system. I started with a good education, $2,500 in capital, and an opportunity to do something-the sky was the limit, and fortunately the same opportunity still exists.

The American free enterprise spirit is something we will be able to maintain only under a Reagan Administration. While Walter Mondale tells us that his plan for this country is better, we've seen what better means: Mondale's recent speeches have promised increased government intervention in the market and our lives and disincentives in the form of higher taxes.

The ill effects of the Carter-Mondale Administration were far-reaching: double-digit inflation-the worst since 1946-unemployment, skyrocketing interest rates, and a crumbling economy. There is no reason to believe that a Mondale-Ferraro Administration would be any different in philosophy or outcome.

All of us realize the importance of strong leadership. It is the greatest attribute any President can have and should be a prime asset of the nation. Lack of leadership ability is one of my greatest concerns about a Mondale-Ferraro Administration. Mondale has given no indication of having such ability either as Carter's Vice President or on his own. How could a nation possibly trust the affairs of state to a person who could not make a decision as to whether Bert Lance or Charles Manatt would chair his party?

America need not take that chance when it is blessed with an incumbent President who has proven leadership qualities. Ronald Reagan has been able to instill a new sense of pride and confidence in our nation. Gone are the days of Carter-Mondale defeatism and national malaise.

In 1980 the American people realized the disastrous economic brink on which this country teetered. They wanted a change for the better, and they chose a President who accomplished that goal. On November 6, Americans will once again ask themselves if a change is in order. I think the resounding answer will be that they wish to stay the course Reagan has charted. We're no longer on the brink of disaster; both feet are planted firmly on solid ground, and the future looks bright.

I'm supporting President Reagan and Vice President Bush for those reasons, and I unabashedly ask others to support them as well. I make no apology for political participation. At stake in this election is the future of the free enterprise system. A commitment from the business community, not just a check, is required to prevent another give-away-now, pay-later disaster. And that commitment will mean for future Americans a vigorous free market, the opportunity to succeed, and an attainable American Dream.

1. *Why should businessmen support Reagan's reelection according to Pickens? What benefit have Reagan's policies been to the success of free enterprise?*
2. *What criticisms are made of Mondale's candidacy?*

30-6 Paul Craig Roberts, The Supply-Side Revolution (1984)

A major tenet of Reagonomics was the supply-side theory. This idea suggested that by cutting taxes, especially for higher-income groups, spending would increase and stimulate the economy.

Prior to February 23, 1977, Republican economic policy focused on balancing the budget by raising taxes and cutting spending, an approach that denied the party a credible economic and political program. The Republicans were not always successful themselves at reducing spending, but if the government was going to spend, they at least wanted to pay for it with cash instead of borrowed money. This put them in conflict with Keynesian economics.

Keynesian theory explained the economy's performance in terms of the level of total spending. A budget deficit adds to total spending and helps keep employment high and the economy running at full capacity. Cutting the deficit, as the Republicans wanted to do, would reduce spending and throw people out of work, thereby lowering national income and raising the unemployment rate. The lower income would produce less tax revenue, and the higher unemployment would require larger budget expenditures for unemployment compensation, food stamps, and other support programs. The budget deficit would thus reappear from a shrunken tax base and higher income-support payments. Patient (and impatient) Democrats, economists, columnists, and editorial writers had explained many times to the obdurate Republicans that cutting the deficit would simply reduce spending on goods and services, drive the economy down, and raise the unemployment rate. Keynesians argued that the way to balance the budget was to run a deficit. Deficit spending would lift the economy, and the government's tax revenues would rise, bringing the budget into balance. Since cutting the deficit was believed to be the surest way to throw people out of work, there were not many Republican economists. When Democrat Alice Rivlin was asked why there were no Republican economists on her "nonpartisan" Congressional Budget Committee staff, she was probably telling the truth when she said she could not find any.

The focus on the deficit had left the Republicans without a competitive political program. They were perceived by the recipients of government benefits as the party always threatening to cut back on government programs such as social security, while the taxpaying part of the electorate saw Republicans as the party that was always threatening to raise taxes in order to pay for the benefits that others were receiving. The party that takes away with both hands competes badly with the party that gives away with both hands, and that simple fact explained the decline of the Republican Party, which had come to be known as the tax collector for Democratic spending programs. . . .

Supply-side economics brought a new perspective to fiscal policy. Instead of stressing the effects on spending, supply-siders showed that tax rates directly affect the supply of goods and services. Lower tax rates mean better incentives to work, to save, to take risks, and to invest. As people respond to the higher after-tax rewards, or greater profitability, incomes rise and the tax base grows, thus feeding back some of the lost revenues to the Treasury. The saving rate also grows, providing more financing for government and private borrowing. Since Keynesian analysis left out such effects, once supply-side economics appeared on the scene the Democrats could no longer claim that government spending stimulated the economy more effectively than tax cuts. Tax cuts were now competitive, and the House Republicans began to make the most of it. . . .

Many people also have the mistaken idea that taxes on personal income have no adverse consequences for business other than reducing the demand for products. They believe that higher tax rates on personal income help business by reducing the federal deficit and lowering interest rates. In actual fact, higher personal tax rates reduce private-sector saving and drive up both the cost of credit and the cost of labor to firms. When the Treasury examined the effects of the Kennedy tax cuts, it was found that the personal saving rate rose. This implies that the saving rate would fall if tax rates rise, and indeed the saving rate declined as bracket creep pushed savers into higher tax brackets.

Higher income tax rates raise labor costs to the firm, thereby undermining the competitiveness of its products at home and abroad. The higher the worker's marginal tax rate, the more expensive it is to the firm to protect wages from being eroded by inflation or to give real wage increases. Since additional income is taxed at the worker's highest bracket, the higher the tax rate, the larger the gross wage necessary to correspond to any net wage.

This does not meant that deficits are good for the economy. But it does mean that the argument that higher taxes are preferable to higher borrowing is at best unproved. The way this unproven argument has been used against the President's efforts to reduce tax rates and improve economic incentives is irresponsible. The key to a successful economy is incentives. Any economic policy that forgets this-even one that reduces deficits-will fail. . . .

We now have many decades of empirical evidence of the effects of disincentives on economic performance, ranging from China and the Soviet Union to the European welfare states. The effects of disincentives clearly thwart the intended results of central planning, government investment programs, and the maintenance of aggregate demand. On the other hand, there is an abundance of evidence of the positive effects of good incentives. Only free people are productive and forward-looking, but they cease to be free when their property rights are sacrificed to interest-group politics. Supply-side economics is the economics of a free society. It will prevail wherever freedom itself prevails.

1. *Explain the different theories outlined in this document regarding the effects of cutting the deficit and balancing the budget.*
2. *What factors are identified as leading to the decline of the Republican Party's popularity?*
3. *What new perspective did supply-side economics add to the discussion on the economy?*

30-7 Bill Chappell, Speech to the American Security Council Foundation (1985)

Seeking to protect the United States against a missile attack, The Reagan administration proposed the Strategic Defense Initiative. This costly, high technology system was called Star Wars by opponents. In 1985, Bill Chappell explained the SDI concept to the Security Council Foundation.

You've asked me today to speak on the subject of "The Need for a Strategic Defense Initiative." That's a pretty big assignment for one so low on the totem pole as I am in matters of defense. You are going to be hearing later from General Abrahamson and several others who are really experts in the field. So I am not going to try to be so technical. Rather, I want to establish a need for SDI-not that you don't already know it. I'll probably not say anything you don't already know. But the fact that we can share together those thoughts gives us a better opportunity to carry those thoughts back to the grass roots where they are so direly needed today.

"To be prepared for war is one of the most effectual means of preserving the peace." How many of you know who said that? And isn't it an ironical statement when you really think about it. To prevent war, we must create a strong peace. Now, that quotation didn't come from President Reagan when he was trying to sell the SDI. It didn't come from some military officer over on the Hill trying to justify a particular program. It came from George Washington, nearly 200 years ago.

That sentiment has been echoed repeatedly in this century by people such as Presidents Woodrow Wilson, Franklin D. Roosevelt, John F. Kennedy and, of course, Ronald Reagan. With today's threat of nuclear welfare, it has become more incumbent upon us than ever before to ensure that peace is maintained through whatever resources we have and can develop.

It is no secret that the Soviet Union is so determined to carry out its policies-and so believes in them-that it would use force to carry out its policies. Allowing that kind of effort to go unchecked will ultimately lead to war of disastrous consequences to the whole of humanity. Its next battleground or base may be space-25 miles above your home. The United States has a vital interest in protecting its outer spaces-as well as its inner spaces-from attack. That is why the President's strategic defensive Initiative-shortened to SDI-has become so critical in our search for a system to defend against nuclear missile attack. It is why we have assembled here today as concerned policymakers and citizens to carry on this dialogue.

The Strategic Defense Initiative is our most vitally important defense program under development. Stated very simply: if we are able to devise a defensive system that negates or significantly reduces the effectiveness of Soviet ICBMs [Intercontinental Ballistic Missiles], we will have regained the lost ground that gave us strategic stability during the '50s and '60s-and into the '70s. And we will have ended our nearly forty years of dependence on an increasingly precarious policy of mutual suicidal standoff-in one form or another. And if we do succeed in reducing the effectiveness of the ICBM, we will make it far easier to negotiate its reduction and eventual elimination.

Perhaps the vital importance of our SDI program can be perceived even more vividly, if we consider another possible outcome. Let us assume that the Soviet SDI effort succeeds and the U.S. is unable to generate comparable strategic defenses-what then? What then?

We, of course, acknowledge that Soviet forces already have us vastly outnumbered in manpower and conventional weaponry. And, avoiding any hairsplitting-we also realize that our nuclear forces have-at best-a rough parity with the Soviet Union at the present time. Obviously, even a partially effective Soviet strategic defense capability would establish a wide margin of Soviet superiority strategically, and thus give them dominance in all major areas of warfare. With the U.S. military in a position of pronounced inferiority, I would not want to speculate on the ultimate fate of Western civilization in general-or our nation-or society-in particular. . . .

Despite its unspecified nature, we are continually bombarded with detailed descriptions of what SDI will consist of and why it won't work.

In the words of one congressional leader, "The Strategic Defense Initiative raises more questions than its supporters have answered so far."

Quite true, and that is a mathematically verifiable fact. But it's an unfair contest. There are many thousands devising questions of widely varying levels of worth and validity-and only a small handful of people trying to provide thoughtful-coherent-integrated-and consistent answers to the Congress-the media-and the organized opposition. Or, to paraphrase Winston Churchill's tribute to the Royal Air Force fighter pilots: "Never have so many provided detailed predictions of what a research program will ultimately determine-for so few."

Another widely quoted statement proposes a slow-down-a smaller-scale SDI research program-because-it is said-it is very unlikely that space-based anti-missile weapons can ever fully protect the U.S. population from nuclear attack.

Such statements, based on false premises, naturally lead to equally false conclusions. No responsible SDI spokesman has yet indicated an intended reliance on space-based anti-missile weapons or given such reliance that they will fully protect the U.S. population from nuclear attack. Such safely ambiguous "straw man" statements tend to raise unfounded doubts and fears, generate endless miles of hysterical newsprint, and contribute nothing to the resolution of this national debate. . . .

With greater public support, Congress should approve the full funding level requested by the President that would allow full integration of all components of SDI. SDI is a research program, not one for the deployment of weapons-and I keep emphasizing that-you can't do piecemeal because there are so many integral parts. Certainly, General Abrahamson, when he speaks to you later, will point that out so vividly: You can't move an important part of this program or cut out one piece of it without affecting the whole. It has to be an integrated program. . . .

Let me invite you, fellow members of the Congressional Advisory Board of the American Security Council Foundation, to learn everything you can about the Strategic Defense Initiative. Learn why it is so important to America. Acquaint yourself with all of the facts that you can. Prepare yourselves at home in the best way you can-in small groups, in study groups, in all kinds of meetings-to get the message across to our people about the importance of this program. I invite you to understand the important part you play.

Together, we can create a peace strong enough to deter war. That's what SDI is all about-a peace strong enough to deter war. But that takes a strong America; it takes initiative, technology, and all of the things we have been talking about. Let's give it our best effort.

Thank you.

---

1. *Explain Chappell opinion regarding the importance and significance of Strategic Defense Initiative.*
2. *Summarize the focus and goal of this address to the American Security Council Foundation.*

30-8 Patricia Morrisroe, "The New Class" (1985)

*The return of prosperity in the early 1980s was not universally shared but a new group of young pro-
fessionals emerged as major beneficiaries. Called Yuppies, these young, urban professionals helped put
their stamp on the era through their consumer practices and lifestyles.*

It's a Saturday night at 96th and Broadway. Inside the new Caramba!!! everybody's drinking frozen maragaritas and talking real estate, while outside on the traffic strip, a derelict swigs Wild Turkey and shouts obscenities. By 11 P.M., he's sound asleep on the bench, but the crowd at Caramba!!! is still going strong.

"These are the most lethal maragaritas in Manhattan," says a man in a blue pinstriped suit by Polo. He staggers out of the restaurant and into David's Cookies next door. "Get the double-chunk chocolate chip," says his girlfriend, who is window-shopping at Pildes Optical.

At the newsstand across the street, a middle-aged woman buys the Sunday *Times* and looks at the dozens of young professionals spilling out of Caramba!!! "Yuppies," she shouts. "Go home!"

But they are home. Ads in the *Times* tout the Upper West Side as "Yuppie Country," and Amsterdam is being called "Cinderella Avenue." According to a study of the years 1970 through 1980 by New York's Department of City Planning, 7,500 people between the ages of 25 and 44 flooded the area between West 70th and 86th Streets. That age-group now makes up 47 percent of the population there. At the same time, the number of singles went up by 31 percent, while the number of families dropped 24 percent. "You want to know who's moving into the West Side?" says a woman who owns an antiques store on Amsterdam Avenue. "It's the young, the rich, and the restless."

Some older West Siders blame the newcomers for the skyrocketing rents and the uprooting of local merchants. They deplore the cuteness of Columbus Avenue and the hordes of tourists who congest the sidewalks. They worry that the neighborhood's solid middle class values will be replaced by the yuppie version of the West Side Dream: a pre-war apartment with a Food Emporium around the corner.

They can't relate to the 30-year-old on Central Park West who takes her husband's shirts to the East Side because she can't find a "quality" laundry in the neighborhood. Or to the tenants at the Sofia on West 61st Street, 50 percent of whom bought their apartments after seeing a model of the bathroom. ("They're big and very Deco," says Richard Zinn, the building's director of sales.)

The Columbia, a condominium on West 96th Street, has been called the "Yuppie Housing Project" by locals who can't believe anyone would *pay* to live on Broadway. "Didn't anyone tell these people it's a *commercial* street?" says an elderly man who is buying Rice Krispies at the Red Apple on the corner. "If I had the money for a condo, I'd move to Florida."

One third of the Columbia's units were bought by lawyers; the average income per apartment is $100,000. "It's a nice first home for couples on their way up," says developer Arthur Zeckendorf, who worked with his father, William, to build the Columbia. Once they've made it, they can move to the Park Belvedere, a condominium on West 79th Street also built by the Zeckendorfs. Sold for an average of $400 per square foot, it has attracted a better-off buyer. "I looked at the Columbia," says a 27-year-old Wall Street bond trader, "but the neighborhood was just too borderline for me." So he bought an apartment in one of the Belvedere's towers and persuaded a friend to buy one, too. "It's a great deal," he says of his $400,000 one-bedroom.

Many West Side co-ops are besieged by Wall Street financiers who use their bonuses to make down payments.

"The last five apartments in my building went to investment bankers," says a woman who owns a co-op on West End Avenue. "I want to protect my property, so it's good to have people with money move in. But I worry about the population in the next ten years. Are you going to need an MBA to get into Zabar's?" . . .

Yet for all the money being poured into the neighborhood, some of the new West Siders have a decidedly old-fashioned point of view. For every yuppie who dreams about moving from Broadway to Central Park West there are others who chose the West Side because it seemed unpretentious. "I always hated everything the East Side represented," says 33-year-old Joe Powers in between feeding mashed carrots to his five-month-old son, Mark. "The West Side always seemed to have less airs about it. To me, it's Zabar's and Fairway. Not Rœelles and Pasta & Cheese." . . .

Ten blocks uptown, 31-year-old Richard Conway is setting up his VCR to tape Jacqueline Bisset in *Anna Karenina*. A vice-president at a Wall Street investment firm, Conway recently bought a twelfth-floor five-room co-op at 106th Street and Riverside Drive. In the past fifteen years, Conway has moved from Greenwich to Harvard to Third Avenue to Yale to Chelsea, and now to Duke Ellington Boulevard.

"This is not a yuppie neighborhood," says Conway, uncorking a bottle of white wine. "That's what I like about it. In my building, we have a wonderful mix of people. The head of the co-op board is a musical director, and we've got artists and writers and movie producers."

When Conway decided to buy a co-op, he wanted to look only north of West 96th Street. "I think a lot of the glamour is gone from the East Side," he says. "Besides, I considered it boring and staid, too much like Greenwich. I like living in a neighborhood that's ethnically diverse. Broadway has a lot of bodegas and mom-and-pop stores. To me, that's nice."

From his living room, Conway has a spectacular view of the Hudson. From the opposite end of the apartment, in the dining room, he can see a cityscape of charming turn-of-the-century brownstones. "I wonder how long they'll last," he says. "It's ironic, but everything I like about the neighborhood will probably disappear. And unfortunately, the reason is that people like me are moving into it." . . .

[Lawyer Jay] Zamansky, who grew up in Philadelphia, now makes his home in a renovated SRO next door to the Salvation Army senior citizen's home on West 95th Street. "I really wanted a place where I could establish roots," he says. Constructed around the turn of the century, the building has 30 apartments, most of which are inhabited by young professionals. "We're a real unique building," he explains. "In the summer, we have barbecues, and when our first co-op baby was born, everybody was thrilled."

Zamansky bought this apartment, a duplex with a roof garden, for a little over $100,000. "I'm real proud of it," he says. "It's the consummate bachelor pad." The ceiling is painted black, with lots of track lighting. "I met an interior designer at the Vertical Club," he explains, "and she helped me with the overall concept."

But Zamansky says he doesn't want to be the kind of person who does nothing but "work, eat at restaurants, and go to a health club. I really want to be a part of this neighborhood," he says. "I attend community-board meetings, and I registered voters in front of Zabar's. I even went into the Salvation Army's old people's home and registered senior citizens. They were just so glad to see a young face that I don't think they cared how they voted. By the way, I'm a Republican. I think it's important to put that in the article.

"I'm also very pro-development," he adds. "It makes me angry when people criticize a lot of the changes. The displacement is unfortunate, but where are we supposed to live? We have rights. We pay taxes. Whether people realize it or not, we're real assets to this community."

Twenty-nine-year-old Paula Handler, who lives with her husband in a three-bedroom apartment in the Eldorado on Central Park West between 90th and 91st Streets agrees. "These big pre-war buildings need young blood," she says. "The old people can't maintain their apartments. They resist everything, from redoing the lobby to putting in new windows. The problem is they can't switch their rental mentalities into a co-op mode."

The Handlers moved from the East Side to the Eldorado a year ago. "Frankly, I didn't know anything about Central Park West," says Paula. "I mean, I knew the Dakota, but the Eldorado? What? All I knew was that I wanted space, and I wanted old. Old is chic."

"Originally, I said no to the West Side," says Scott, a quiet man who is involved in commercial real estate.

"That's right, he did," Paula says. "He didn't like it because it was dirty and nobody we knew lived there. But I fell in love with this apartment. It was a total wreck, but it was me. We gave them an offer the minute we saw it. We even offered more than they asked because we wanted it so much."

The Handlers put in two new bathrooms and a new kitchen, and redid the plumbing and wiring. Today, the apartment, which faces the park, is completely renovated. "See what I mean about new blood?" Paula says. "It doesn't take money. It just takes creativity."

Six floors above the Handlers, Linda and Mark Reiner also had to redo their apartment completely. "It was considered the worst disaster in the building," Linda says. "The walls, which were painted magenta, royal blue, and orange, were falling down. But we really wanted to live here. We recognized how the West Side was growing, and we wanted to be a part of that."

Two years ago, they moved from a house in Hewlett Harbor, where Mark Reiner had a medical practice. "It was a risk giving up everything," he says, "but Hewlett Harbor was very sterile and uniform."

"That's why we didn't want the East Side," adds Linda, who until recently was a practicing psychologist. "Now I sell real estate," she says. "I became addicted to it while we were looking for this apartment." The au pair brings their two-year-old son into the living room to say good night. "You wouldn't believe the children's playground in the park," Linda says. "You can barely get a place for your kid in the sandbox."

"Everybody wants to come here," says Mark. "There's nothing more exciting than living in a neighborhood in transition. It's sad, because a lot of people who live here can't afford to shop in the stores. But they're being pushed out of Manhattan, not just the West Side."

"The West Side makes you feel the difference between the haves and the have-nots," says Linda, who is dressed in a silk Chanel shirt, black pants, and pumps. "Right in our building, there's a real schism between the pre-conversion and post-conversion people. A new breed is taking over, and there's a lot of hostility. People are separated by age and economic class. The senior citizens got insider prices so low that there's a lot of resentment on all sides. At a recent meeting, one elderly person shouted, 'Well, I'm not rich like you.' But what can you do?"

"Basically, we're very optimistic," Mark says. "We feel good about the changes. The neighborhood is going to continue to improve."

Linda nods. "Definitely," she says. "For the West Side, there's no turning back."

1. *How do these accounts represent the sudden fortunes brought about by the growth of technology and business?*
2. *What tensions are present in these accounts? Identify the varying attitudes expressed about the changing class structures and demographics?*

30-9 George Bush, Address to the Nation Announcing Allied Military Action in the Persian Gulf (1991)

The invasion of Kuwait by Iraq stimulated a broad military coalition of nations led by the United States and backed by the United Nations. In 1991, this coalition attacked Iraq, beginning the Gulf War.

Just 2 hours ago, allied air forces began an attack on military targets in Iraq and Kuwait. These attacks continue as I speak. Ground forces are not engaged.

This conflict started August 2d when the dictator of Iraq invaded a small and helpless neighbor. Kuwait-a member of the Arab League and a member of the United Nations-was crushed; its people, brutalized. Five months ago, Saddam Hussein [President of Iraq] Saddam Hussein started this cruel war against Kuwait. Tonight, the battle has been joined.

This military action, taken in accord with United Nations resolutions and with the consent of the Untied States Congress, follows months of constant and virtually endless diplomatic activity on the part of the United Nations, the United States, and many, many other countries. Arab leaders sought what became known as an Arab solution, only to conclude that Saddam Hussein was unwilling to leave Kuwait. Others traveled to Baghdad in a variety of efforts to restore peace and justice. Our Secretary of State, James Baker, held an historic meeting in Geneva, only to be totally rebuffed. This past weekend, in a last-ditch effort, the Secretary-General of the United Nations went to the Middle East with peace in his heart-his second such mission. And he came back from Baghdad with no progress at all in getting Saddam Hussein to withdraw from Kuwait.

Now the twenty-eight countries with forces in the Gulf area have exhausted all reasonable efforts to reach a peaceful resolution-have no choice but to drive Saddam from Kuwait by force. We will not fail.

As I report to you, air attacks are underway against military targets in Iraq. We are determined to knock out Saddam Hussein's nuclear-bomb potential. We will also destroy his chemical-weapons facilities. Much of Saddam's artillery and tanks will be destroyed. Our operations are designed to best protect the lives of all the coalition forces by targeting Saddam's vast military arsenal. Initial reports from General Schwarzkopf are that our operations are proceeding according to plan.

Our objectives are clear: Saddam Hussein's forces will leave Kuwait. The legitimate government of Kuwait will be restored to its rightful place, and Kuwait will once again be free. Iraq will eventually comply with all relevant United Nations resolutions, and then, when peace is restored, it is our hope that Iraq will live as a peaceful and cooperative member of the family of nations, thus enhancing the security and stability of the Gulf.

Some may ask: Why act now? Why not wait? The answer is clear: The world could wait no longer. Sanctions, though having some effect, showed no signs of accomplishing their objective. Sanctions were tried for well over five months, and we and our allies concluded that sanctions alone would not force Saddam from Kuwait.

While the world waited, Saddam Hussein systematically raped, pillaged, and plundered a tiny nation, no threat to his own. He subjected the people of Kuwait to unspeakable atrocities-and among those maimed and murdered, innocent children.

While the world waited, Saddam sought to add to the chemical weapons arsenal he now possesses, and infinitely more dangerous weapon of mass destruction-a nuclear weapon. And while the world waited, while the world talked peace and withdrawal, Saddam Hussein dug in and moved massive forces into Kuwait.

While the world waited, while Saddam stalled, more damage was being done to the fragile economies of the Third World, emerging democracies of Eastern Europe, to the entire world, including to our own economy.

The United States, together with the United Nations, exhausted every means at our disposal to bring this crisis to a peaceful end. However, Saddam clearly felt that by stalling and threatening and defying the United Nations, he could weaken the forces arrayed against him.

While the world waited, Saddam Hussein met every overture of peace with open contempt. While the world prayed for peace, Saddam prepared for war.

I had hoped that when the United States Congress, in historic debate, took its resolute action, Saddam would realize the could not prevail and would move out of Kuwait in accord with the United Nation resolutions. He did not do that. Instead, he remained intransigent, certain that time was on his side.

Saddam was warned over and over again to comply with the will of the United Nations: Leave Kuwait, or be driven out. Saddam has arrogantly rejected all warnings. Instead, he tried to make this a dispute between Iraq and the United States of America.

Well, he failed. tonight, twenty-eight nations-countries from five continents, Europe and Asia, Africa, and the Arab League-have forces in the Gulf area standing shoulder to shoulder against Saddam Hussein. These countries had hoped the use of force could be avoided. Regrettably, we now believe that only force will make him leave.

Prior to ordering our forces into battle, I instructed our military commanders to take every necessary step to prevail as quickly as possible, and with the greatest degree of protection possible for American and allied service men and women. I've told the American people before that this will not be another Vietnam, and I repeat this here tonight. Our troops will have the best possible support in the entire world, and they will not be asked to fight with one hand tied behind their back. I'm hopeful that this fighting will not go on for long and that casualties will be held to an absolute minimum.

This is an historic moment. We have in this past year made great progress in ending the long era of conflict and cold war. We have before us the opportunity to forge for ourselves and for future generations a new world order-a world where the rule of law, not the law of the jungle, governs the conduct of nations. When we are successful-and we will be-we have a real chance at this new world order, an order in which a credible United Nations can use its peacekeeping role to fulfill the promise and vision of the U.N.'s founders.

We have no argument with the people of Iraq. Indeed, for the innocents caught in this conflict, I pray for their safety. Our goal is not the conquest of Iraq. It is the liberation of Kuwait. It is my hope that somehow the Iraqi people can, even now, convince their dictator that he must lay down his arms, leave Kuwait and let Iraq itself rejoin the family of peace-loving nations.

Thomas Paine wrote many years ago: "These are the times that try men's souls." Those well-known words are so very true today. But even as planes of the multinational forces attack Iraq, I prefer to think of peace, not war. I am convinced not only that we will prevail but that out of the horror of combat will come the recognition that no nation can stand against a world united. No nation will be permitted to brutally assault its neighbor.

No president can easily commit our sons and daughters to war. They are the Nation's finest. Ours is an all-volunteer force, magnificently trained, highly motivated. The troops know why they're there. And listen to what they say, for they've said it better than any President or Prime Minister ever could.

Listen to Hollywood Huddleston, marine lance corporal. He says, "Let's free these people, so we can go home and be free again." And he's right. The terrible crimes and tortures committed by Saddam's henchmen against the innocent people of Kuwait are an affront to mankind and a challenge to the freedom of all.

Listen to one of our great officers out there, Marine Lieutenant General Walter Boomer. He said: "There are things worth fighting for. A world in which brutality and lawlessness are allowed to go unchecked isn't the kind of world we're going to want to live in."

Listen to Master Sergeant J. P. Kendall of the 82d Airborne: "We're here for more than just the price of a gallon of gas. What we're doing is going to chart the future of the world for the next 100 years. It's better to deal with this guy now than five years from now."

And finally, we should all sit up and listen to Jackie Jones, an army lieutenant, when she says, "If we let him get away with this, who knows what's going to be next?"

I have called upon Hollywood and Walter and J. P. and Jackie and all their courageous comrades-in-arms to do what must be done. Tonight, America and the world are deeply grateful to them and to their families. And let me say to everyone listening or watching tonight: When the troops we've sent in finish their work, I am determined to bring them home as soon as possible.

Tonight, as our forces fight, they and their families are in our prayers. May God bless each and every one of them, and the coalition forces at our side in the Gulf, and may He continue to bless our nation, the United States of America.

1. What justification is provided in this address for engaging in military strikes against Iraq?
2. Describe the "new world" order mentioned in this address and its impact on international relations.
3. How does President Bush use the words of common citizens and soldiers to support his argument? What is the effect of this method of persuasion?